SATURDAY AM

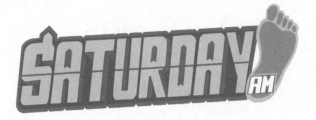

PRESENTS...

# APPLE BLACK

## VOLUME 1

### NEO FREEDOM

STORY AND ART BY ODUNZE OGUGUO

ROCKPORT

# CONTENTS

# APPLE BLACK

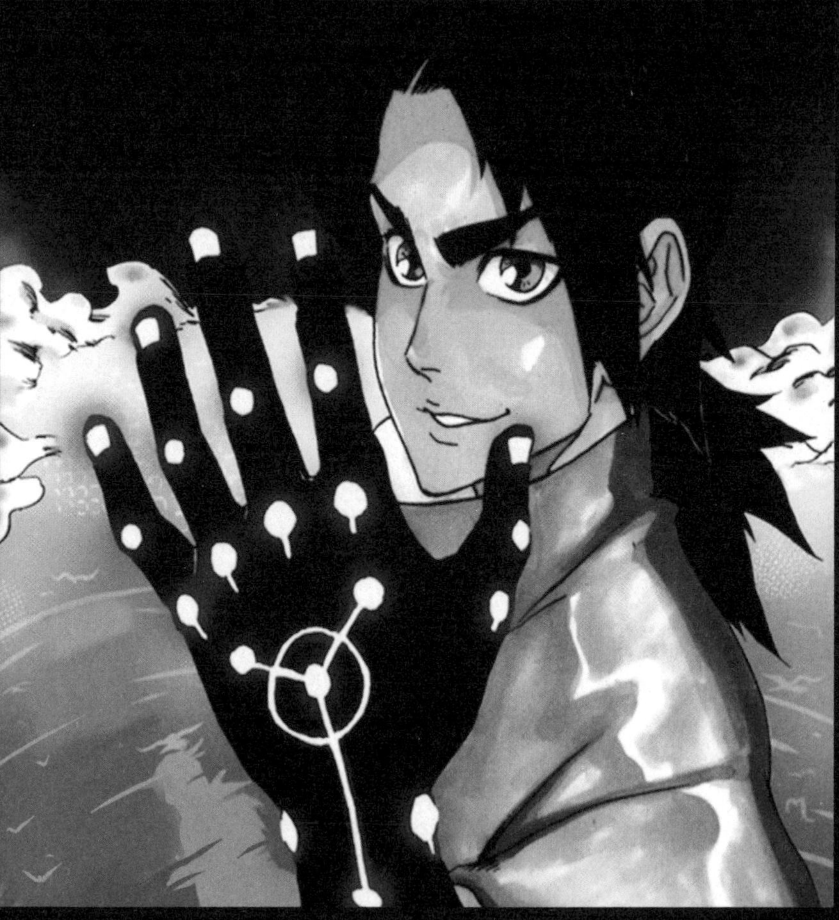

## CHAPTER 1 | FREEDOM DAY

APPLE BLACK

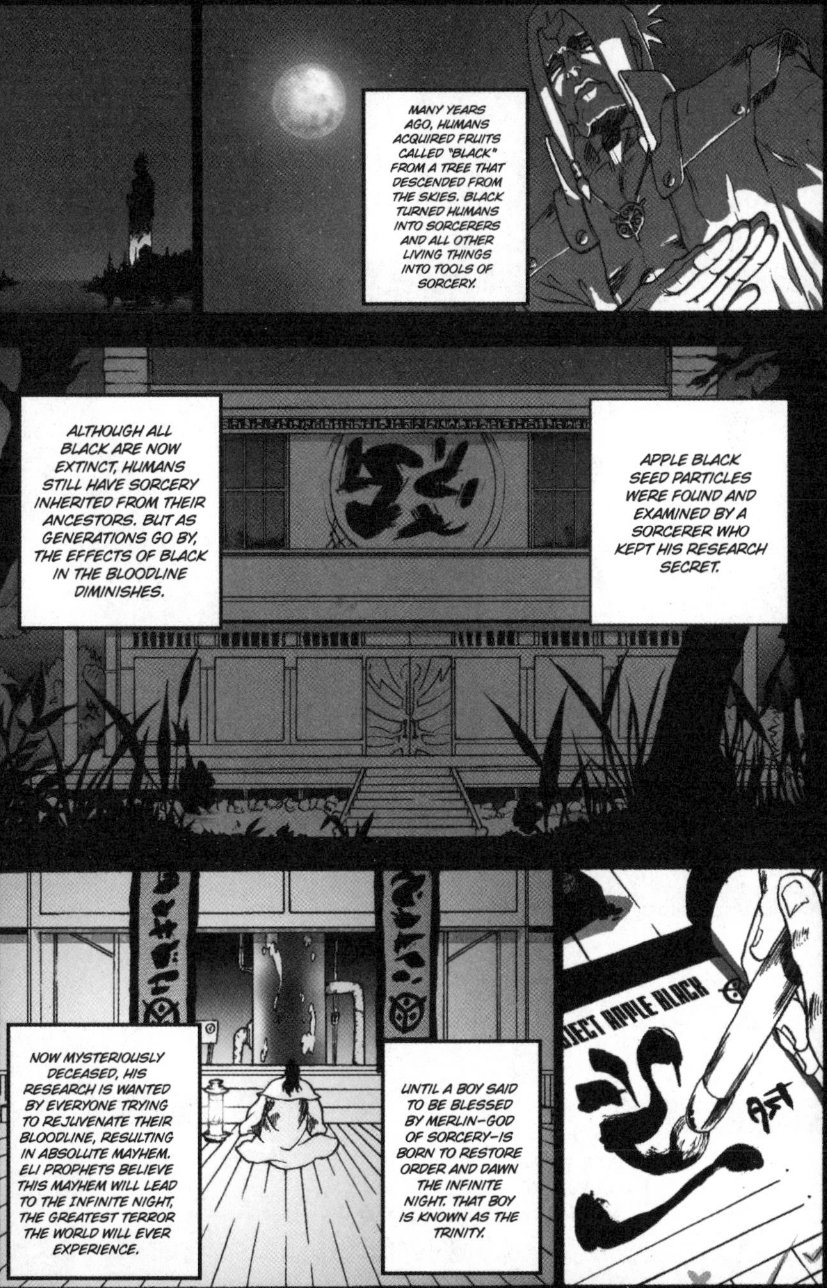
MANY YEARS AGO, HUMANS ACQUIRED FRUITS CALLED "BLACK" FROM A TREE THAT DESCENDED FROM THE SKIES. BLACK TURNED HUMANS INTO SORCERERS AND ALL OTHER LIVING THINGS INTO TOOLS OF SORCERY.
ALTHOUGH ALL BLACK ARE NOW EXTINCT, HUMANS STILL HAVE SORCERY INHERITED FROM THEIR ANCESTORS. BUT AS GENERATIONS GO BY, THE EFFECTS OF BLACK IN THE BLOODLINE DIMINISHES.
APPLE BLACK SEED PARTICLES WERE FOUND AND EXAMINED BY A SORCERER WHO KEPT HIS RESEARCH SECRET.
NOW MYSTERIOUSLY DECEASED, HIS RESEARCH IS WANTED BY EVERYONE TRYING TO REJUVENATE THEIR BLOODLINE, RESULTING IN ABSOLUTE MAYHEM. ELI PROPHETS BELIEVE THIS MAYHEM WILL LEAD TO THE INFINITE NIGHT, THE GREATEST TERROR THE WORLD WILL EVER EXPERIENCE.
UNTIL A BOY SAID TO BE BLESSED BY MERLIN—GOD OF SORCERY—IS BORN TO RESTORE ORDER AND DAWN THE INFINITE NIGHT. THAT BOY IS KNOWN AS THE TRINITY.

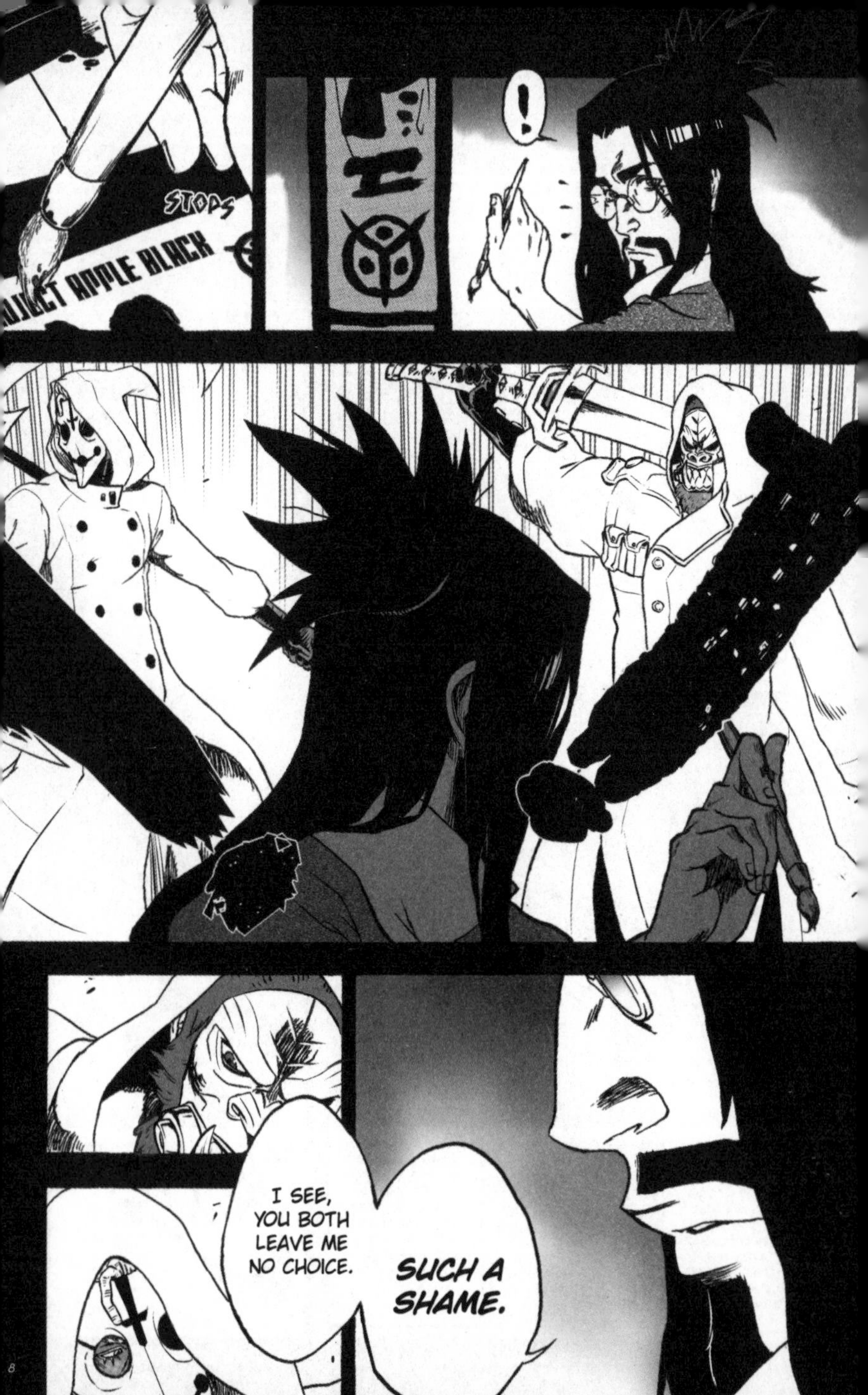
STOPS
APPLE BLACK
!
I SEE, YOU BOTH LEAVE ME NO CHOICE.
SUCH A SHAME.

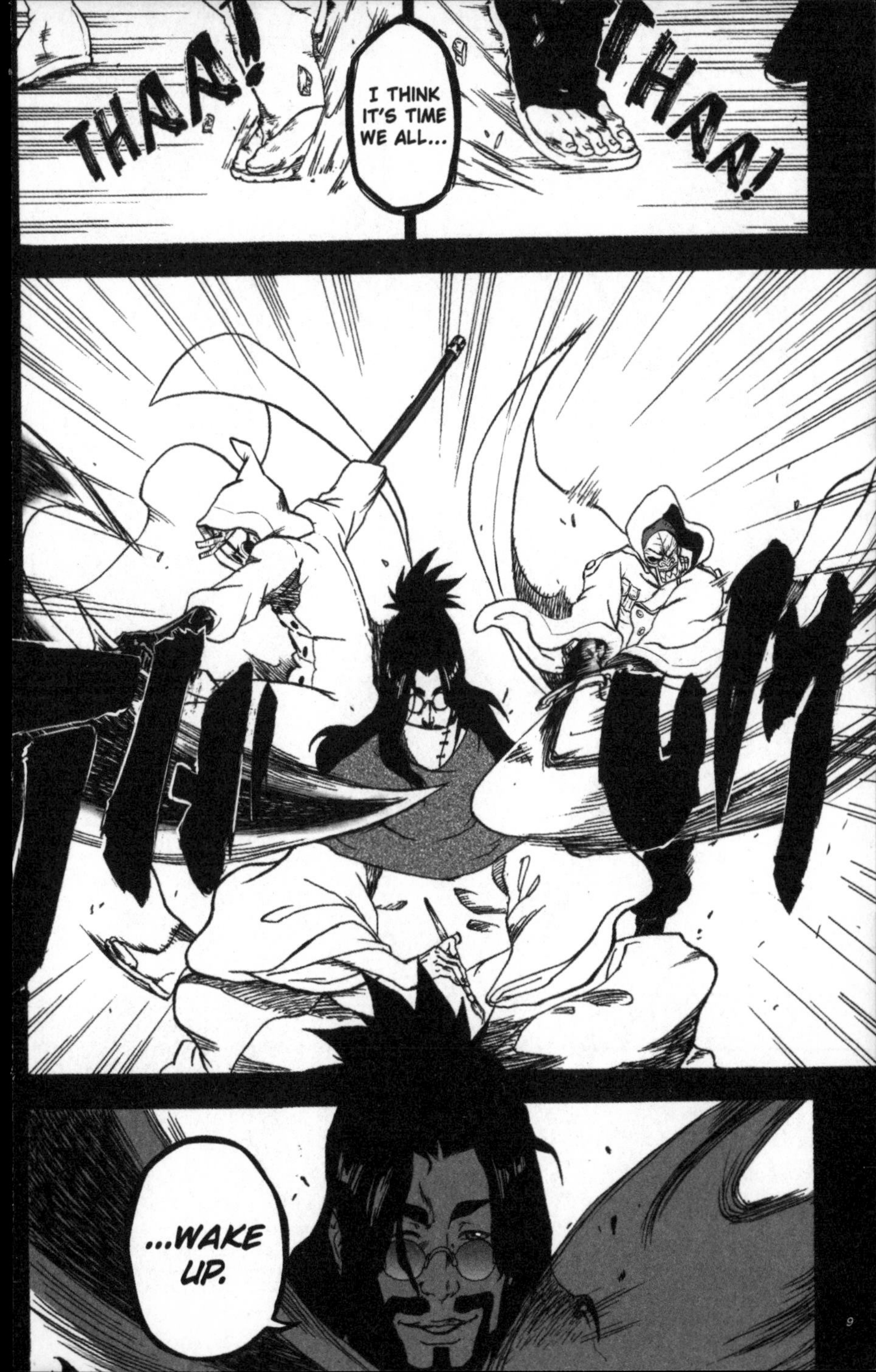
THAA!
I THINK IT'S TIME WE ALL...
THAA!
THUM
...WAKE UP.

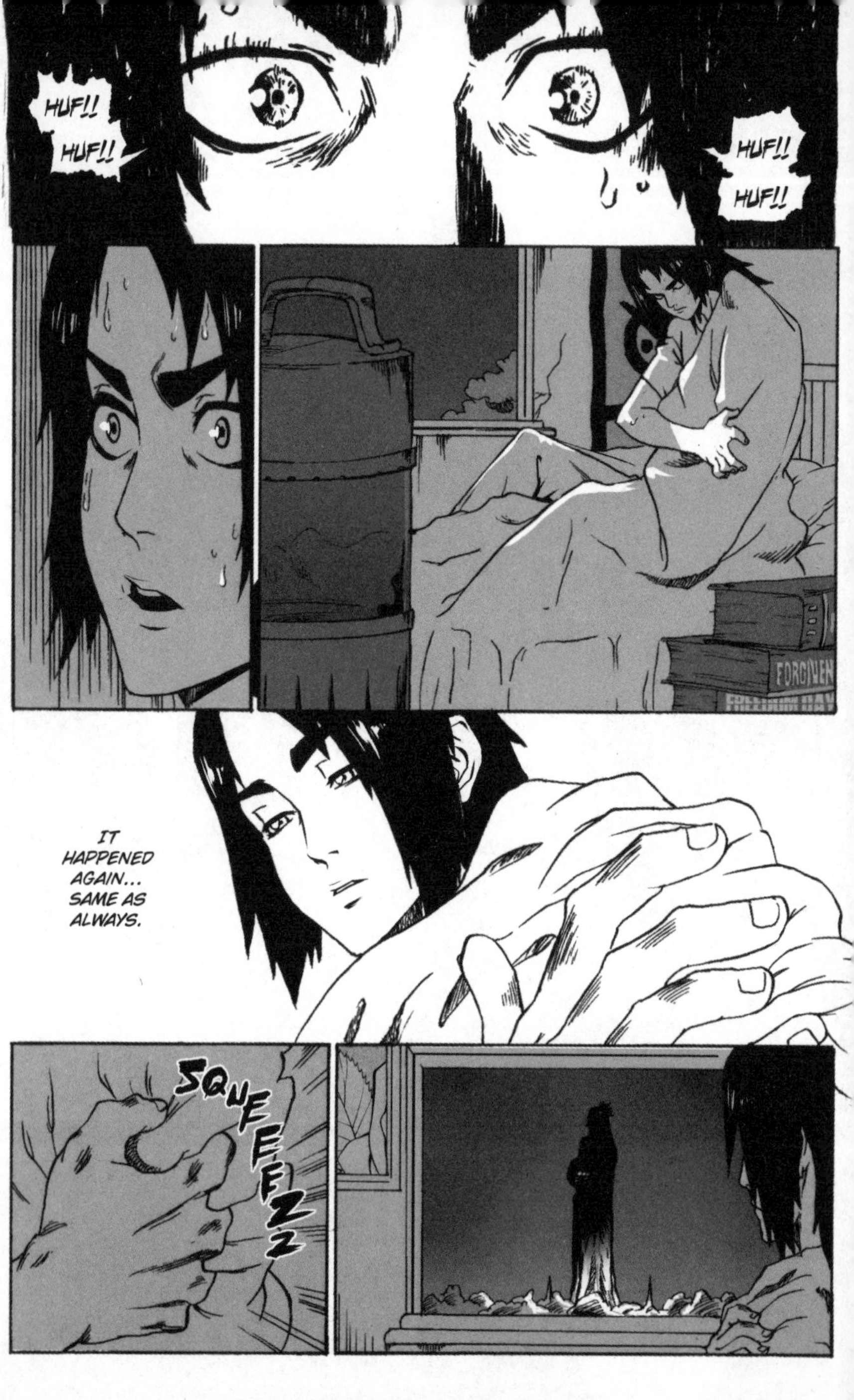
HUF!!
HUF!!
HUF!!
HUF!!
IT HAPPENED AGAIN... SAME AS ALWAYS.
SQUEEEZZ

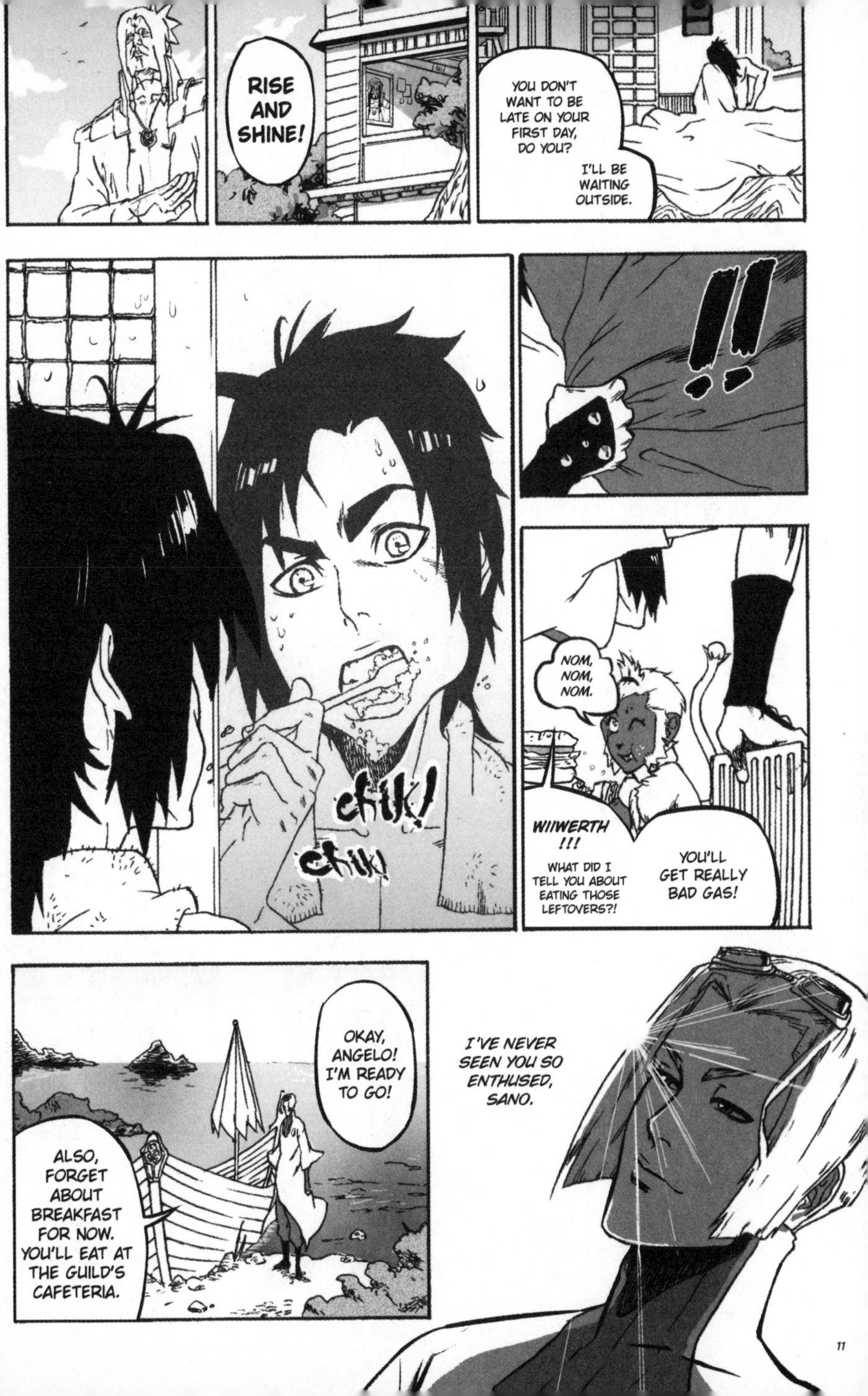
RISE AND SHINE!
YOU DON'T WANT TO BE LATE ON YOUR FIRST DAY, DO YOU?
I'LL BE WAITING OUTSIDE.
chik!
chik!
!!
NOM, NOM, NOM.
WIIWERTH !!!
WHAT DID I TELL YOU ABOUT EATING THOSE LEFTOVERS?!
YOU'LL GET REALLY BAD GAS!
OKAY, ANGELO! I'M READY TO GO!
ALSO, FORGET ABOUT BREAKFAST FOR NOW. YOU'LL EAT AT THE GUILD'S CAFETERIA.
I'VE NEVER SEEN YOU SO ENTHUSED, SANO.

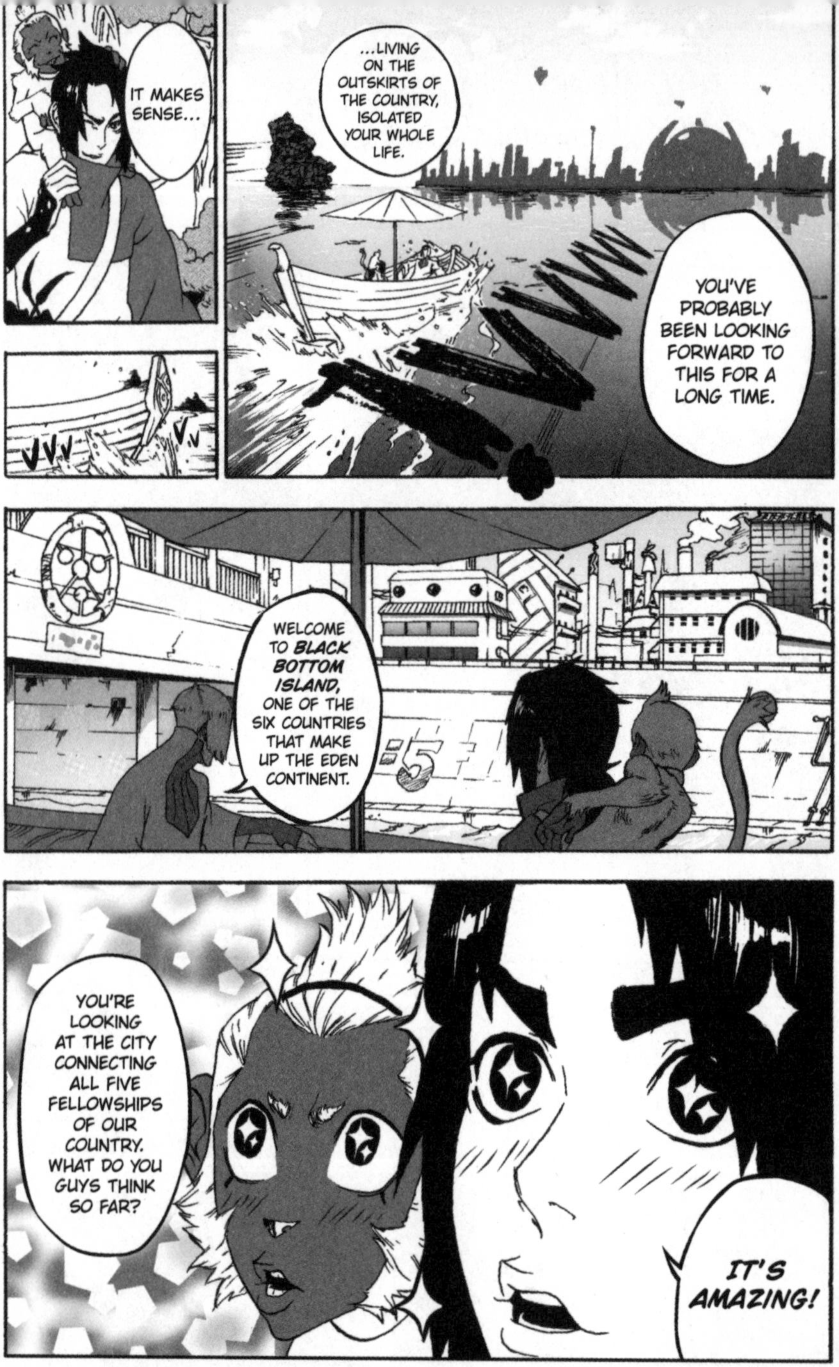
IT MAKES SENSE...
...LIVING ON THE OUTSKIRTS OF THE COUNTRY, ISOLATED YOUR WHOLE LIFE.
YOU'VE PROBABLY BEEN LOOKING FORWARD TO THIS FOR A LONG TIME.
WELCOME TO *BLACK BOTTOM ISLAND,* ONE OF THE SIX COUNTRIES THAT MAKE UP THE EDEN CONTINENT.
YOU'RE LOOKING AT THE CITY CONNECTING ALL FIVE FELLOWSHIPS OF OUR COUNTRY. WHAT DO YOU GUYS THINK SO FAR?
*IT'S AMAZING!*

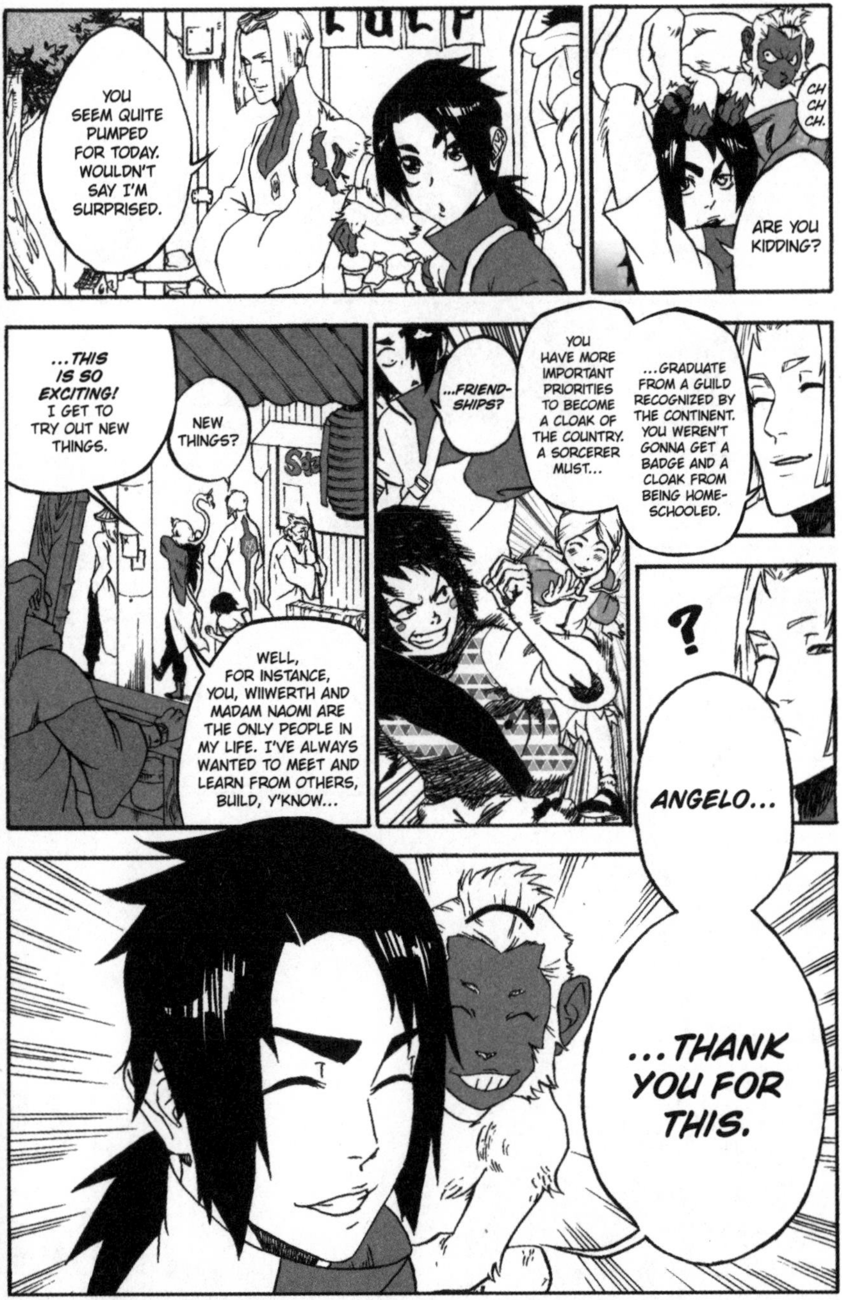
YOU SEEM QUITE PUMPED FOR TODAY. WOULDN'T SAY I'M SURPRISED.
CH CH CH.
ARE YOU KIDDING?
...THIS IS SO EXCITING! I GET TO TRY OUT NEW THINGS.
NEW THINGS?
WELL, FOR INSTANCE, YOU, WIIWERTH AND MADAM NAOMI ARE THE ONLY PEOPLE IN MY LIFE. I'VE ALWAYS WANTED TO MEET AND LEARN FROM OTHERS, BUILD, Y'KNOW...
...FRIEND-SHIPS?
YOU HAVE MORE IMPORTANT PRIORITIES TO BECOME A CLOAK OF THE COUNTRY. A SORCERER MUST...
...GRADUATE FROM A GUILD RECOGNIZED BY THE CONTINENT. YOU WEREN'T GONNA GET A BADGE AND A CLOAK FROM BEING HOME-SCHOOLED.
?
ANGELO...
...THANK YOU FOR THIS.

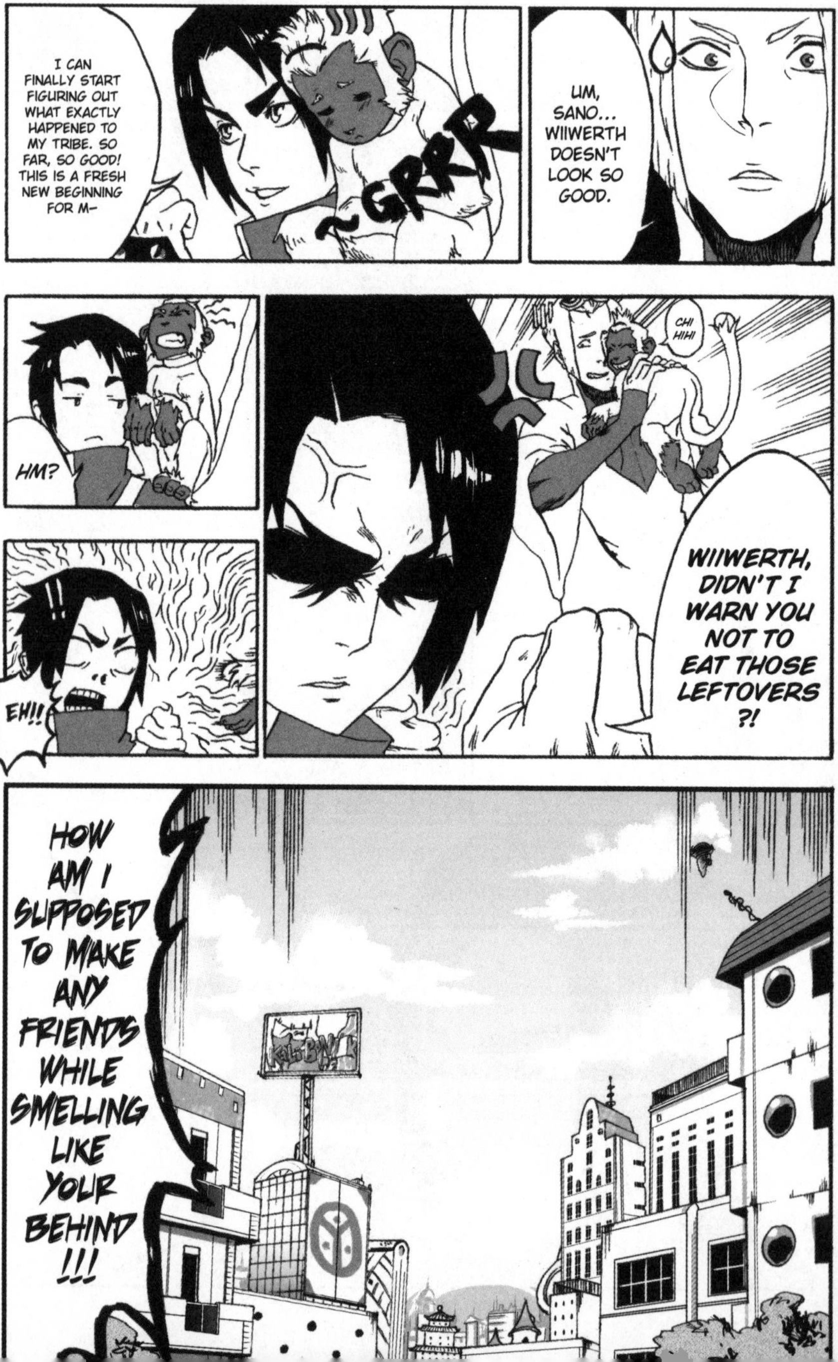
I CAN FINALLY START FIGURING OUT WHAT EXACTLY HAPPENED TO MY TRIBE. SO FAR, SO GOOD! THIS IS A FRESH NEW BEGINNING FOR M-
~GRRR
UM, SANO... WIIWERTH DOESN'T LOOK SO GOOD.
HM?
EH!!
CHI HIHI
WIIWERTH, DIDN'T I WARN YOU NOT TO EAT THOSE LEFTOVERS?!
HOW AM I SUPPOSED TO MAKE ANY FRIENDS WHILE SMELLING LIKE YOUR BEHIND!!!

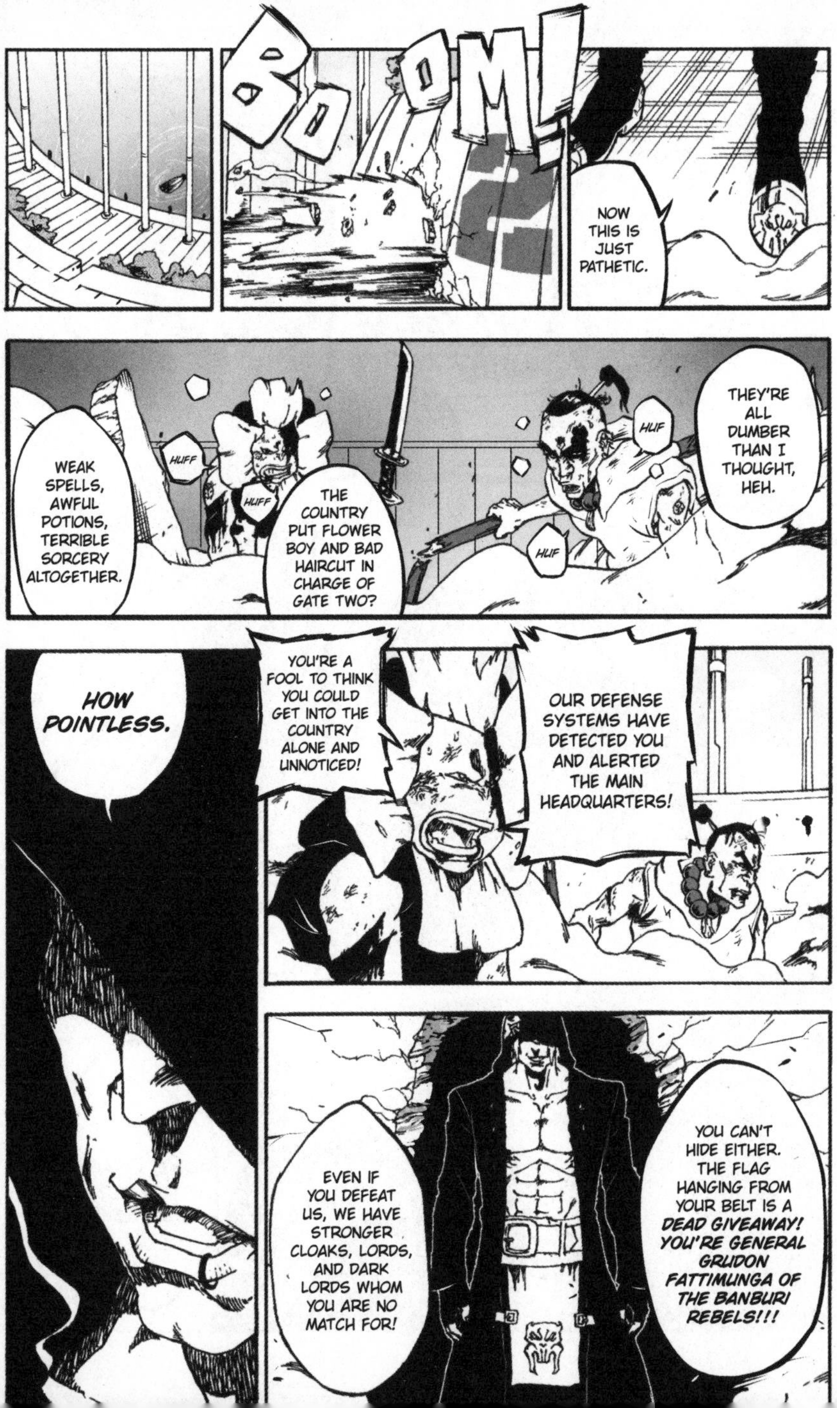
BOOM!
NOW THIS IS JUST PATHETIC.
WEAK SPELLS, AWFUL POTIONS, TERRIBLE SORCERY ALTOGETHER.
HUFF
HUFF
THE COUNTRY PUT FLOWER BOY AND BAD HAIRCUT IN CHARGE OF GATE TWO?
HUF
HUF
THEY'RE ALL DUMBER THAN I THOUGHT, HEH.
HOW POINTLESS.
YOU'RE A FOOL TO THINK YOU COULD GET INTO THE COUNTRY ALONE AND UNNOTICED!
OUR DEFENSE SYSTEMS HAVE DETECTED YOU AND ALERTED THE MAIN HEADQUARTERS!
EVEN IF YOU DEFEAT US, WE HAVE STRONGER CLOAKS, LORDS, AND DARK LORDS WHOM YOU ARE NO MATCH FOR!
YOU CAN'T HIDE EITHER. THE FLAG HANGING FROM YOUR BELT IS A DEAD GIVEAWAY! YOU'RE GENERAL GRUDON FATTIMUNGA OF THE BANBURI REBELS!!!

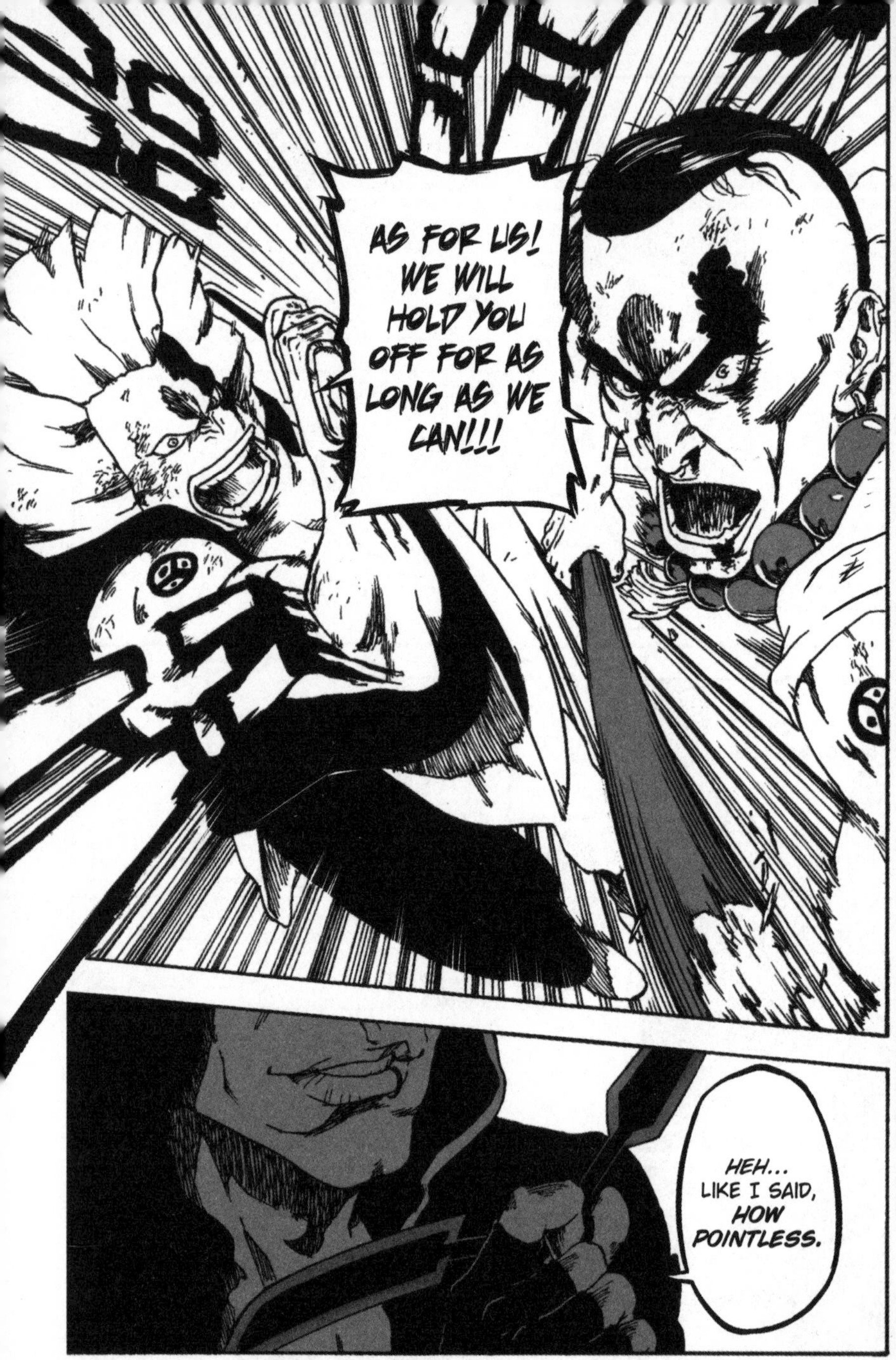
AS FOR US! WE WILL HOLD YOU OFF FOR AS LONG AS WE CAN!!!
HEH... LIKE I SAID, HOW POINTLESS.

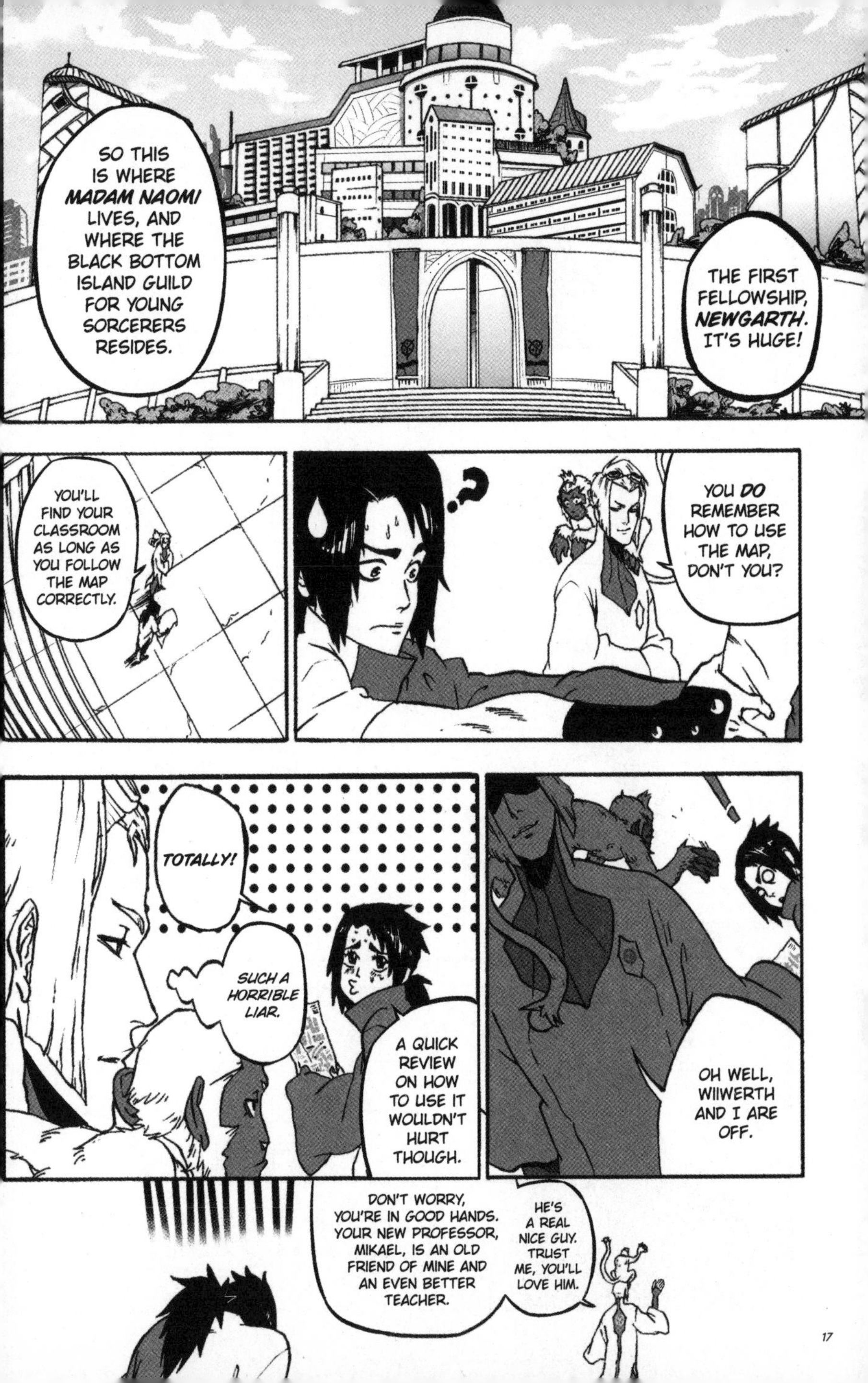
SO THIS IS WHERE MADAM NAOMI LIVES, AND WHERE THE BLACK BOTTOM ISLAND GUILD FOR YOUNG SORCERERS RESIDES.
THE FIRST FELLOWSHIP, NEWGARTH. IT'S HUGE!
YOU'LL FIND YOUR CLASSROOM AS LONG AS YOU FOLLOW THE MAP CORRECTLY.
YOU DO REMEMBER HOW TO USE THE MAP, DON'T YOU?
TOTALLY!
SUCH A HORRIBLE LIAR.
A QUICK REVIEW ON HOW TO USE IT WOULDN'T HURT THOUGH.
OH WELL, WIIWERTH AND I ARE OFF.
DON'T WORRY, YOU'RE IN GOOD HANDS. YOUR NEW PROFESSOR, MIKAEL, IS AN OLD FRIEND OF MINE AND AN EVEN BETTER TEACHER.
HE'S A REAL NICE GUY. TRUST ME, YOU'LL LOVE HIM.

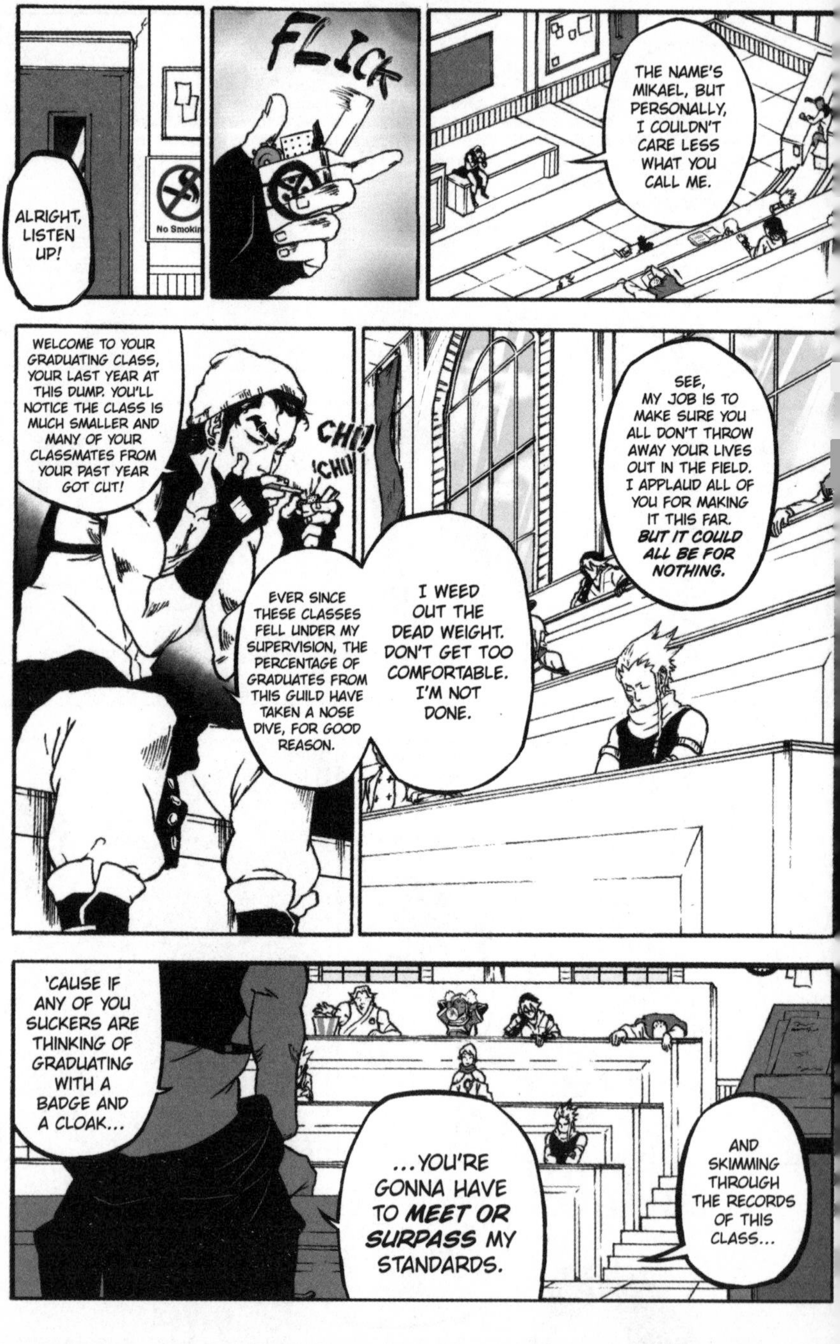
ALRIGHT, LISTEN UP!
No Smokin
FLICK
THE NAME'S MIKAEL, BUT PERSONALLY, I COULDN'T CARE LESS WHAT YOU CALL ME.
WELCOME TO YOUR GRADUATING CLASS, YOUR LAST YEAR AT THIS DUMP. YOU'LL NOTICE THE CLASS IS MUCH SMALLER AND MANY OF YOUR CLASSMATES FROM YOUR PAST YEAR GOT CUT!
CHI!
CHI!
EVER SINCE THESE CLASSES FELL UNDER MY SUPERVISION, THE PERCENTAGE OF GRADUATES FROM THIS GUILD HAVE TAKEN A NOSE DIVE, FOR GOOD REASON.
I WEED OUT THE DEAD WEIGHT. DON'T GET TOO COMFORTABLE. I'M NOT DONE.
SEE, MY JOB IS TO MAKE SURE YOU ALL DON'T THROW AWAY YOUR LIVES OUT IN THE FIELD. I APPLAUD ALL OF YOU FOR MAKING IT THIS FAR. ***BUT IT COULD ALL BE FOR NOTHING.***
'CAUSE IF ANY OF YOU SUCKERS ARE THINKING OF GRADUATING WITH A BADGE AND A CLOAK...
...YOU'RE GONNA HAVE TO ***MEET OR SURPASS*** MY STANDARDS.
AND SKIMMING THROUGH THE RECORDS OF THIS CLASS...

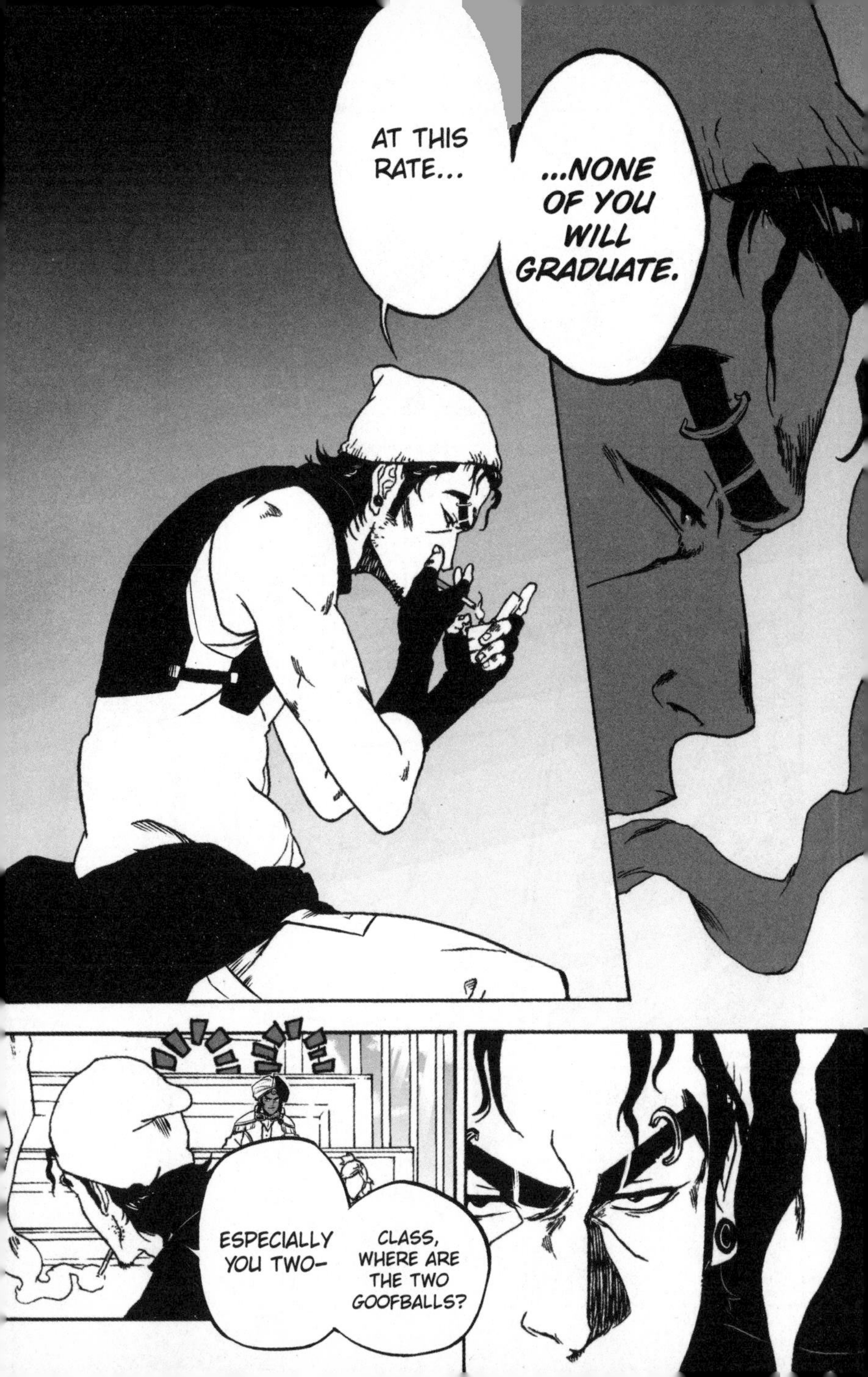
AT THIS RATE...
...NONE OF YOU WILL GRADUATE.
ESPECIALLY YOU TWO-
CLASS, WHERE ARE THE TWO GOOFBALLS?

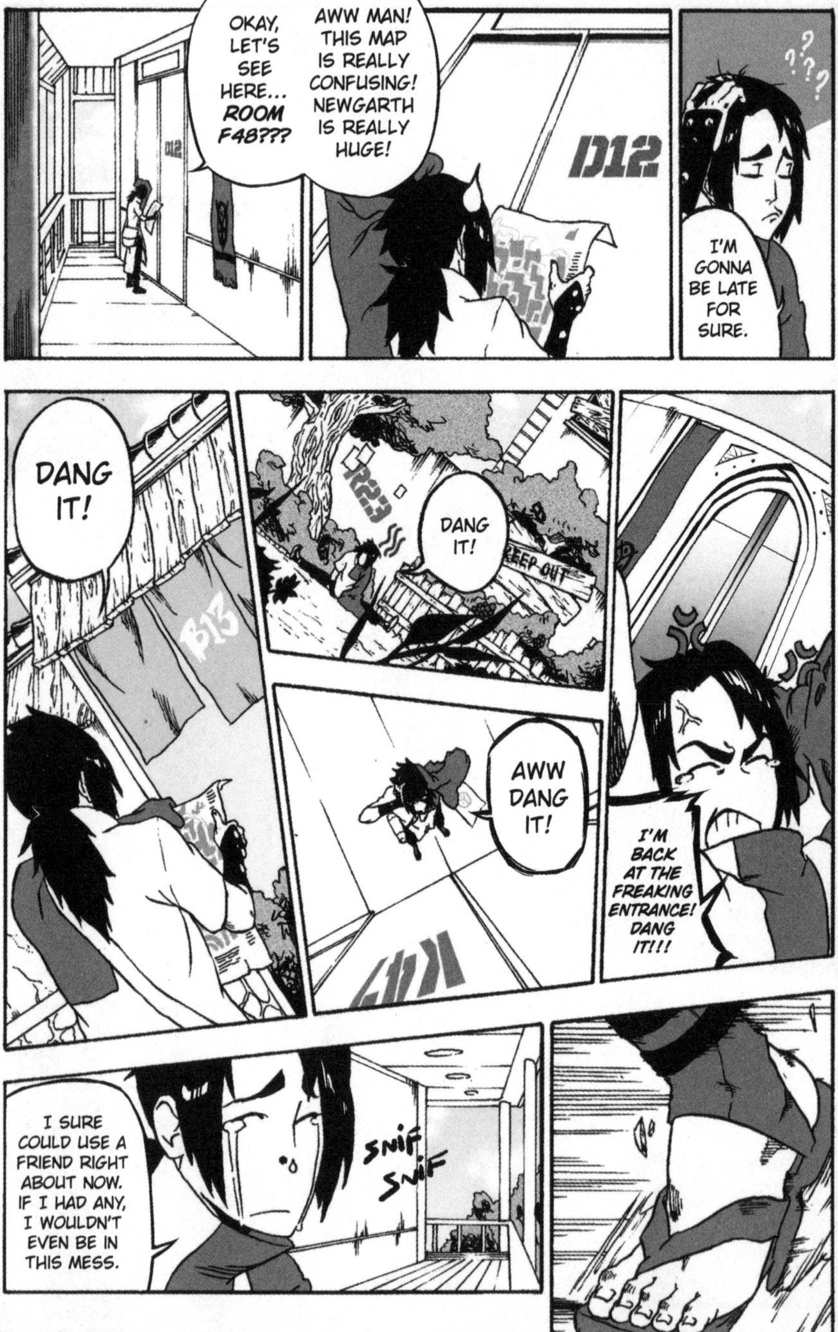
D12
OKAY, LET'S SEE HERE... *ROOM F48???*
AWW MAN! THIS MAP IS REALLY CONFUSING! NEWGARTH IS REALLY HUGE!
D12
???
I'M GONNA BE LATE FOR SURE.
DANG IT!
B13
DANG IT!
AWW DANG IT!
*I'M BACK AT THE FREAKING ENTRANCE! DANG IT!!!*
I SURE COULD USE A FRIEND RIGHT ABOUT NOW. IF I HAD ANY, I WOULDN'T EVEN BE IN THIS MESS.
SNIF SNIF

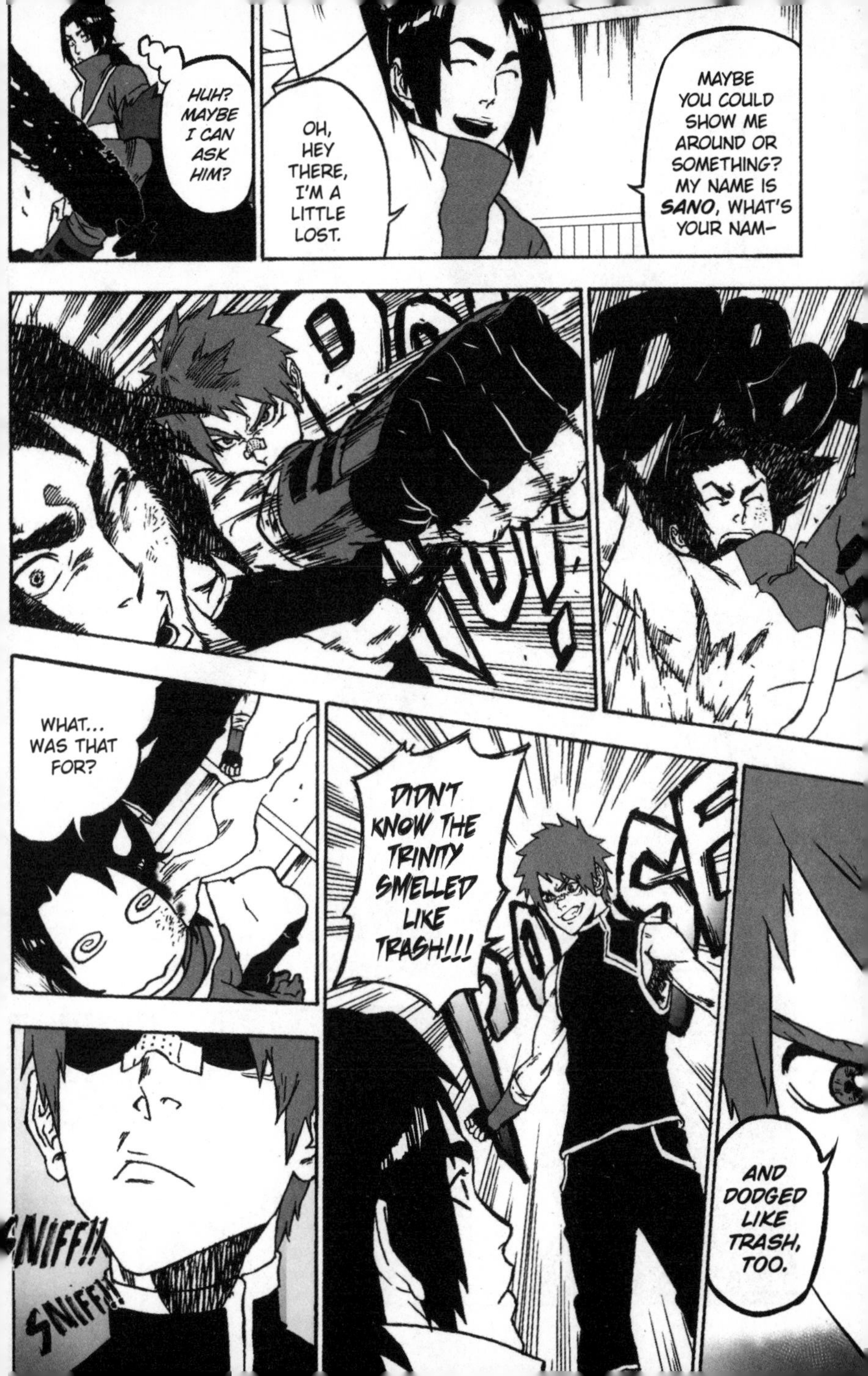
HUH? MAYBE I CAN ASK HIM?
OH, HEY THERE, I'M A LITTLE LOST.
MAYBE YOU COULD SHOW ME AROUND OR SOMETHING? MY NAME IS SANO, WHAT'S YOUR NAM-
WHAT... WAS THAT FOR?
SNIFF!!
SNIFF!!
DIDN'T KNOW THE TRINITY SMELLED LIKE TRASH!!!
AND DODGED LIKE TRASH, TOO.

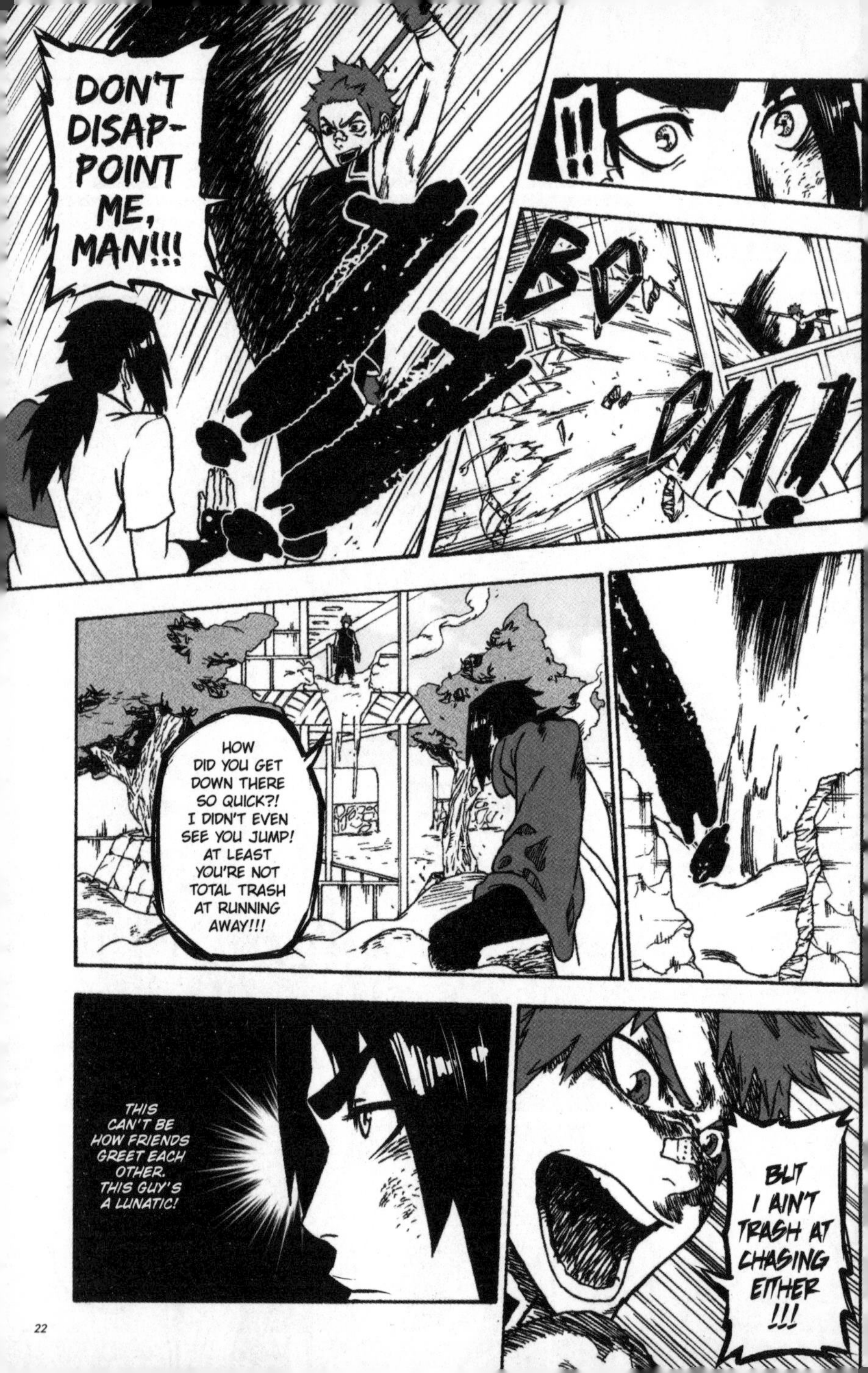
DON'T DISAP-POINT ME, MAN!!!
!!
BOOM!
HOW DID YOU GET DOWN THERE SO QUICK?! I DIDN'T EVEN SEE YOU JUMP! AT LEAST YOU'RE NOT TOTAL TRASH AT RUNNING AWAY!!!
THIS CAN'T BE HOW FRIENDS GREET EACH OTHER. THIS GUY'S A LUNATIC!
BUT I AIN'T TRASH AT CHASING EITHER!!!

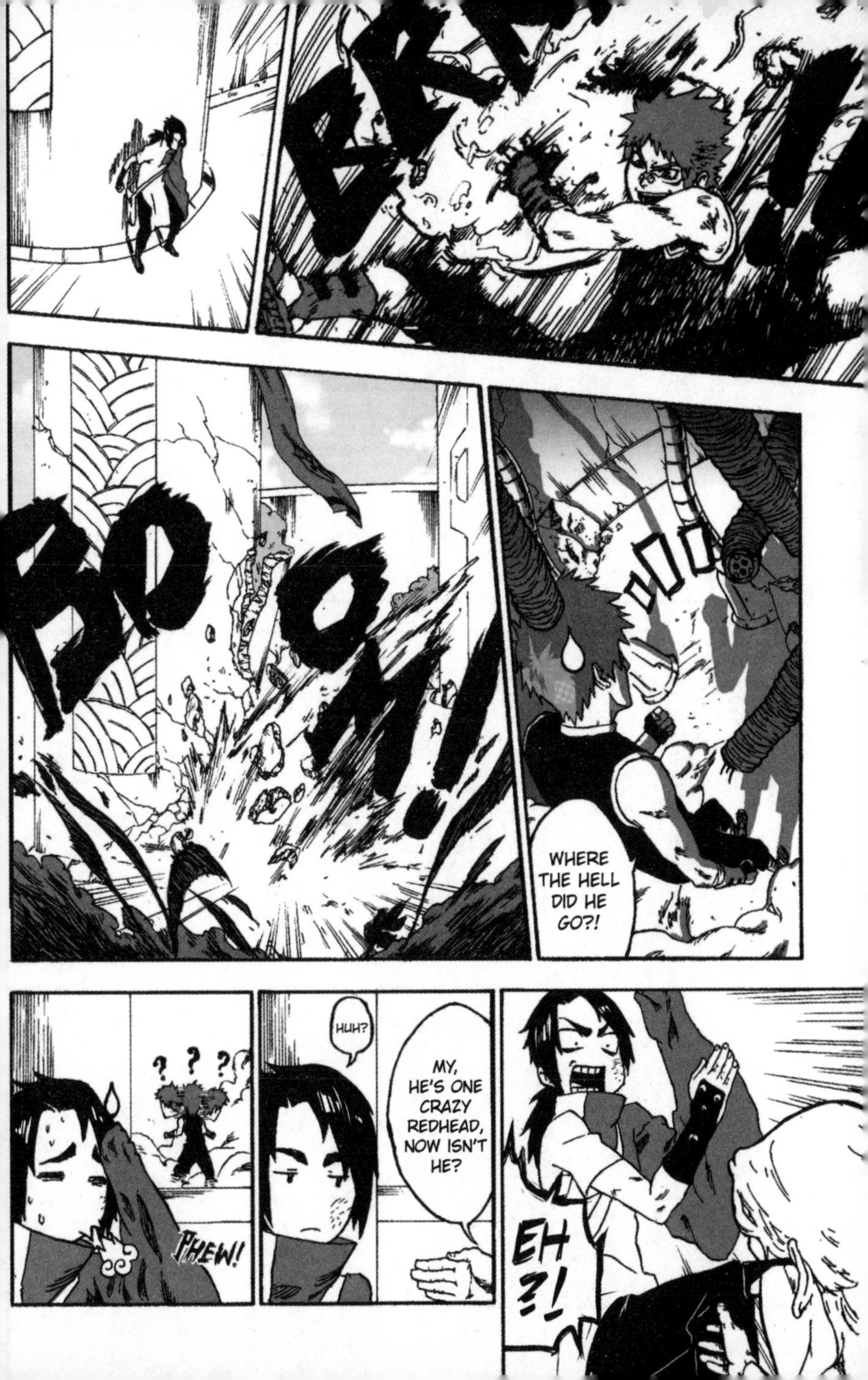
BOOM!!
WHERE THE HELL DID HE GO?!
? ? ?
PHEW!
HUH?
MY, HE'S ONE CRAZY REDHEAD, NOW ISN'T HE?
EH?!

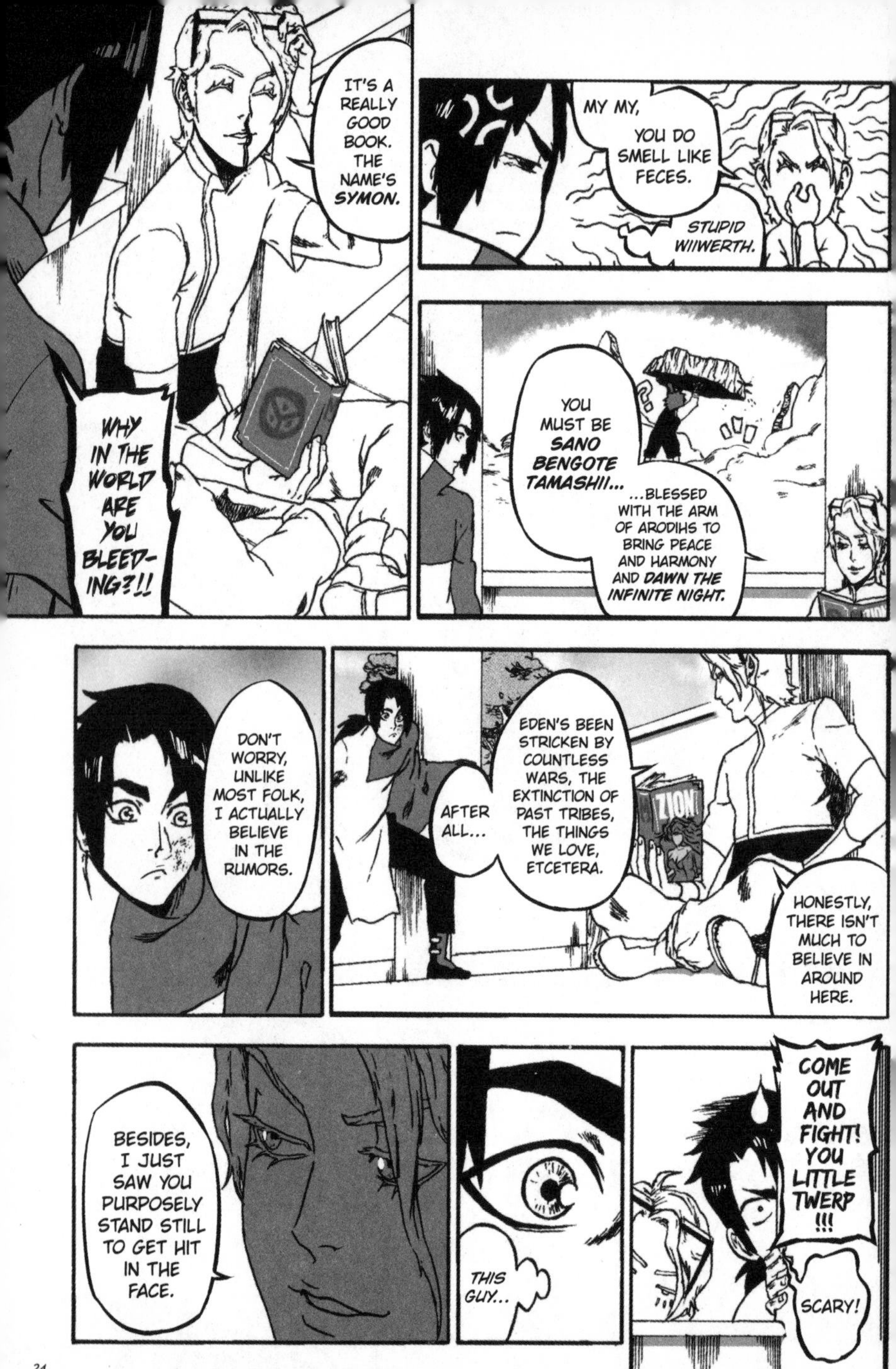
IT'S A REALLY GOOD BOOK. THE NAME'S SYMON.
WHY IN THE WORLD ARE YOU BLEED-ING?!!
MY MY,
YOU DO SMELL LIKE FECES.
STUPID WIIWERTH.
YOU MUST BE SANO BENGOTE TAMASHII...
...BLESSED WITH THE ARM OF ARODIHS TO BRING PEACE AND HARMONY AND DAWN THE INFINITE NIGHT.
DON'T WORRY, UNLIKE MOST FOLK, I ACTUALLY BELIEVE IN THE RUMORS.
AFTER ALL...
EDEN'S BEEN STRICKEN BY COUNTLESS WARS, THE EXTINCTION OF PAST TRIBES, THE THINGS WE LOVE, ETCETERA.
ZION
HONESTLY, THERE ISN'T MUCH TO BELIEVE IN AROUND HERE.
BESIDES, I JUST SAW YOU PURPOSELY STAND STILL TO GET HIT IN THE FACE.
THIS GUY...
COME OUT AND FIGHT! YOU LITTLE TWERP!!!
SCARY!

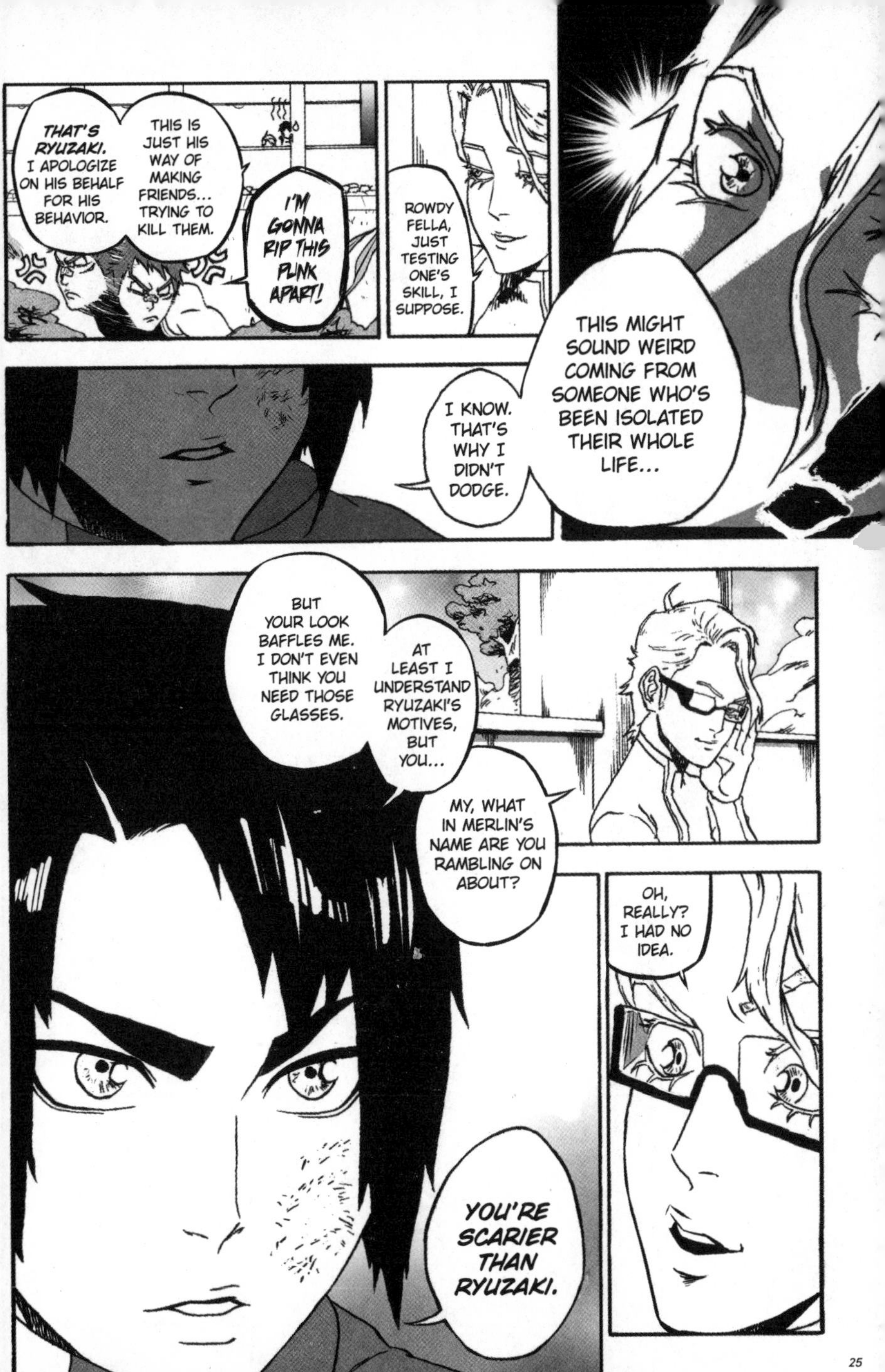
THAT'S RYUZAKI. I APOLOGIZE ON HIS BEHALF FOR HIS BEHAVIOR.
THIS IS JUST HIS WAY OF MAKING FRIENDS... TRYING TO KILL THEM.
I'M GONNA RIP THIS PUNK APART!
ROWDY FELLA, JUST TESTING ONE'S SKILL, I SUPPOSE.
I KNOW. THAT'S WHY I DIDN'T DODGE.
THIS MIGHT SOUND WEIRD COMING FROM SOMEONE WHO'S BEEN ISOLATED THEIR WHOLE LIFE...
BUT YOUR LOOK BAFFLES ME. I DON'T EVEN THINK YOU NEED THOSE GLASSES.
AT LEAST I UNDERSTAND RYUZAKI'S MOTIVES, BUT YOU...
YOU'RE SCARIER THAN RYUZAKI.
MY, WHAT IN MERLIN'S NAME ARE YOU RAMBLING ON ABOUT?
OH, REALLY? I HAD NO IDEA.

I COULD BE WRONG, I GUESS...

THERE YOU ARE!!!

WHAT'S THE MATTER, TWERP? YOU LOOK PALE!

oi!!

WHAT THE HELL IS GOING ON HERE?!

YOU GOOFBALLS HAVE GOT A LOT OF EXPLAINING TO DO!

PRO-FESSOR MIKAEL!!

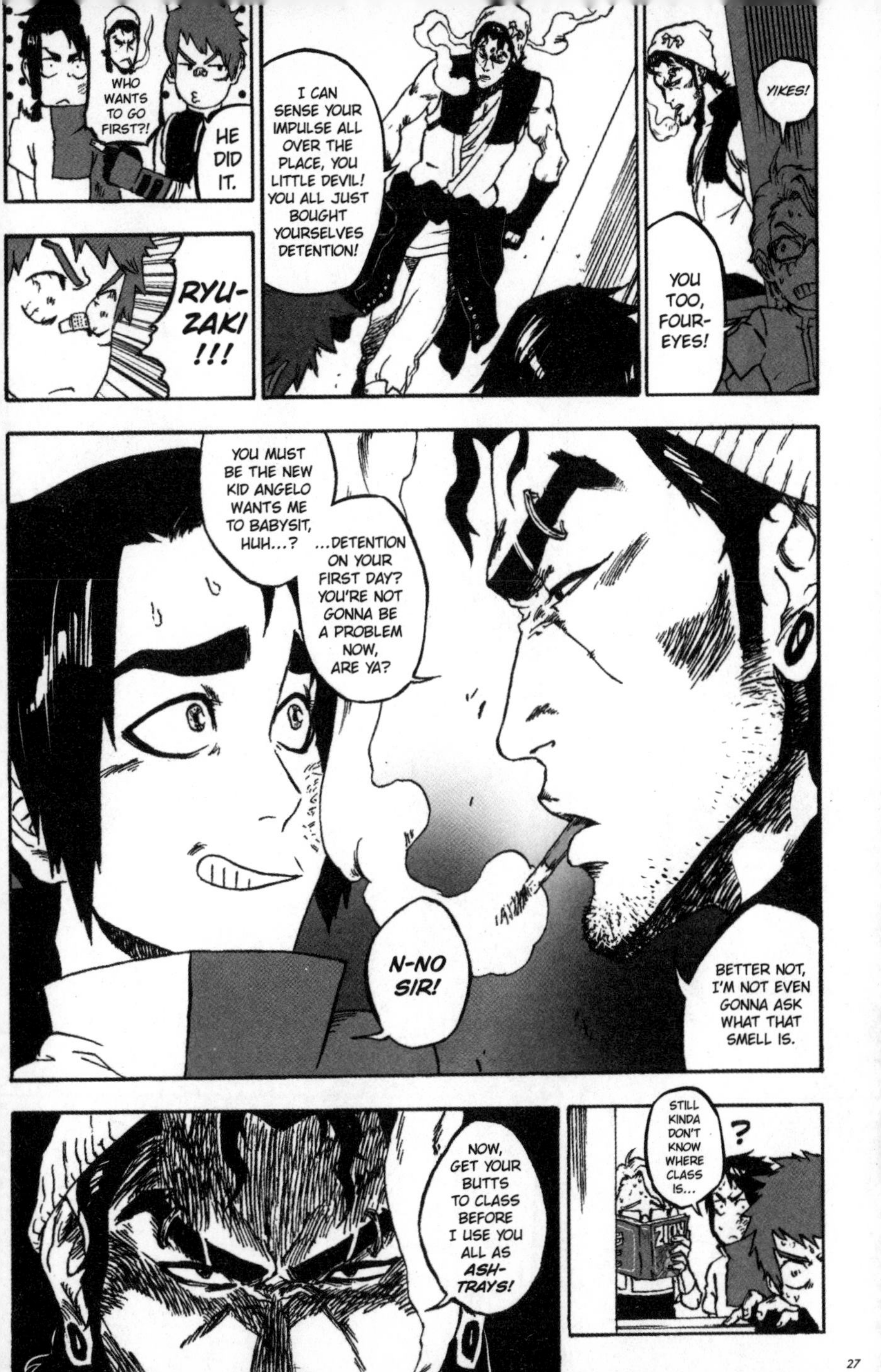
WHO WANTS TO GO FIRST?!
HE DID IT.
RYU-ZAKI !!!
I CAN SENSE YOUR IMPULSE ALL OVER THE PLACE, YOU LITTLE DEVIL! YOU ALL JUST BOUGHT YOURSELVES DETENTION!
YIKES!
YOU TOO, FOUR-EYES!
YOU MUST BE THE NEW KID ANGELO WANTS ME TO BABYSIT, HUH...?
...DETENTION ON YOUR FIRST DAY? YOU'RE NOT GONNA BE A PROBLEM NOW, ARE YA?
N-NO SIR!
BETTER NOT, I'M NOT EVEN GONNA ASK WHAT THAT SMELL IS.
NOW, GET YOUR BUTTS TO CLASS BEFORE I USE YOU ALL AS ASH-TRAYS!
STILL KINDA DON'T KNOW WHERE CLASS IS...
?

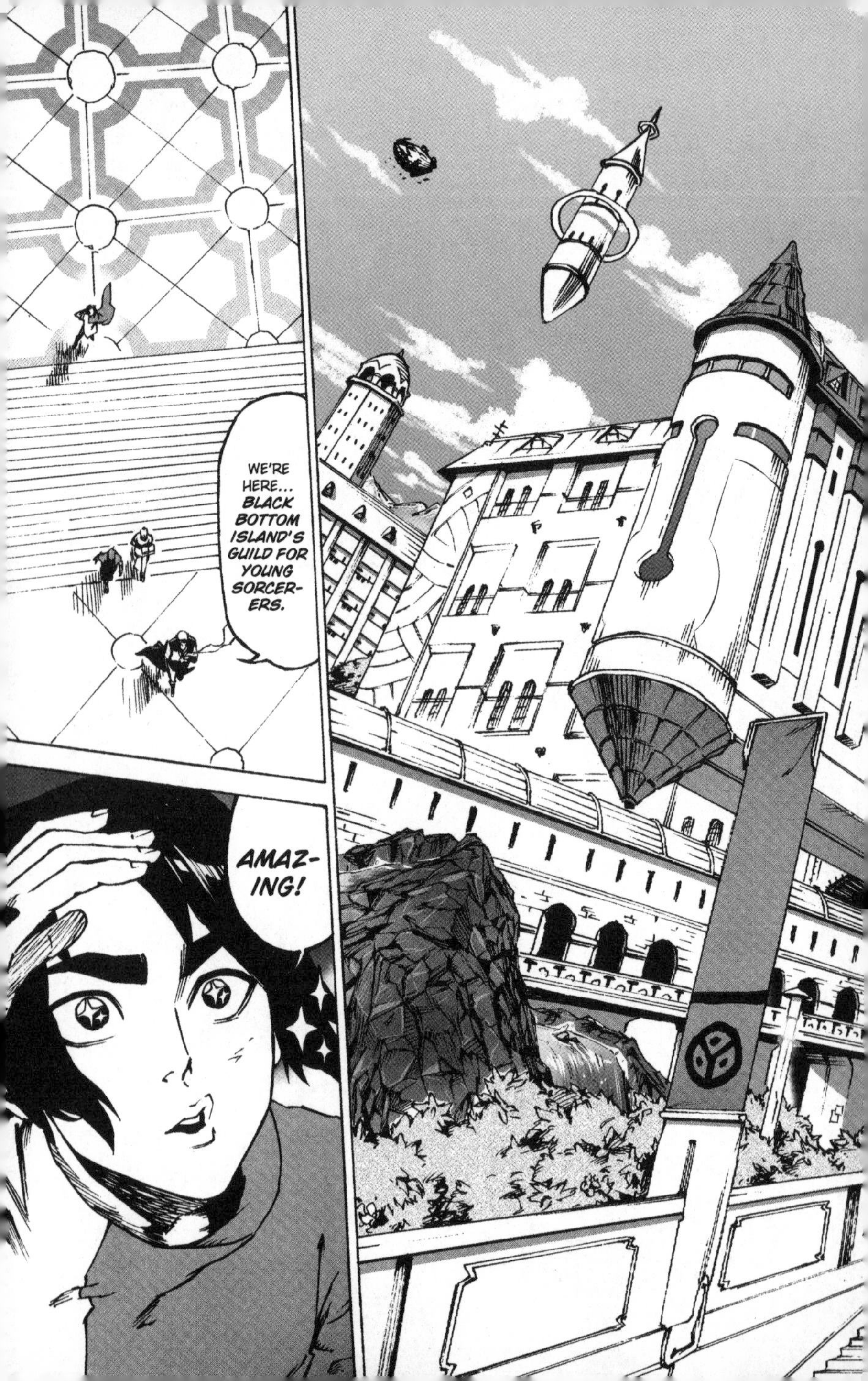
WE'RE HERE... BLACK BOTTOM ISLAND'S GUILD FOR YOUNG SORCERERS.
AMAZ-ING!

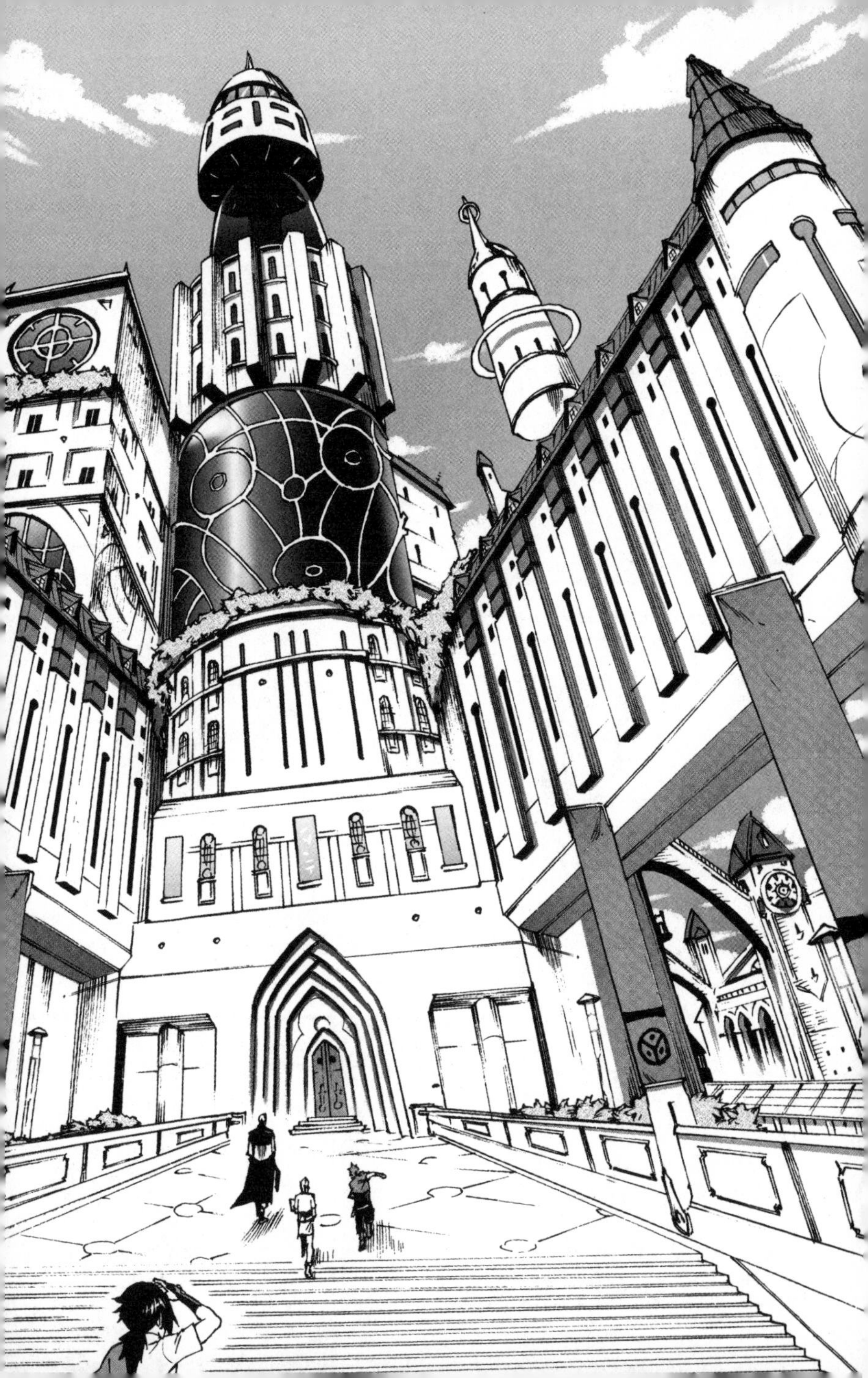

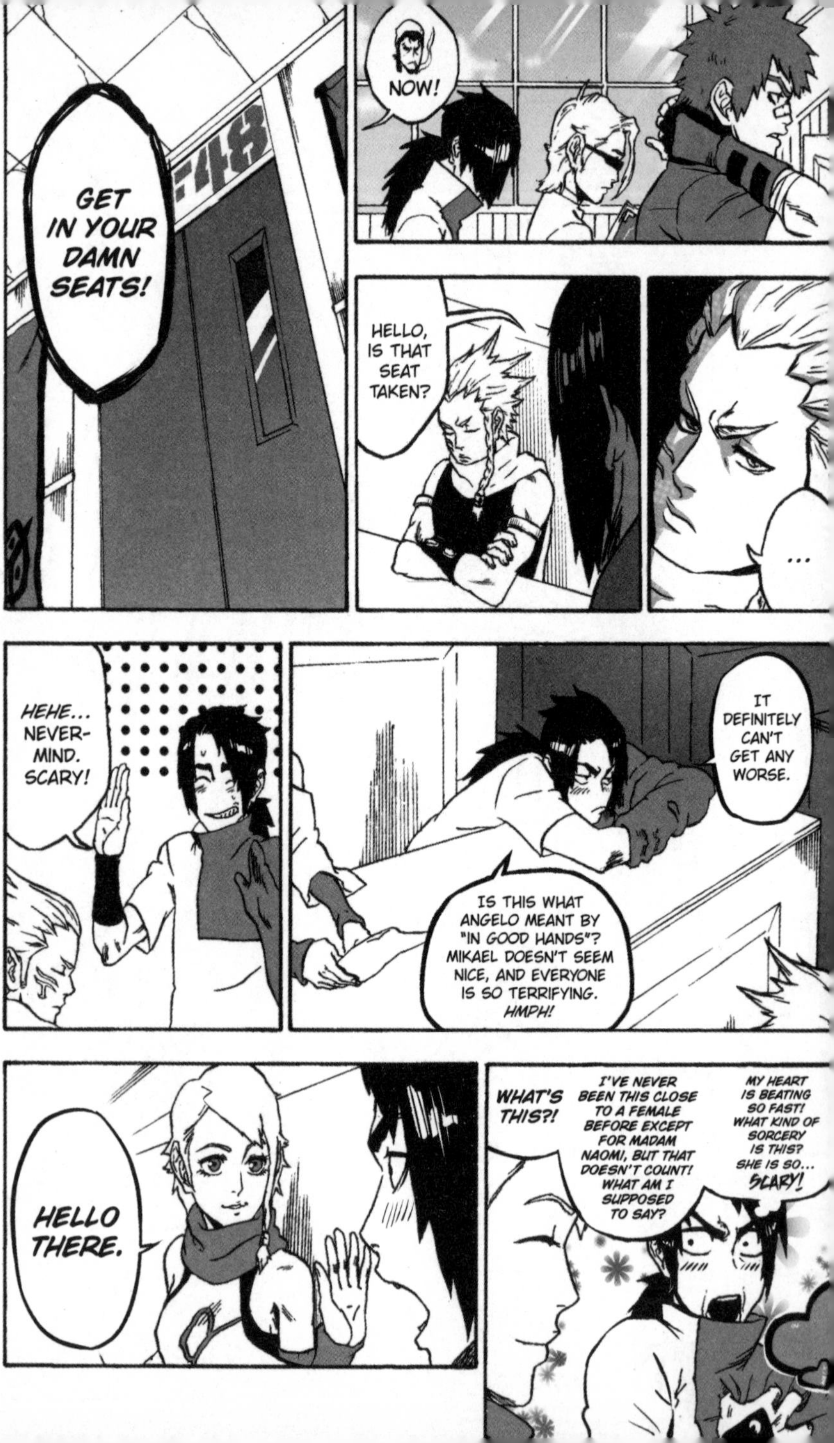
GET IN YOUR DAMN SEATS!
NOW!
HELLO, IS THAT SEAT TAKEN?
...
HEHE... NEVER-MIND. SCARY!
IT DEFINITELY CAN'T GET ANY WORSE.
IS THIS WHAT ANGELO MEANT BY "IN GOOD HANDS"? MIKAEL DOESN'T SEEM NICE, AND EVERYONE IS SO TERRIFYING. HMPH!
HELLO THERE.
WHAT'S THIS?!
I'VE NEVER BEEN THIS CLOSE TO A FEMALE BEFORE EXCEPT FOR MADAM NAOMI, BUT THAT DOESN'T COUNT! WHAT AM I SUPPOSED TO SAY?
MY HEART IS BEATING SO FAST! WHAT KIND OF SORCERY IS THIS? SHE IS SO... SCARY!

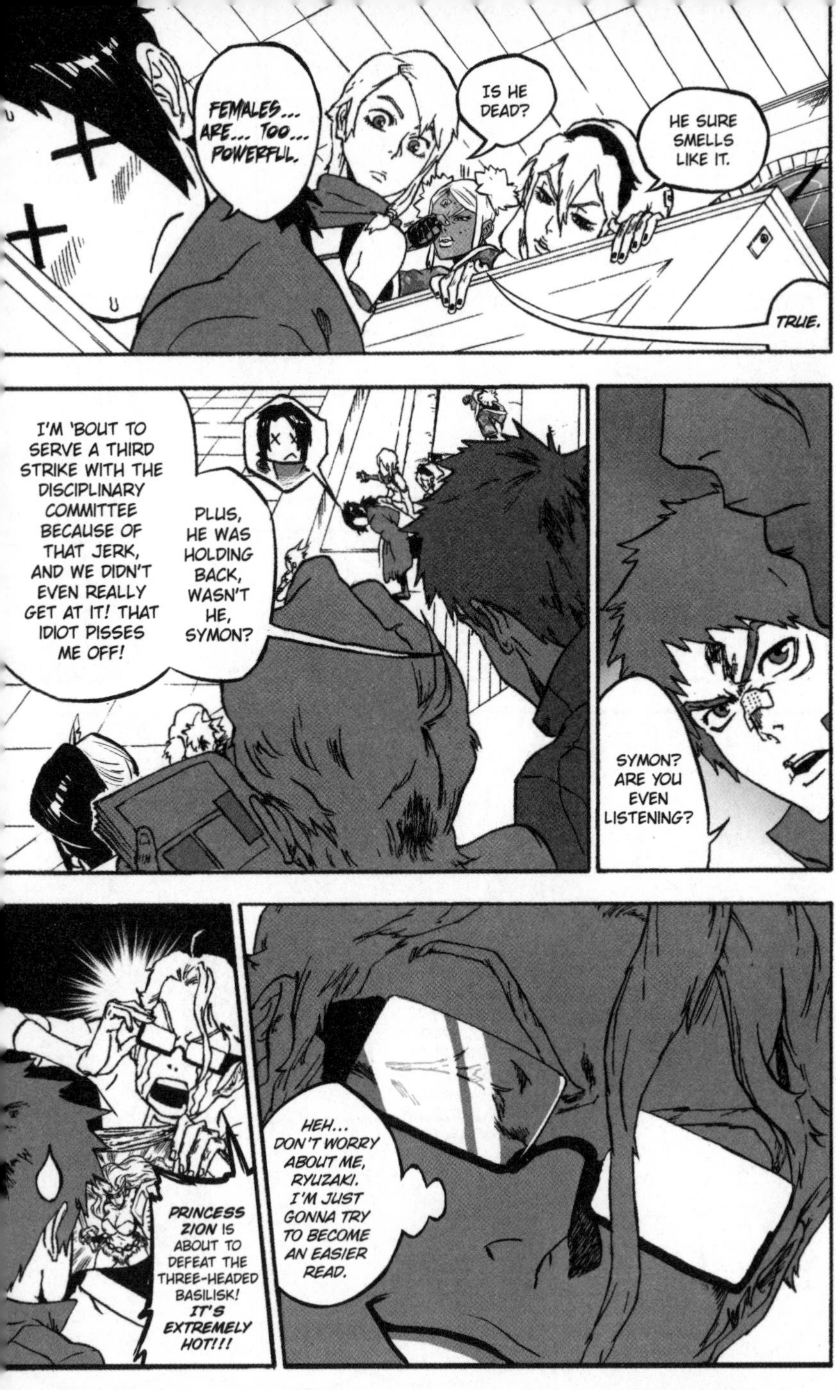
FEMALES... ARE... TOO... POWERFUL.
IS HE DEAD?
HE SURE SMELLS LIKE IT.
TRUE.
I'M 'BOUT TO SERVE A THIRD STRIKE WITH THE DISCIPLINARY COMMITTEE BECAUSE OF THAT JERK, AND WE DIDN'T EVEN REALLY GET AT IT! THAT IDIOT PISSES ME OFF!
PLUS, HE WAS HOLDING BACK, WASN'T HE, SYMON?
SYMON? ARE YOU EVEN LISTENING?
PRINCESS ZION IS ABOUT TO DEFEAT THE THREE-HEADED BASILISK! IT'S EXTREMELY HOT!!!
HEH... DON'T WORRY ABOUT ME, RYUZAKI. I'M JUST GONNA TRY TO BECOME AN EASIER READ.

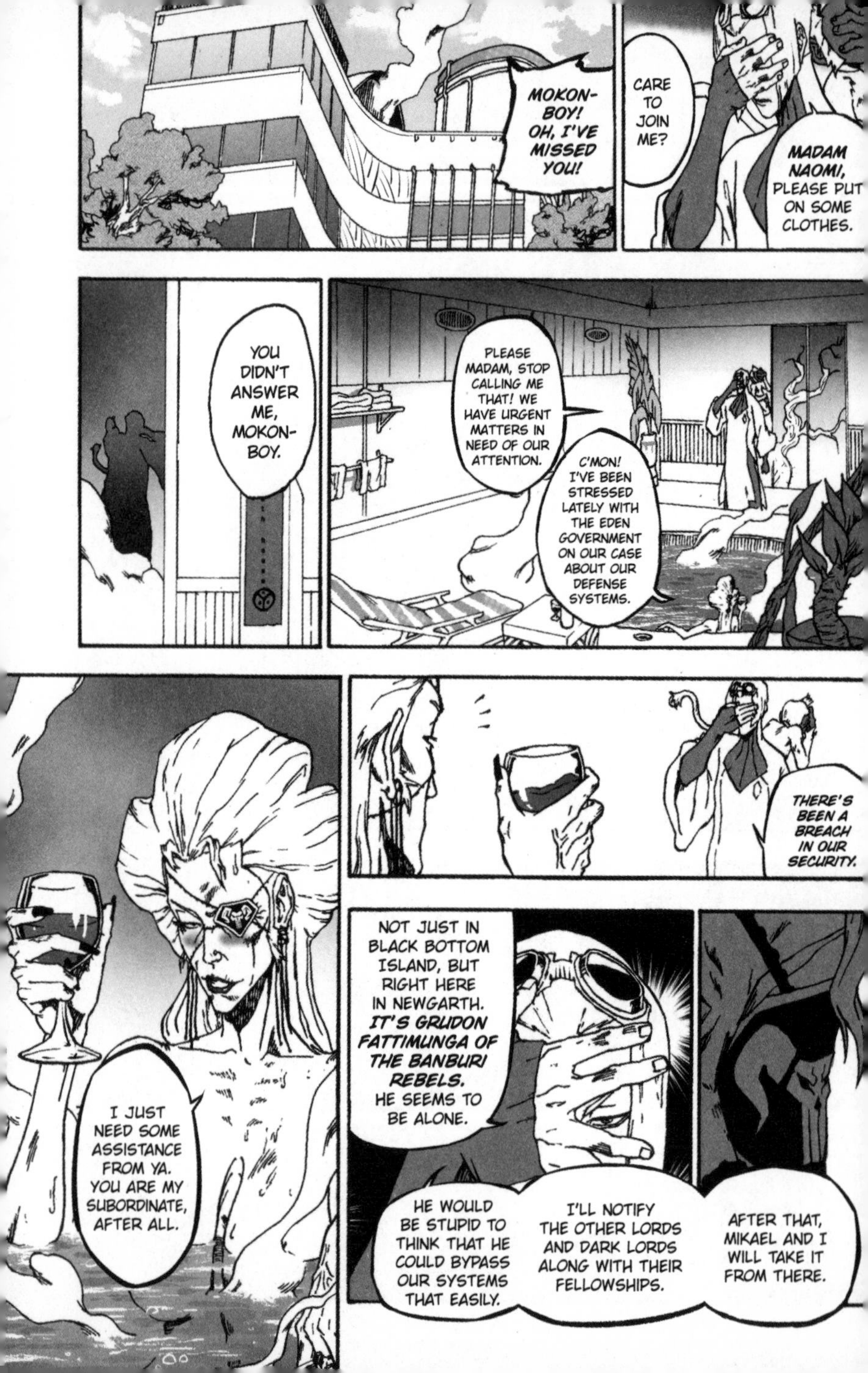
MOKON-BOY! OH, I'VE MISSED YOU!
CARE TO JOIN ME?
MADAM NAOMI, PLEASE PUT ON SOME CLOTHES.
YOU DIDN'T ANSWER ME, MOKON-BOY.
PLEASE MADAM, STOP CALLING ME THAT! WE HAVE URGENT MATTERS IN NEED OF OUR ATTENTION.
C'MON! I'VE BEEN STRESSED LATELY WITH THE EDEN GOVERNMENT ON OUR CASE ABOUT OUR DEFENSE SYSTEMS.
I JUST NEED SOME ASSISTANCE FROM YA. YOU ARE MY SUBORDINATE, AFTER ALL.
THERE'S BEEN A BREACH IN OUR SECURITY.
NOT JUST IN BLACK BOTTOM ISLAND, BUT RIGHT HERE IN NEWGARTH. IT'S GRUDON FATTIMUNGA OF THE BANBURI REBELS. HE SEEMS TO BE ALONE.
HE WOULD BE STUPID TO THINK THAT HE COULD BYPASS OUR SYSTEMS THAT EASILY.
I'LL NOTIFY THE OTHER LORDS AND DARK LORDS ALONG WITH THEIR FELLOWSHIPS.
AFTER THAT, MIKAEL AND I WILL TAKE IT FROM THERE.

HOW'S THE BOY?

STILL IN DEVELOP-MENT.

ANGELO, DO YOU REALLY BELIEVE THIS WILL WORK?

HE'S BEEN IN THE DARK LONG ENOUGH. THIS EXPOSURE WILL SERVE AS A CATALYST TOWARD HIS GROWTH.

THAT'S WHAT I'M AFRAID OF. WE'RE JEOPARDIZING EVERYTHING WE'VE WORKED FOR.

MADAM NAOMI, THE GROWTH OF THE APPLE BLACK SEED CANNOT BE COMPROMISED BY SUBJECTS OF LOWER LIFEFORMS. SANO WILL BE SAFE, YOU'VE HEARD THIS FROM THE GREAT *ELI PROPHETS* YOURSELF. ARODIHS IS THE *KEY OF DREAMS*. WE BOTH HAVE WITNESSED ITS IMMENSE POWER.

THE ARODIHS ARM, HUH... WE BOTH KNOW WHAT THAT ARM *TRULY IS.*

...

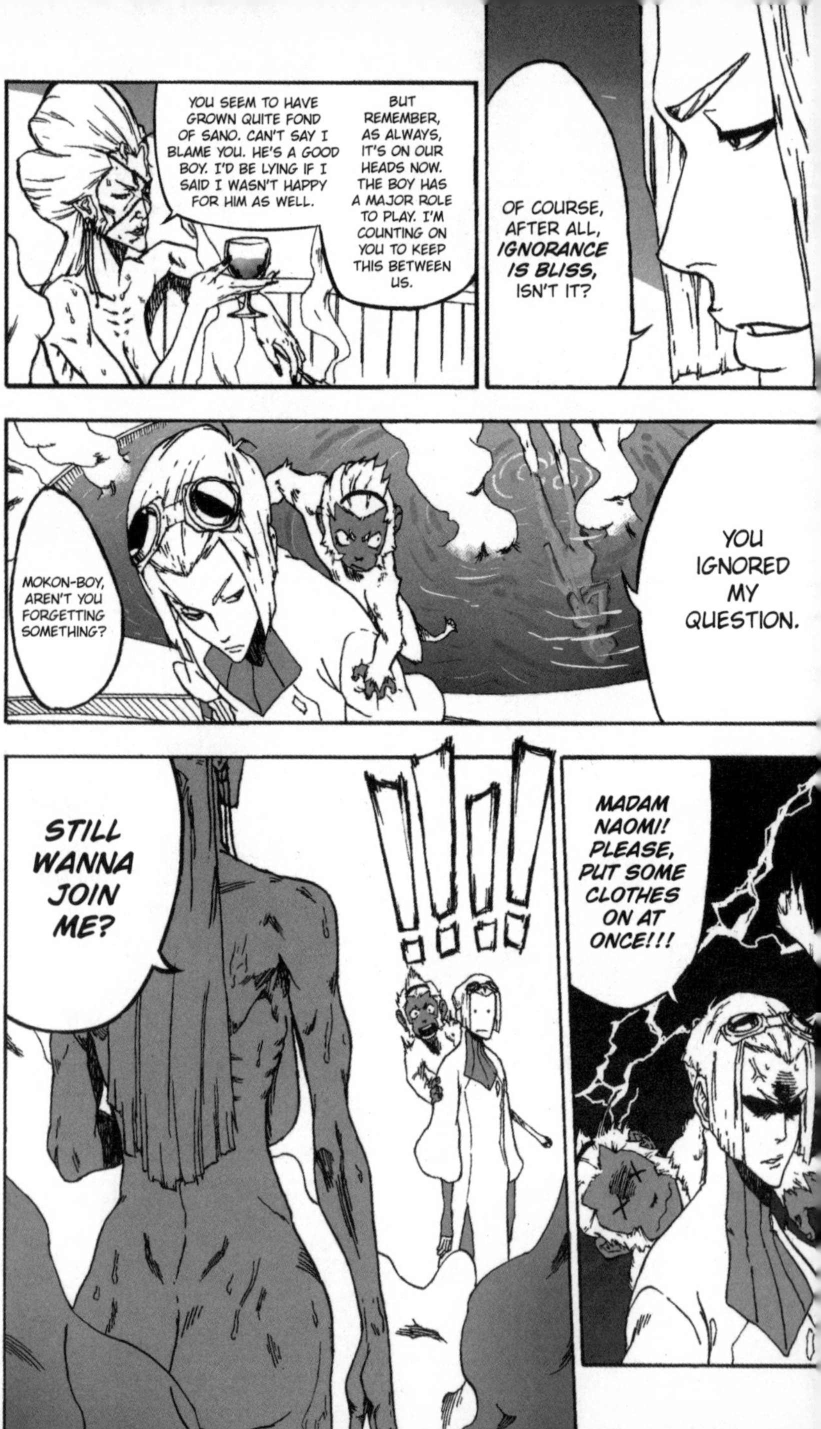
YOU SEEM TO HAVE GROWN QUITE FOND OF SANO. CAN'T SAY I BLAME YOU. HE'S A GOOD BOY. I'D BE LYING IF I SAID I WASN'T HAPPY FOR HIM AS WELL.
BUT REMEMBER, AS ALWAYS, IT'S ON OUR HEADS NOW. THE BOY HAS A MAJOR ROLE TO PLAY. I'M COUNTING ON YOU TO KEEP THIS BETWEEN US.
OF COURSE, AFTER ALL, IGNORANCE IS BLISS, ISN'T IT?
MOKON-BOY, AREN'T YOU FORGETTING SOMETHING?
YOU IGNORED MY QUESTION.
STILL WANNA JOIN ME?
!!!!
MADAM NAOMI! PLEASE, PUT SOME CLOTHES ON AT ONCE!!!

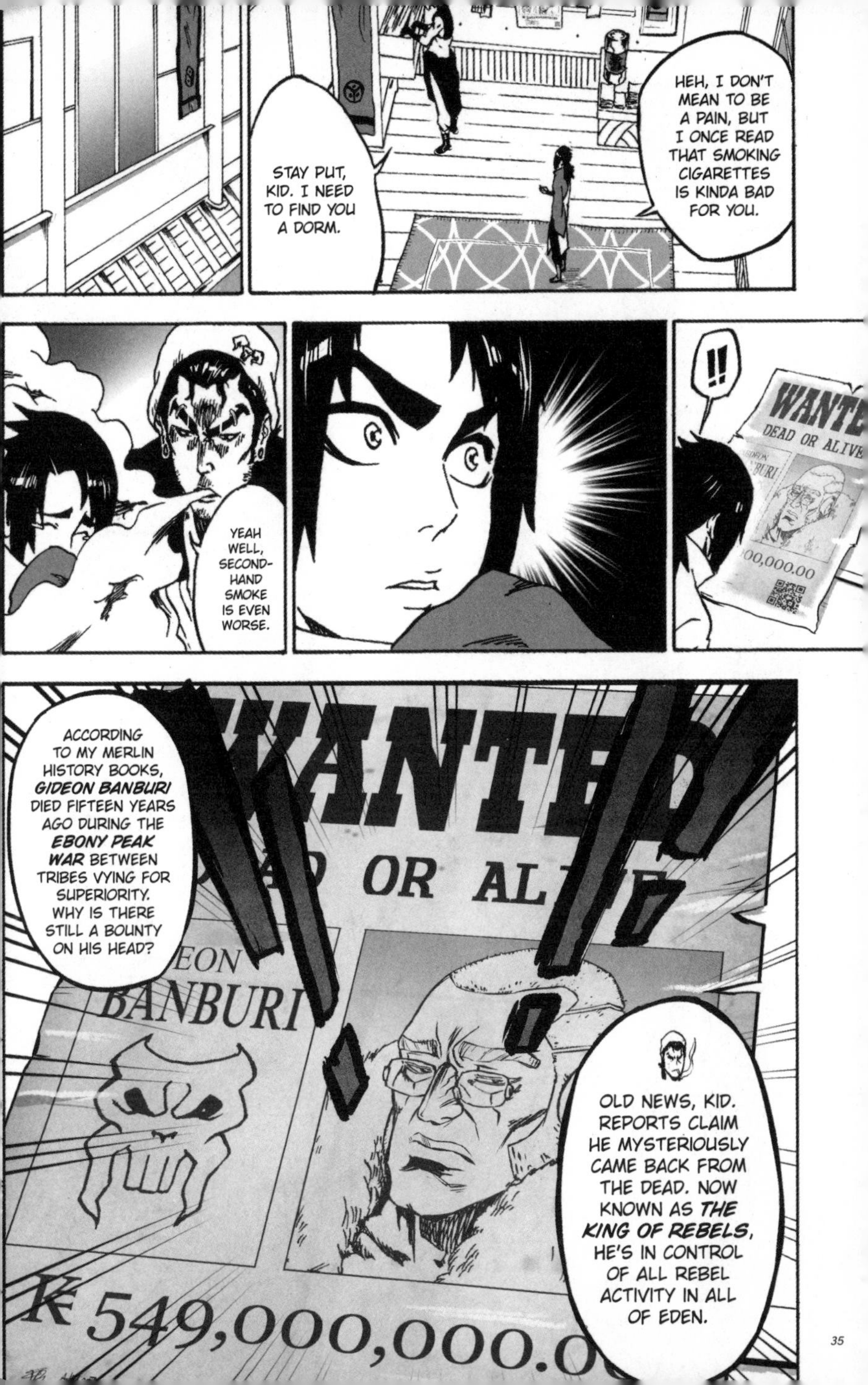
STAY PUT, KID. I NEED TO FIND YOU A DORM.
HEH, I DON'T MEAN TO BE A PAIN, BUT I ONCE READ THAT SMOKING CIGARETTES IS KINDA BAD FOR YOU.
YEAH WELL, SECOND-HAND SMOKE IS EVEN WORSE.
!!
ACCORDING TO MY MERLIN HISTORY BOOKS, ***GIDEON BANBURI*** DIED FIFTEEN YEARS AGO DURING THE ***EBONY PEAK WAR*** BETWEEN TRIBES VYING FOR SUPERIORITY. WHY IS THERE STILL A BOUNTY ON HIS HEAD?
BANBURI
OLD NEWS, KID. REPORTS CLAIM HE MYSTERIOUSLY CAME BACK FROM THE DEAD. NOW KNOWN AS ***THE KING OF REBELS***, HE'S IN CONTROL OF ALL REBEL ACTIVITY IN ALL OF EDEN.

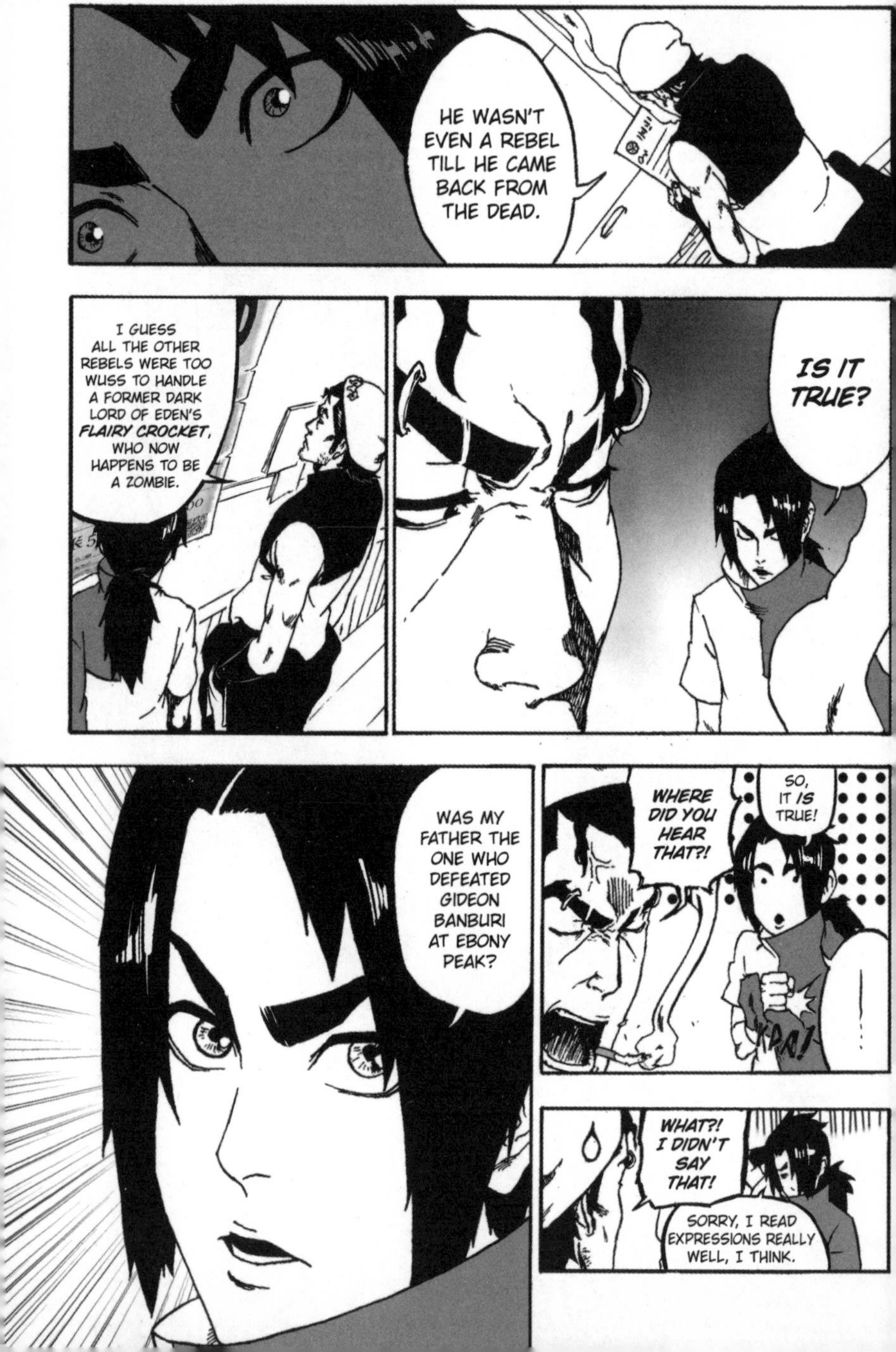
HE WASN'T EVEN A REBEL TILL HE CAME BACK FROM THE DEAD.
I GUESS ALL THE OTHER REBELS WERE TOO WUSS TO HANDLE A FORMER DARK LORD OF EDEN'S *FLAIRY CROCKET*, WHO NOW HAPPENS TO BE A ZOMBIE.
*IS IT TRUE?*
WAS MY FATHER THE ONE WHO DEFEATED GIDEON BANBURI AT EBONY PEAK?
*WHERE DID YOU HEAR THAT?!*
SO, IT *IS* TRUE!
*WHAT?! I DIDN'T SAY THAT!*
SORRY, I READ EXPRESSIONS REALLY WELL, I THINK.

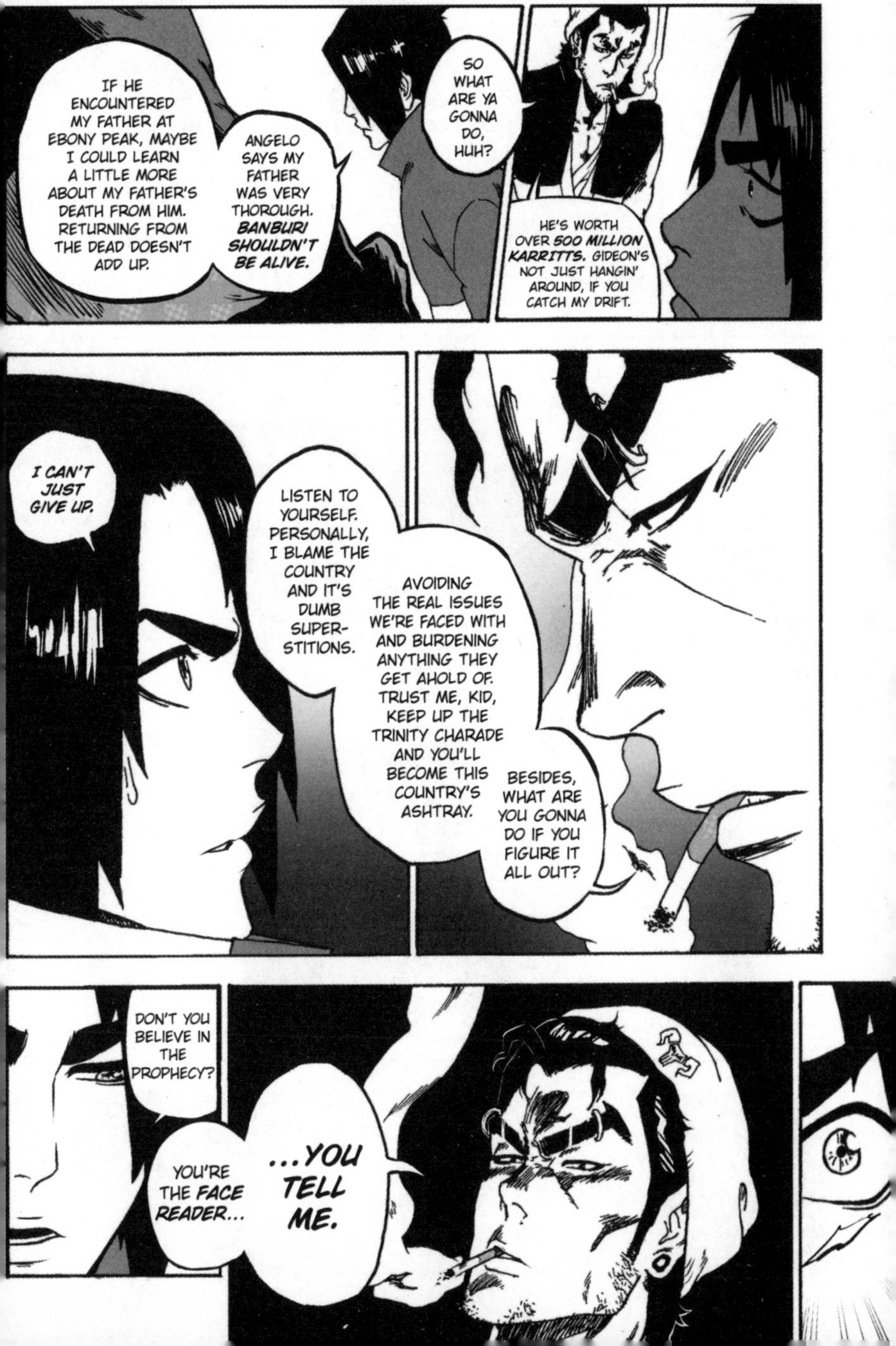
IF HE ENCOUNTERED MY FATHER AT EBONY PEAK, MAYBE I COULD LEARN A LITTLE MORE ABOUT MY FATHER'S DEATH FROM HIM. RETURNING FROM THE DEAD DOESN'T ADD UP.
ANGELO SAYS MY FATHER WAS VERY THOROUGH. BANBURI SHOULDN'T BE ALIVE.
SO WHAT ARE YA GONNA DO, HUH?
HE'S WORTH OVER 500 MILLION KARRITTS. GIDEON'S NOT JUST HANGIN' AROUND, IF YOU CATCH MY DRIFT.
I CAN'T JUST GIVE UP.
LISTEN TO YOURSELF. PERSONALLY, I BLAME THE COUNTRY AND IT'S DUMB SUPER-STITIONS.
AVOIDING THE REAL ISSUES WE'RE FACED WITH AND BURDENING ANYTHING THEY GET AHOLD OF. TRUST ME, KID, KEEP UP THE TRINITY CHARADE AND YOU'LL BECOME THIS COUNTRY'S ASHTRAY.
BESIDES, WHAT ARE YOU GONNA DO IF YOU FIGURE IT ALL OUT?
DON'T YOU BELIEVE IN THE PROPHECY?
YOU'RE THE FACE READER...
...YOU TELL ME.

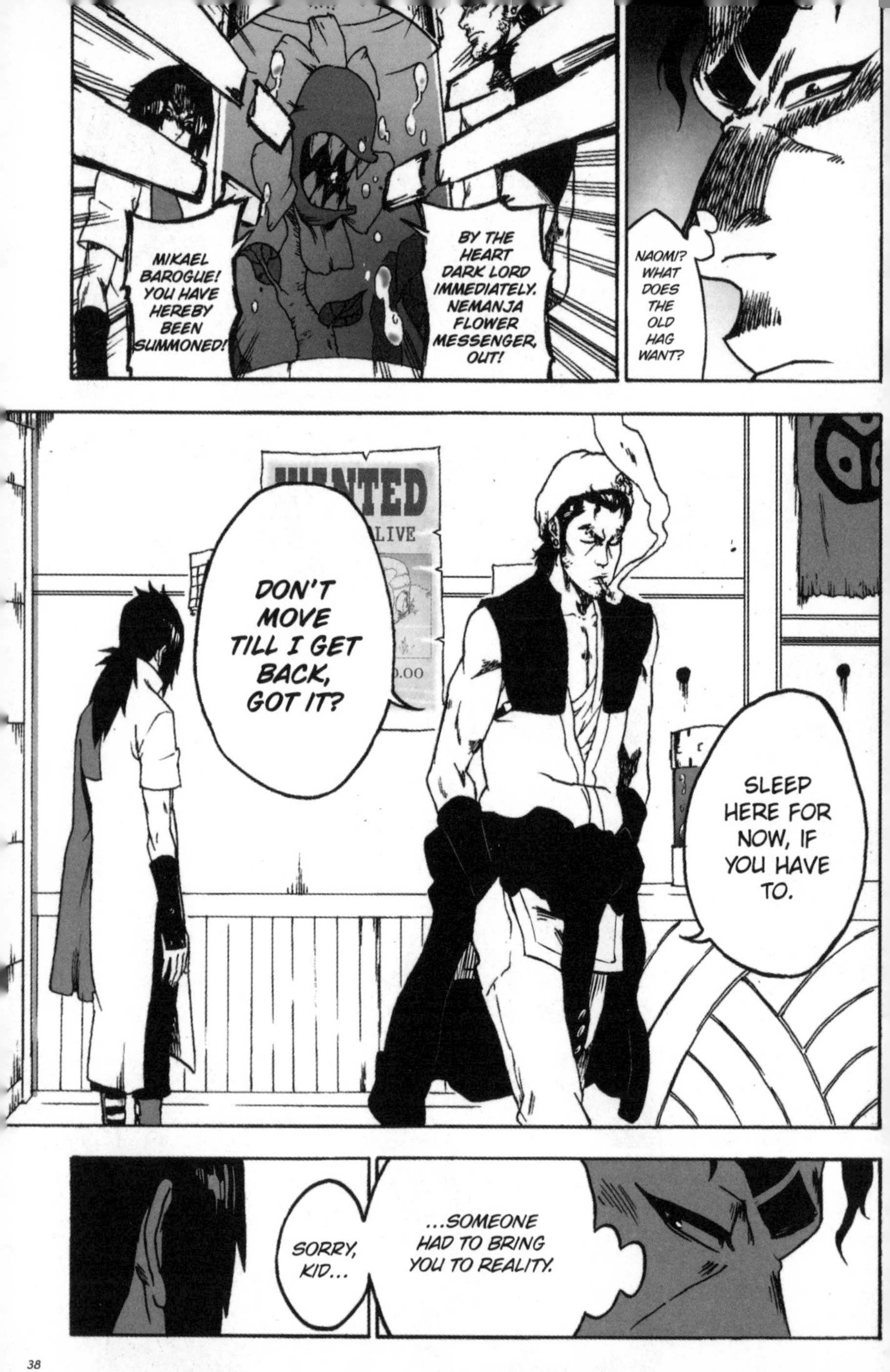
MIKAEL BAROGUE! YOU HAVE HEREBY BEEN SUMMONED!
BY THE HEART DARK LORD IMMEDIATELY. NEMANJA FLOWER MESSENGER, OUT!
NAOMI? WHAT DOES THE OLD HAG WANT?
DON'T MOVE TILL I GET BACK, GOT IT?
SLEEP HERE FOR NOW, IF YOU HAVE TO.
SORRY, KID...
...SOMEONE HAD TO BRING YOU TO REALITY.

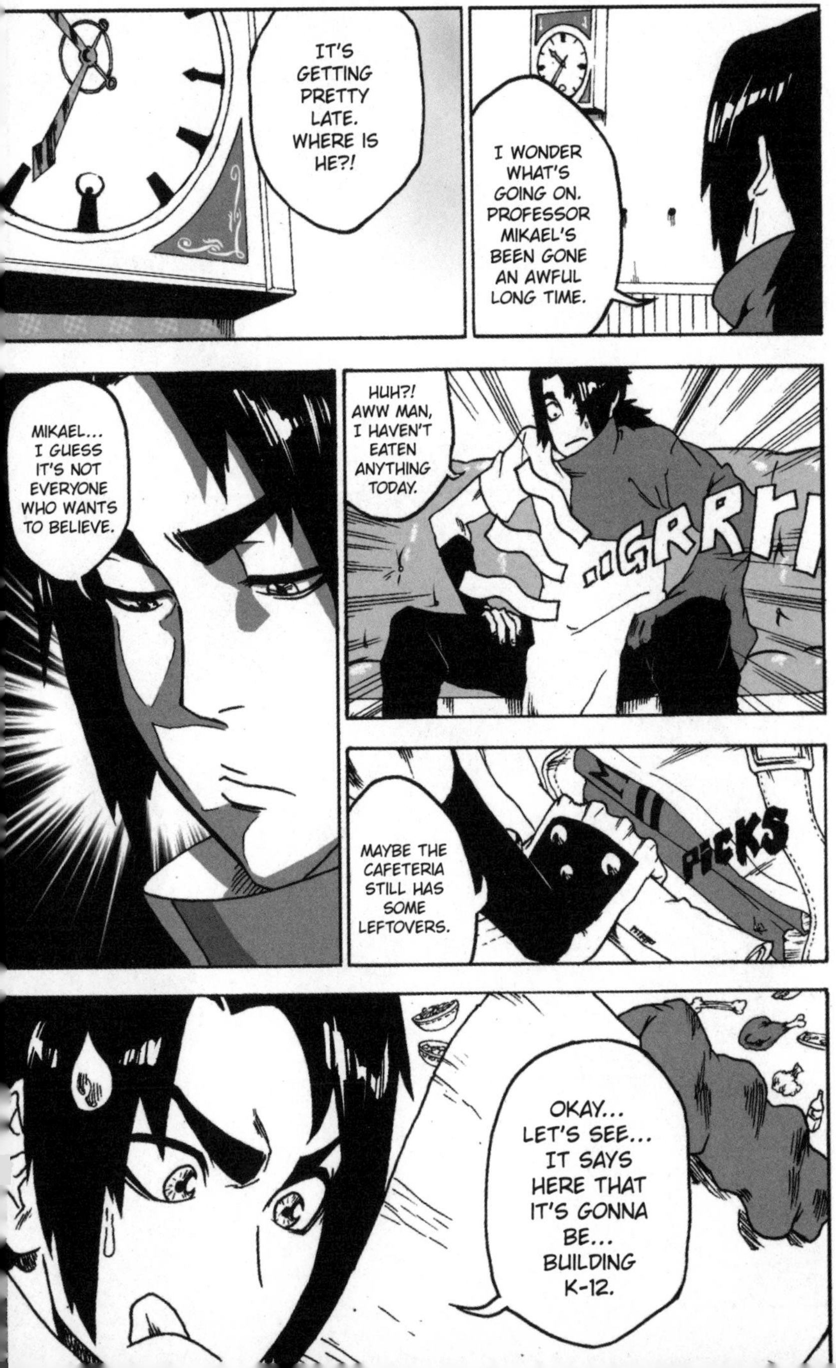
IT'S GETTING PRETTY LATE. WHERE IS HE?!
I WONDER WHAT'S GOING ON. PROFESSOR MIKAEL'S BEEN GONE AN AWFUL LONG TIME.
MIKAEL... I GUESS IT'S NOT EVERYONE WHO WANTS TO BELIEVE.
HUH?! AWW MAN, I HAVEN'T EATEN ANYTHING TODAY.
GRRR
MAYBE THE CAFETERIA STILL HAS SOME LEFTOVERS.
PICKS
OKAY... LET'S SEE... IT SAYS HERE THAT IT'S GONNA BE... BUILDING K-12.

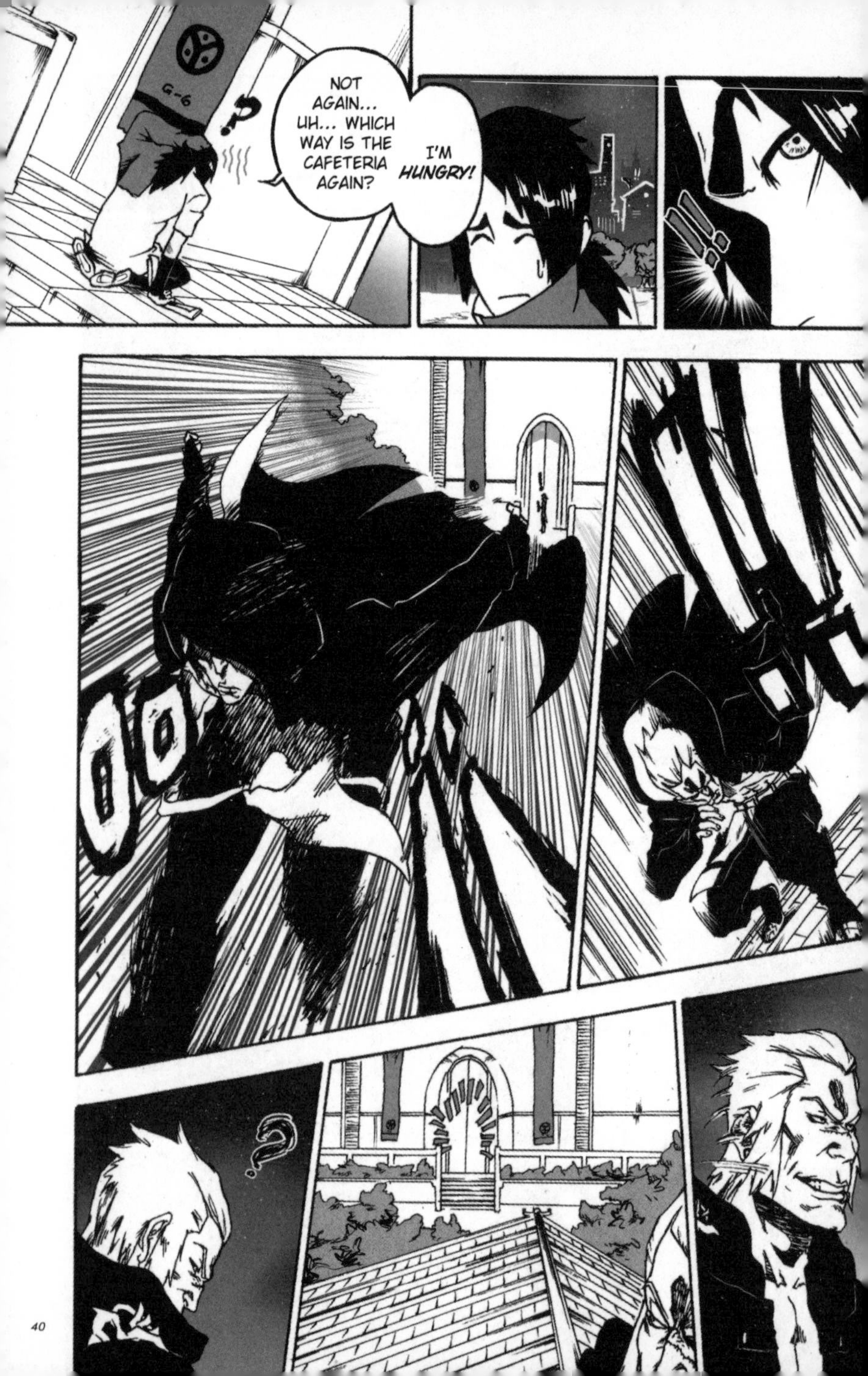
?
NOT AGAIN... UH... WHICH WAY IS THE CAFETERIA AGAIN?
I'M *HUNGRY!*
!!
?

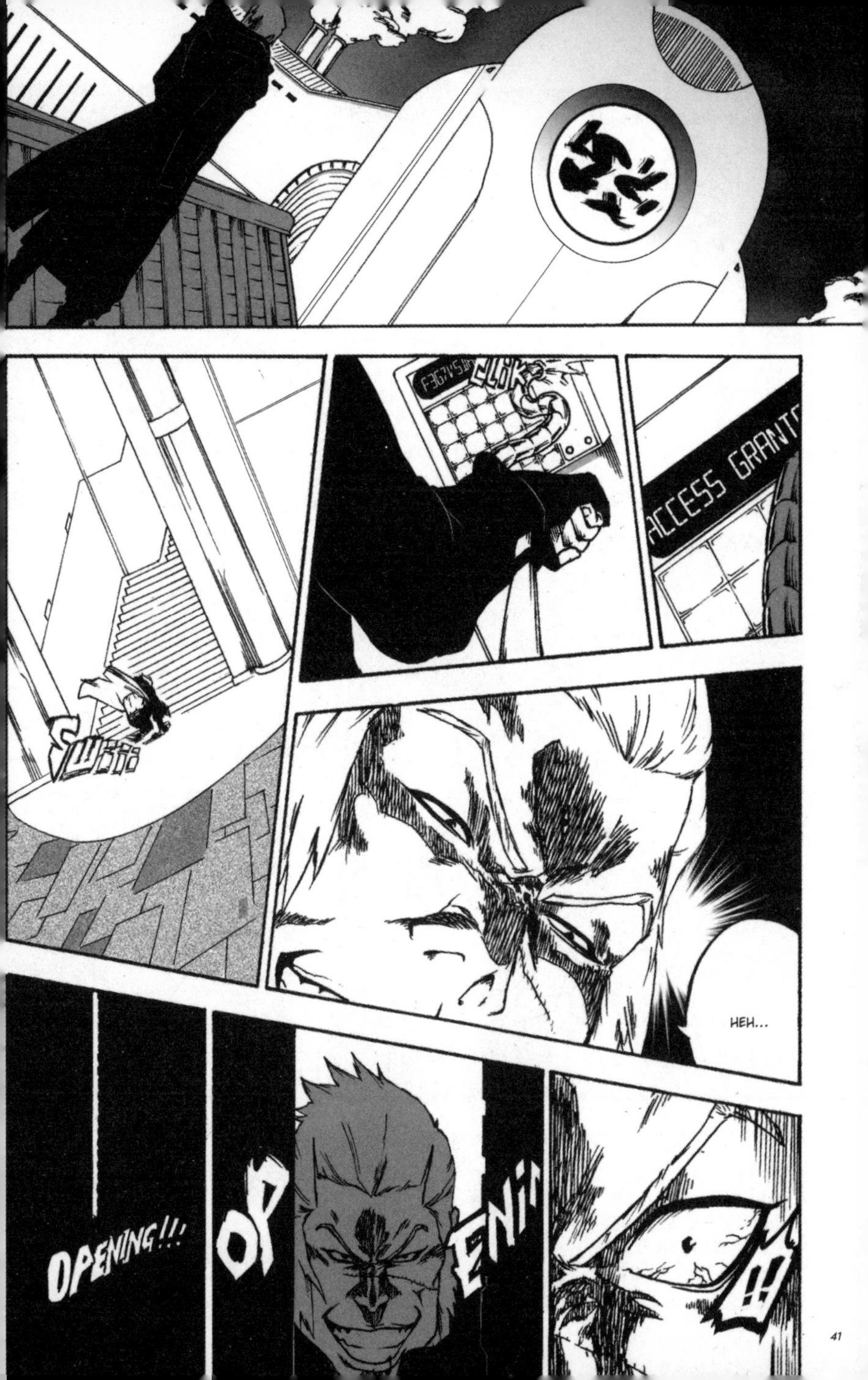
CLIK
ACCESS GRANTE
HEH...
OPENING!!!
OP
ENI
!!

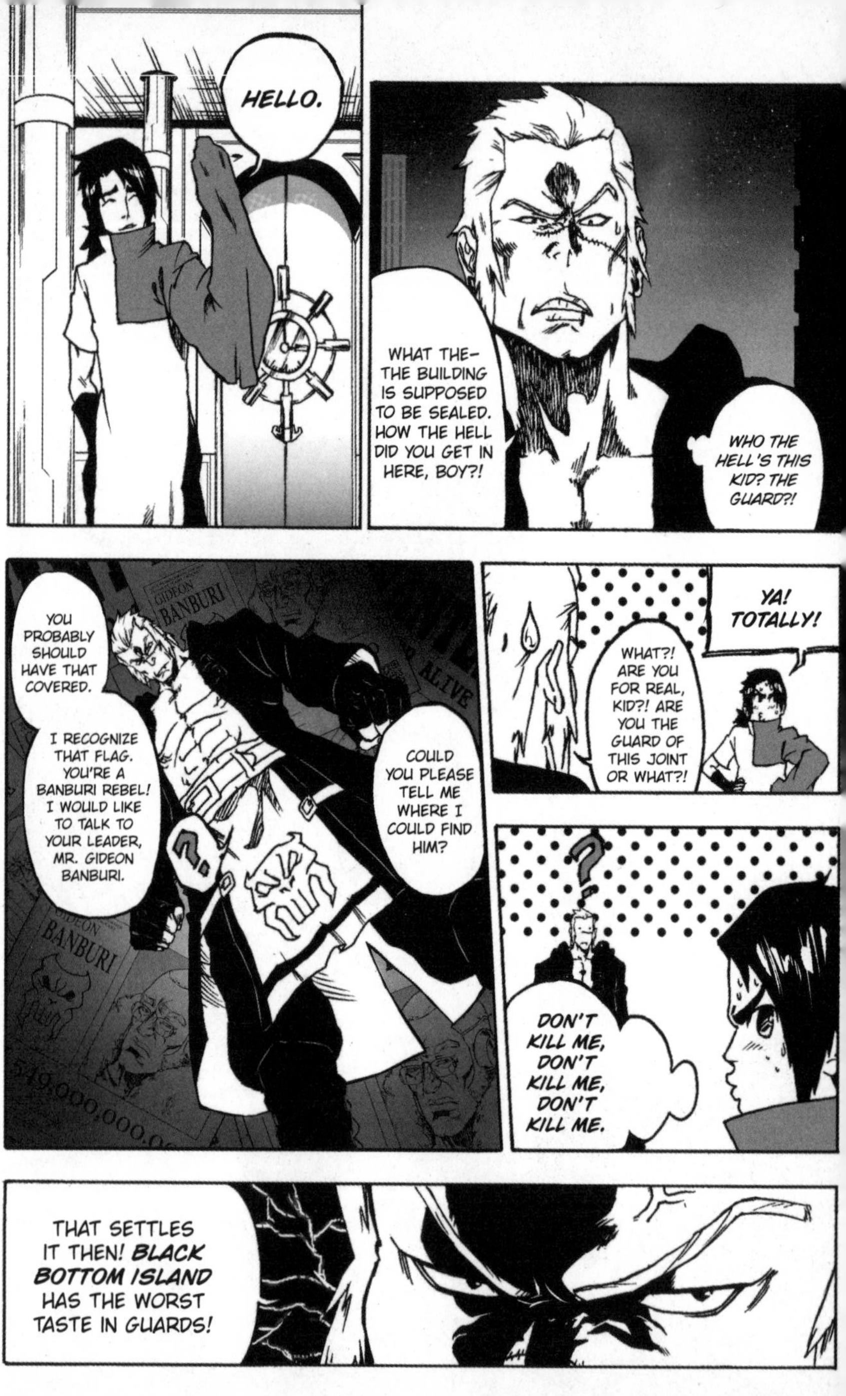
HELLO.
WHAT THE— THE BUILDING IS SUPPOSED TO BE SEALED. HOW THE HELL DID YOU GET IN HERE, BOY?!
WHO THE HELL'S THIS KID? THE GUARD?!
YOU PROBABLY SHOULD HAVE THAT COVERED.
I RECOGNIZE THAT FLAG. YOU'RE A BANBURI REBEL! I WOULD LIKE TO TALK TO YOUR LEADER, MR. GIDEON BANBURI.
COULD YOU PLEASE TELL ME WHERE I COULD FIND HIM?
GIDEON BANBURI
ALIVE
GIDEON BANBURI
519,000,000.00
WHAT?! ARE YOU FOR REAL, KID?! ARE YOU THE GUARD OF THIS JOINT OR WHAT?!
YA! TOTALLY!
DON'T KILL ME, DON'T KILL ME, DON'T KILL ME.
THAT SETTLES IT THEN! BLACK BOTTOM ISLAND HAS THE WORST TASTE IN GUARDS!

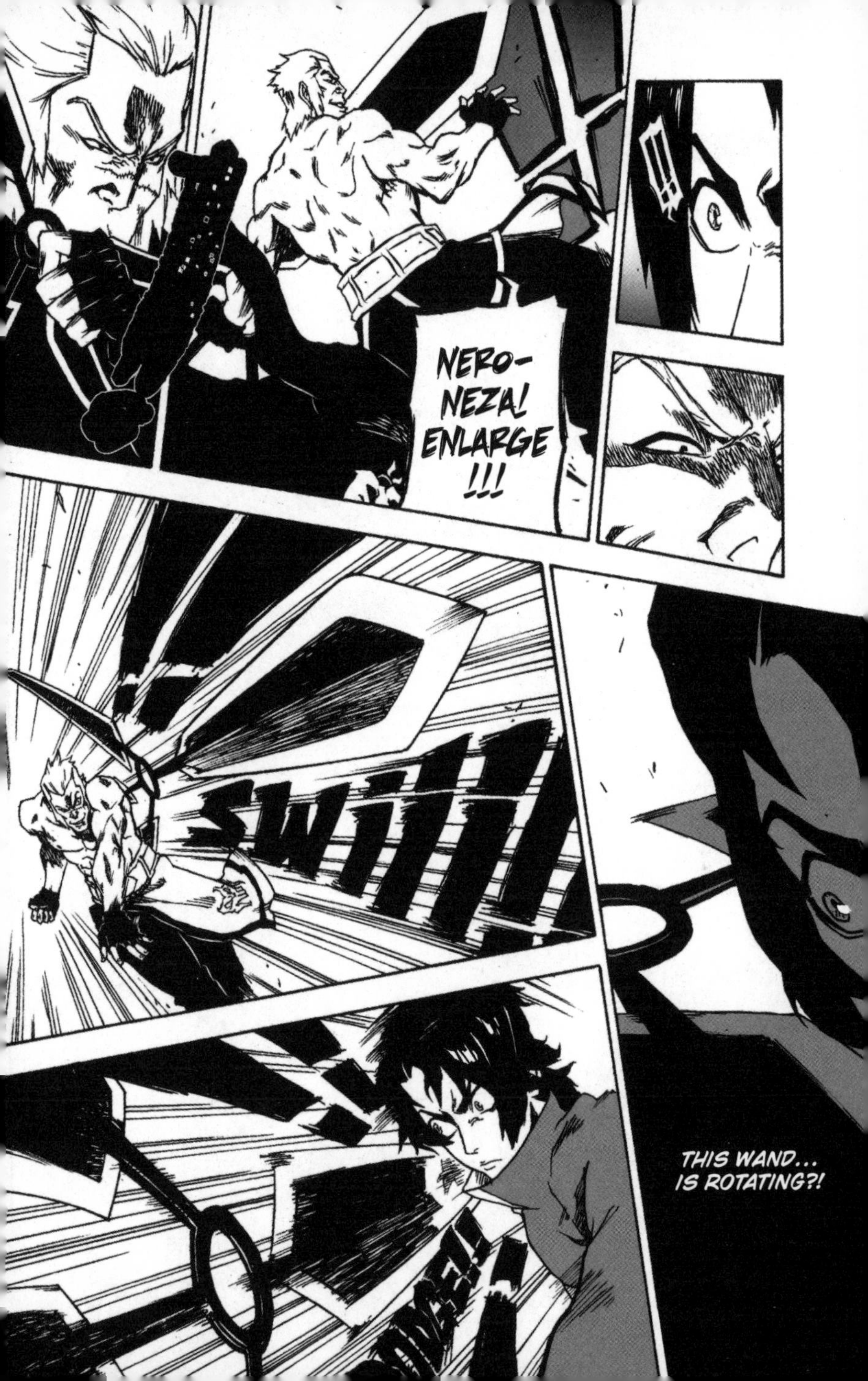
NERO-NEZA! ENLARGE !!!
SWIII
THIS WAND... IS ROTATING?!

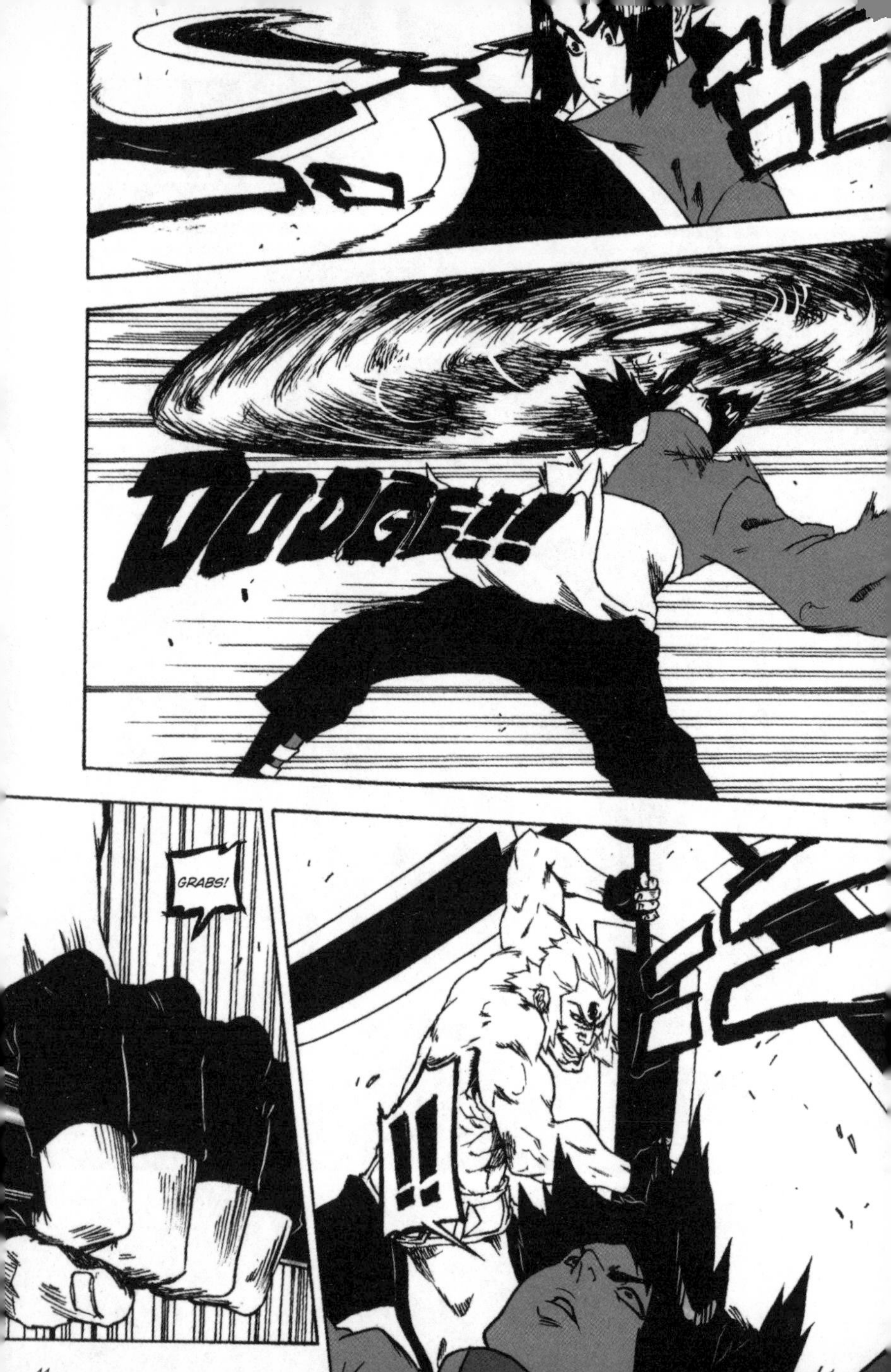
DODGE!!
GRABS!
!!

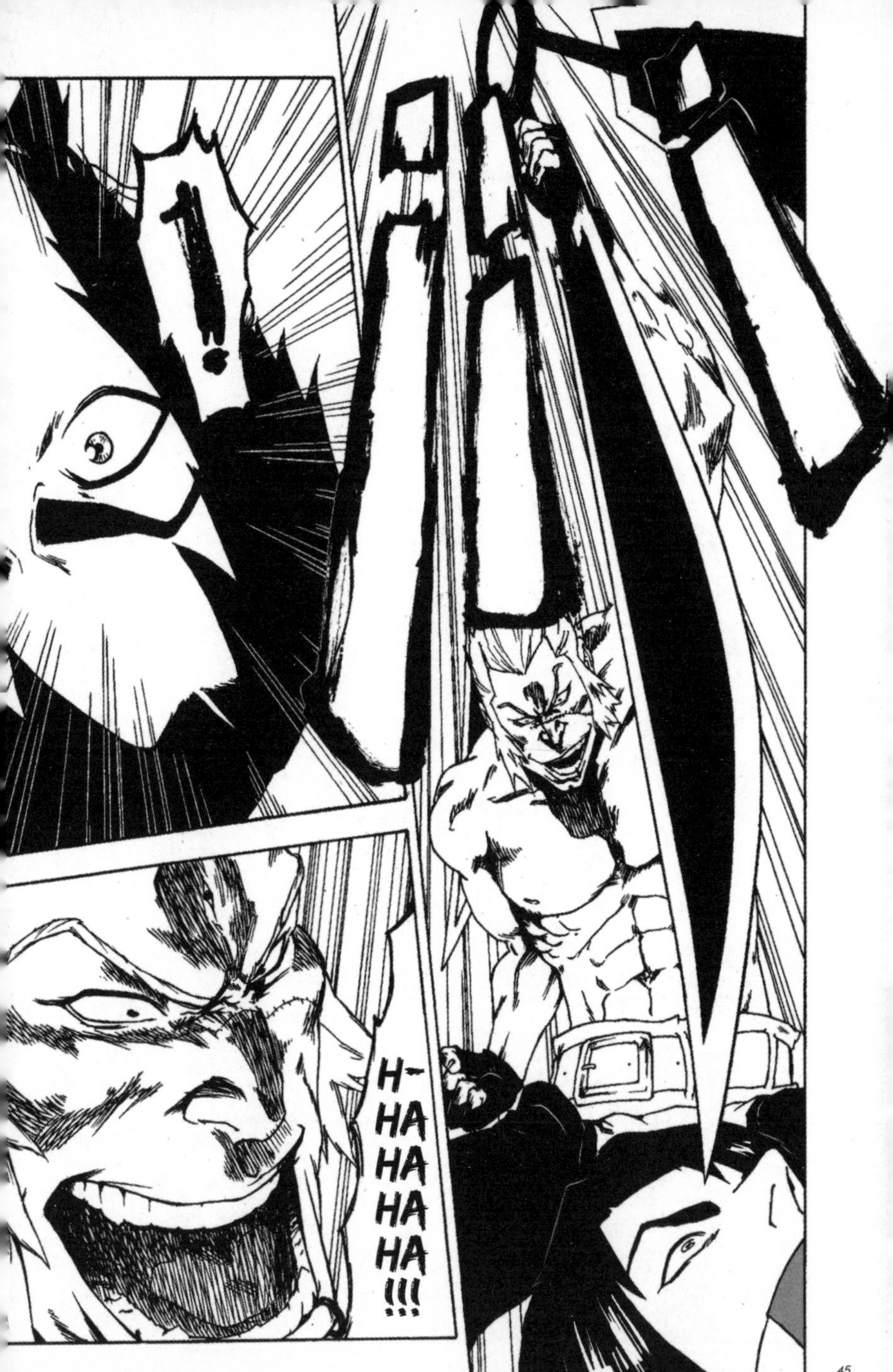
!!
H-
HA
HA
HA
HA
!!!

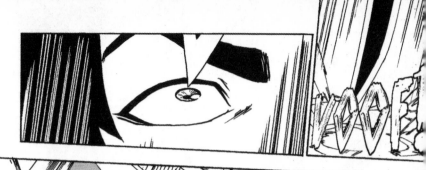

A TELE-PORTER, HUH? THAT EXPLAINS HOW YOU GOT IN HERE.

HUF

YOU MUST BE FROM THE OLD TAMASHII TRIBE.

HUF

YOU ALL NEARED EXTINCTION AFTER THE EBONY PEAK WARS.

LEAD BY THE ALMIGHTY WARLOCK...

SERGO ABRAHAM TAMASHII! BUT HE'S DEAD NOW ISN'T HE?

HUF

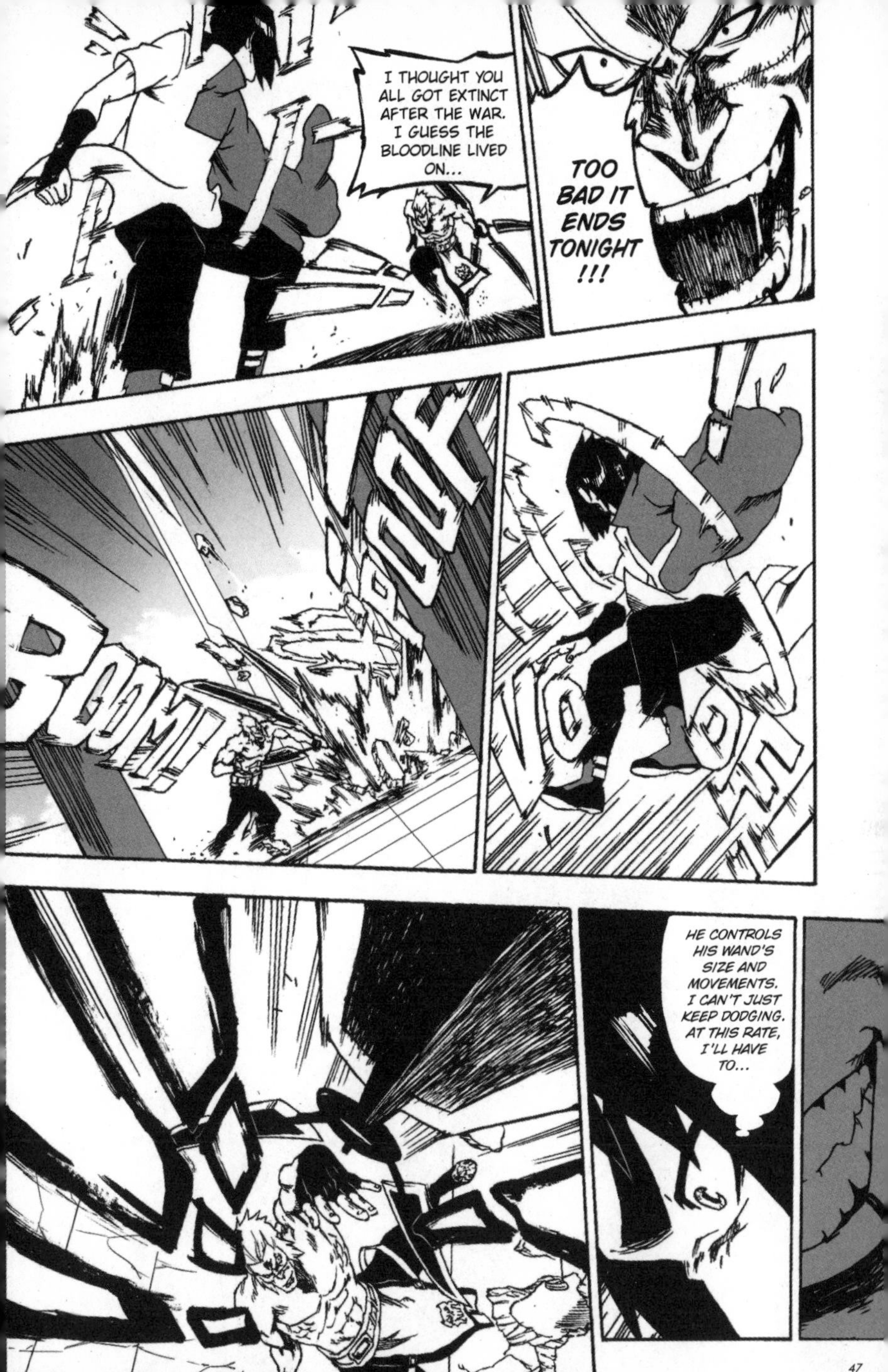

I THOUGHT YOU ALL GOT EXTINCT AFTER THE WAR. I GUESS THE BLOODLINE LIVED ON...
TOO BAD IT ENDS TONIGHT !!!
BOOM
HE CONTROLS HIS WAND'S SIZE AND MOVEMENTS. I CAN'T JUST KEEP DODGING. AT THIS RATE, I'LL HAVE TO...

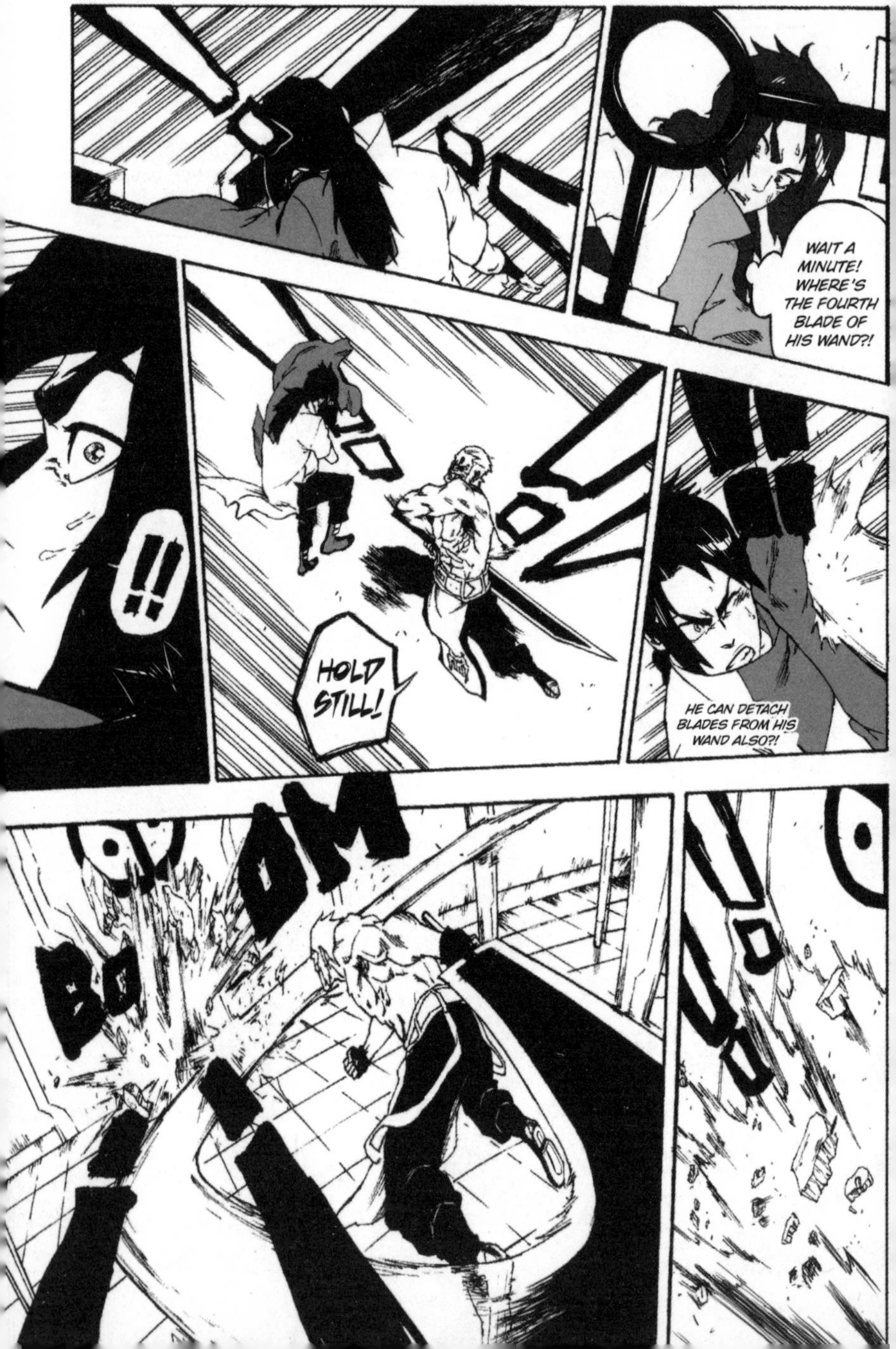
WAIT A MINUTE! WHERE'S THE FOURTH BLADE OF HIS WAND?!
!!
HOLD STILL!
HE CAN DETACH BLADES FROM HIS WAND ALSO?!

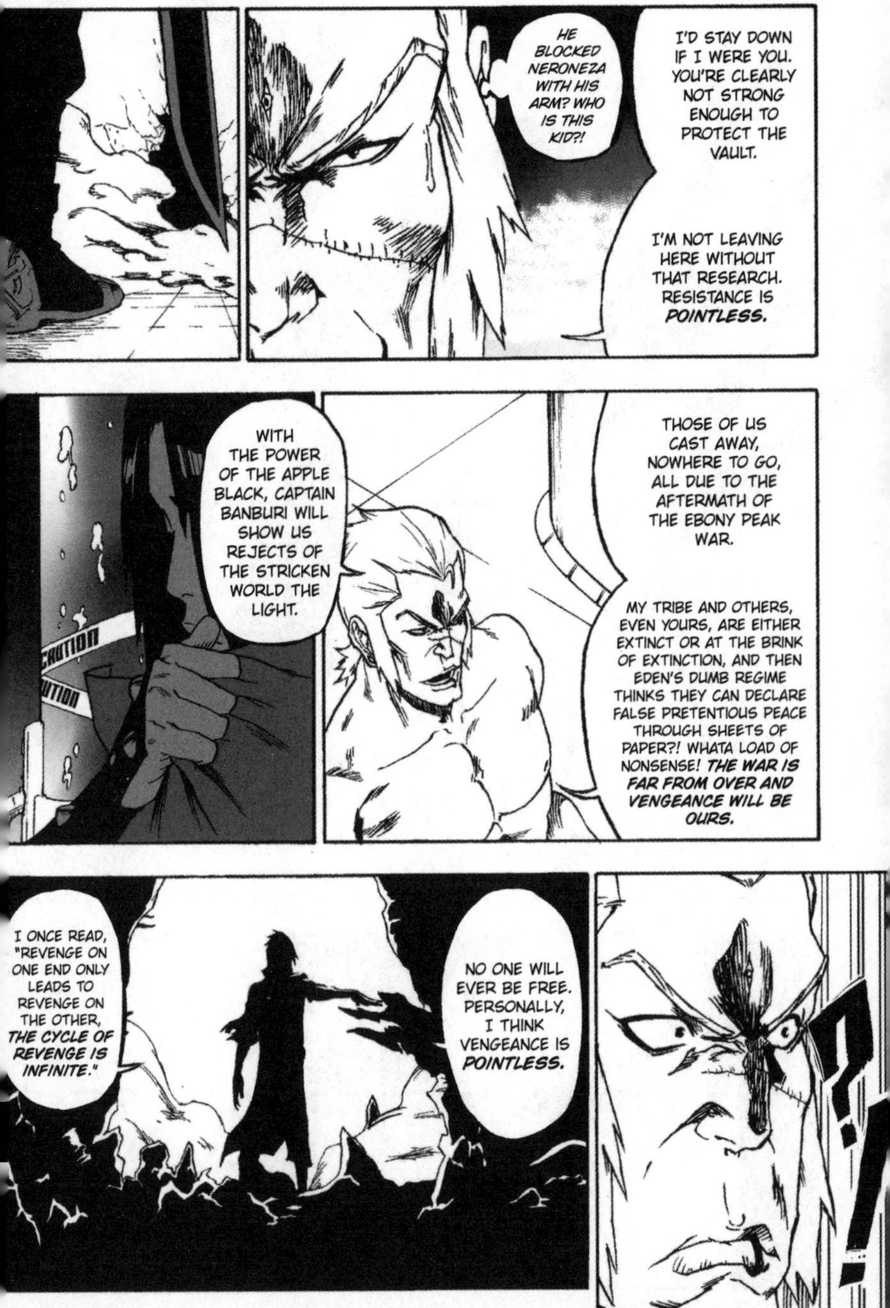
HE BLOCKED NERONEZA WITH HIS ARM? WHO IS THIS KID?!
I'D STAY DOWN IF I WERE YOU. YOU'RE CLEARLY NOT STRONG ENOUGH TO PROTECT THE VAULT.
I'M NOT LEAVING HERE WITHOUT THAT RESEARCH. RESISTANCE IS ***POINTLESS.***
CAUTION
WITH THE POWER OF THE APPLE BLACK, CAPTAIN BANBURI WILL SHOW US REJECTS OF THE STRICKEN WORLD THE LIGHT.
THOSE OF US CAST AWAY, NOWHERE TO GO, ALL DUE TO THE AFTERMATH OF THE EBONY PEAK WAR.
MY TRIBE AND OTHERS, EVEN YOURS, ARE EITHER EXTINCT OR AT THE BRINK OF EXTINCTION, AND THEN EDEN'S DUMB REGIME THINKS THEY CAN DECLARE FALSE PRETENTIOUS PEACE THROUGH SHEETS OF PAPER?! WHATA LOAD OF NONSENSE! ***THE WAR IS FAR FROM OVER AND VENGEANCE WILL BE OURS.***
I ONCE READ, "REVENGE ON ONE END ONLY LEADS TO REVENGE ON THE OTHER, ***THE CYCLE OF REVENGE IS INFINITE.***"
NO ONE WILL EVER BE FREE. PERSONALLY, I THINK VENGEANCE IS ***POINTLESS.***
?!

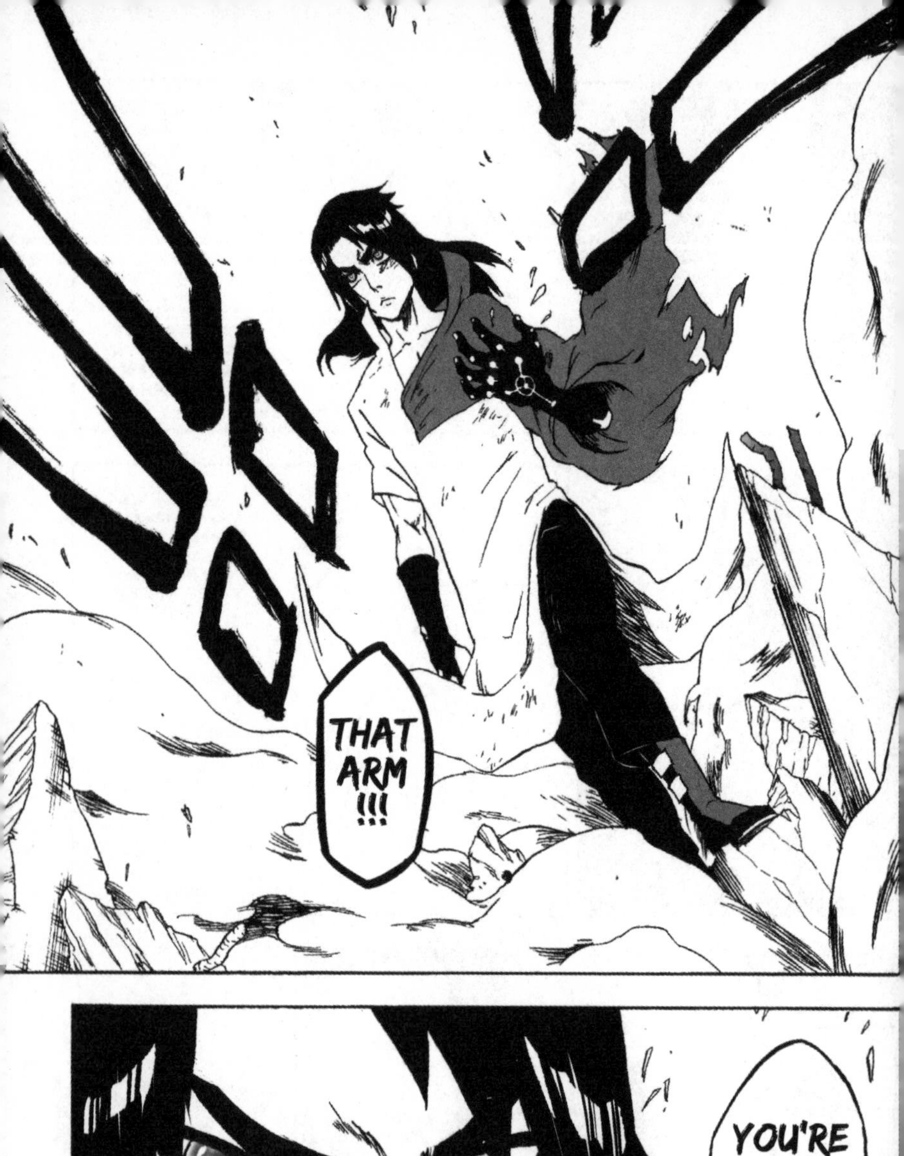
THAT ARM !!!

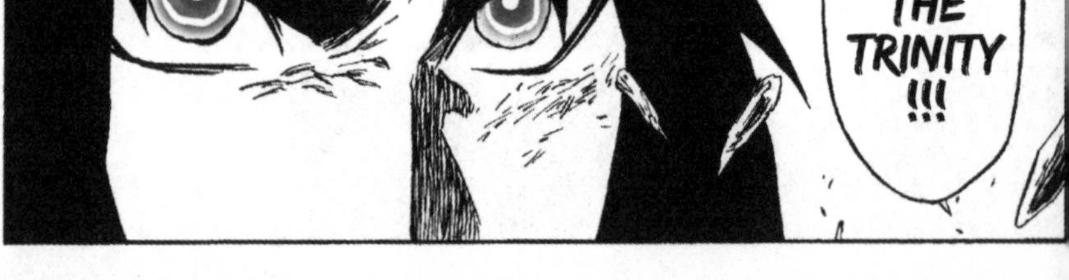
YOU'RE THE TRINITY !!!

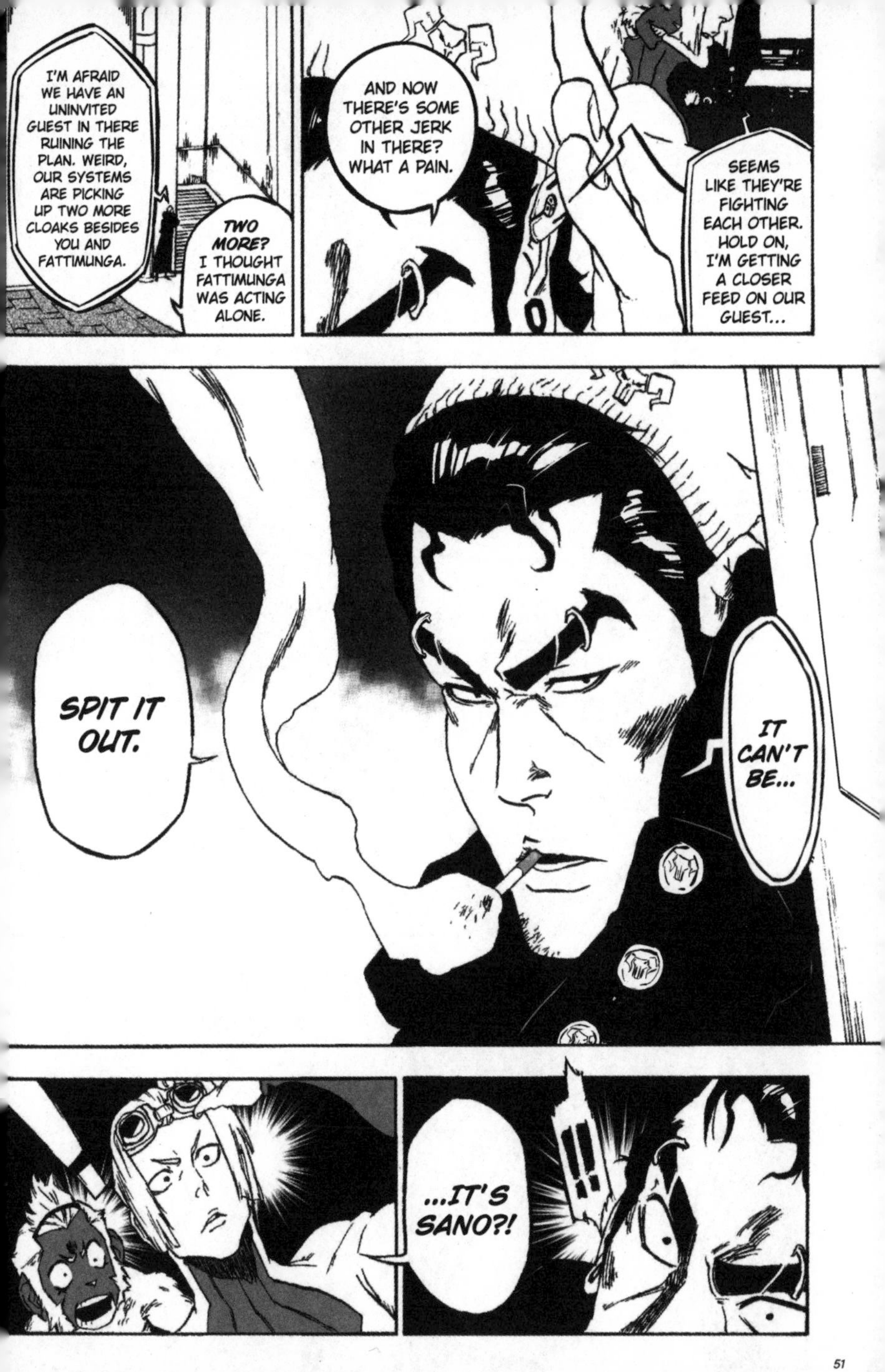
I'M AFRAID WE HAVE AN UNINVITED GUEST IN THERE RUINING THE PLAN. WEIRD, OUR SYSTEMS ARE PICKING UP TWO MORE CLOAKS BESIDES YOU AND FATTIMUNGA.
TWO MORE? I THOUGHT FATTIMUNGA WAS ACTING ALONE.
AND NOW THERE'S SOME OTHER JERK IN THERE? WHAT A PAIN.
SEEMS LIKE THEY'RE FIGHTING EACH OTHER. HOLD ON, I'M GETTING A CLOSER FEED ON OUR GUEST...
SPIT IT OUT.
IT CAN'T BE...
...IT'S SANO?!
!!

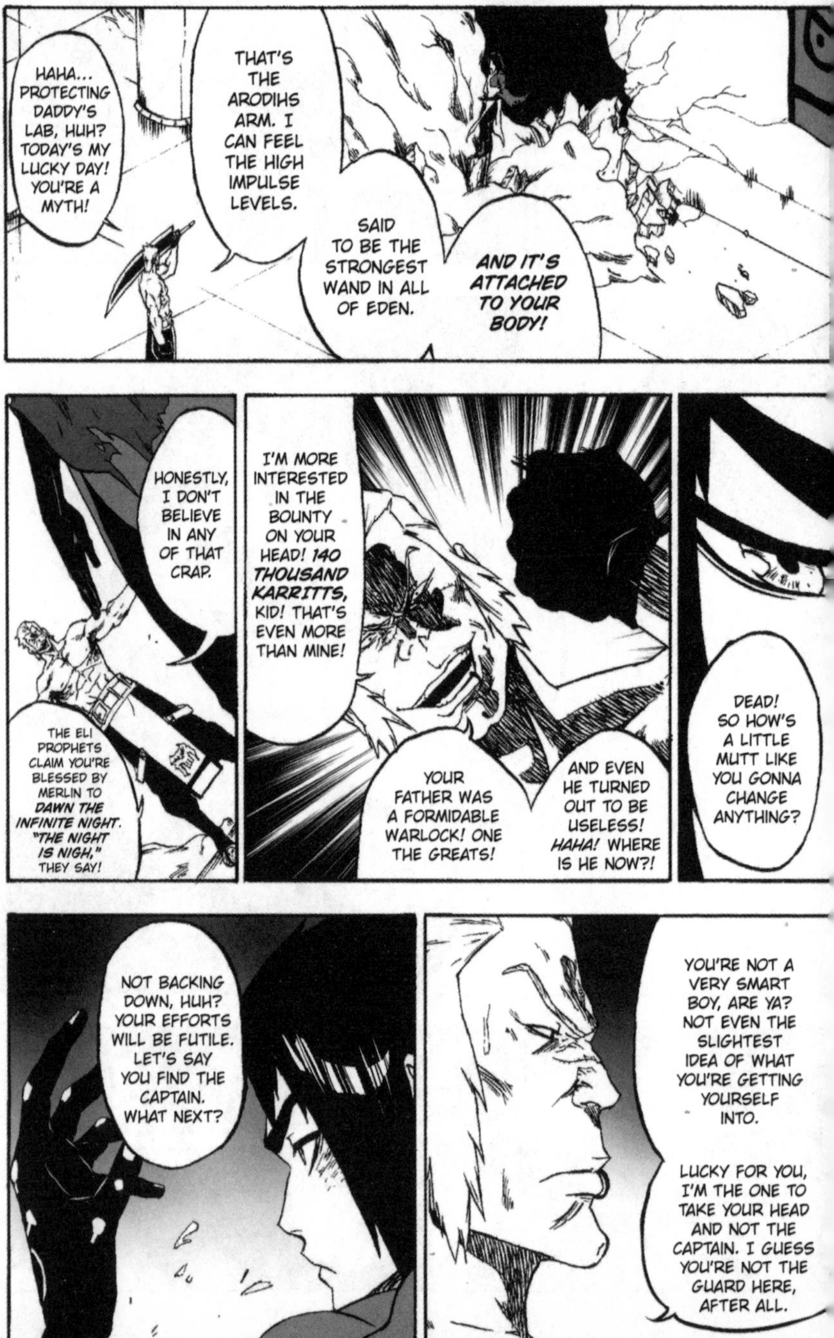
HAHA... PROTECTING DADDY'S LAB, HUH? TODAY'S MY LUCKY DAY! YOU'RE A MYTH!
THAT'S THE ARODIHS ARM. I CAN FEEL THE HIGH IMPULSE LEVELS.
SAID TO BE THE STRONGEST WAND IN ALL OF EDEN.
AND IT'S ATTACHED TO YOUR BODY!
HONESTLY, I DON'T BELIEVE IN ANY OF THAT CRAP.
THE ELI PROPHETS CLAIM YOU'RE BLESSED BY MERLIN TO DAWN THE INFINITE NIGHT. "THE NIGHT IS NIGH," THEY SAY!
I'M MORE INTERESTED IN THE BOUNTY ON YOUR HEAD! 140 THOUSAND KARRITTS, KID! THAT'S EVEN MORE THAN MINE!
YOUR FATHER WAS A FORMIDABLE WARLOCK! ONE THE GREATS!
AND EVEN HE TURNED OUT TO BE USELESS! HAHA! WHERE IS HE NOW?!
DEAD! SO HOW'S A LITTLE MUTT LIKE YOU GONNA CHANGE ANYTHING?
NOT BACKING DOWN, HUH? YOUR EFFORTS WILL BE FUTILE. LET'S SAY YOU FIND THE CAPTAIN. WHAT NEXT?
YOU'RE NOT A VERY SMART BOY, ARE YA? NOT EVEN THE SLIGHTEST IDEA OF WHAT YOU'RE GETTING YOURSELF INTO.
LUCKY FOR YOU, I'M THE ONE TO TAKE YOUR HEAD AND NOT THE CAPTAIN. I GUESS YOU'RE NOT THE GUARD HERE, AFTER ALL.

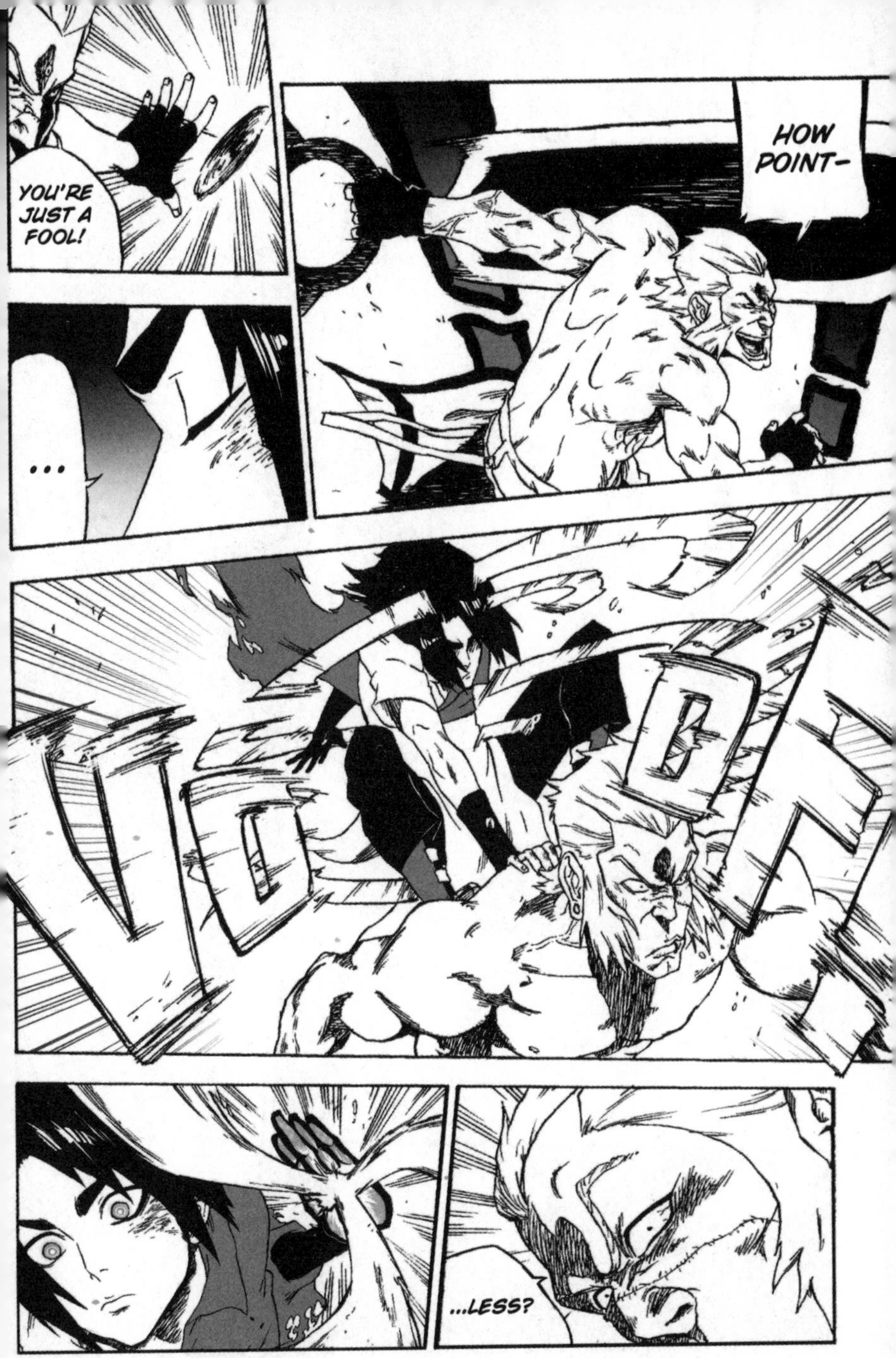
YOU'RE JUST A FOOL!
...
HOW POINT-
...LESS?

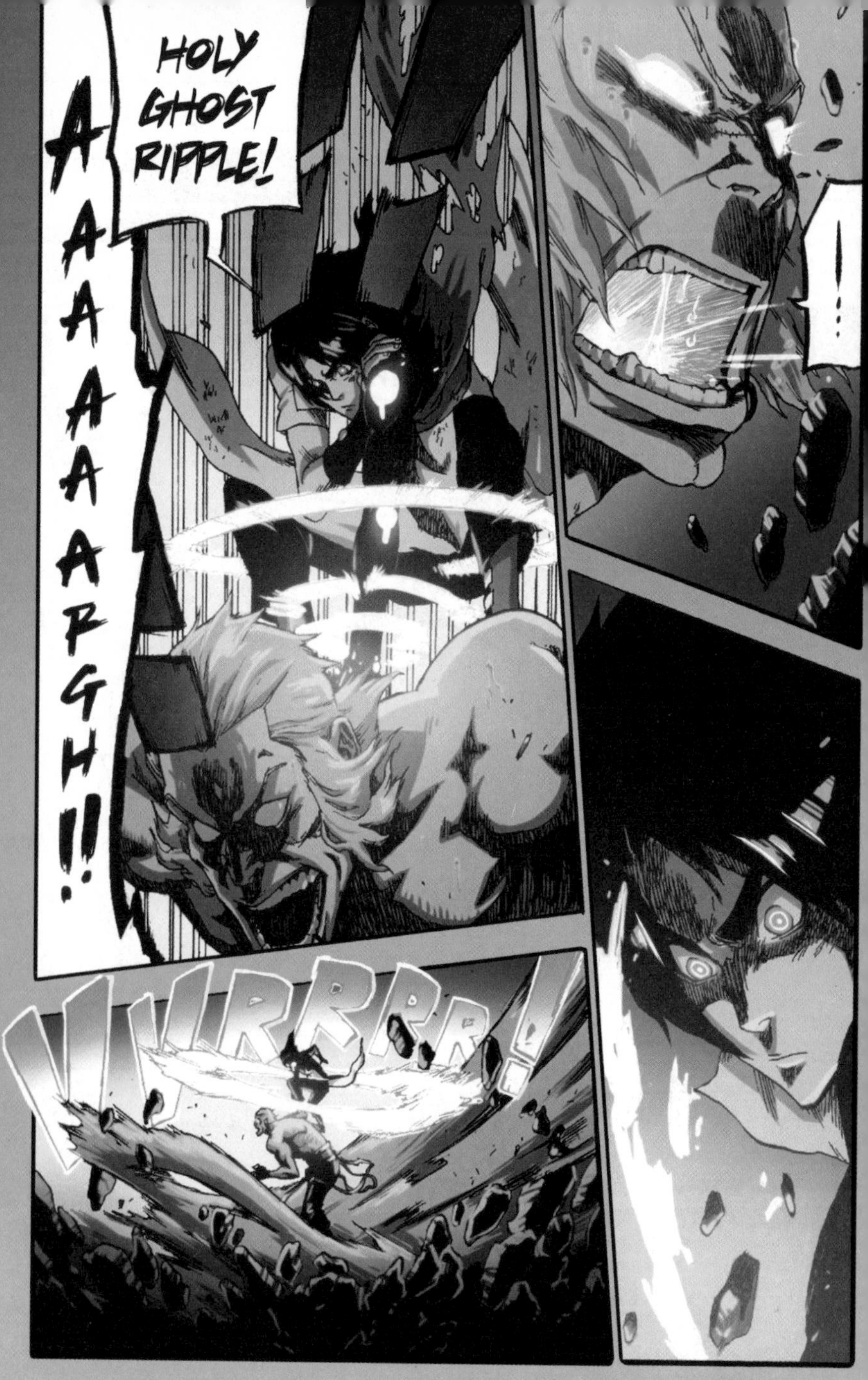
HOLY GHOST RIPPLE!
AAAAAAARGH!!
!
VVVRRRR!

SANO!! ARE YOU OKAY?!

A SPELL STRONG ENOUGH TO KNOCK FATTIMLINGA OUT?

U R G H...

HOW THE HELL?

YOU JUST MIGHT BE A WORSE GOOFBALL THAN THE ONES I ALREADY GOT.

I THOUGHT I TOLD YOU TO STAY IN THE ROOM?! *YOU COULD'VE GOTTEN YOURSELF KILLED!*

WE HAVE FORCES FOR SITUATIONS LIKE THIS! WHY THE HELL DID YOU COME OUT HERE?! TO SHOW OFF?! THIS WAS A DECOY OPERATION! WE ALREADY LURED FATTIMLINGA TO THE WRONG VAULT! *YOU ALMOST RUINED EVERYTHING!*

I UNDER-STAND.

BECAUSE THE REAL VAULT IS RIGHT IN FRONT OF ME.

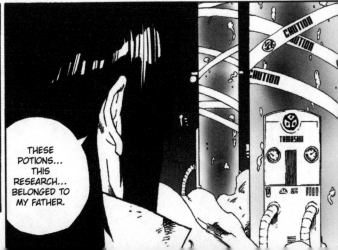

THESE POTIONS... THIS RESEARCH... BELONGED TO MY FATHER.

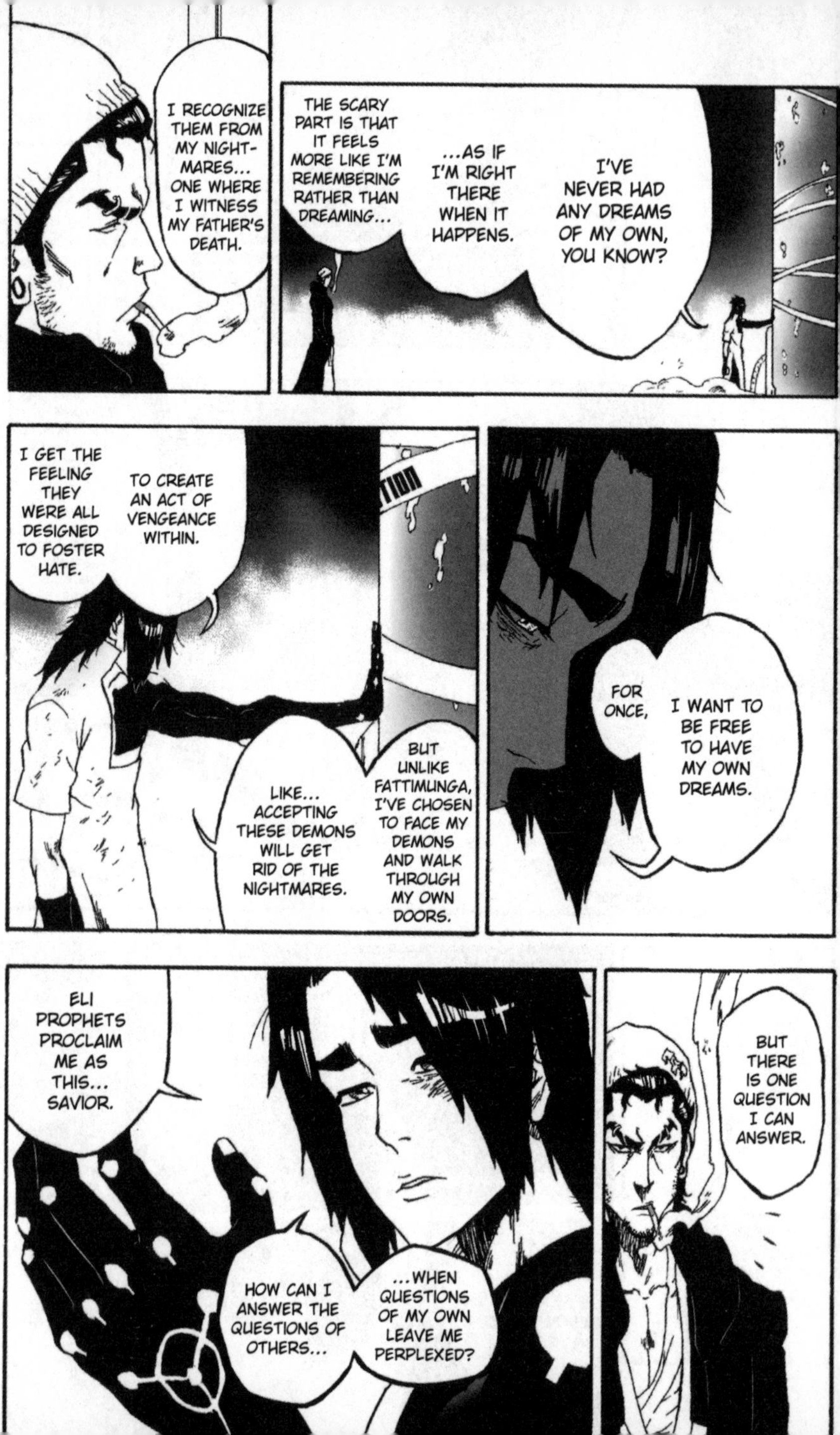
I RECOGNIZE THEM FROM MY NIGHTMARES... ONE WHERE I WITNESS MY FATHER'S DEATH.
THE SCARY PART IS THAT IT FEELS MORE LIKE I'M REMEMBERING RATHER THAN DREAMING...
...AS IF I'M RIGHT THERE WHEN IT HAPPENS.
I'VE NEVER HAD ANY DREAMS OF MY OWN, YOU KNOW?
I GET THE FEELING THEY WERE ALL DESIGNED TO FOSTER HATE.
TO CREATE AN ACT OF VENGEANCE WITHIN.
LIKE... ACCEPTING THESE DEMONS WILL GET RID OF THE NIGHTMARES.
BUT UNLIKE FATTIMUNGA, I'VE CHOSEN TO FACE MY DEMONS AND WALK THROUGH MY OWN DOORS.
FOR ONCE,
I WANT TO BE FREE TO HAVE MY OWN DREAMS.
ELI PROPHETS PROCLAIM ME AS THIS... SAVIOR.
HOW CAN I ANSWER THE QUESTIONS OF OTHERS...
...WHEN QUESTIONS OF MY OWN LEAVE ME PERPLEXED?
BUT THERE IS ONE QUESTION I CAN ANSWER.

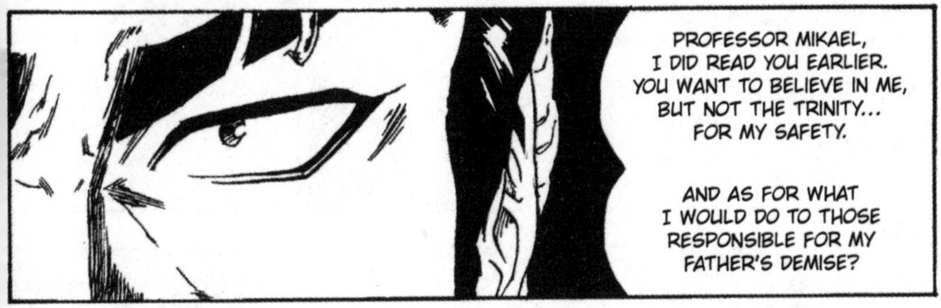
PROFESSOR MIKAEL, I DID READ YOU EARLIER. YOU WANT TO BELIEVE IN ME, BUT NOT THE TRINITY... FOR MY SAFETY.
AND AS FOR WHAT I WOULD DO TO THOSE RESPONSIBLE FOR MY FATHER'S DEMISE?
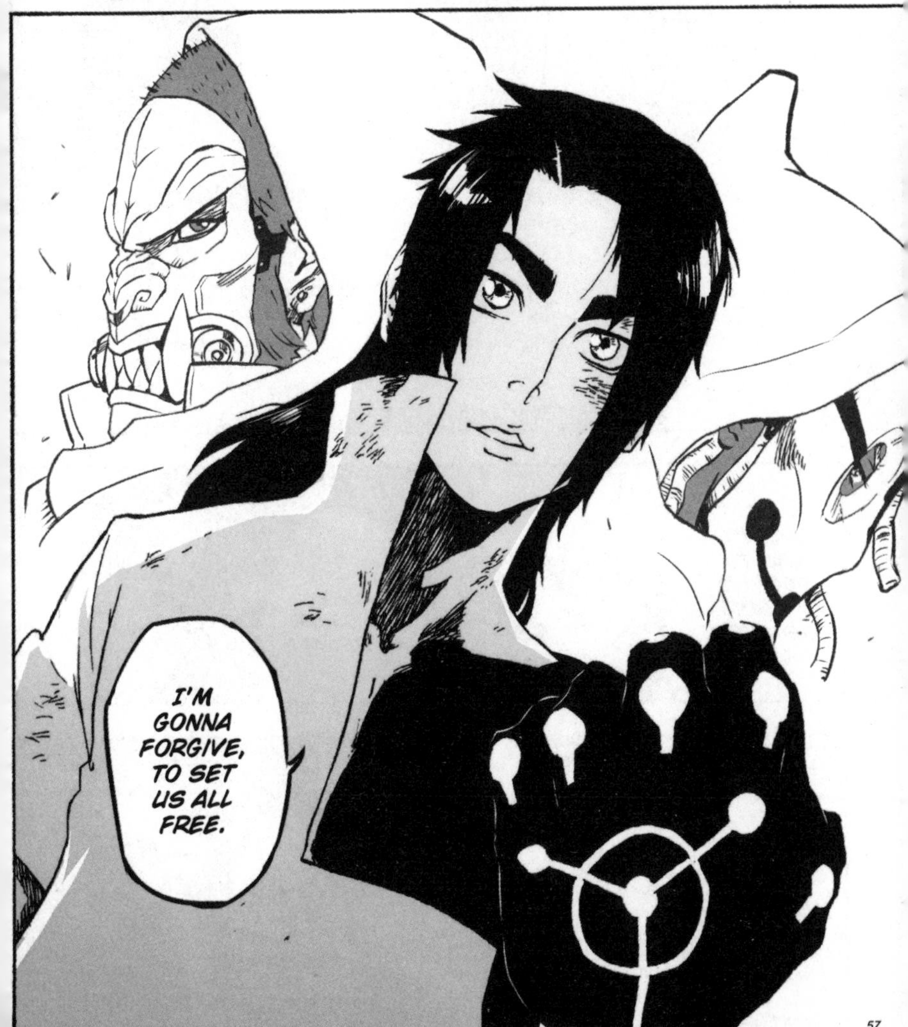
I'M GONNA FORGIVE, TO SET US ALL FREE.

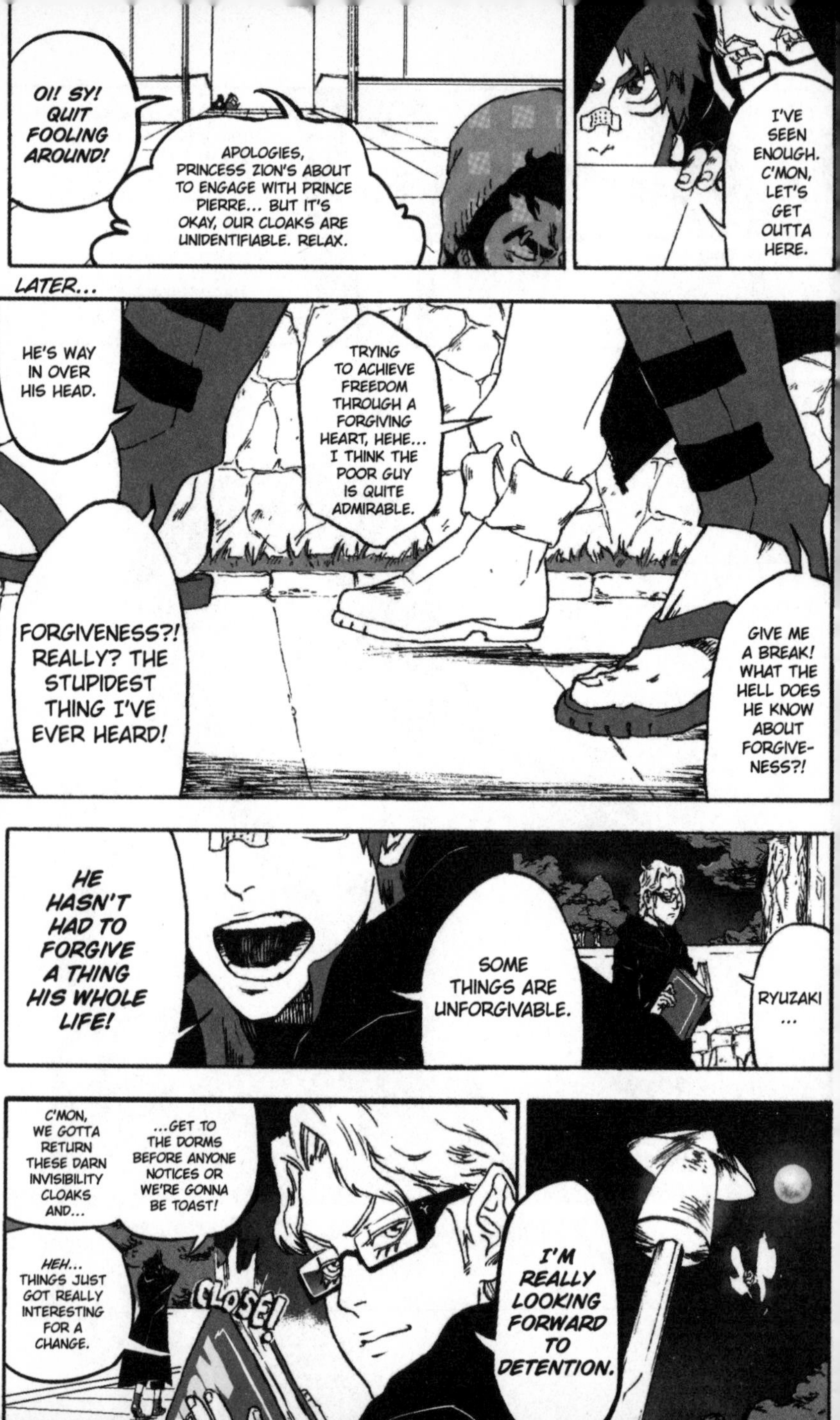
OI! SY! QUIT FOOLING AROUND!
APOLOGIES, PRINCESS ZION'S ABOUT TO ENGAGE WITH PRINCE PIERRE... BUT IT'S OKAY, OUR CLOAKS ARE UNIDENTIFIABLE. RELAX.
I'VE SEEN ENOUGH. C'MON, LET'S GET OUTTA HERE.
LATER...
HE'S WAY IN OVER HIS HEAD.
TRYING TO ACHIEVE FREEDOM THROUGH A FORGIVING HEART, HEHE... I THINK THE POOR GUY IS QUITE ADMIRABLE.
FORGIVENESS?! REALLY? THE STUPIDEST THING I'VE EVER HEARD!
GIVE ME A BREAK! WHAT THE HELL DOES HE KNOW ABOUT FORGIVE-NESS?!
HE HASN'T HAD TO FORGIVE A THING HIS WHOLE LIFE!
SOME THINGS ARE UNFORGIVABLE.
RYUZAKI ...
C'MON, WE GOTTA RETURN THESE DARN INVISIBILITY CLOAKS AND...
...GET TO THE DORMS BEFORE ANYONE NOTICES OR WE'RE GONNA BE TOAST!
HEH... THINGS JUST GOT REALLY INTERESTING FOR A CHANGE.
CLOSE!
I'M REALLY LOOKING FORWARD TO DETENTION.

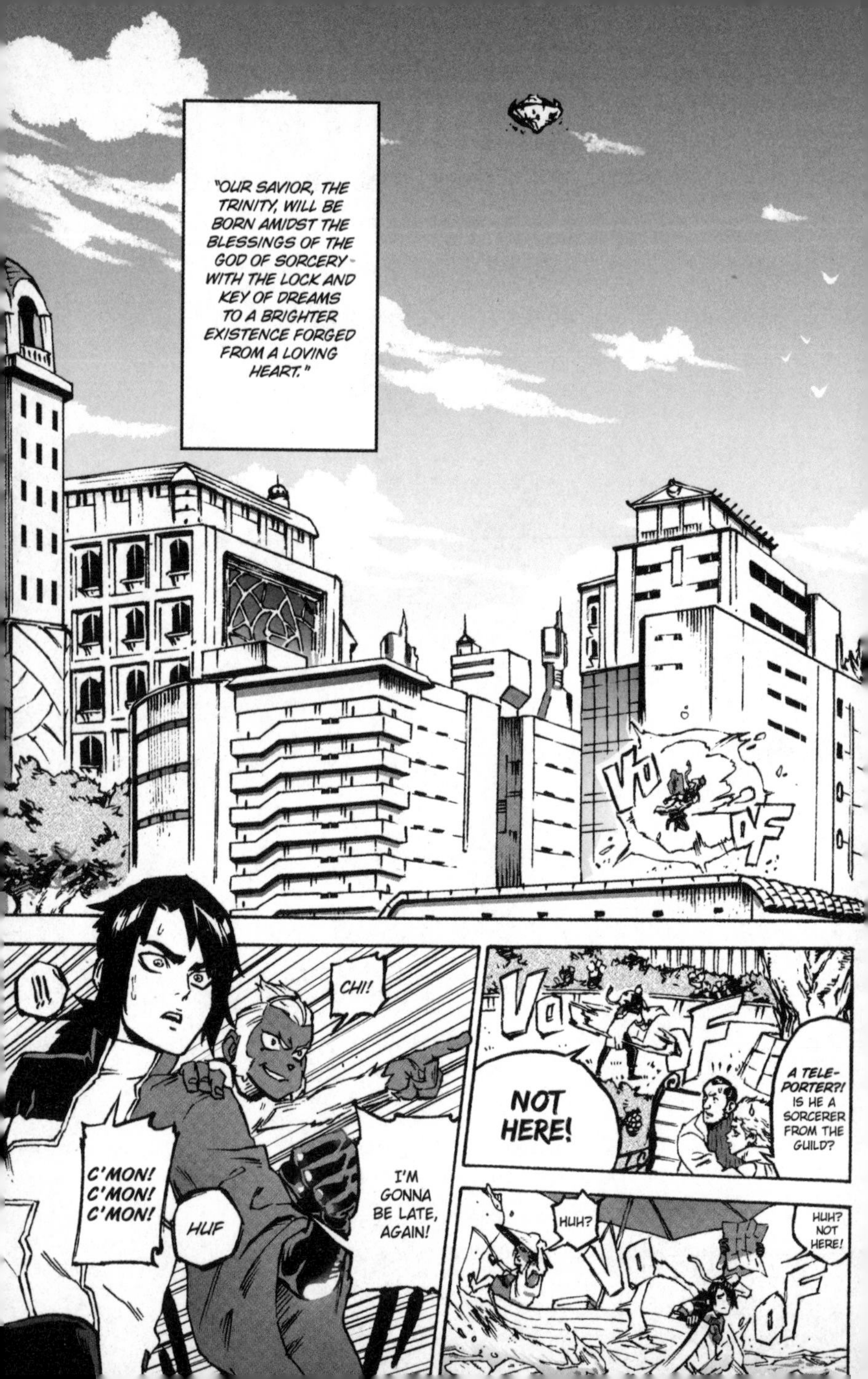
"OUR SAVIOR, THE TRINITY, WILL BE BORN AMIDST THE BLESSINGS OF THE GOD OF SORCERY - WITH THE LOCK AND KEY OF DREAMS TO A BRIGHTER EXISTENCE FORGED FROM A LOVING HEART."
VOOF
!!
CHI!
C'MON! C'MON! C'MON!
HUF
I'M GONNA BE LATE, AGAIN!
VOOF
NOT HERE!
A TELE-PORTER?! IS HE A SORCERER FROM THE GUILD?
HUH?
VOOF
HUH? NOT HERE!

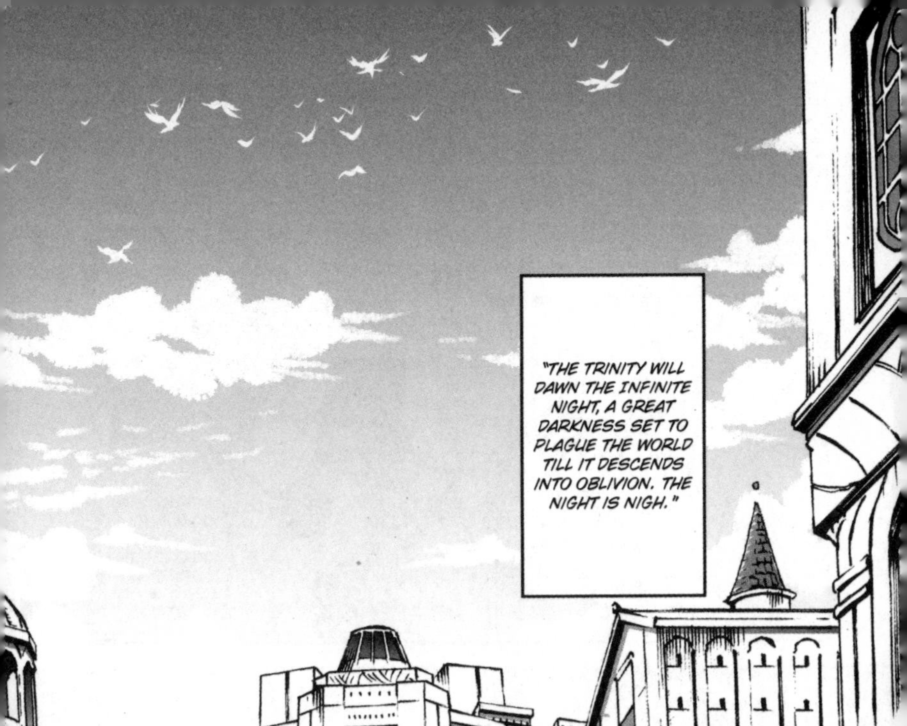
"THE TRINITY WILL DAWN THE INFINITE NIGHT, A GREAT DARKNESS SET TO PLAGUE THE WORLD TILL IT DESCENDS INTO OBLIVION. THE NIGHT IS NIGH."

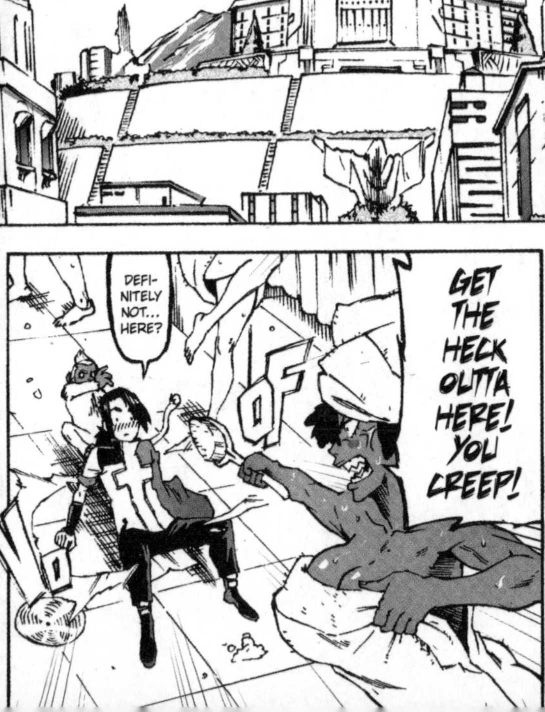
DEFI-NITELY NOT... HERE?
GET THE HECK OUTTA HERE! YOU CREEP!

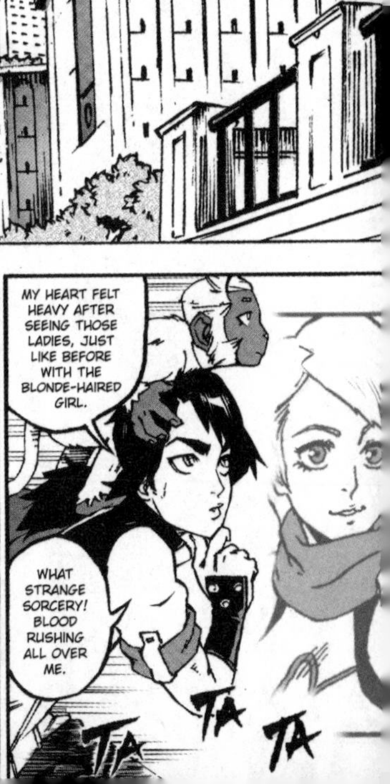
MY HEART FELT HEAVY AFTER SEEING THOSE LADIES, JUST LIKE BEFORE WITH THE BLONDE-HAIRED GIRL.
WHAT STRANGE SORCERY! BLOOD RUSHING ALL OVER ME.
TA TA TA

DO NOT MISS OUR NEXT CLASS SESSION. COME PREPARED, OR DON'T COME AT ALL!

WHAT ARE WE GONNA DO? PROFESSOR MIKAEL HAS IT OUT FOR ME, TOO.

THIS PLACE IS HUGE, AND THE MAP IS STILL WEIRDLY COMPLEX FOR NEWBIES LIKE ME! RIGHT, WIIWERTH?

I SHOULD'VE TOLD ANGELO THE TRUTH ABOUT NOT GRASPING HOW THE MAP WORKS!

EH?!

DROPS!

K8,,

?!

Daily Garden

CAPTURED!!

IS THE TRINITY A HOAX?

YOU'RE THE FACE MAKER!

YOU TELL ME.

WHAT DO I CARE ANYWAY...?

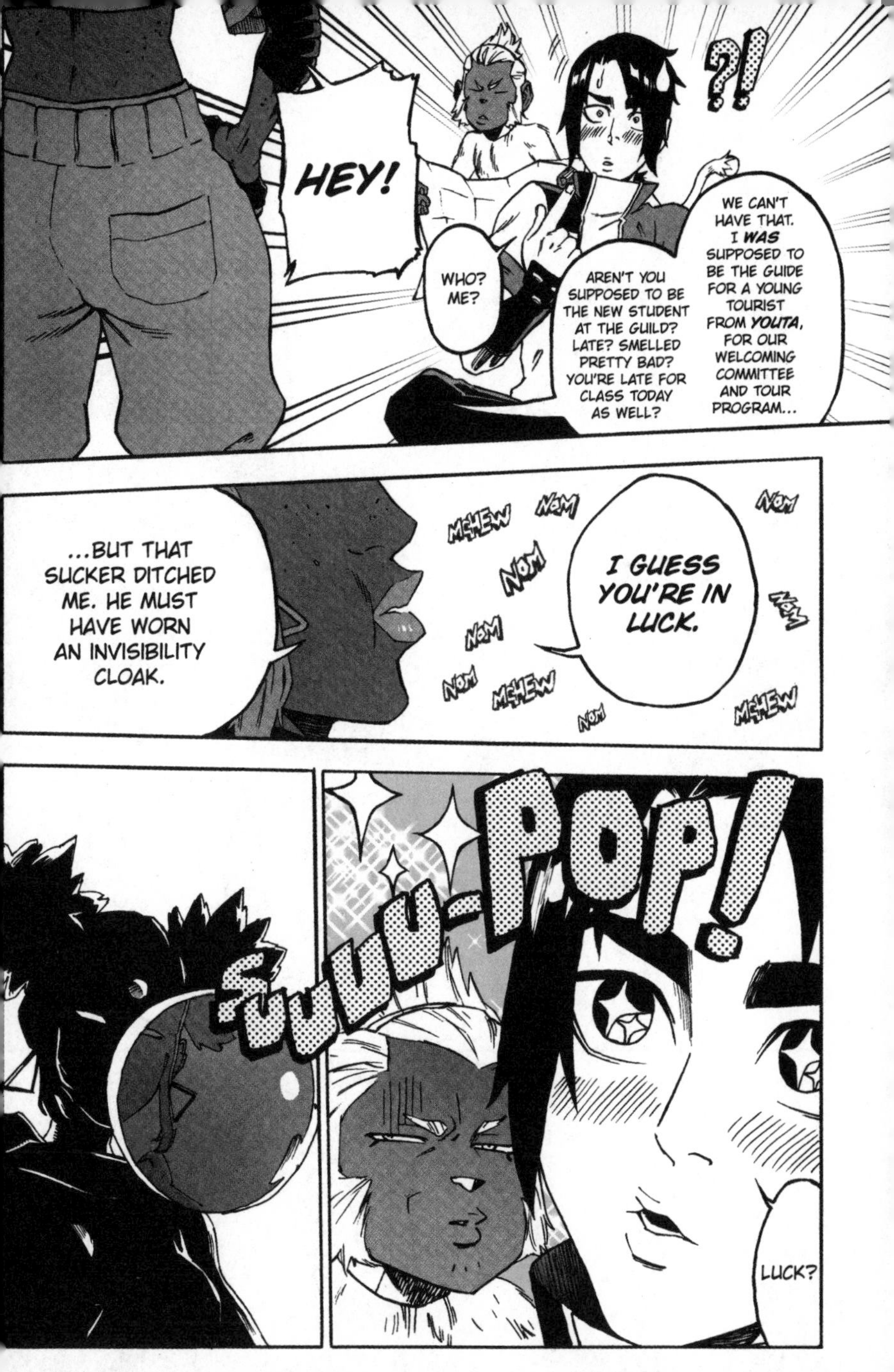
HEY!
?!
WHO? ME?
AREN'T YOU SUPPOSED TO BE THE NEW STUDENT AT THE GUILD? LATE? SMELLED PRETTY BAD? YOU'RE LATE FOR CLASS TODAY AS WELL?
WE CAN'T HAVE THAT. I **WAS** SUPPOSED TO BE THE GUIDE FOR A YOUNG TOURIST FROM **YOUTA**, FOR OUR WELCOMING COMMITTEE AND TOUR PROGRAM...
...BUT THAT SUCKER DITCHED ME. HE MUST HAVE WORN AN INVISIBILITY CLOAK.
MCHEW NOM NOM NOM NOM MCHEW NOM
I GUESS YOU'RE IN LUCK.
NOM NOM MCHEW
SUUUU-POP!
LUCK?

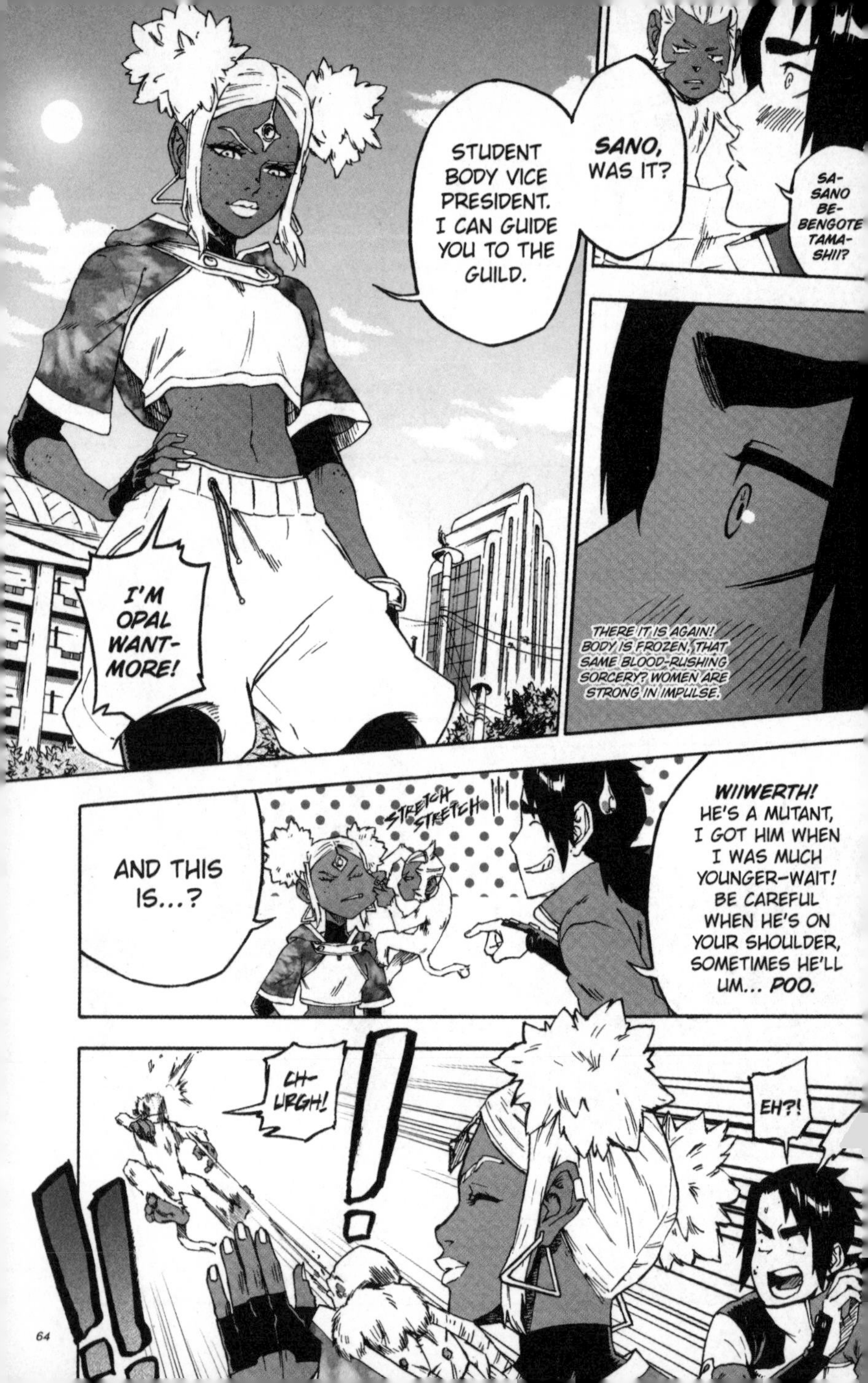
I'M OPAL WANT-MORE!
STUDENT BODY VICE PRESIDENT. I CAN GUIDE YOU TO THE GUILD.
SANO, WAS IT?
SA-SANO BE-BENGOTE TAMA-SHII?
THERE IT IS AGAIN! BODY IS FROZEN, THAT SAME BLOOD-RUSHING SORCERY? WOMEN ARE STRONG IN IMPULSE.
AND THIS IS...?
STRETCH STRETCH
WIIWERTH! HE'S A MUTANT, I GOT HIM WHEN I WAS MUCH YOUNGER—WAIT! BE CAREFUL WHEN HE'S ON YOUR SHOULDER, SOMETIMES HE'LL UM... POO.
CH-URGH!
EH?!

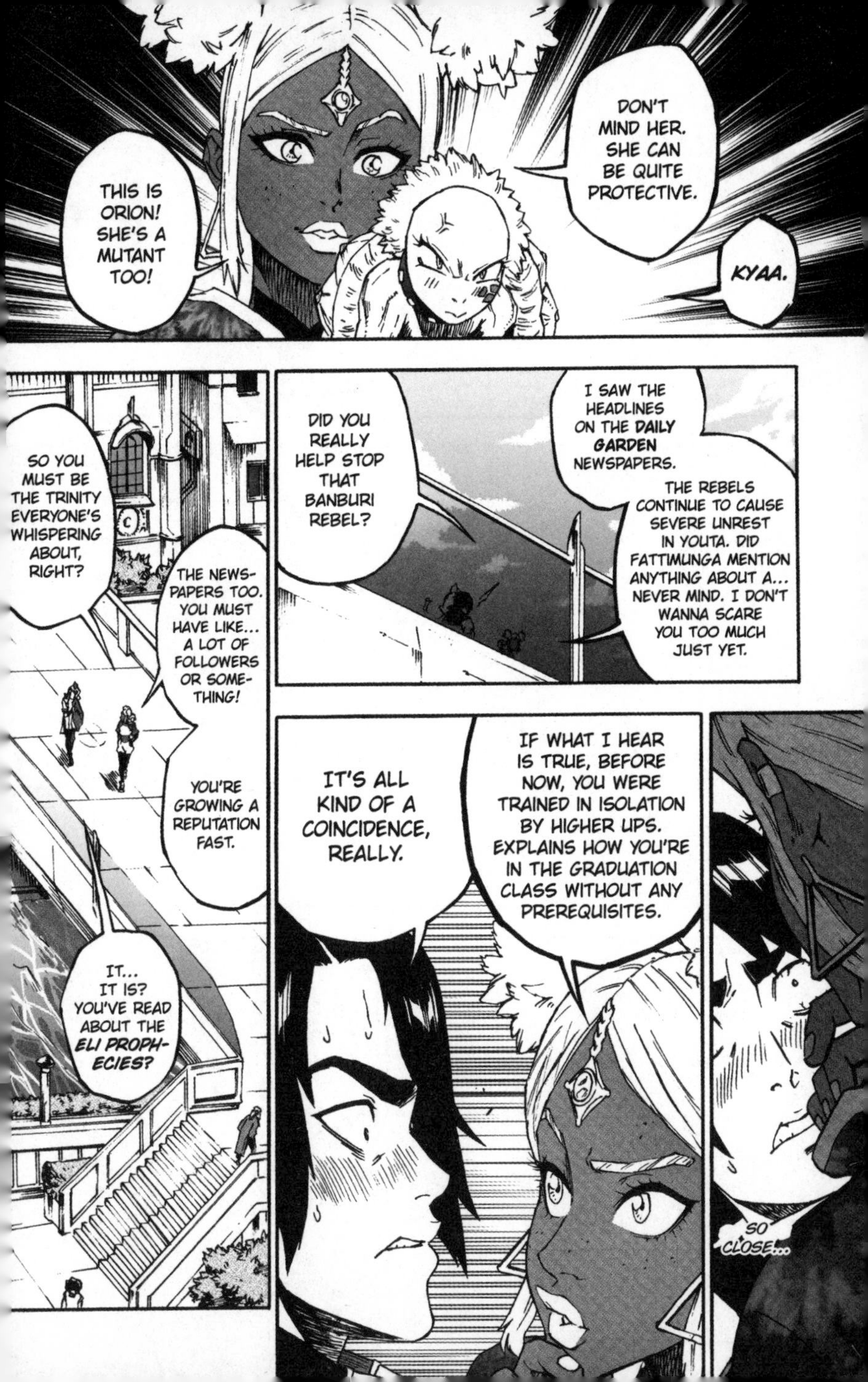
THIS IS ORION! SHE'S A MUTANT TOO!
DON'T MIND HER. SHE CAN BE QUITE PROTECTIVE.
KYAA.
SO YOU MUST BE THE TRINITY EVERYONE'S WHISPERING ABOUT, RIGHT?
THE NEWS-PAPERS TOO. YOU MUST HAVE LIKE... A LOT OF FOLLOWERS OR SOME-THING!
YOU'RE GROWING A REPUTATION FAST.
IT... IT IS? YOU'VE READ ABOUT THE ELI PROPH-ECIES?
DID YOU REALLY HELP STOP THAT BANBURI REBEL?
I SAW THE HEADLINES ON THE DAILY GARDEN NEWSPAPERS.
THE REBELS CONTINUE TO CAUSE SEVERE UNREST IN YOUTA. DID FATTIMUNGA MENTION ANYTHING ABOUT A... NEVER MIND. I DON'T WANNA SCARE YOU TOO MUCH JUST YET.
IT'S ALL KIND OF A COINCIDENCE, REALLY.
IF WHAT I HEAR IS TRUE, BEFORE NOW, YOU WERE TRAINED IN ISOLATION BY HIGHER UPS. EXPLAINS HOW YOU'RE IN THE GRADUATION CLASS WITHOUT ANY PREREQUISITES.
SO CLOSE...

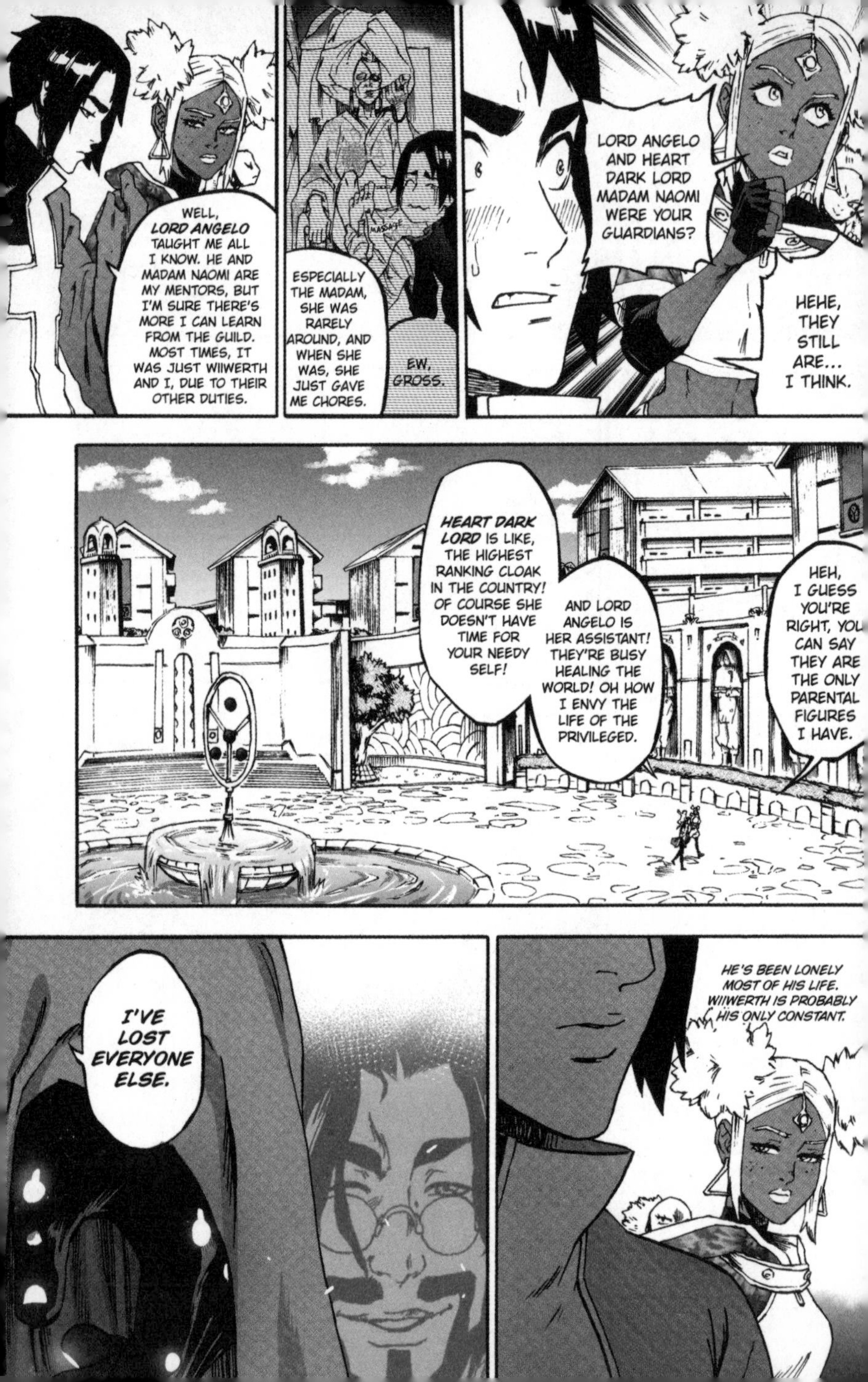
WELL, LORD ANGELO TAUGHT ME ALL I KNOW. HE AND MADAM NAOMI ARE MY MENTORS, BUT I'M SURE THERE'S MORE I CAN LEARN FROM THE GUILD. MOST TIMES, IT WAS JUST WIIWERTH AND I, DUE TO THEIR OTHER DUTIES.
MASSAGE
ESPECIALLY THE MADAM, SHE WAS RARELY AROUND, AND WHEN SHE WAS, SHE JUST GAVE ME CHORES.
EW, GROSS.
LORD ANGELO AND HEART DARK LORD MADAM NAOMI WERE YOUR GUARDIANS?
HEHE, THEY STILL ARE... I THINK.
HEART DARK LORD IS LIKE, THE HIGHEST RANKING CLOAK IN THE COUNTRY! OF COURSE SHE DOESN'T HAVE TIME FOR YOUR NEEDY SELF!
AND LORD ANGELO IS HER ASSISTANT! THEY'RE BUSY HEALING THE WORLD! OH HOW I ENVY THE LIFE OF THE PRIVILEGED.
HEH, I GUESS YOU'RE RIGHT, YOU CAN SAY THEY ARE THE ONLY PARENTAL FIGURES I HAVE.
I'VE LOST EVERYONE ELSE.
HE'S BEEN LONELY MOST OF HIS LIFE. WIIWERTH IS PROBABLY HIS ONLY CONSTANT.

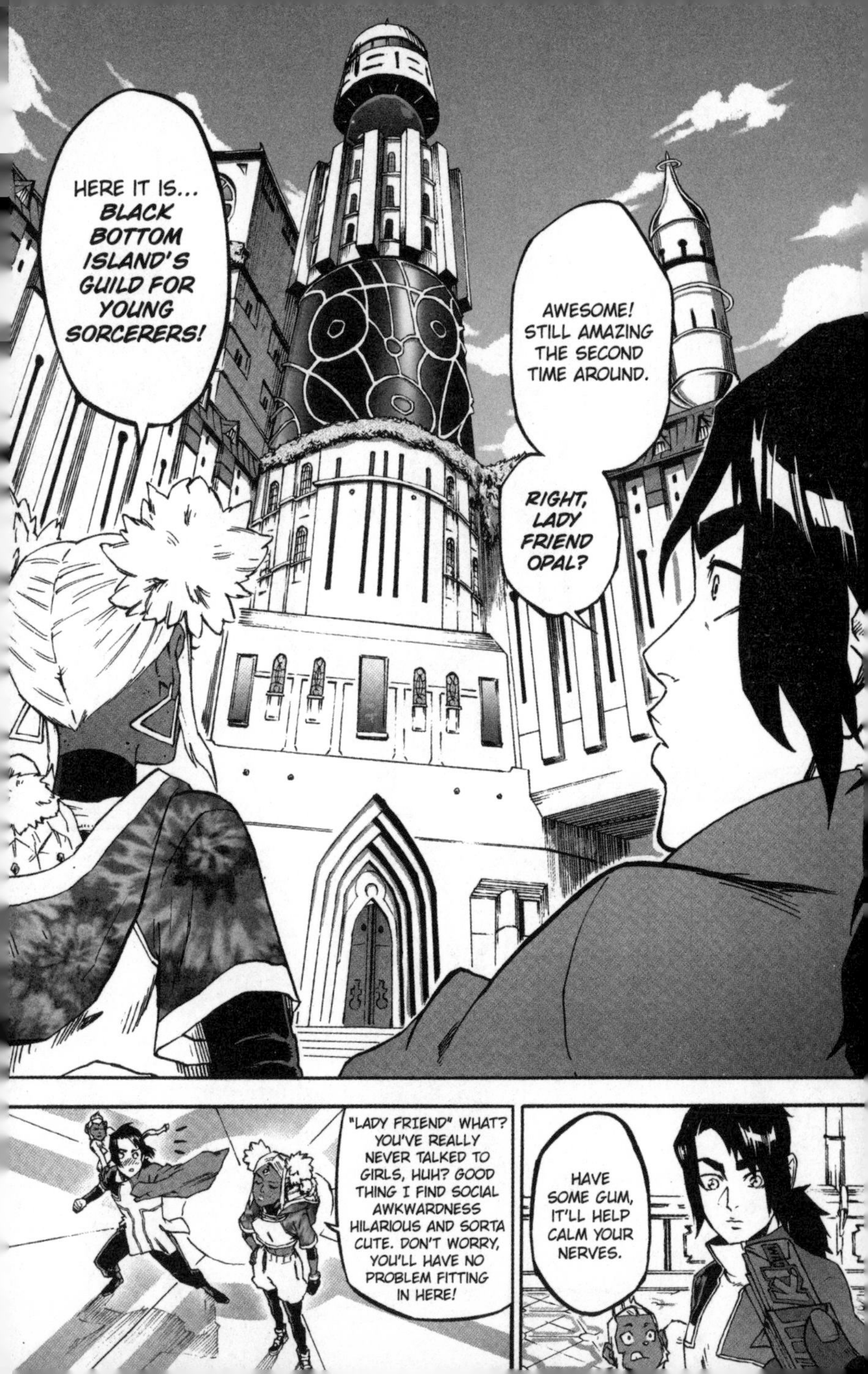
HERE IT IS... BLACK BOTTOM ISLAND'S GUILD FOR YOUNG SORCERERS!
AWESOME! STILL AMAZING THE SECOND TIME AROUND.
RIGHT, LADY FRIEND OPAL?
"LADY FRIEND" WHAT? YOU'VE REALLY NEVER TALKED TO GIRLS, HUH? GOOD THING I FIND SOCIAL AWKWARDNESS HILARIOUS AND SORTA CUTE. DON'T WORRY, YOU'LL HAVE NO PROBLEM FITTING IN HERE!
HAVE SOME GUM, IT'LL HELP CALM YOUR NERVES.

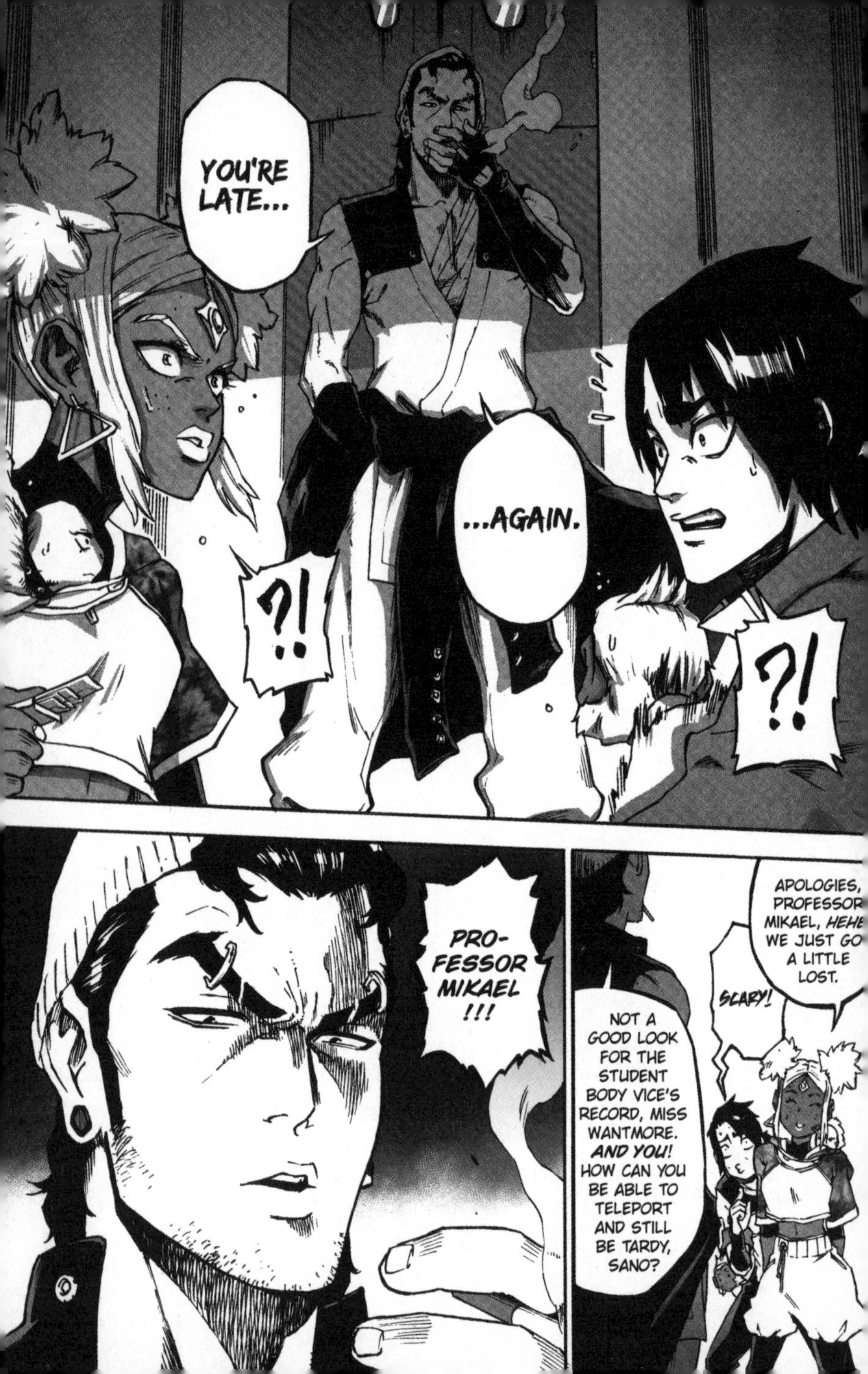
YOU'RE LATE...
...AGAIN.
?!
?!
PRO-FESSOR MIKAEL!!!
NOT A GOOD LOOK FOR THE STUDENT BODY VICE'S RECORD, MISS WANTMORE. AND YOU! HOW CAN YOU BE ABLE TO TELEPORT AND STILL BE TARDY, SANO?
APOLOGIES, PROFESSOR MIKAEL, HEHE WE JUST GO A LITTLE LOST.
SCARY!

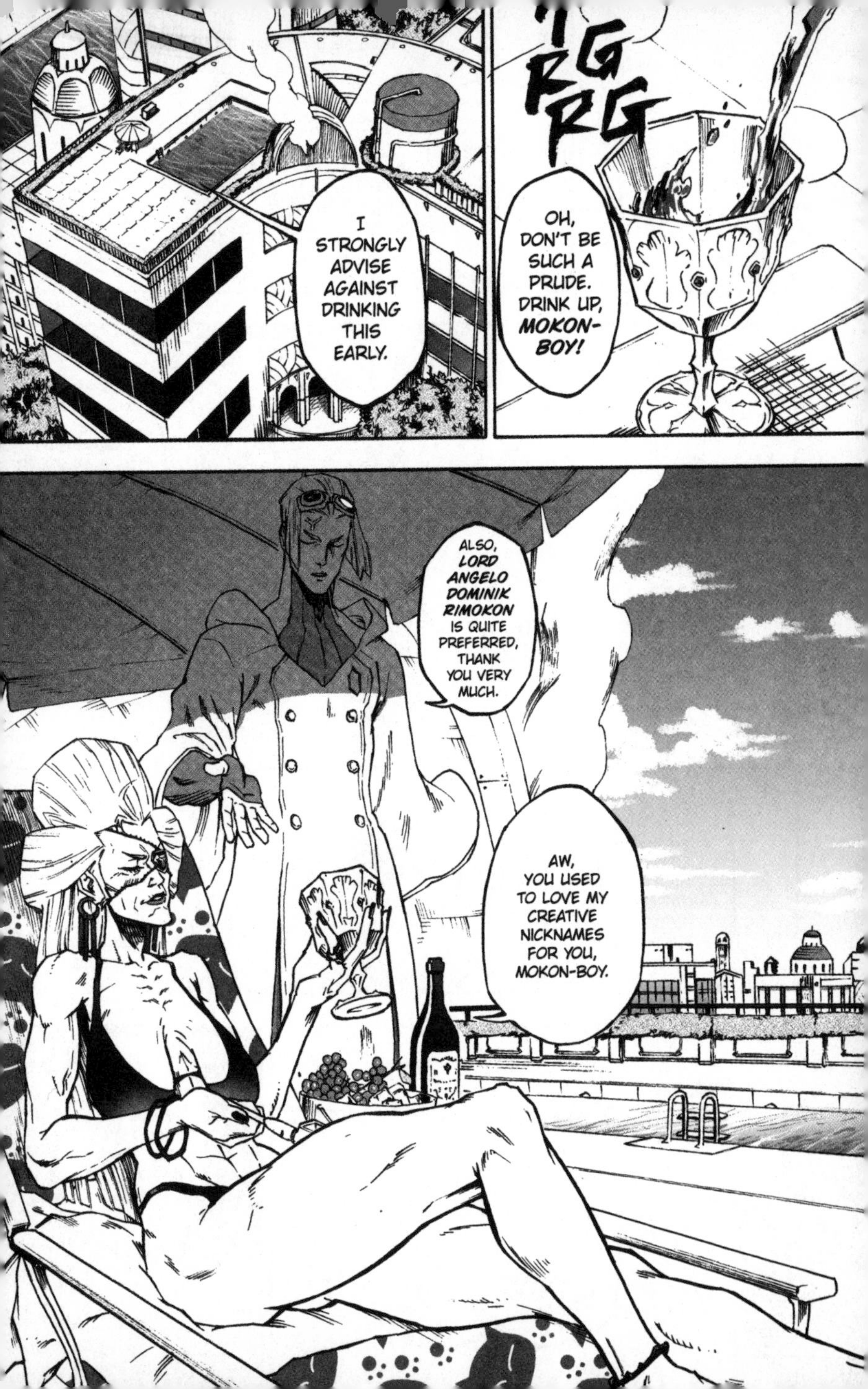
I STRONGLY ADVISE AGAINST DRINKING THIS EARLY.
RG RG
OH, DON'T BE SUCH A PRUDE. DRINK UP, ***MOKON-BOY!***
ALSO, ***LORD ANGELO DOMINIK RIMOKON*** IS QUITE PREFERRED, THANK YOU VERY MUCH.
AW, YOU USED TO LOVE MY CREATIVE NICKNAMES FOR YOU, MOKON-BOY.

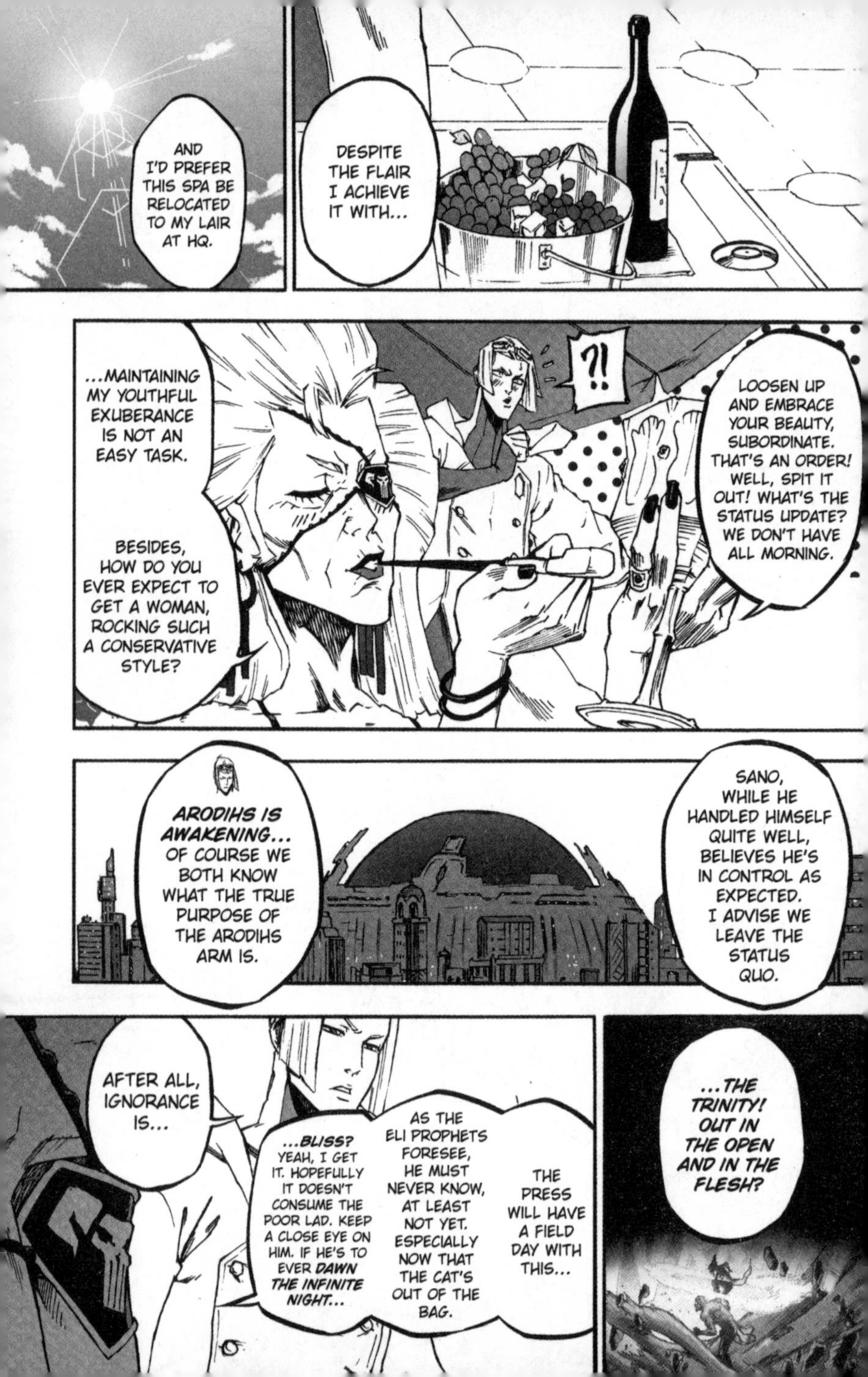
AND I'D PREFER THIS SPA BE RELOCATED TO MY LAIR AT HQ.
DESPITE THE FLAIR I ACHIEVE IT WITH...
...MAINTAINING MY YOUTHFUL EXUBERANCE IS NOT AN EASY TASK.
BESIDES, HOW DO YOU EVER EXPECT TO GET A WOMAN, ROCKING SUCH A CONSERVATIVE STYLE?
?!
LOOSEN UP AND EMBRACE YOUR BEAUTY, SUBORDINATE. THAT'S AN ORDER! WELL, SPIT IT OUT! WHAT'S THE STATUS UPDATE? WE DON'T HAVE ALL MORNING.
ARODIHS IS AWAKENING... OF COURSE WE BOTH KNOW WHAT THE TRUE PURPOSE OF THE ARODIHS ARM IS.
SANO, WHILE HE HANDLED HIMSELF QUITE WELL, BELIEVES HE'S IN CONTROL AS EXPECTED. I ADVISE WE LEAVE THE STATUS QUO.
AFTER ALL, IGNORANCE IS...
...BLISS? YEAH, I GET IT. HOPEFULLY IT DOESN'T CONSUME THE POOR LAD. KEEP A CLOSE EYE ON HIM. IF HE'S TO EVER DAWN THE INFINITE NIGHT...
AS THE ELI PROPHETS FORESEE, HE MUST NEVER KNOW, AT LEAST NOT YET. ESPECIALLY NOW THAT THE CAT'S OUT OF THE BAG.
THE PRESS WILL HAVE A FIELD DAY WITH THIS...
...THE TRINITY! OUT IN THE OPEN AND IN THE FLESH?

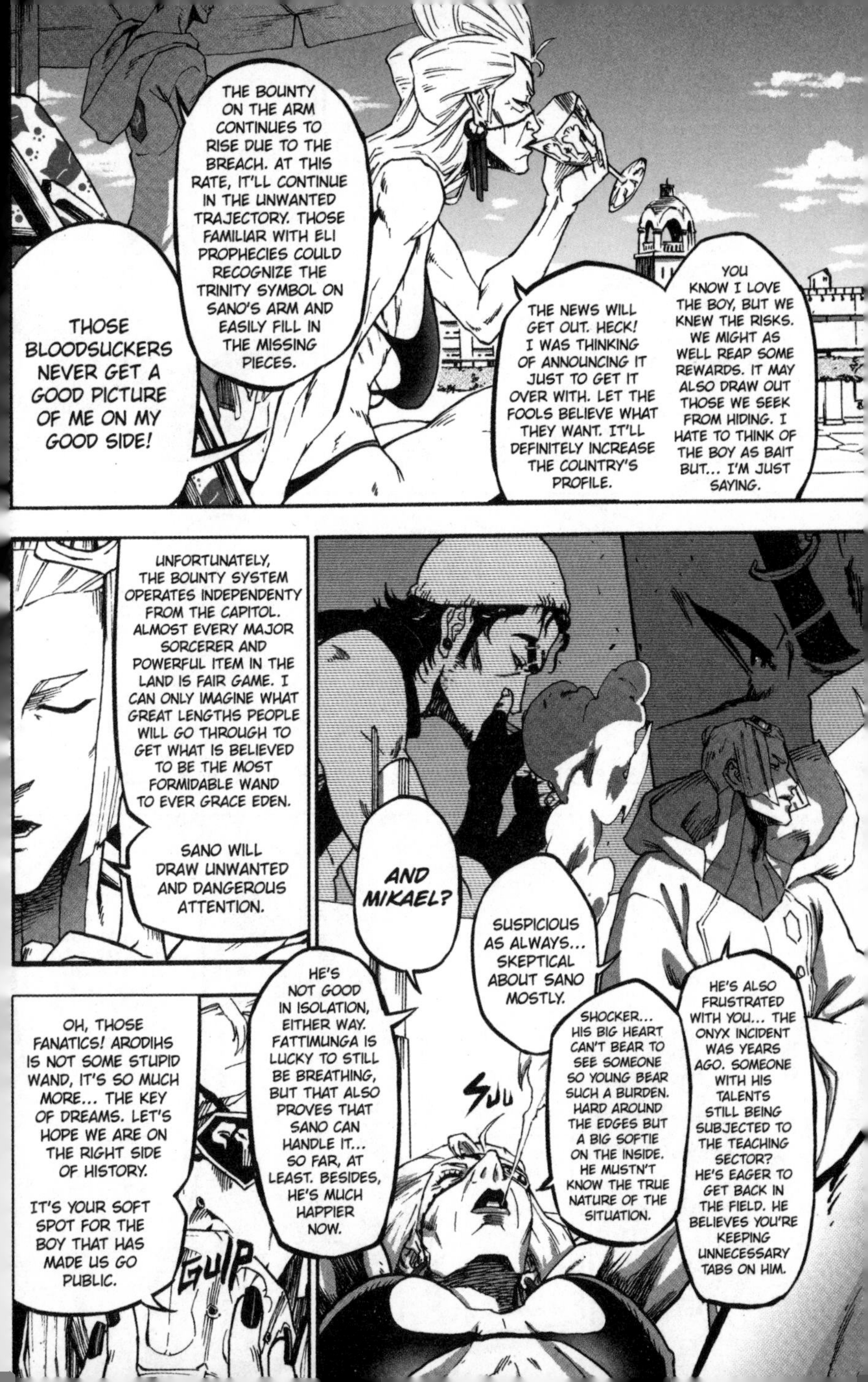
THE BOUNTY ON THE ARM CONTINUES TO RISE DUE TO THE BREACH. AT THIS RATE, IT'LL CONTINUE IN THE UNWANTED TRAJECTORY. THOSE FAMILIAR WITH ELI PROPHECIES COULD RECOGNIZE THE TRINITY SYMBOL ON SANO'S ARM AND EASILY FILL IN THE MISSING PIECES.
THOSE BLOODSUCKERS NEVER GET A GOOD PICTURE OF ME ON MY GOOD SIDE!
THE NEWS WILL GET OUT. HECK! I WAS THINKING OF ANNOUNCING IT JUST TO GET IT OVER WITH. LET THE FOOLS BELIEVE WHAT THEY WANT. IT'LL DEFINITELY INCREASE THE COUNTRY'S PROFILE.
YOU KNOW I LOVE THE BOY, BUT WE KNEW THE RISKS. WE MIGHT AS WELL REAP SOME REWARDS. IT MAY ALSO DRAW OUT THOSE WE SEEK FROM HIDING. I HATE TO THINK OF THE BOY AS BAIT BUT... I'M JUST SAYING.
UNFORTUNATELY, THE BOUNTY SYSTEM OPERATES INDEPENDENTLY FROM THE CAPITOL. ALMOST EVERY MAJOR SORCERER AND POWERFUL ITEM IN THE LAND IS FAIR GAME. I CAN ONLY IMAGINE WHAT GREAT LENGTHS PEOPLE WILL GO THROUGH TO GET WHAT IS BELIEVED TO BE THE MOST FORMIDABLE WAND TO EVER GRACE EDEN.
SANO WILL DRAW UNWANTED AND DANGEROUS ATTENTION.
AND MIKAEL?
SUSPICIOUS AS ALWAYS... SKEPTICAL ABOUT SANO MOSTLY.
OH, THOSE FANATICS! ARODIHS IS NOT SOME STUPID WAND, IT'S SO MUCH MORE... THE KEY OF DREAMS. LET'S HOPE WE ARE ON THE RIGHT SIDE OF HISTORY.
IT'S YOUR SOFT SPOT FOR THE BOY THAT HAS MADE US GO PUBLIC.
HE'S NOT GOOD IN ISOLATION, EITHER WAY. FATTIMUNGA IS LUCKY TO STILL BE BREATHING, BUT THAT ALSO PROVES THAT SANO CAN HANDLE IT... SO FAR, AT LEAST. BESIDES, HE'S MUCH HAPPIER NOW.
SUU
SHOCKER... HIS BIG HEART CAN'T BEAR TO SEE SOMEONE SO YOUNG BEAR SUCH A BURDEN. HARD AROUND THE EDGES BUT A BIG SOFTIE ON THE INSIDE. HE MUSTN'T KNOW THE TRUE NATURE OF THE SITUATION.
HE'S ALSO FRUSTRATED WITH YOU... THE ONYX INCIDENT WAS YEARS AGO. SOMEONE WITH HIS TALENTS STILL BEING SUBJECTED TO THE TEACHING SECTOR? HE'S EAGER TO GET BACK IN THE FIELD. HE BELIEVES YOU'RE KEEPING UNNECESSARY TABS ON HIM.
GULP

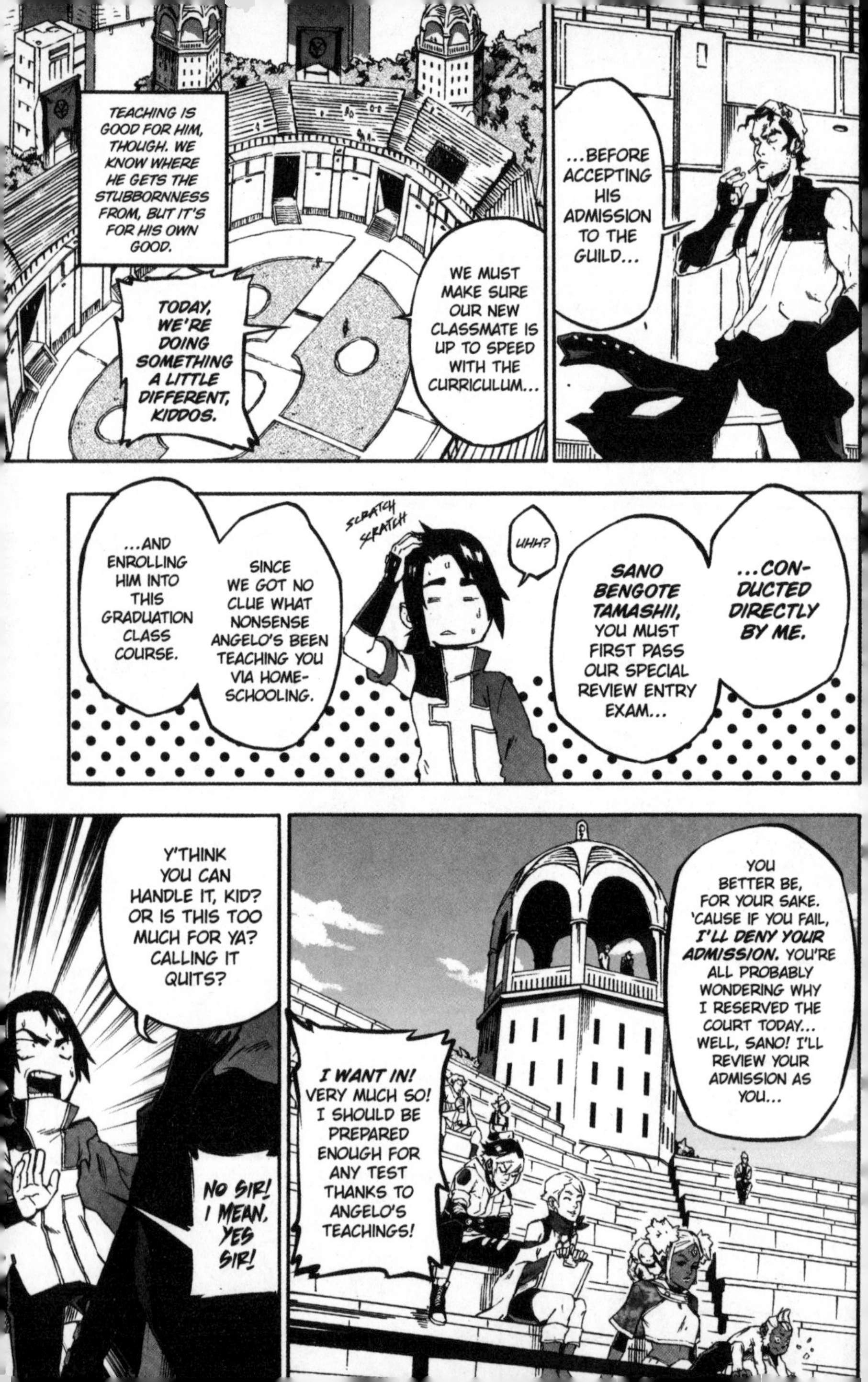
TEACHING IS GOOD FOR HIM, THOUGH. WE KNOW WHERE HE GETS THE STUBBORNNESS FROM, BUT IT'S FOR HIS OWN GOOD.
TODAY, WE'RE DOING SOMETHING A LITTLE DIFFERENT, KIDDOS.
WE MUST MAKE SURE OUR NEW CLASSMATE IS UP TO SPEED WITH THE CURRICULUM...
...BEFORE ACCEPTING HIS ADMISSION TO THE GUILD...
...AND ENROLLING HIM INTO THIS GRADUATION CLASS COURSE.
SINCE WE GOT NO CLUE WHAT NONSENSE ANGELO'S BEEN TEACHING YOU VIA HOME-SCHOOLING.
SCRATCH SCRATCH
UHH?
SANO BENGOTE TAMASHII, YOU MUST FIRST PASS OUR SPECIAL REVIEW ENTRY EXAM...
...CONDUCTED DIRECTLY BY ME.
Y'THINK YOU CAN HANDLE IT, KID? OR IS THIS TOO MUCH FOR YA? CALLING IT QUITS?
NO SIR! I MEAN, YES SIR!
I WANT IN! VERY MUCH SO! I SHOULD BE PREPARED ENOUGH FOR ANY TEST THANKS TO ANGELO'S TEACHINGS!
YOU BETTER BE, FOR YOUR SAKE. 'CAUSE IF YOU FAIL, I'LL DENY YOUR ADMISSION. YOU'RE ALL PROBABLY WONDERING WHY I RESERVED THE COURT TODAY... WELL, SANO! I'LL REVIEW YOUR ADMISSION AS YOU...

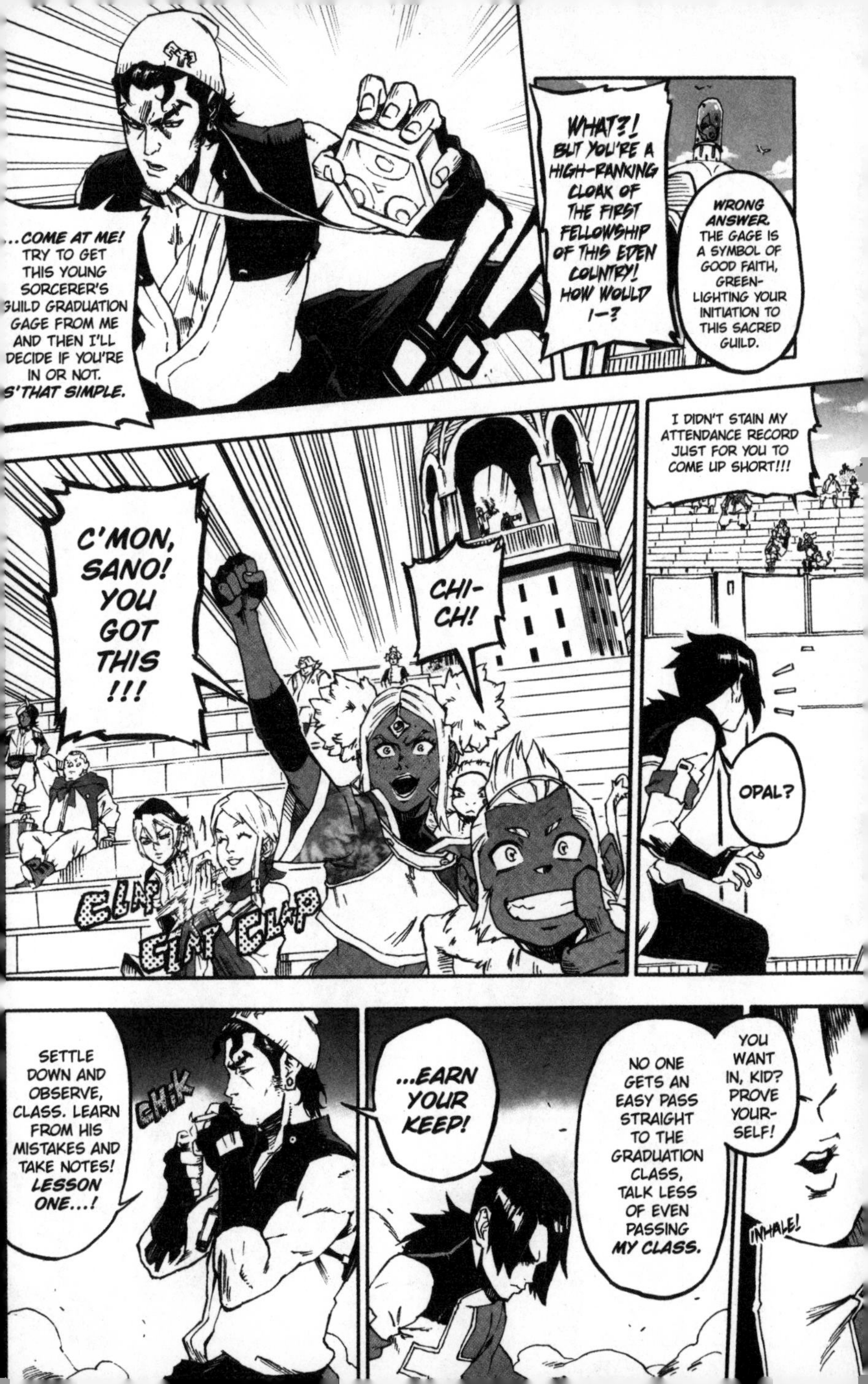
...COME AT ME! TRY TO GET THIS YOUNG SORCERER'S GUILD GRADUATION GAGE FROM ME AND THEN I'LL DECIDE IF YOU'RE IN OR NOT. S'THAT SIMPLE.
WHAT?! BUT YOU'RE A HIGH-RANKING CLOAK OF THE FIRST FELLOWSHIP OF THIS EDEN COUNTRY! HOW WOULD I—?
WRONG ANSWER. THE GAGE IS A SYMBOL OF GOOD FAITH, GREEN-LIGHTING YOUR INITIATION TO THIS SACRED GUILD.
C'MON, SANO! YOU GOT THIS!!!
CHI-CH!
CLAP CLAP CLAP
I DIDN'T STAIN MY ATTENDANCE RECORD JUST FOR YOU TO COME UP SHORT!!!
OPAL?
SETTLE DOWN AND OBSERVE, CLASS. LEARN FROM HIS MISTAKES AND TAKE NOTES! LESSON ONE...!
CHIK
...EARN YOUR KEEP!
NO ONE GETS AN EASY PASS STRAIGHT TO THE GRADUATION CLASS, TALK LESS OF EVEN PASSING MY CLASS.
YOU WANT IN, KID? PROVE YOURSELF!
INHALE!

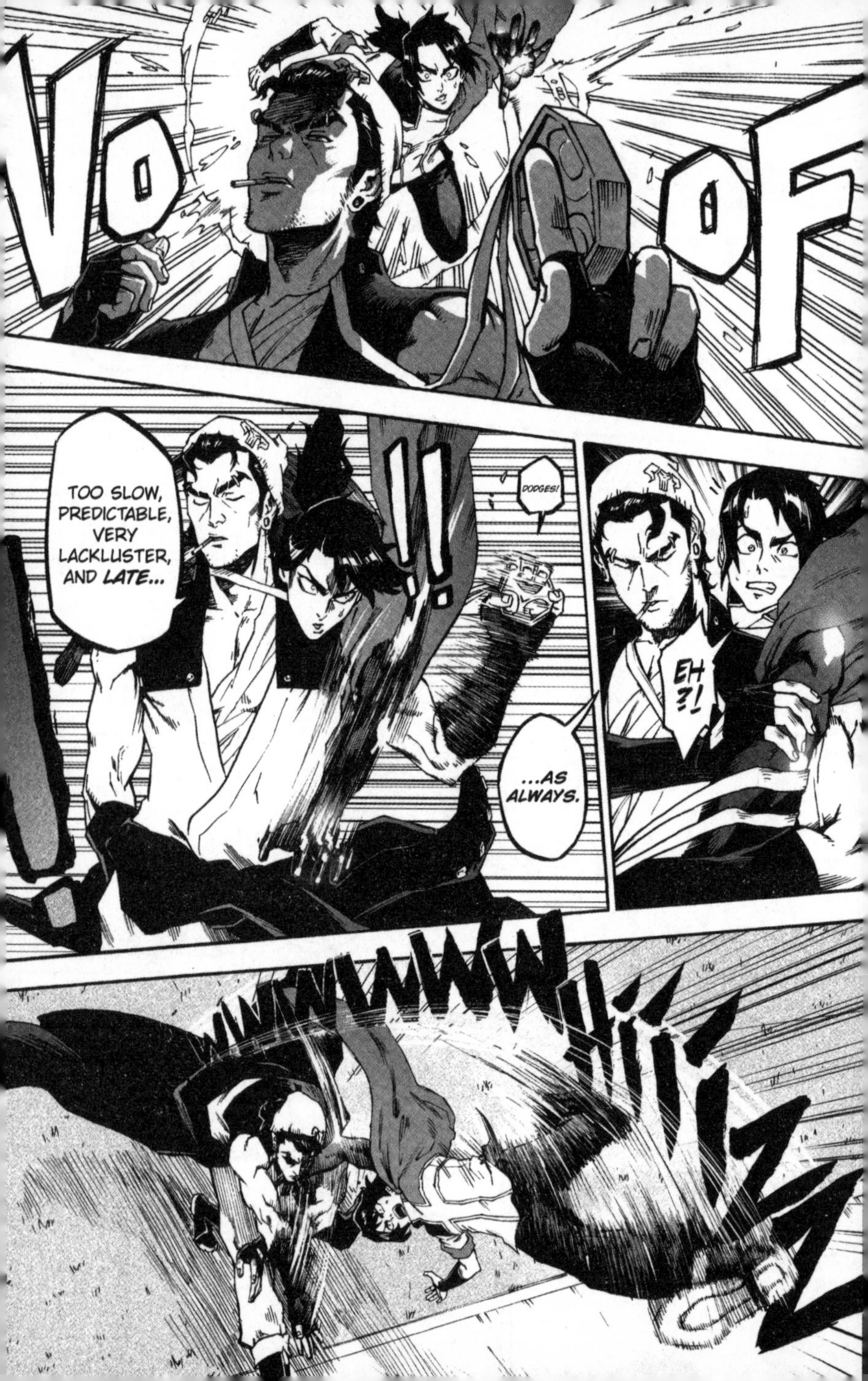
VOOOF
TOO SLOW, PREDICTABLE, VERY LACKLUSTER, AND *LATE*...
!!
DODGES!
EH ?!
...AS ALWAYS.
WHHHIIIZZ

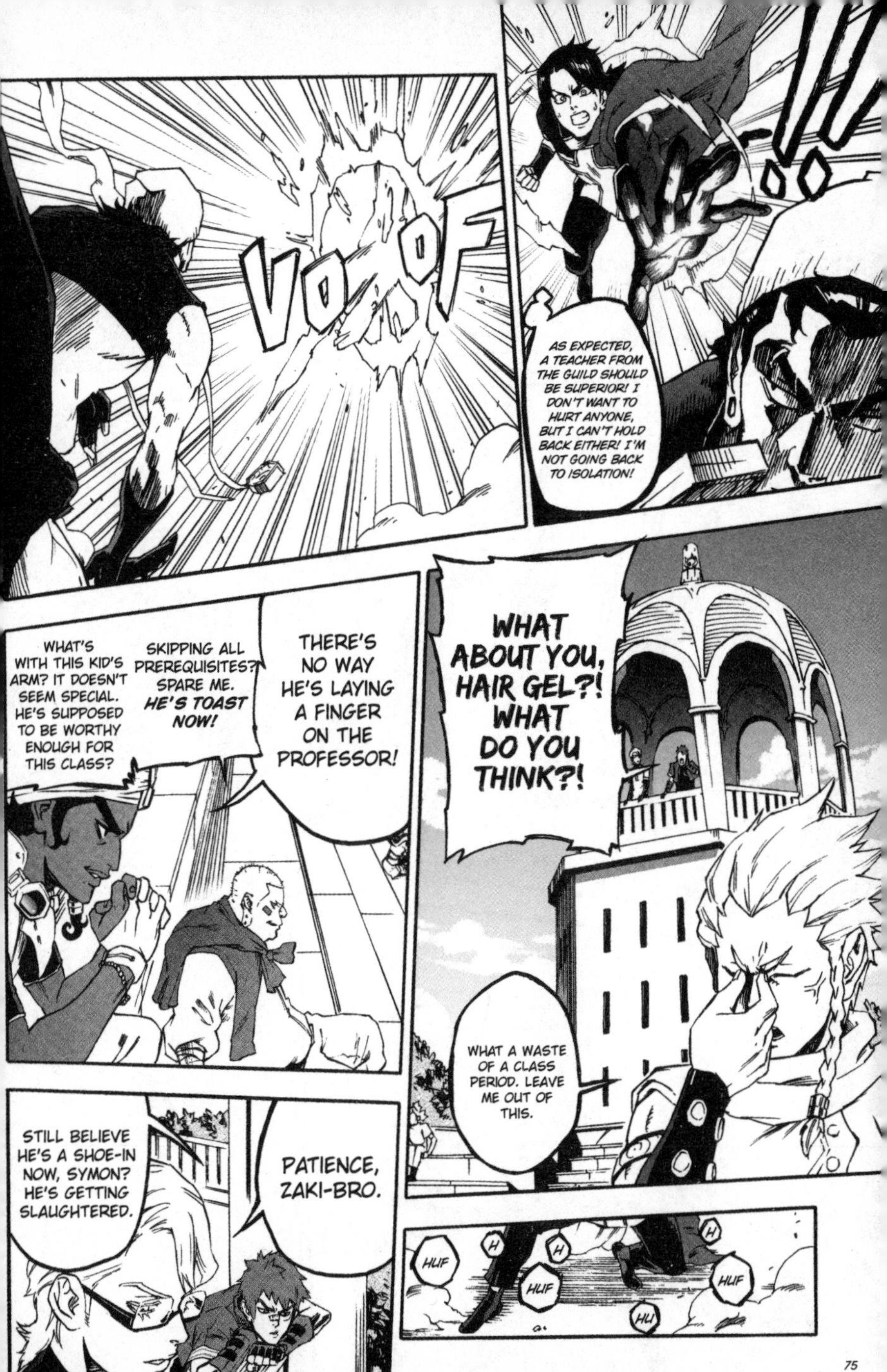
VOOF
AS EXPECTED, A TEACHER FROM THE GUILD SHOULD BE SUPERIOR! I DON'T WANT TO HURT ANYONE, BUT I CAN'T HOLD BACK EITHER! I'M NOT GOING BACK TO ISOLATION!
WHAT'S WITH THIS KID'S ARM? IT DOESN'T SEEM SPECIAL. HE'S SUPPOSED TO BE WORTHY ENOUGH FOR THIS CLASS?
SKIPPING ALL PREREQUISITES? SPARE ME. HE'S TOAST NOW!
THERE'S NO WAY HE'S LAYING A FINGER ON THE PROFESSOR!
WHAT ABOUT YOU, HAIR GEL?! WHAT DO YOU THINK?!
WHAT A WASTE OF A CLASS PERIOD. LEAVE ME OUT OF THIS.
STILL BELIEVE HE'S A SHOE-IN NOW, SYMON? HE'S GETTING SLAUGHTERED.
PATIENCE, ZAKI-BRO.
H
H
H
HUF
HUF
HUF
HU

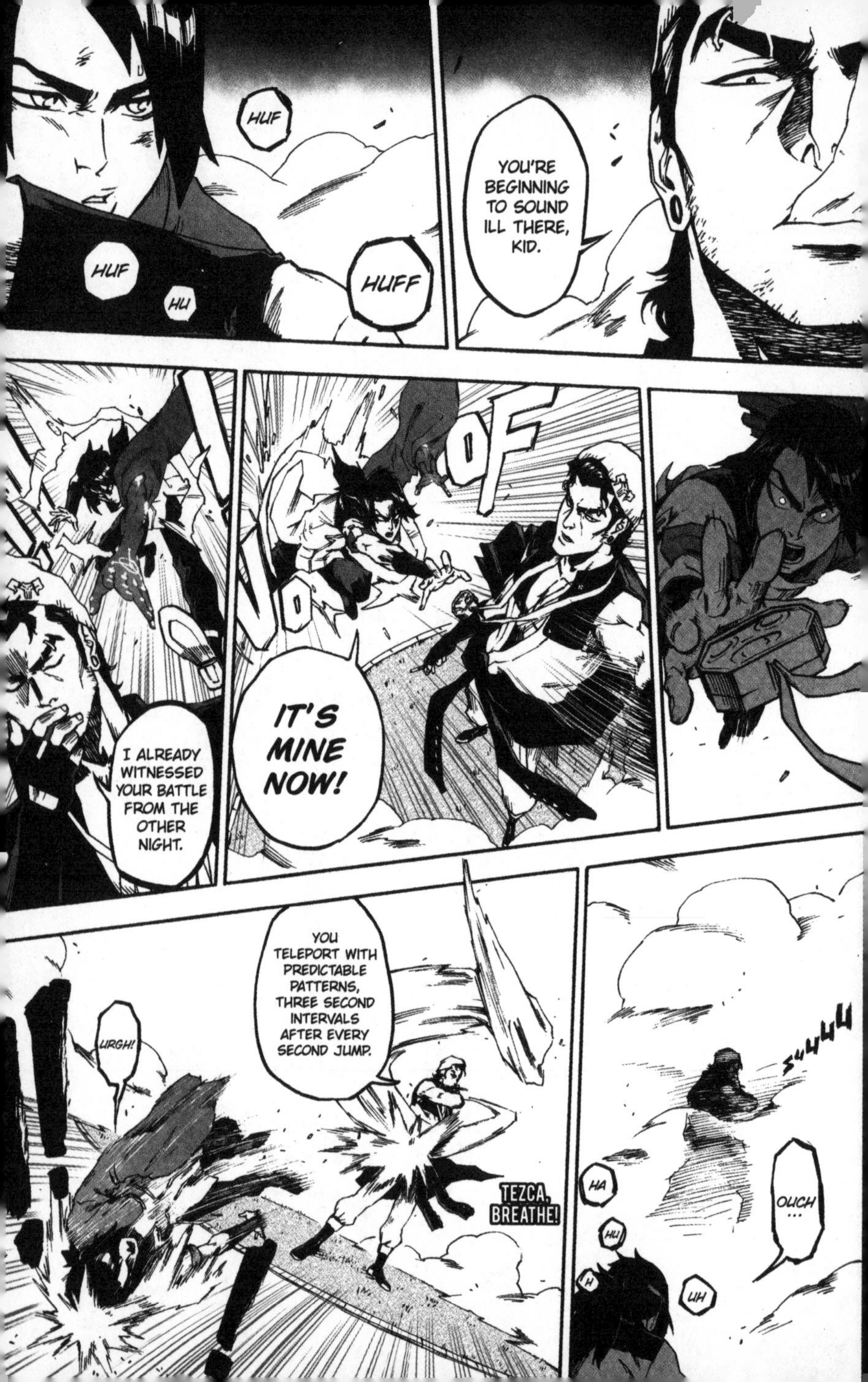
HUF
HUF
HU
HUFF
YOU'RE BEGINNING TO SOUND ILL THERE, KID.
I ALREADY WITNESSED YOUR BATTLE FROM THE OTHER NIGHT.
VOOF
IT'S MINE NOW!
URGH!
YOU TELEPORT WITH PREDICTABLE PATTERNS, THREE SECOND INTERVALS AFTER EVERY SECOND JUMP.
TEZCA, BREATHE!
SHUUU
HA
HU
H
UH
OUCH ...

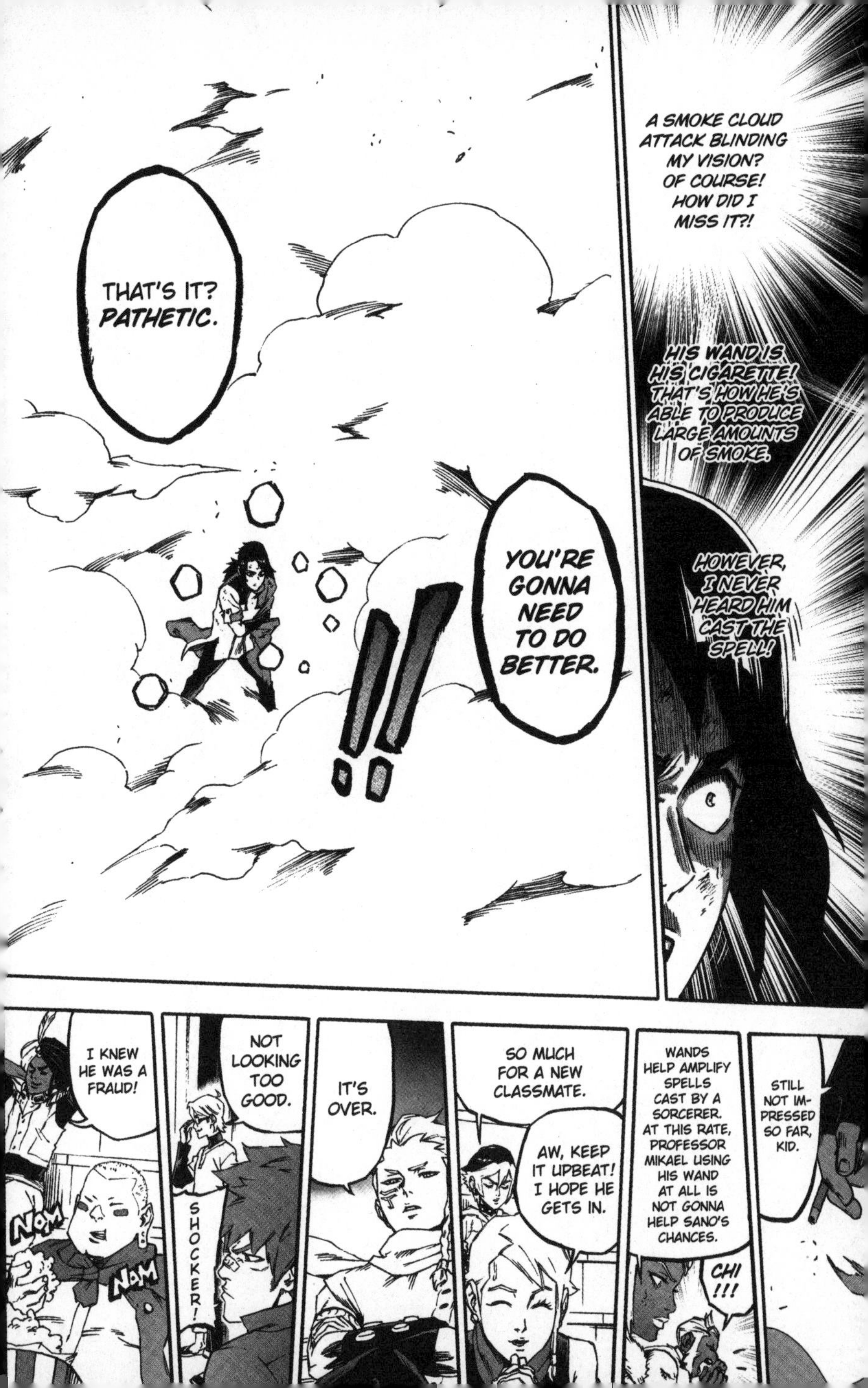
THAT'S IT? PATHETIC.
YOU'RE GONNA NEED TO DO BETTER.
A SMOKE CLOUD ATTACK BLINDING MY VISION? OF COURSE! HOW DID I MISS IT?!
HIS WAND IS HIS CIGARETTE! THAT'S HOW HE'S ABLE TO PRODUCE LARGE AMOUNTS OF SMOKE.
HOWEVER, I NEVER HEARD HIM CAST THE SPELL!
I KNEW HE WAS A FRAUD!
NOM
NOM
NOT LOOKING TOO GOOD.
SHOCKER!
IT'S OVER.
SO MUCH FOR A NEW CLASSMATE.
AW, KEEP IT UPBEAT! I HOPE HE GETS IN.
WANDS HELP AMPLIFY SPELLS CAST BY A SORCERER. AT THIS RATE, PROFESSOR MIKAEL USING HIS WAND AT ALL IS NOT GONNA HELP SANO'S CHANCES.
CHI !!!
STILL NOT IMPRESSED SO FAR, KID.

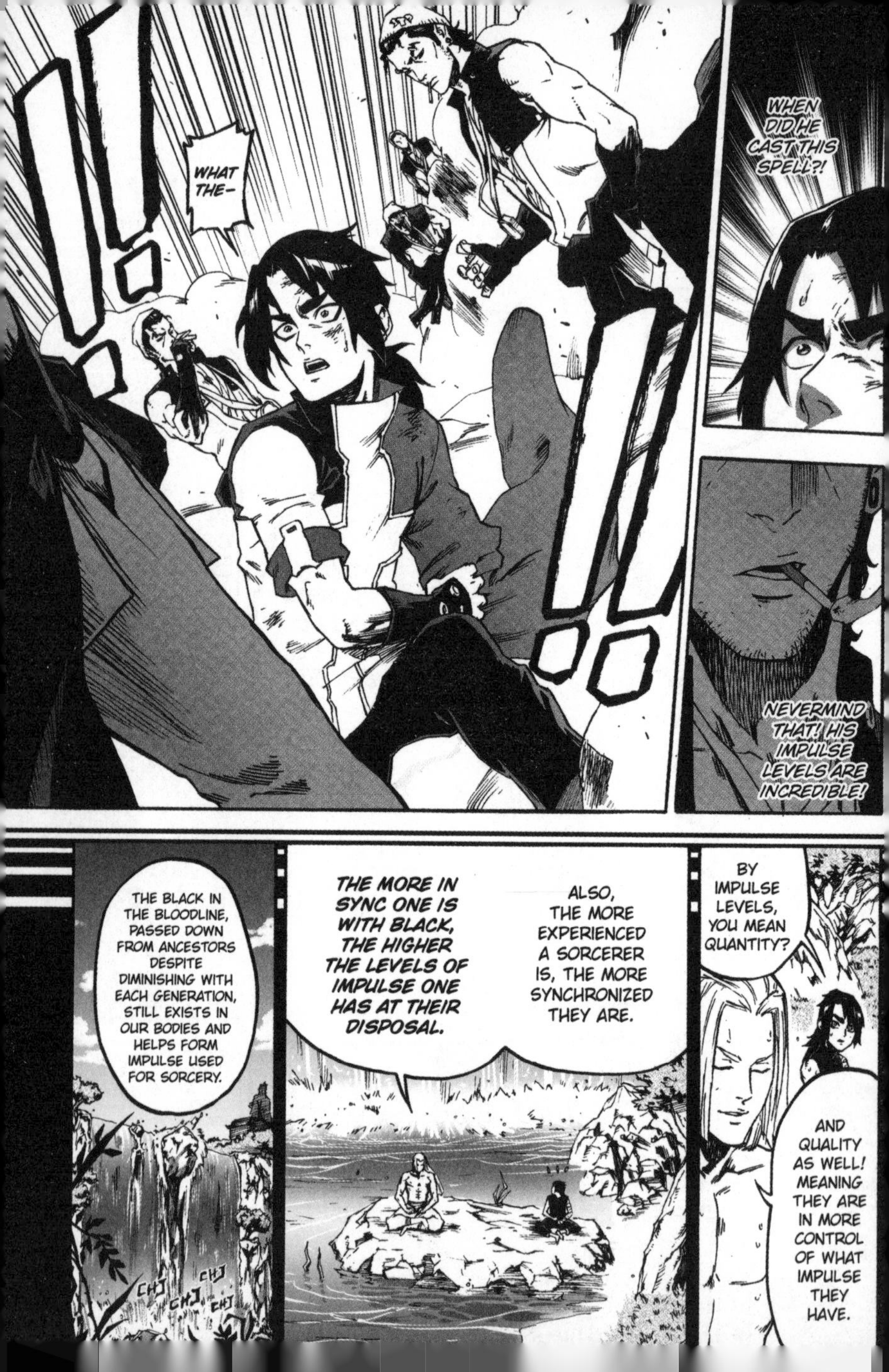
WHAT THE-
WHEN DID HE CAST THIS SPELL?!
NEVERMIND THAT! HIS IMPULSE LEVELS ARE INCREDIBLE!
THE BLACK IN THE BLOODLINE, PASSED DOWN FROM ANCESTORS DESPITE DIMINISHING WITH EACH GENERATION, STILL EXISTS IN OUR BODIES AND HELPS FORM IMPULSE USED FOR SORCERY.
THE MORE IN SYNC ONE IS WITH BLACK, THE HIGHER THE LEVELS OF IMPULSE ONE HAS AT THEIR DISPOSAL.
ALSO, THE MORE EXPERIENCED A SORCERER IS, THE MORE SYNCHRONIZED THEY ARE.
BY IMPULSE LEVELS, YOU MEAN QUANTITY?
AND QUALITY AS WELL! MEANING THEY ARE IN MORE CONTROL OF WHAT IMPULSE THEY HAVE.

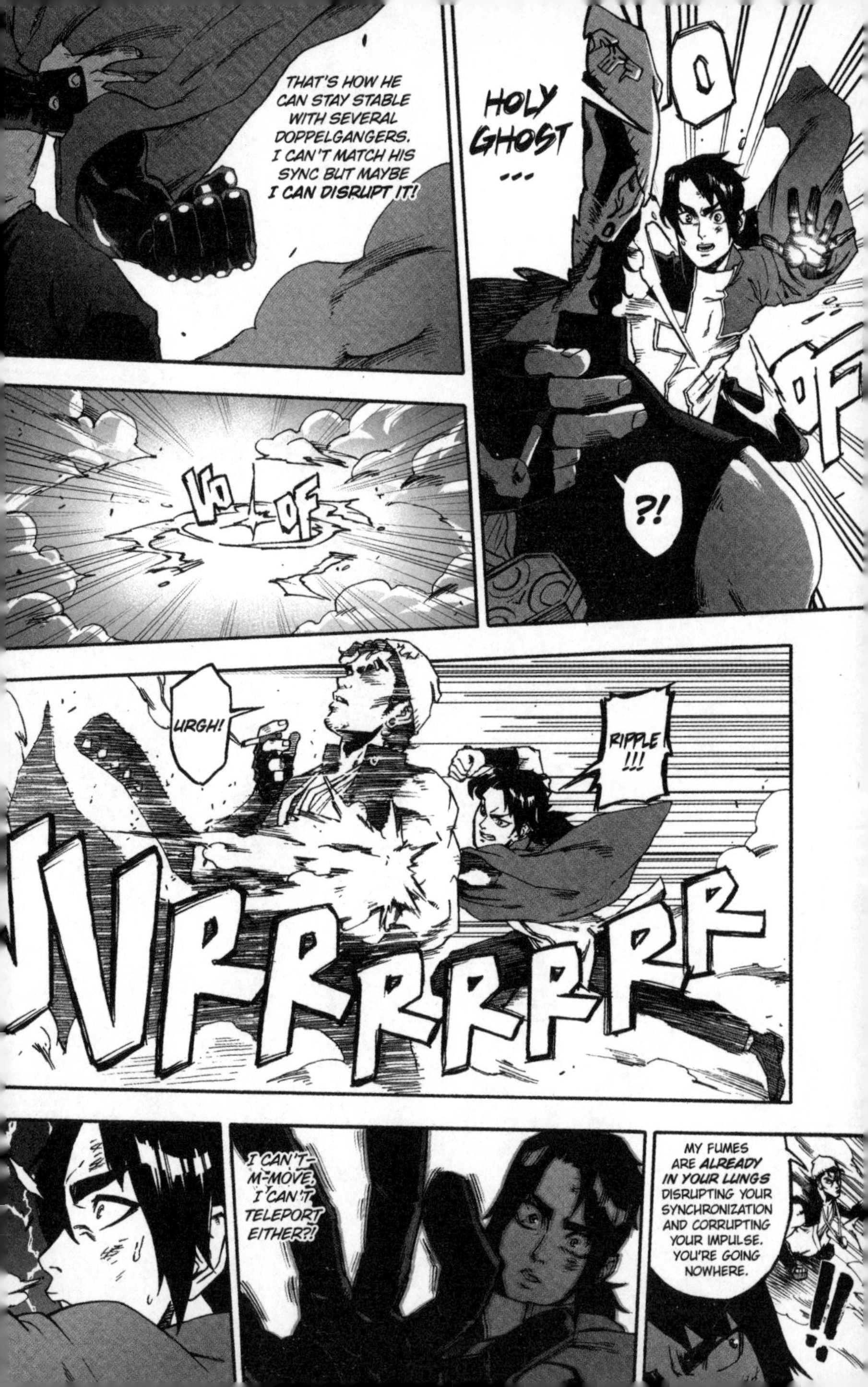
THAT'S HOW HE CAN STAY STABLE WITH SEVERAL DOPPELGANGERS. I CAN'T MATCH HIS SYNC BUT MAYBE ***I CAN DISRUPT IT!***
VO OF
HOLY GHOST ...
O
OF
?!
URGH!
RIPPLE !!!
VRRRRRRR
I CAN'T- M-MOVE. I CAN'T TELEPORT EITHER?!
MY FUMES ARE ***ALREADY IN YOUR LUNGS*** DISRUPTING YOUR SYNCHRONIZATION AND CORRUPTING YOUR IMPULSE. YOU'RE GOING NOWHERE.
!!

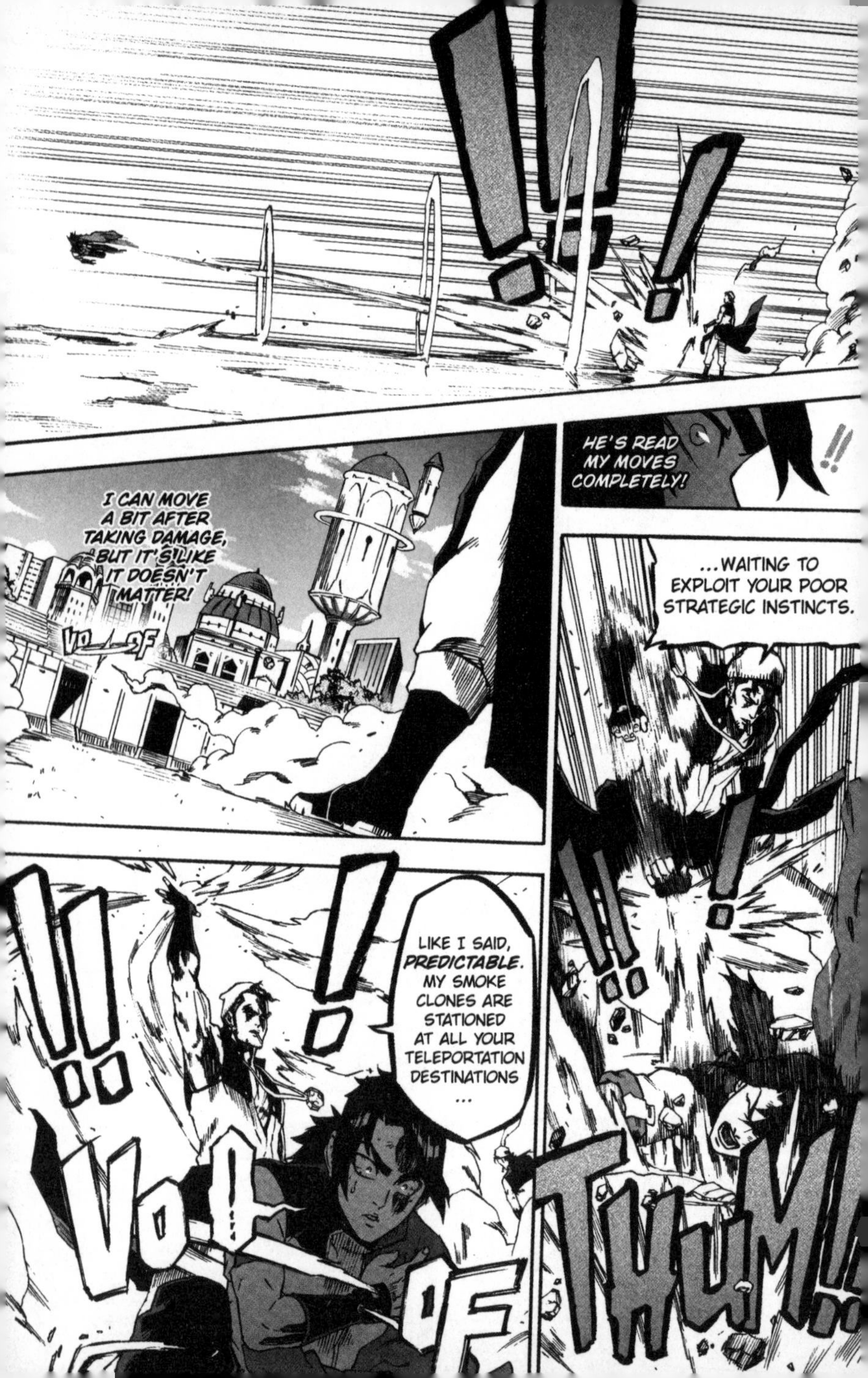
I CAN MOVE A BIT AFTER TAKING DAMAGE, BUT IT'S LIKE IT DOESN'T MATTER!
HE'S READ MY MOVES COMPLETELY!
LIKE I SAID, PREDICTABLE. MY SMOKE CLONES ARE STATIONED AT ALL YOUR TELEPORTATION DESTINATIONS ...
...WAITING TO EXPLOIT YOUR POOR STRATEGIC INSTINCTS.

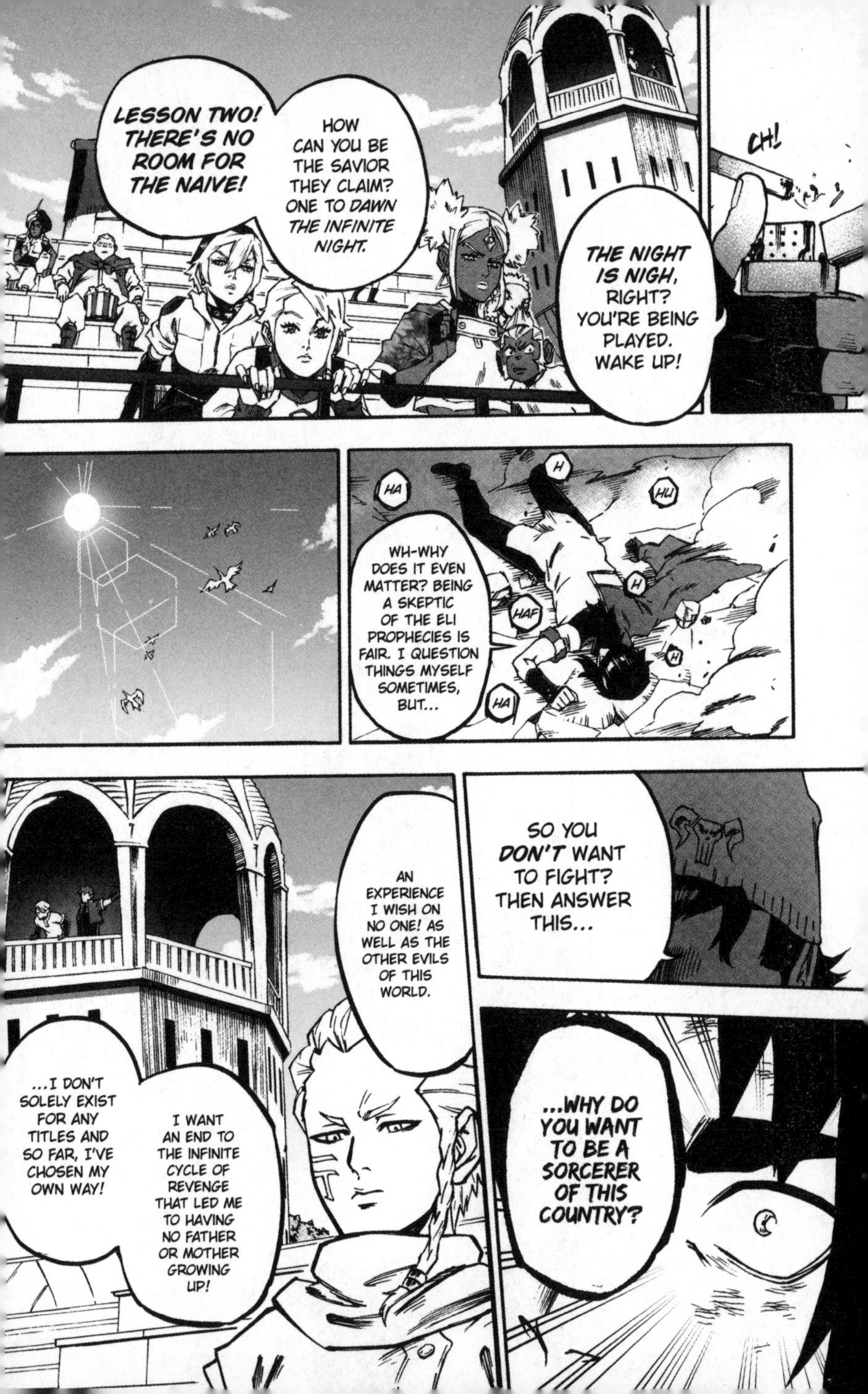
LESSON TWO! THERE'S NO ROOM FOR THE NAIVE!
HOW CAN YOU BE THE SAVIOR THEY CLAIM? ONE TO DAWN THE INFINITE NIGHT.
CH!
THE NIGHT IS NIGH, RIGHT? YOU'RE BEING PLAYED. WAKE UP!
HA
H
HU
WH-WHY DOES IT EVEN MATTER? BEING A SKEPTIC OF THE ELI PROPHECIES IS FAIR. I QUESTION THINGS MYSELF SOMETIMES, BUT...
H
HAF
H
HA
AN EXPERIENCE I WISH ON NO ONE! AS WELL AS THE OTHER EVILS OF THIS WORLD.
...I DON'T SOLELY EXIST FOR ANY TITLES AND SO FAR, I'VE CHOSEN MY OWN WAY!
I WANT AN END TO THE INFINITE CYCLE OF REVENGE THAT LED ME TO HAVING NO FATHER OR MOTHER GROWING UP!
SO YOU DON'T WANT TO FIGHT? THEN ANSWER THIS...
...WHY DO YOU WANT TO BE A SORCERER OF THIS COUNTRY?

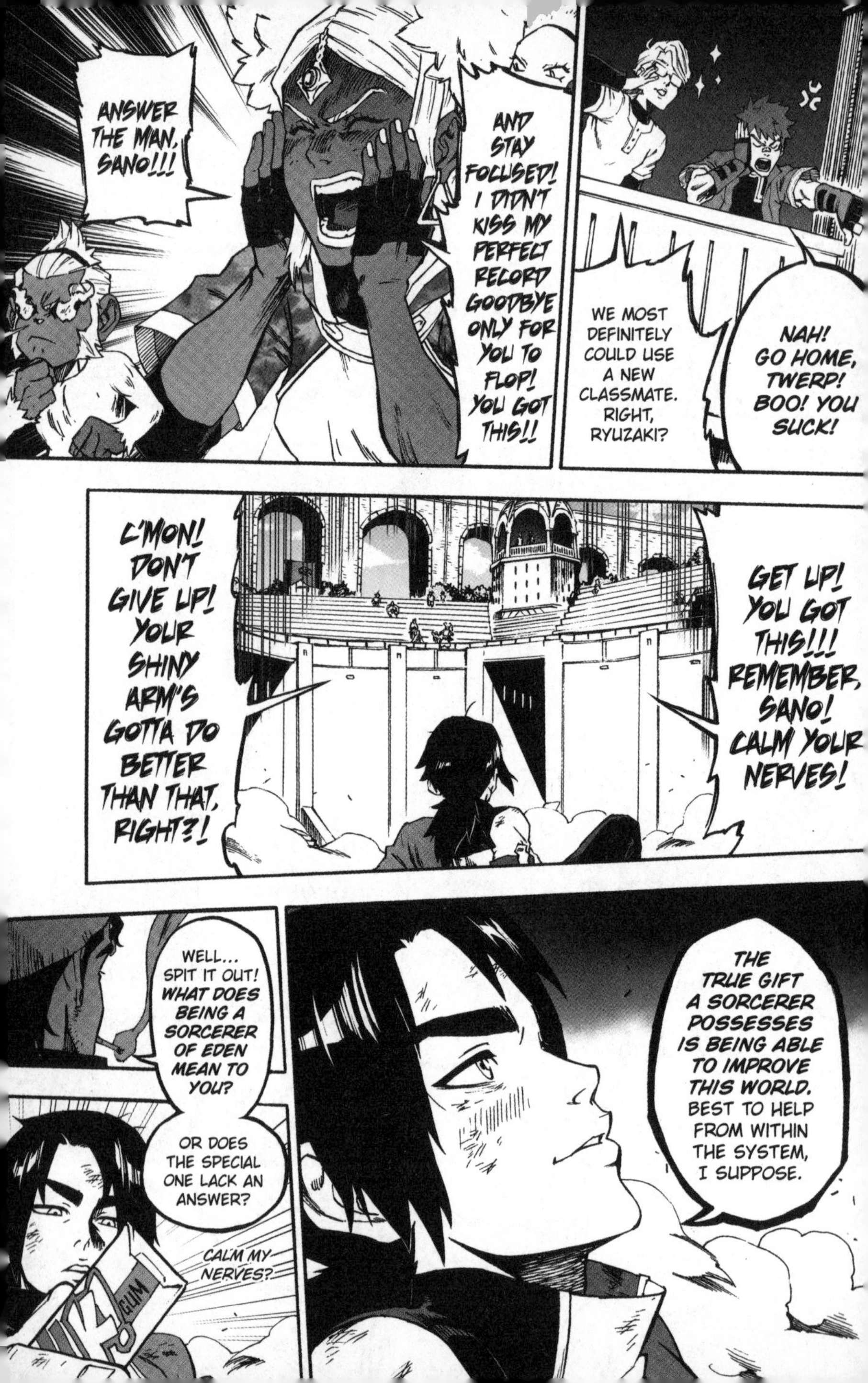
ANSWER THE MAN, SANO!!!
AND STAY FOCUSED! I DIDN'T KISS MY PERFECT RECORD GOODBYE ONLY FOR YOU TO FLOP! YOU GOT THIS!!
WE MOST DEFINITELY COULD USE A NEW CLASSMATE. RIGHT, RYUZAKI?
NAH! GO HOME, TWERP! BOO! YOU SUCK!
C'MON! DON'T GIVE UP! YOUR SHINY ARM'S GOTTA DO BETTER THAN THAT, RIGHT?!
GET UP! YOU GOT THIS!!! REMEMBER, SANO! CALM YOUR NERVES!
WELL... SPIT IT OUT! WHAT DOES BEING A SORCERER OF EDEN MEAN TO YOU?
OR DOES THE SPECIAL ONE LACK AN ANSWER?
CALM MY NERVES?
GUM
THE TRUE GIFT A SORCERER POSSESSES IS BEING ABLE TO IMPROVE THIS WORLD. BEST TO HELP FROM WITHIN THE SYSTEM, I SUPPOSE.

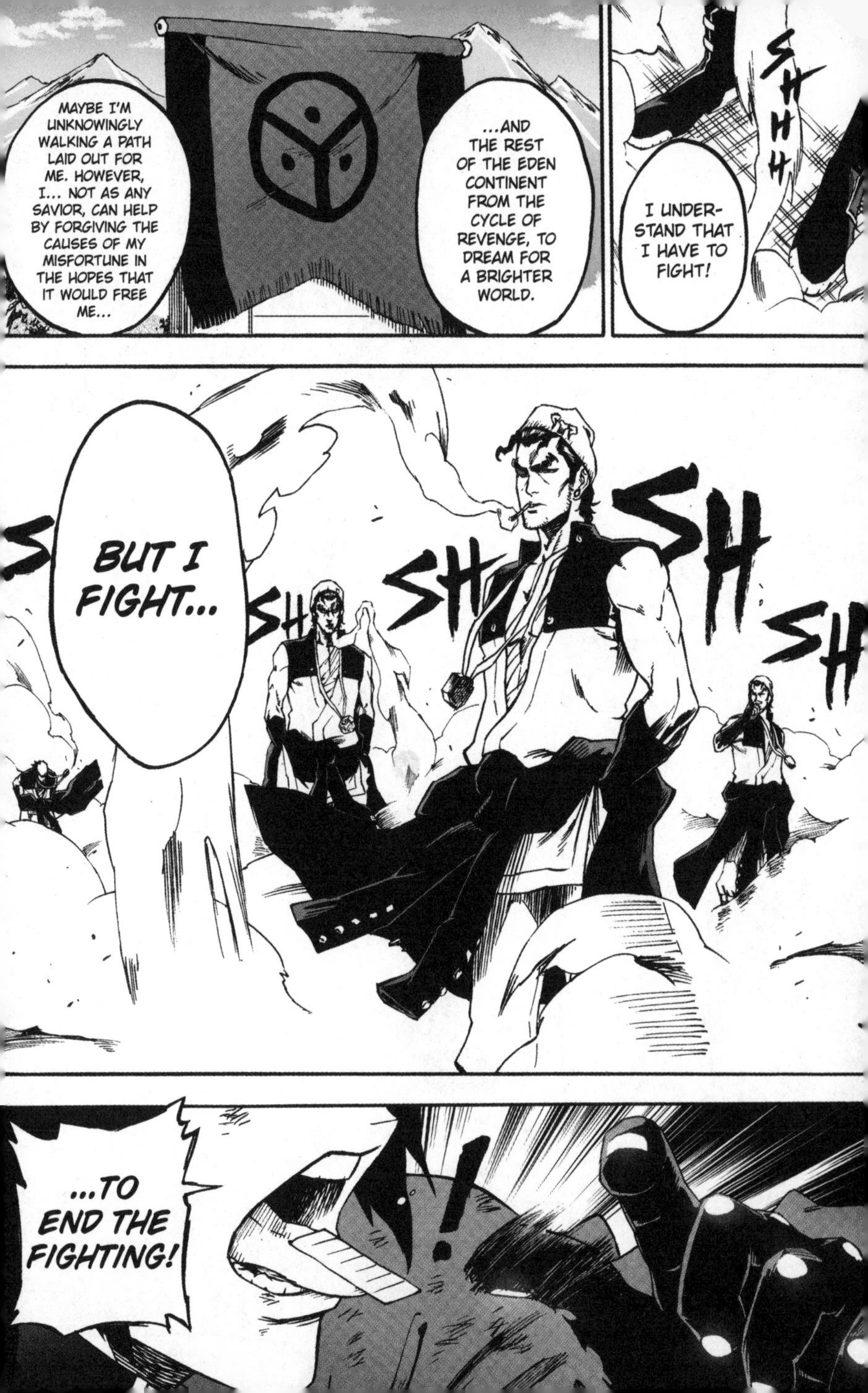
MAYBE I'M UNKNOWINGLY WALKING A PATH LAID OUT FOR ME. HOWEVER, I... NOT AS ANY SAVIOR, CAN HELP BY FORGIVING THE CAUSES OF MY MISFORTUNE IN THE HOPES THAT IT WOULD FREE ME...
...AND THE REST OF THE EDEN CONTINENT FROM THE CYCLE OF REVENGE, TO DREAM FOR A BRIGHTER WORLD.
SHHHH
I UNDER-STAND THAT I HAVE TO FIGHT!
BUT I FIGHT...
SH
SH
SH
SH
SH
...TO END THE FIGHTING!
!

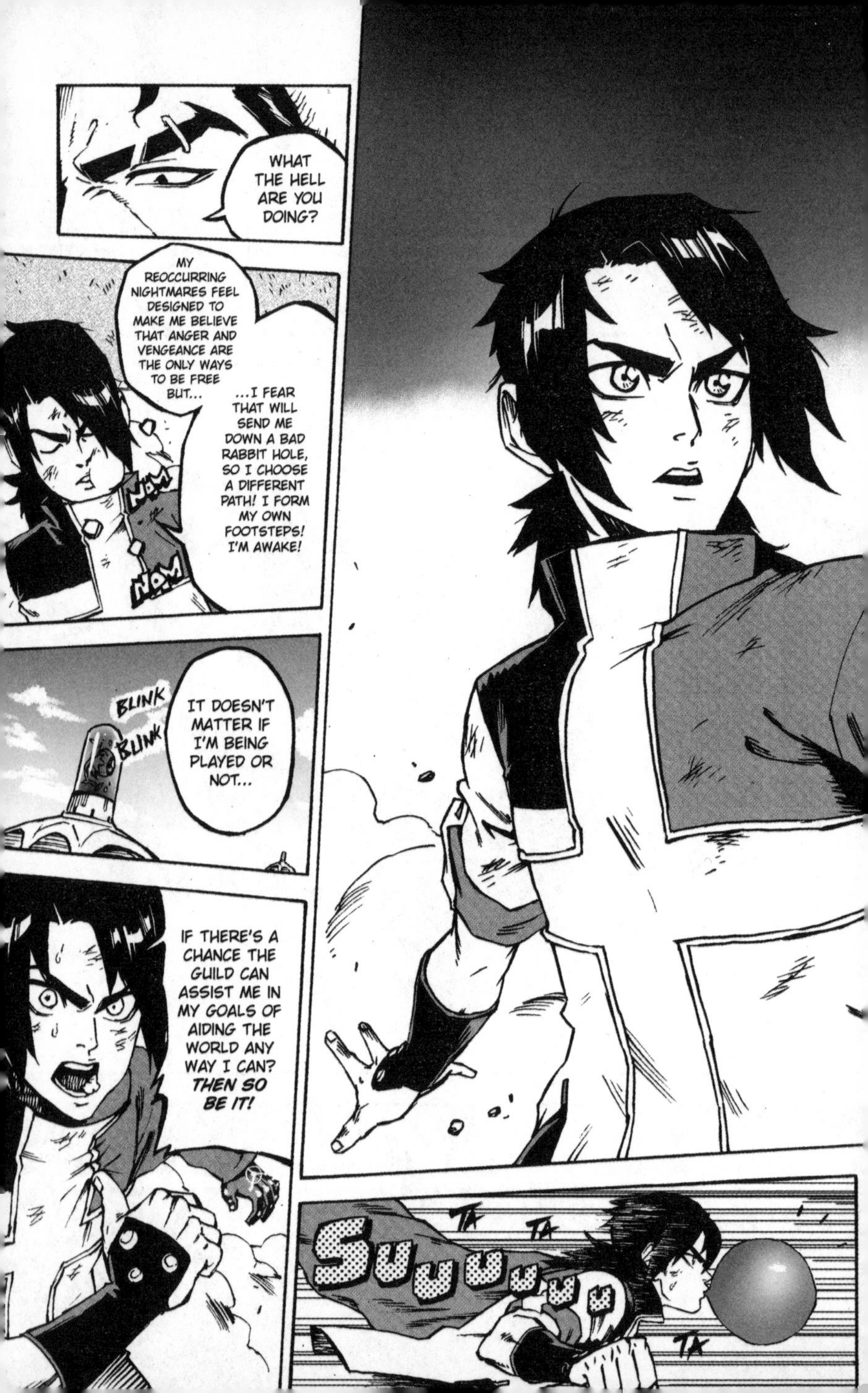
WHAT THE HELL ARE YOU DOING?
MY REOCCURRING NIGHTMARES FEEL DESIGNED TO MAKE ME BELIEVE THAT ANGER AND VENGEANCE ARE THE ONLY WAYS TO BE FREE BUT...
...I FEAR THAT WILL SEND ME DOWN A BAD RABBIT HOLE, SO I CHOOSE A DIFFERENT PATH! I FORM MY OWN FOOTSTEPS! I'M AWAKE!
NOM
NOM
BLINK
BLINK
IT DOESN'T MATTER IF I'M BEING PLAYED OR NOT...
IF THERE'S A CHANCE THE GUILD CAN ASSIST ME IN MY GOALS OF AIDING THE WORLD ANY WAY I CAN? *THEN SO BE IT!*
SUUUUUU
TA
TA
TA

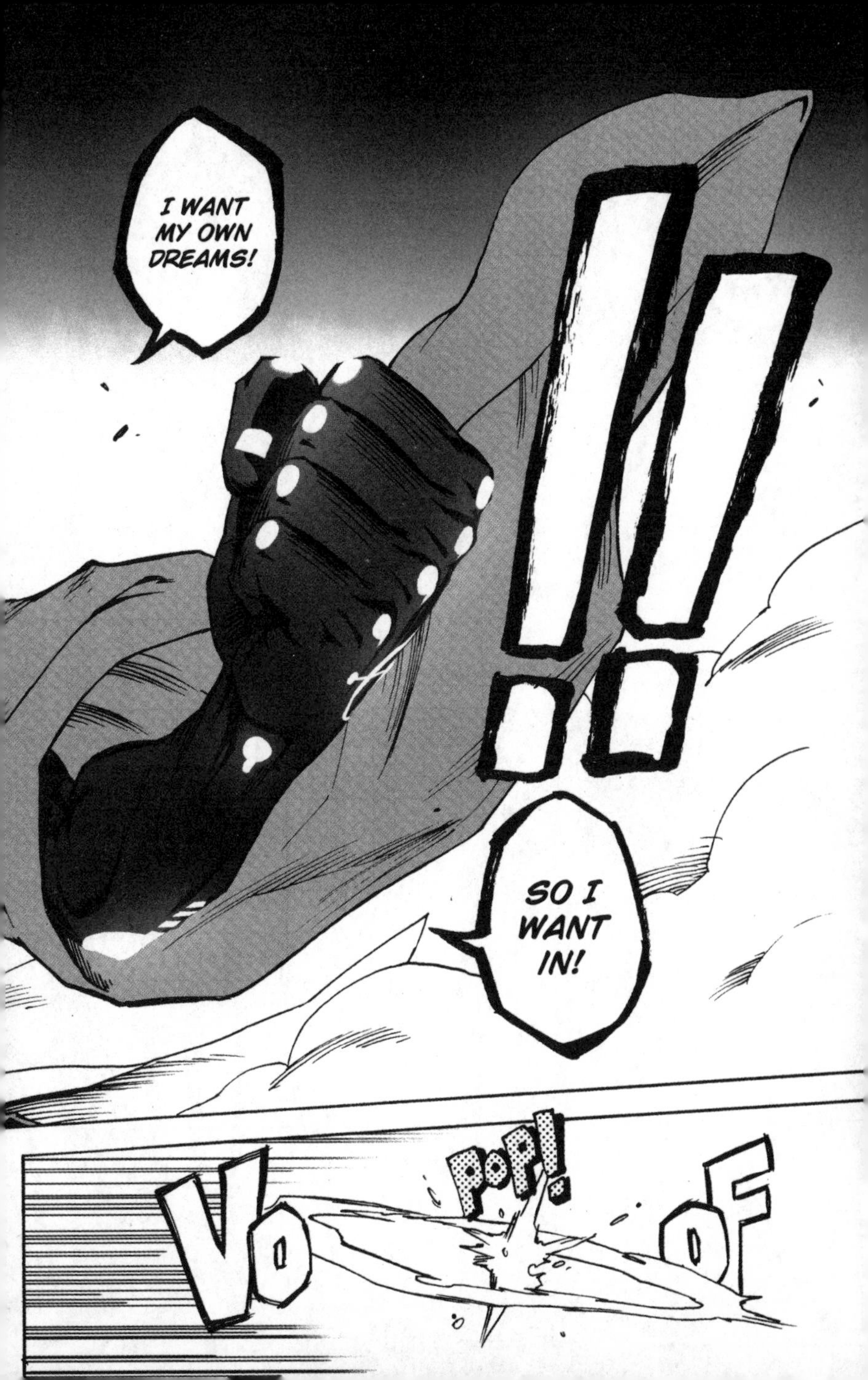
I WANT MY OWN DREAMS!
!!
SO I WANT IN!
VO
POP!
OF

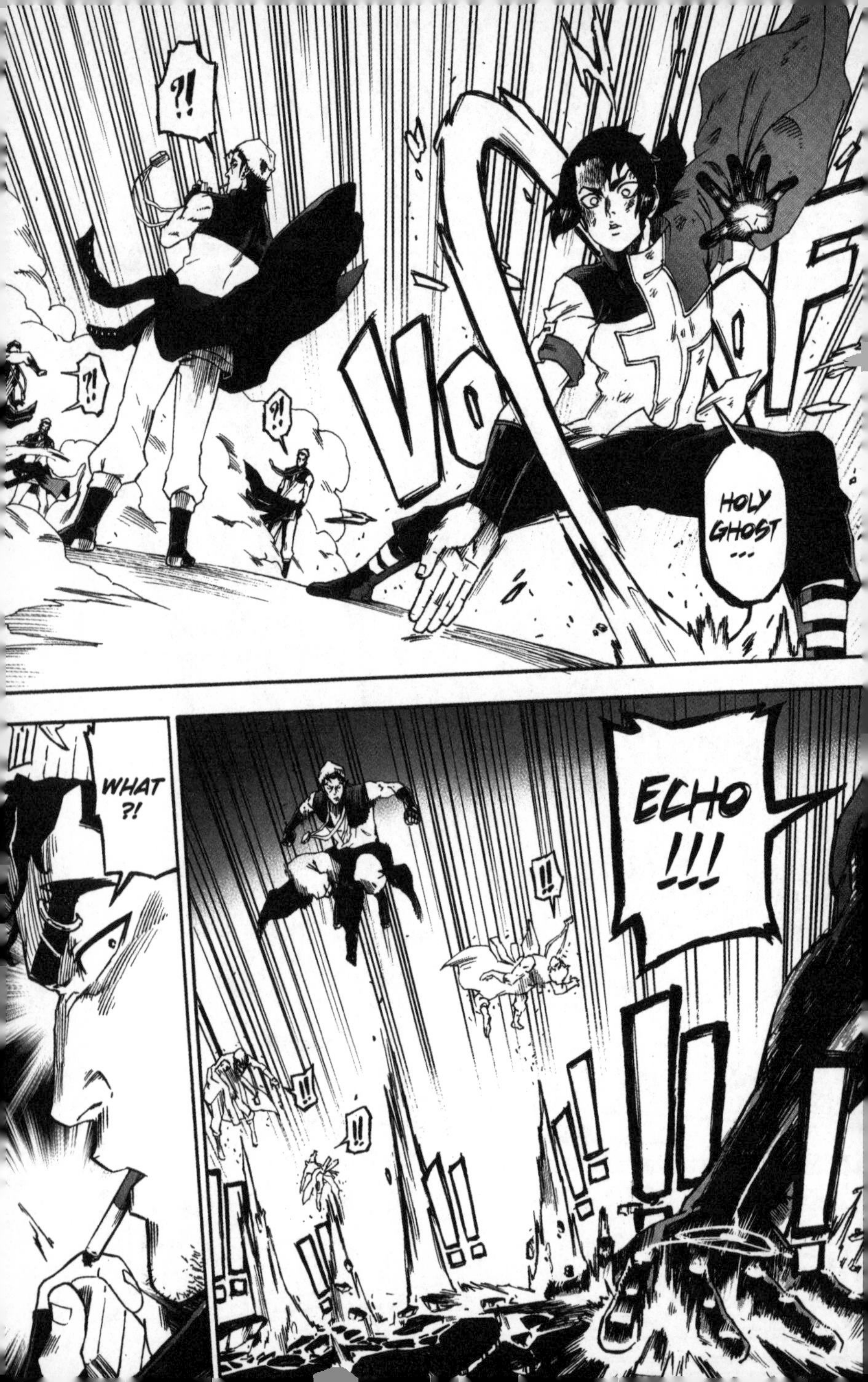
?!
?!
?!
HOLY GHOST ...
WHAT ?!
ECHO !!!
!!
!!
!!

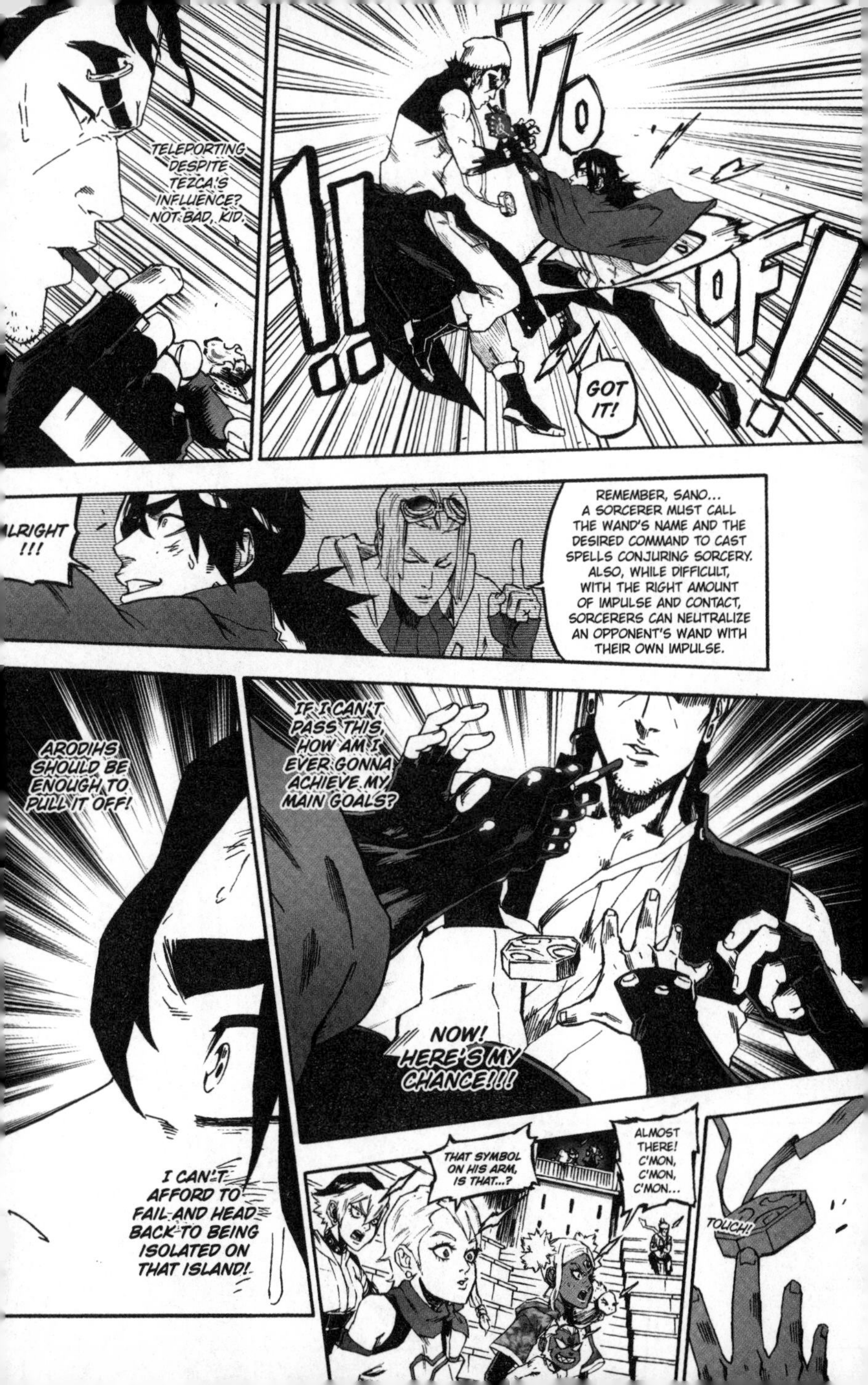
TELEPORTING DESPITE TEZCA'S INFLUENCE? NOT BAD, KID.
VOOF!
!!
GOT IT!
LRIGHT !!!
REMEMBER, SANO... A SORCERER MUST CALL THE WAND'S NAME AND THE DESIRED COMMAND TO CAST SPELLS CONJURING SORCERY. ALSO, WHILE DIFFICULT, WITH THE RIGHT AMOUNT OF IMPULSE AND CONTACT, SORCERERS CAN NEUTRALIZE AN OPPONENT'S WAND WITH THEIR OWN IMPULSE.
ARODIHS SHOULD BE ENOUGH TO PULL IT OFF!
IF I CAN'T PASS THIS, HOW AM I EVER GONNA ACHIEVE MY MAIN GOALS?
NOW! HERE'S MY CHANCE!!!
I CAN'T AFFORD TO FAIL AND HEAD BACK TO BEING ISOLATED ON THAT ISLAND!
THAT SYMBOL ON HIS ARM, IS THAT...?
ALMOST THERE! C'MON, C'MON, C'MON...
TOUCH!

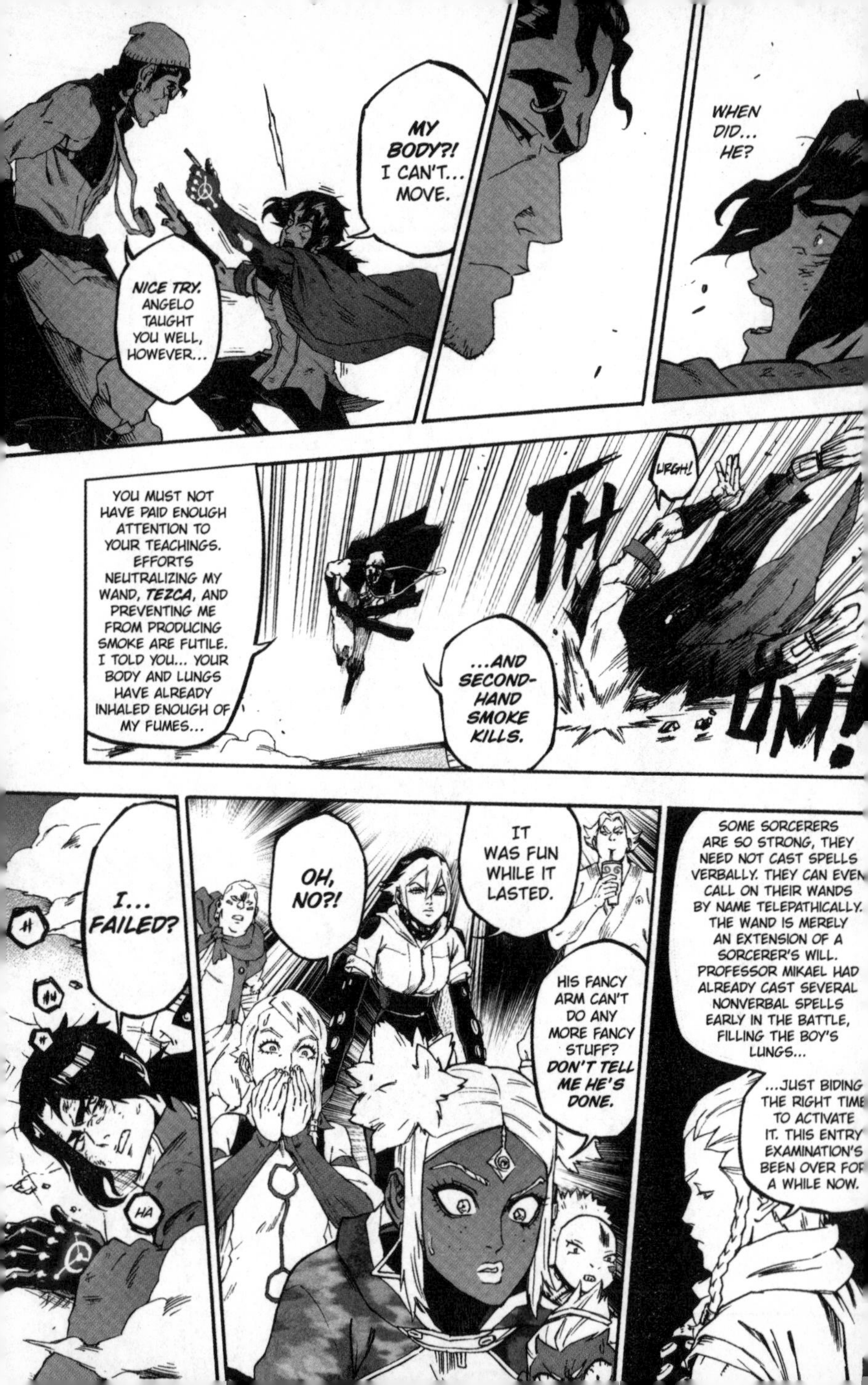
NICE TRY. ANGELO TAUGHT YOU WELL, HOWEVER...
MY BODY?! I CAN'T... MOVE.
WHEN DID... HE?
YOU MUST NOT HAVE PAID ENOUGH ATTENTION TO YOUR TEACHINGS. EFFORTS NEUTRALIZING MY WAND, TEZCA, AND PREVENTING ME FROM PRODUCING SMOKE ARE FUTILE. I TOLD YOU... YOUR BODY AND LUNGS HAVE ALREADY INHALED ENOUGH OF MY FUMES...
TH
URGH!
...AND SECOND-HAND SMOKE KILLS.
UM!
I... FAILED?
H
HU
H
HA
OH, NO?!
IT WAS FUN WHILE IT LASTED.
HIS FANCY ARM CAN'T DO ANY MORE FANCY STUFF? DON'T TELL ME HE'S DONE.
SOME SORCERERS ARE SO STRONG, THEY NEED NOT CAST SPELLS VERBALLY. THEY CAN EVEN CALL ON THEIR WANDS BY NAME TELEPATHICALLY. THE WAND IS MERELY AN EXTENSION OF A SORCERER'S WILL. PROFESSOR MIKAEL HAD ALREADY CAST SEVERAL NONVERBAL SPELLS EARLY IN THE BATTLE, FILLING THE BOY'S LUNGS...
...JUST BIDING THE RIGHT TIME TO ACTIVATE IT. THIS ENTRY EXAMINATION'S BEEN OVER FOR A WHILE NOW.

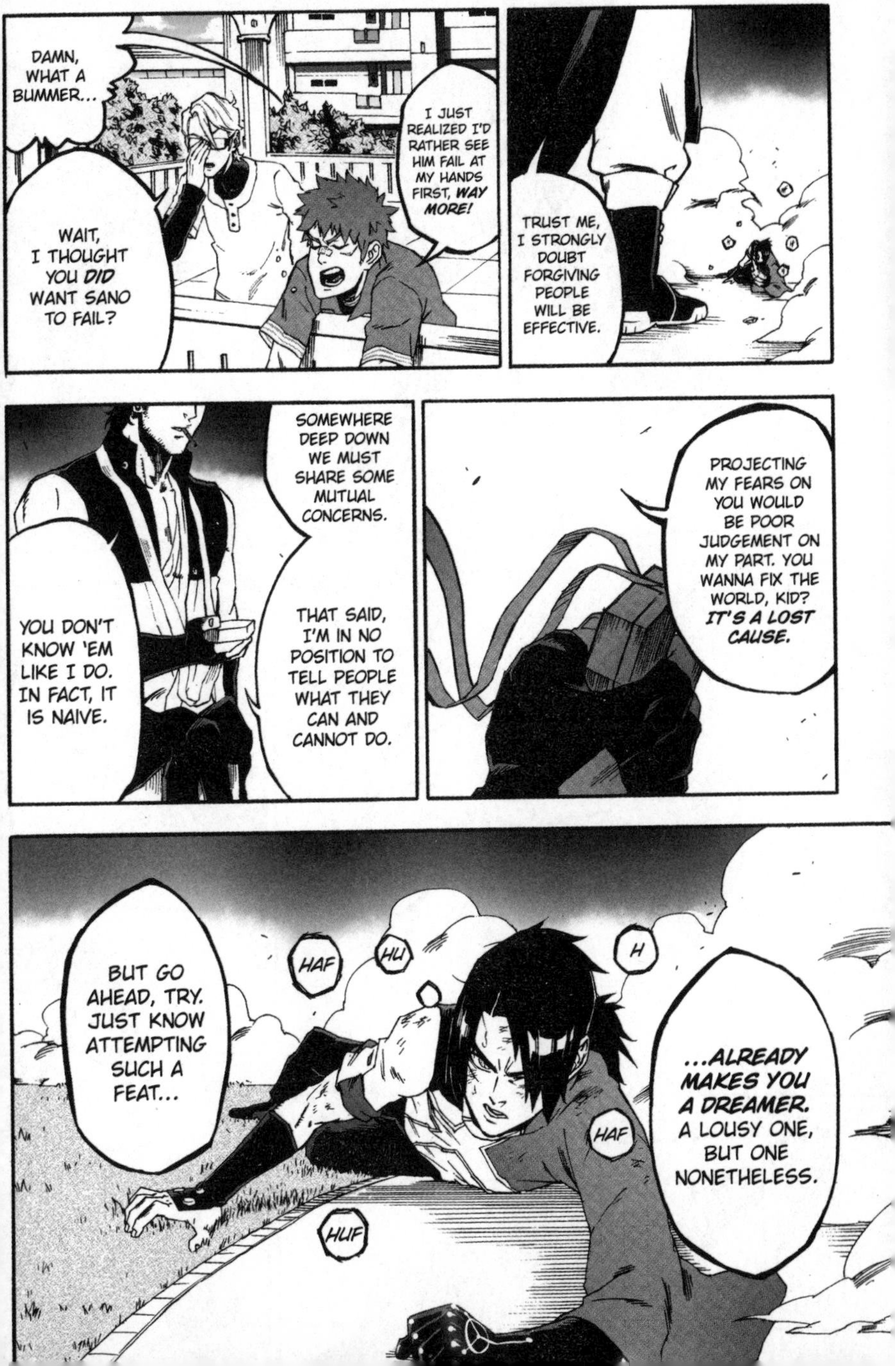
DAMN, WHAT A BUMMER...
WAIT, I THOUGHT YOU *DID* WANT SANO TO FAIL?
I JUST REALIZED I'D RATHER SEE HIM FAIL AT MY HANDS FIRST, *WAY MORE!*
TRUST ME, I STRONGLY DOUBT FORGIVING PEOPLE WILL BE EFFECTIVE.
YOU DON'T KNOW 'EM LIKE I DO. IN FACT, IT IS NAIVE.
SOMEWHERE DEEP DOWN WE MUST SHARE SOME MUTUAL CONCERNS.
THAT SAID, I'M IN NO POSITION TO TELL PEOPLE WHAT THEY CAN AND CANNOT DO.
PROJECTING MY FEARS ON YOU WOULD BE POOR JUDGEMENT ON MY PART. YOU WANNA FIX THE WORLD, KID? *IT'S A LOST CAUSE.*
BUT GO AHEAD, TRY. JUST KNOW ATTEMPTING SUCH A FEAT...
HAF
HU
H
HAF
HUF
*...ALREADY MAKES YOU A DREAMER.* A LOUSY ONE, BUT ONE NONETHELESS.

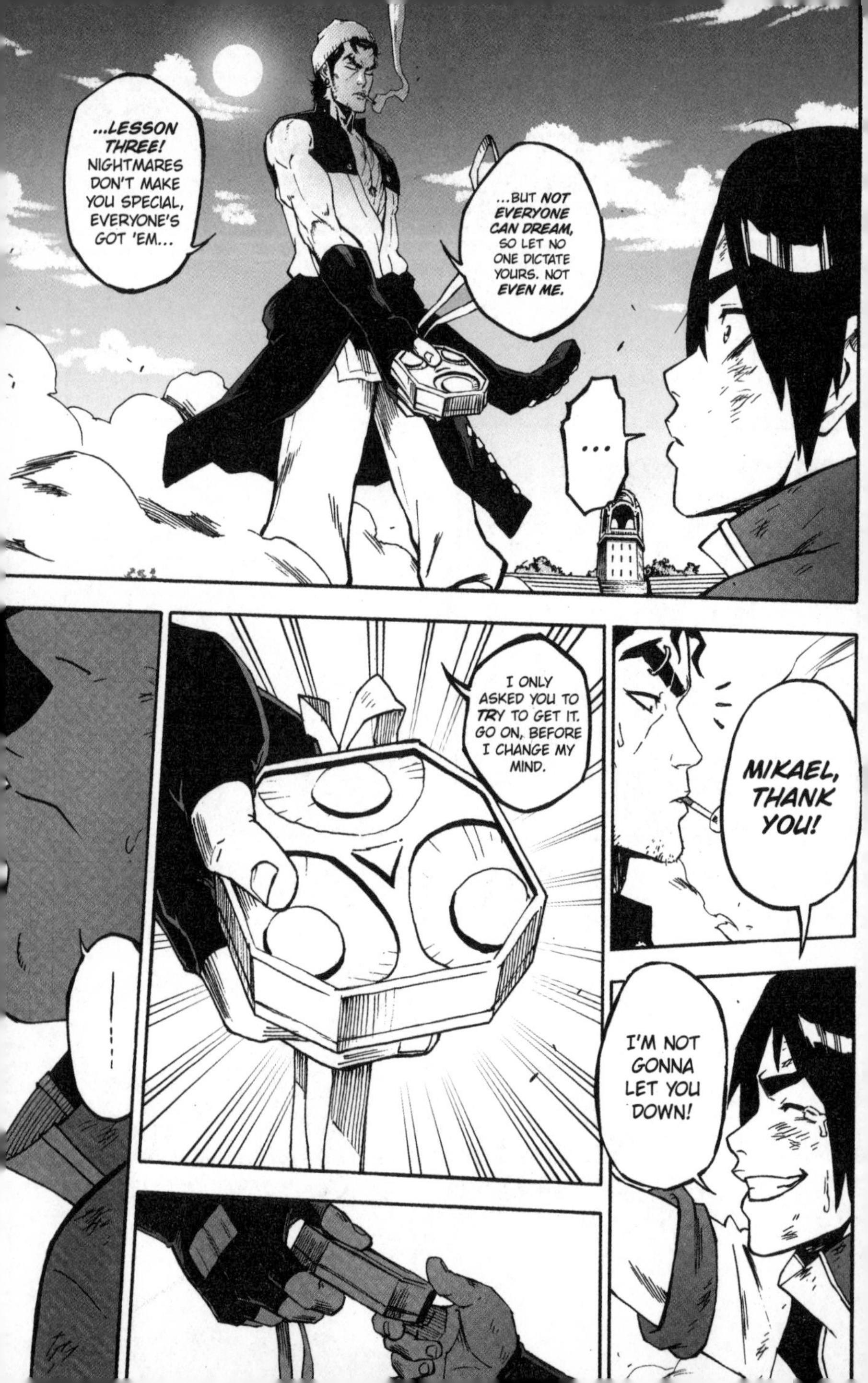
...LESSON THREE! NIGHTMARES DON'T MAKE YOU SPECIAL, EVERYONE'S GOT 'EM...
...BUT NOT EVERYONE CAN DREAM, SO LET NO ONE DICTATE YOURS. NOT EVEN ME.
...
I ONLY ASKED YOU TO TRY TO GET IT. GO ON, BEFORE I CHANGE MY MIND.
MIKAEL, THANK YOU!
I'M NOT GONNA LET YOU DOWN!

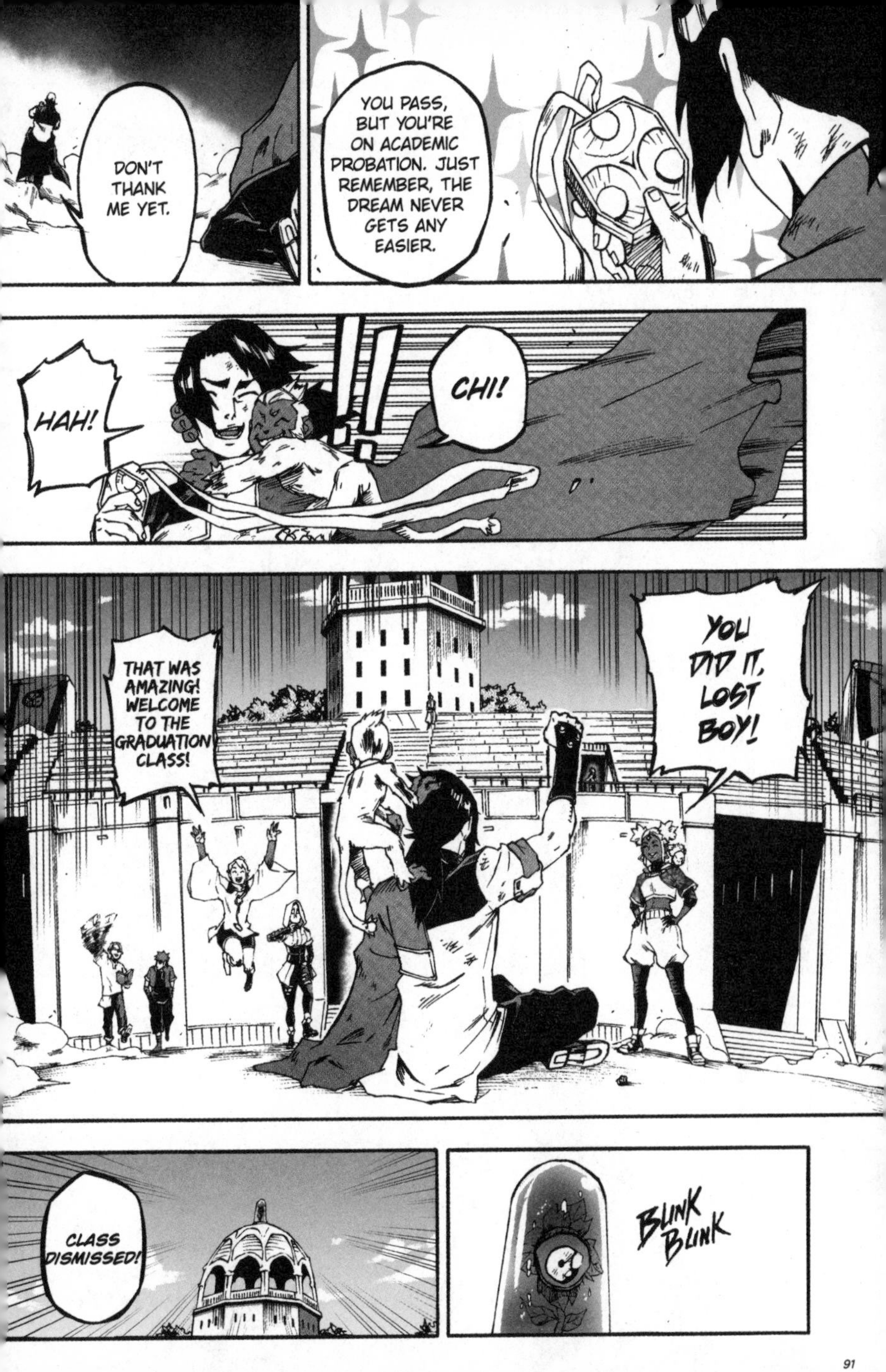

DON'T THANK ME YET.
YOU PASS, BUT YOU'RE ON ACADEMIC PROBATION. JUST REMEMBER, THE DREAM NEVER GETS ANY EASIER.
HAH!
!!
CHI!
THAT WAS AMAZING! WELCOME TO THE GRADUATION CLASS!
YOU DID IT, LOST BOY!
CLASS DISMISSED!
BLINK BLINK

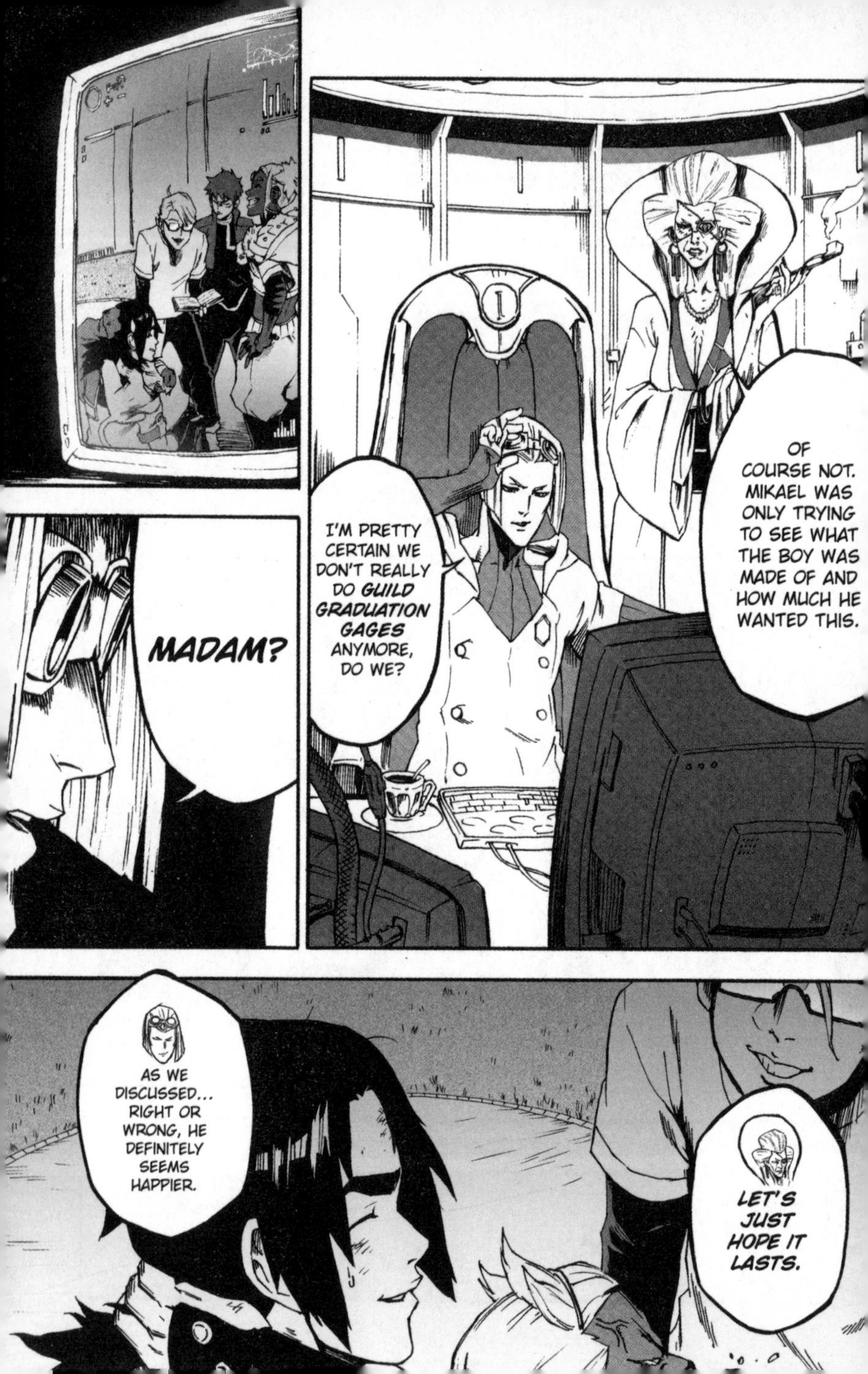

I'M PRETTY CERTAIN WE DON'T REALLY DO **GUILD GRADUATION GAGES** ANYMORE, DO WE?
OF COURSE NOT. MIKAEL WAS ONLY TRYING TO SEE WHAT THE BOY WAS MADE OF AND HOW MUCH HE WANTED THIS.
*MADAM?*
AS WE DISCUSSED... RIGHT OR WRONG, HE DEFINITELY SEEMS HAPPIER.
*LET'S JUST HOPE IT LASTS.*

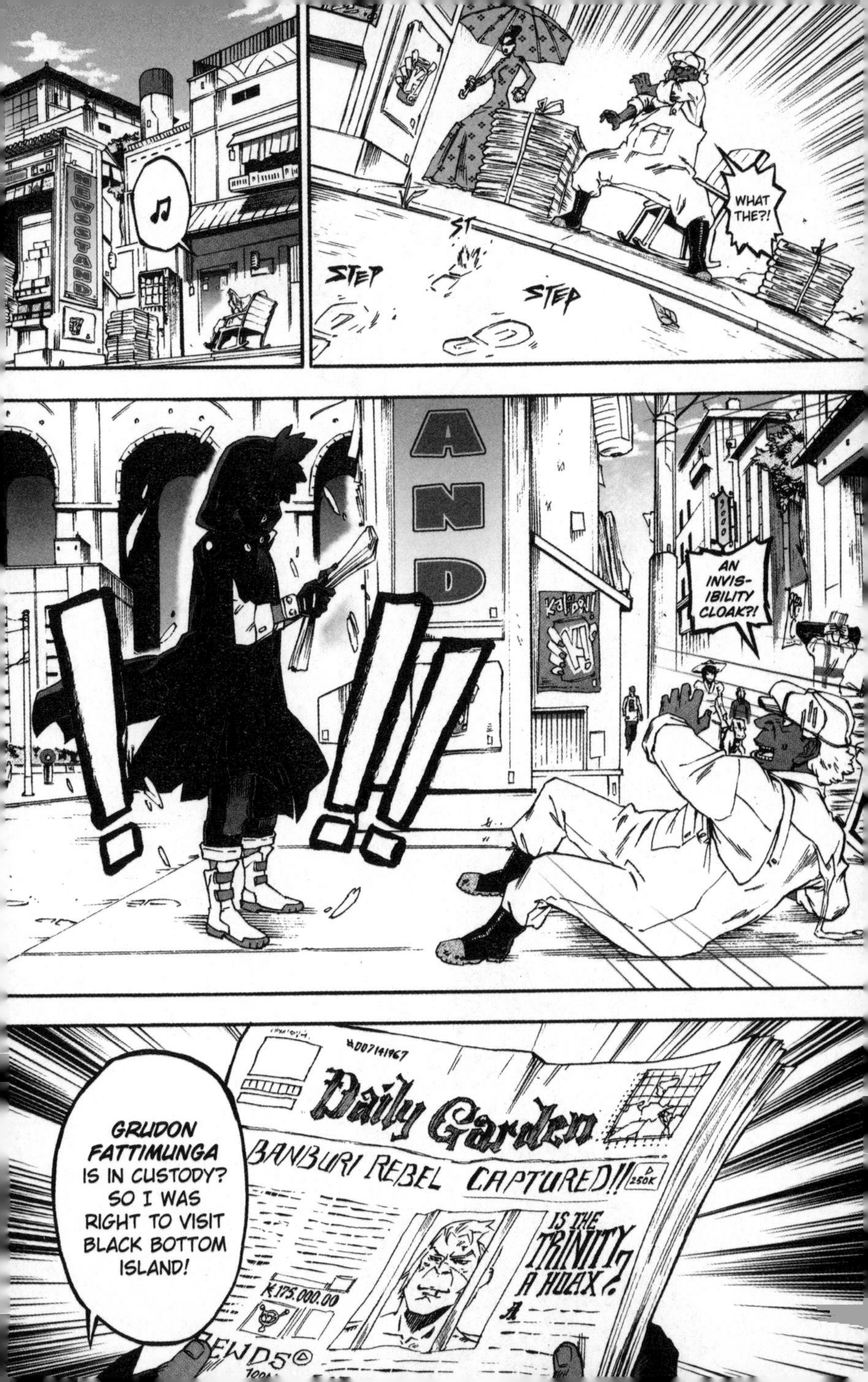
NEWSSTAND
♪
STEP
ST
STEP
WHAT THE?!
AND
AN INVISIBILITY CLOAK?!
Daily Garden
BANBURI REBEL CAPTURED!!
250K
IS THE TRINITY A HOAX?
GRUDON FATTIMUNGA IS IN CUSTODY? SO I WAS RIGHT TO VISIT BLACK BOTTOM ISLAND!

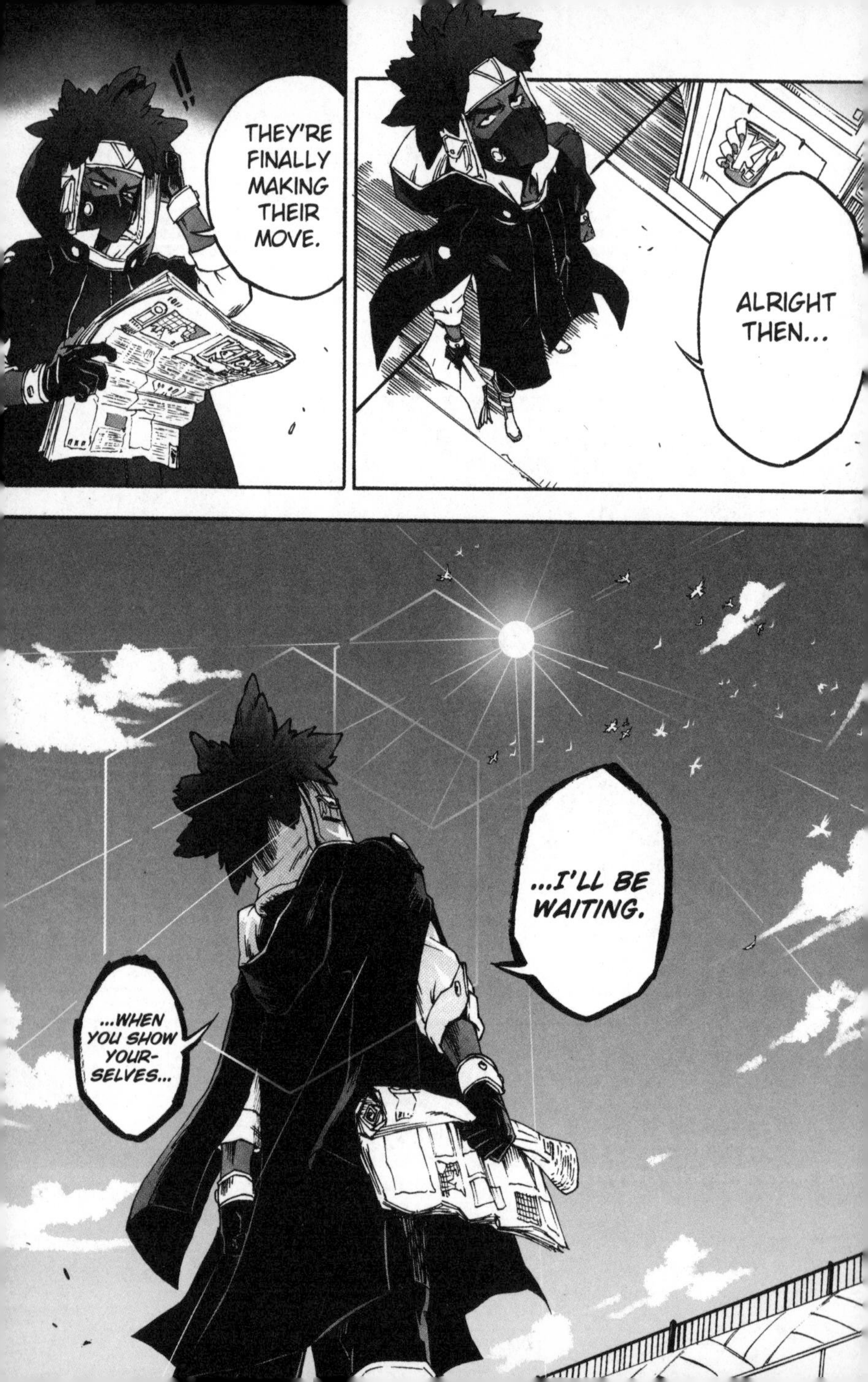
!!
THEY'RE FINALLY MAKING THEIR MOVE.
ALRIGHT THEN...
...I'LL BE WAITING.
...WHEN YOU SHOW YOUR-SELVES...

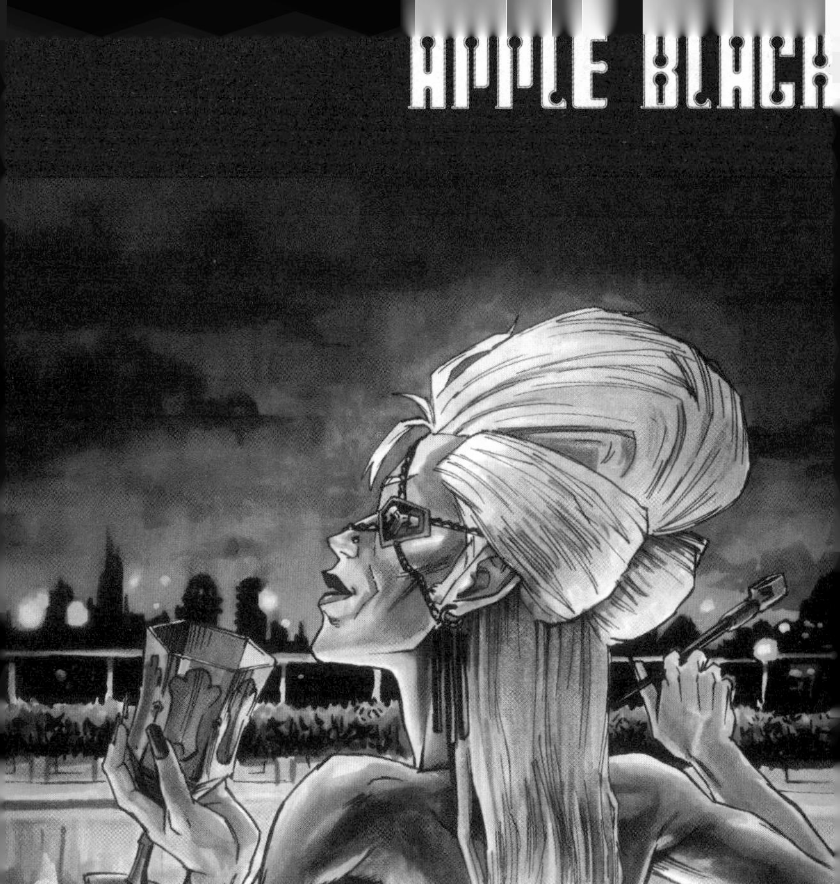
APPLE BLACK

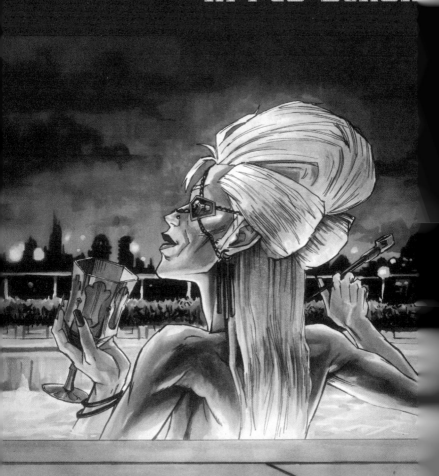

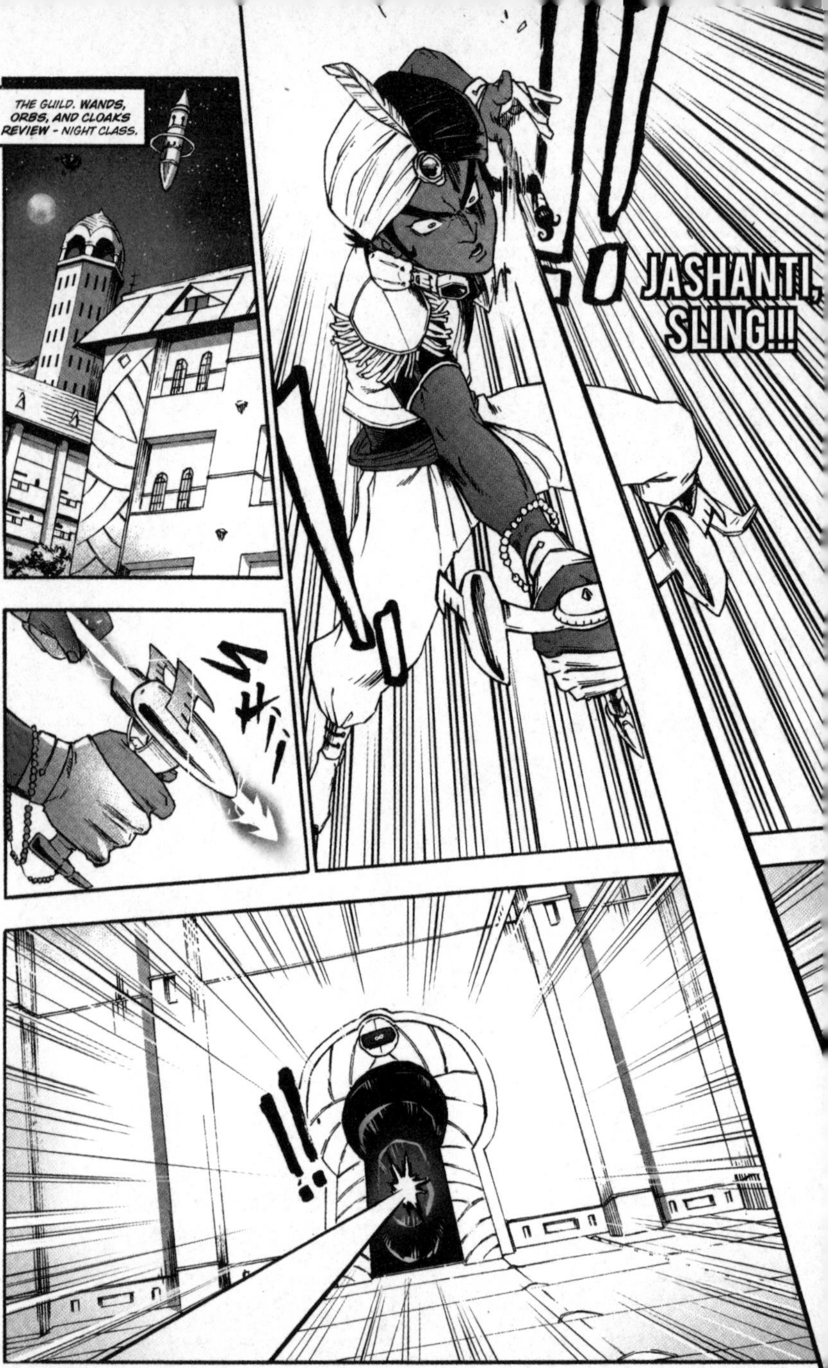
THE GUILD. WANDS, ORBS, AND CLOAKS REVIEW - NIGHT CLASS.
JASHANTI, SLING!!!

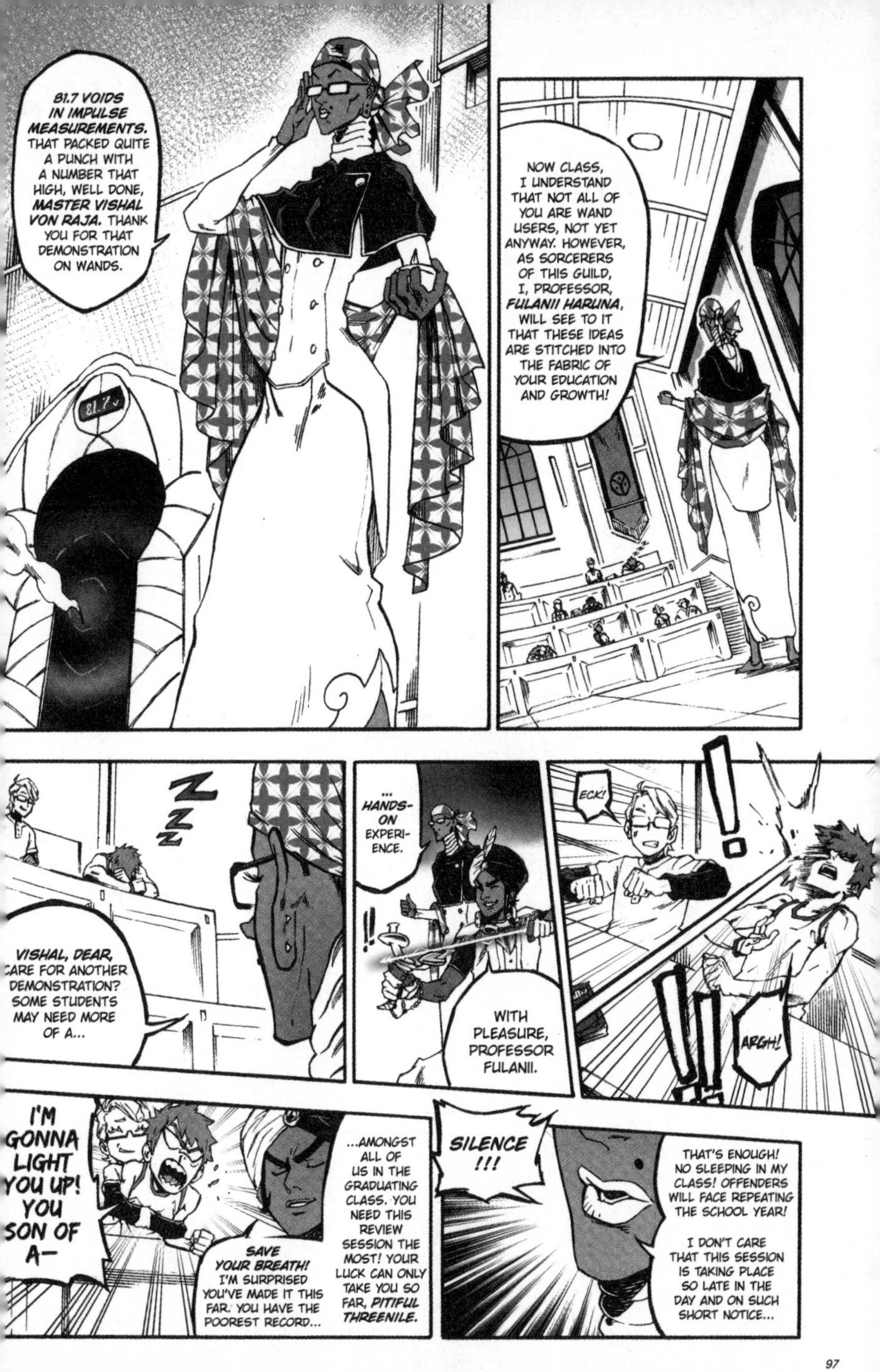

81.7 VOIDS IN IMPULSE MEASUREMENTS. THAT PACKED QUITE A PUNCH WITH A NUMBER THAT HIGH, WELL DONE, MASTER VISHAL VON RAJA. THANK YOU FOR THAT DEMONSTRATION ON WANDS.
81.7
NOW CLASS, I UNDERSTAND THAT NOT ALL OF YOU ARE WAND USERS, NOT YET ANYWAY. HOWEVER, AS SORCERERS OF THIS GUILD, I, PROFESSOR, FULANII HARUNA, WILL SEE TO IT THAT THESE IDEAS ARE STITCHED INTO THE FABRIC OF YOUR EDUCATION AND GROWTH!
Z Z Z
VISHAL, DEAR, CARE FOR ANOTHER DEMONSTRATION? SOME STUDENTS MAY NEED MORE OF A...
... HANDS-ON EXPERI-ENCE.
!!
WITH PLEASURE, PROFESSOR FULANII.
ECK!
!
ARGH!
I'M GONNA LIGHT YOU UP! YOU SON OF A—
SAVE YOUR BREATH! I'M SURPRISED YOU'VE MADE IT THIS FAR. YOU HAVE THE POOREST RECORD...
...AMONGST ALL OF US IN THE GRADUATING CLASS. YOU NEED THIS REVIEW SESSION THE MOST! YOUR LUCK CAN ONLY TAKE YOU SO FAR, PITIFUL THREENILE.
SILENCE !!!
THAT'S ENOUGH! NO SLEEPING IN MY CLASS! OFFENDERS WILL FACE REPEATING THE SCHOOL YEAR!
I DON'T CARE THAT THIS SESSION IS TAKING PLACE SO LATE IN THE DAY AND ON SUCH SHORT NOTICE...

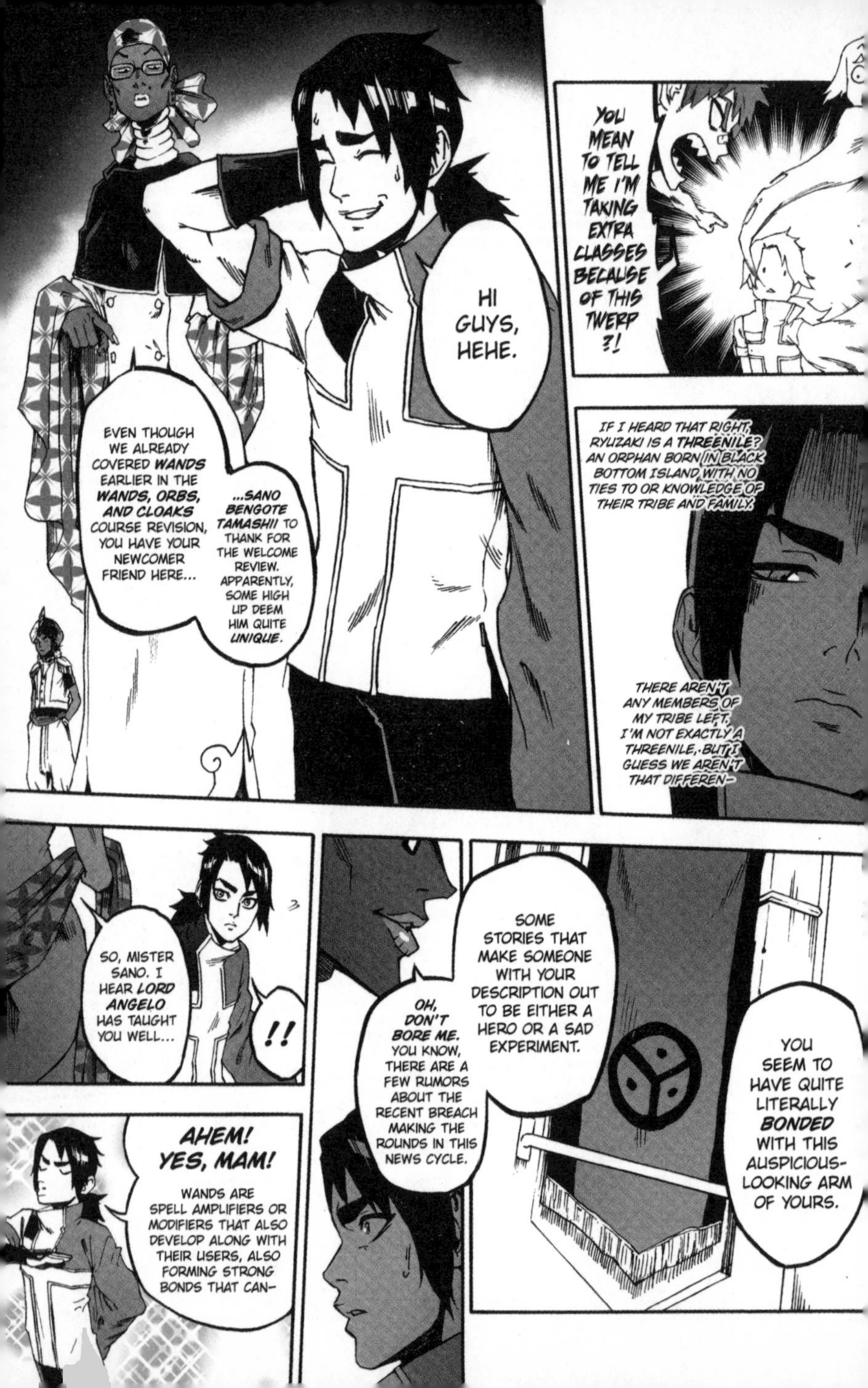
HI GUYS, HEHE.
EVEN THOUGH WE ALREADY COVERED WANDS EARLIER IN THE WANDS, ORBS, AND CLOAKS COURSE REVISION, YOU HAVE YOUR NEWCOMER FRIEND HERE...
...SANO BENGOTE TAMASHII TO THANK FOR THE WELCOME REVIEW. APPARENTLY, SOME HIGH UP DEEM HIM QUITE UNIQUE.
YOU MEAN TO TELL ME I'M TAKING EXTRA CLASSES BECAUSE OF THIS TWERP ?!
IF I HEARD THAT RIGHT, RYUZAKI IS A THREENILE? AN ORPHAN BORN IN BLACK BOTTOM ISLAND WITH NO TIES TO OR KNOWLEDGE OF THEIR TRIBE AND FAMILY.
THERE AREN'T ANY MEMBERS OF MY TRIBE LEFT. I'M NOT EXACTLY A THREENILE, BUT I GUESS WE AREN'T THAT DIFFEREN-
SO, MISTER SANO. I HEAR LORD ANGELO HAS TAUGHT YOU WELL...
!!
AHEM! YES, MAM!
WANDS ARE SPELL AMPLIFIERS OR MODIFIERS THAT ALSO DEVELOP ALONG WITH THEIR USERS, ALSO FORMING STRONG BONDS THAT CAN-
OH, DON'T BORE ME. YOU KNOW, THERE ARE A FEW RUMORS ABOUT THE RECENT BREACH MAKING THE ROUNDS IN THIS NEWS CYCLE.
SOME STORIES THAT MAKE SOMEONE WITH YOUR DESCRIPTION OUT TO BE EITHER A HERO OR A SAD EXPERIMENT.
YOU SEEM TO HAVE QUITE LITERALLY BONDED WITH THIS AUSPICIOUS-LOOKING ARM OF YOURS.

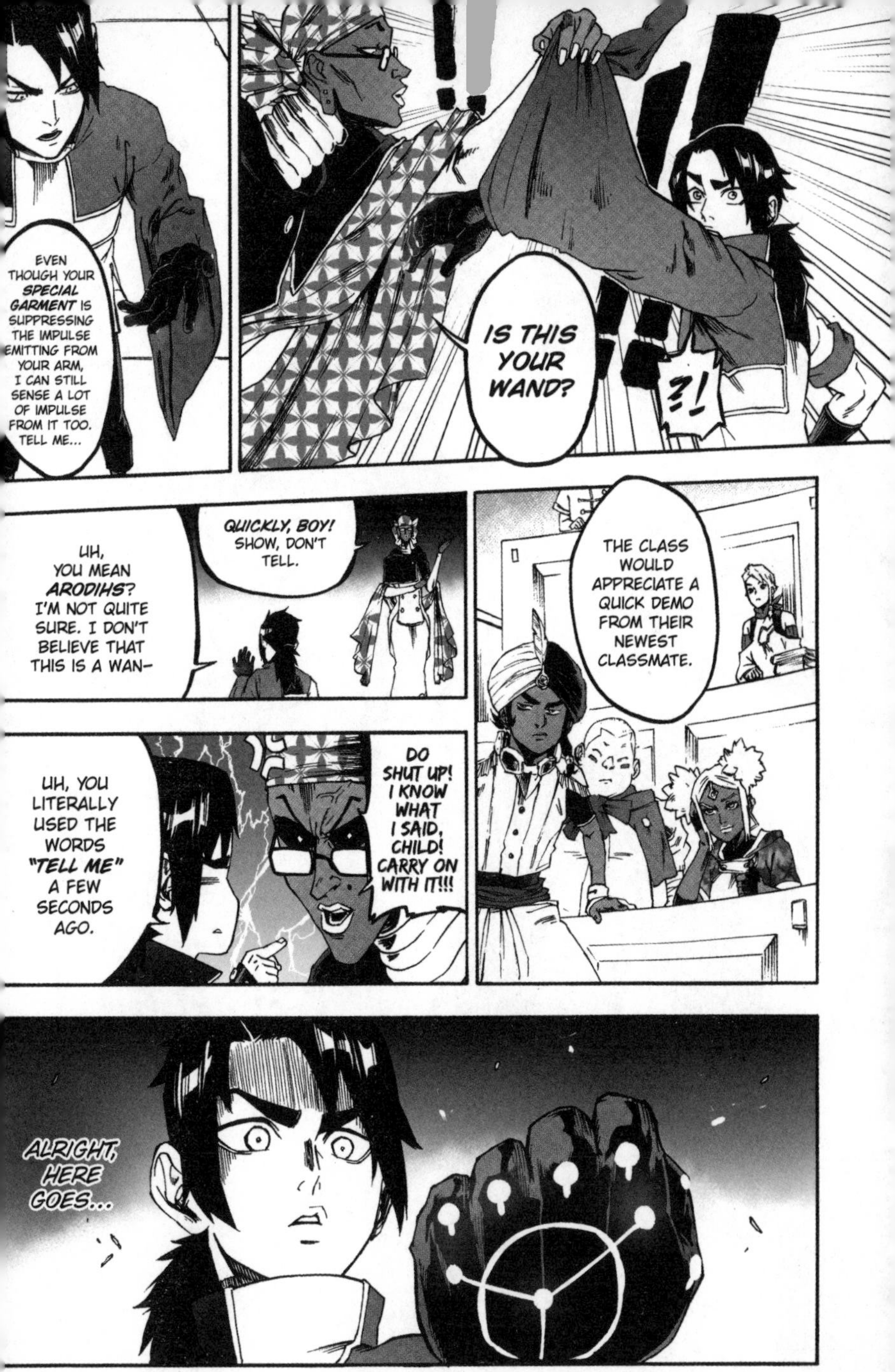
EVEN THOUGH YOUR ***SPECIAL GARMENT*** IS SUPPRESSING THE IMPULSE EMITTING FROM YOUR ARM, I CAN STILL SENSE A LOT OF IMPULSE FROM IT TOO. TELL ME...
!!
IS THIS YOUR WAND?
?!
UH, YOU MEAN ***ARODIHS***? I'M NOT QUITE SURE. I DON'T BELIEVE THAT THIS IS A WAN–
***QUICKLY, BOY!*** SHOW, DON'T TELL.
UH, YOU LITERALLY USED THE WORDS ***"TELL ME"*** A FEW SECONDS AGO.
DO SHUT UP! I KNOW WHAT I SAID, CHILD! CARRY ON WITH IT!!!
THE CLASS WOULD APPRECIATE A QUICK DEMO FROM THEIR NEWEST CLASSMATE.
ALRIGHT, HERE GOES...

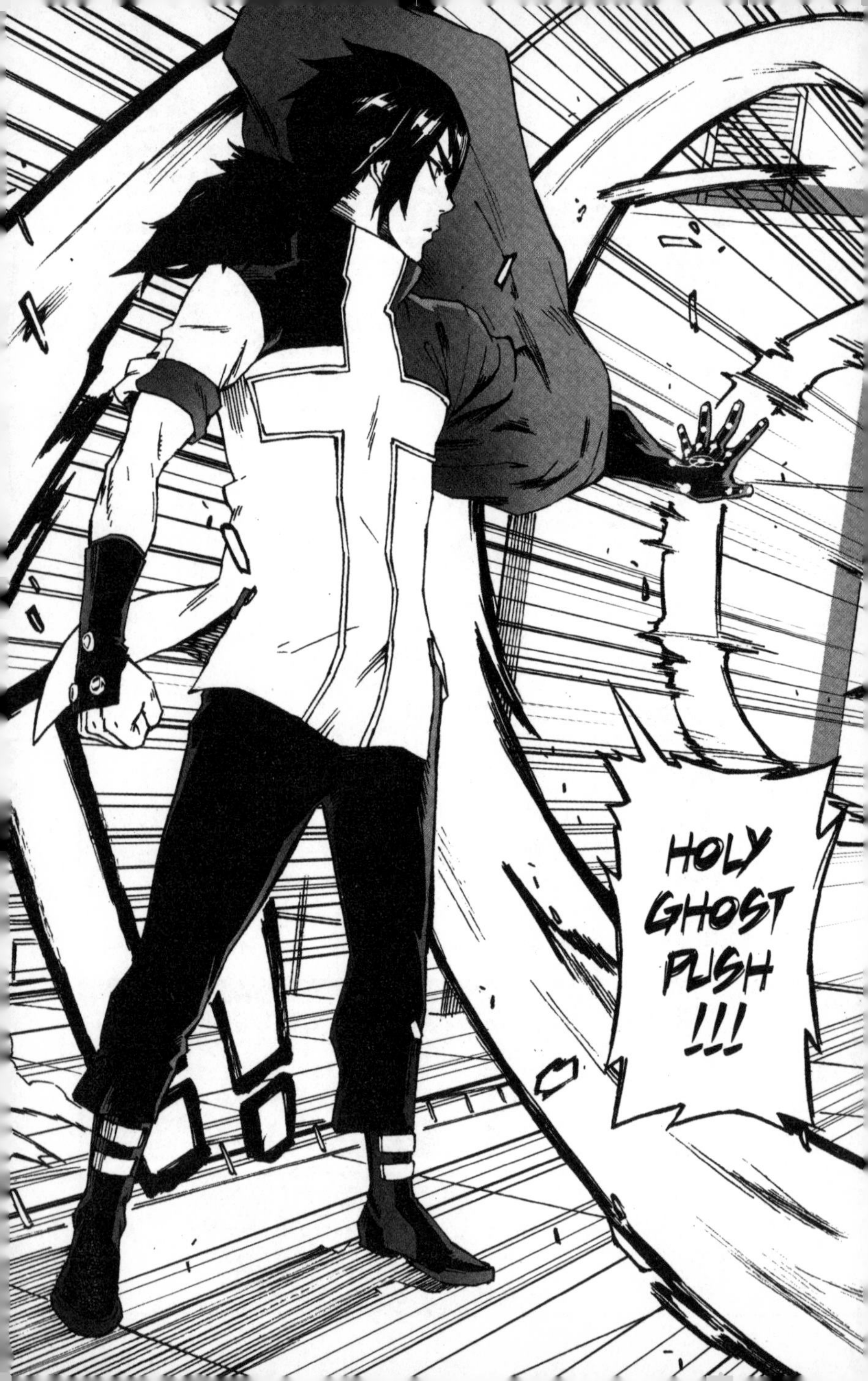
HOLY GHOST PUSH !!!

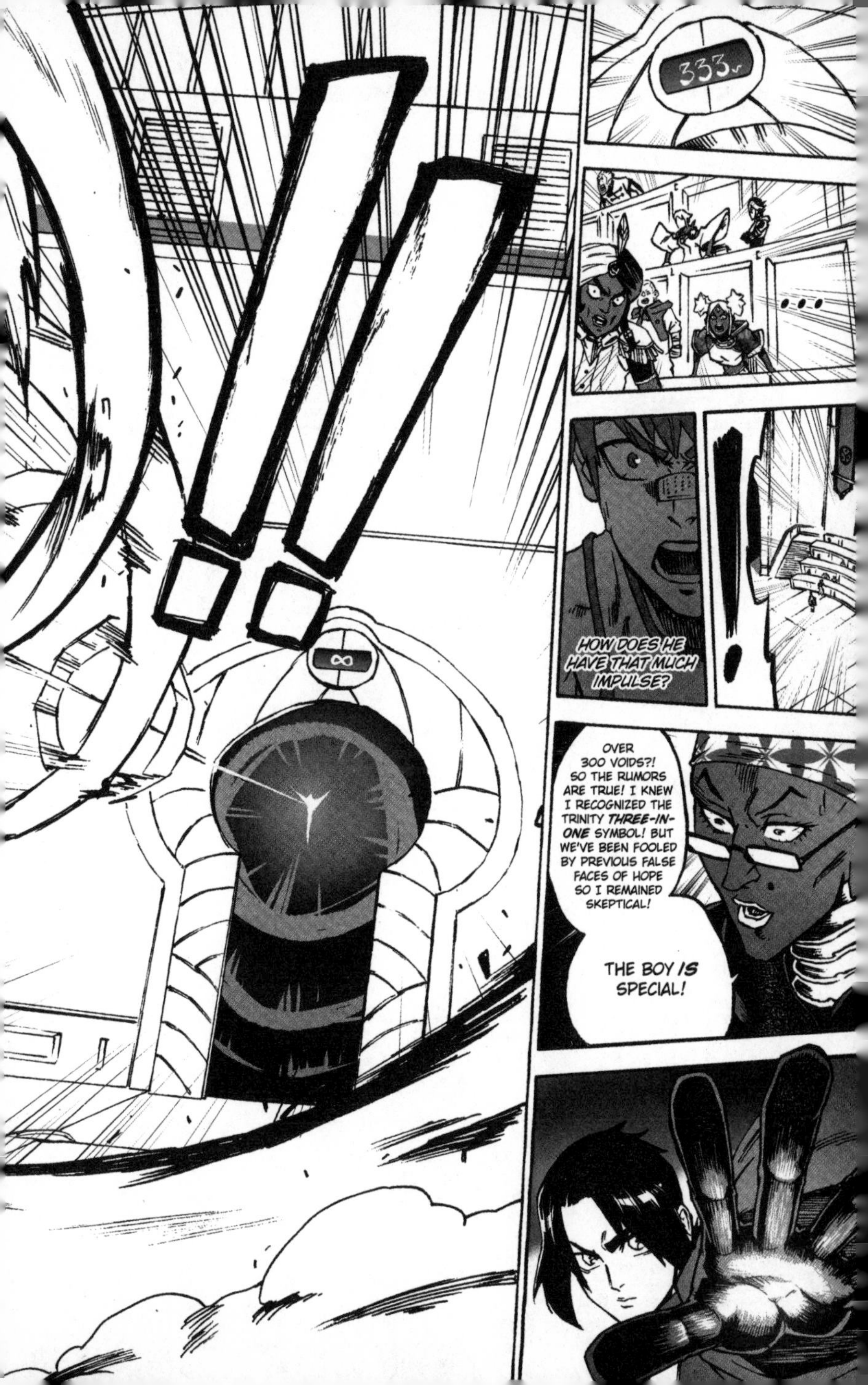
333
...
HOW DOES HE HAVE THAT MUCH IMPULSE?
OVER 300 VOIDS?! SO THE RUMORS ARE TRUE! I KNEW I RECOGNIZED THE TRINITY *THREE-IN-ONE* SYMBOL! BUT WE'VE BEEN FOOLED BY PREVIOUS FALSE FACES OF HOPE SO I REMAINED SKEPTICAL!
THE BOY *IS* SPECIAL!

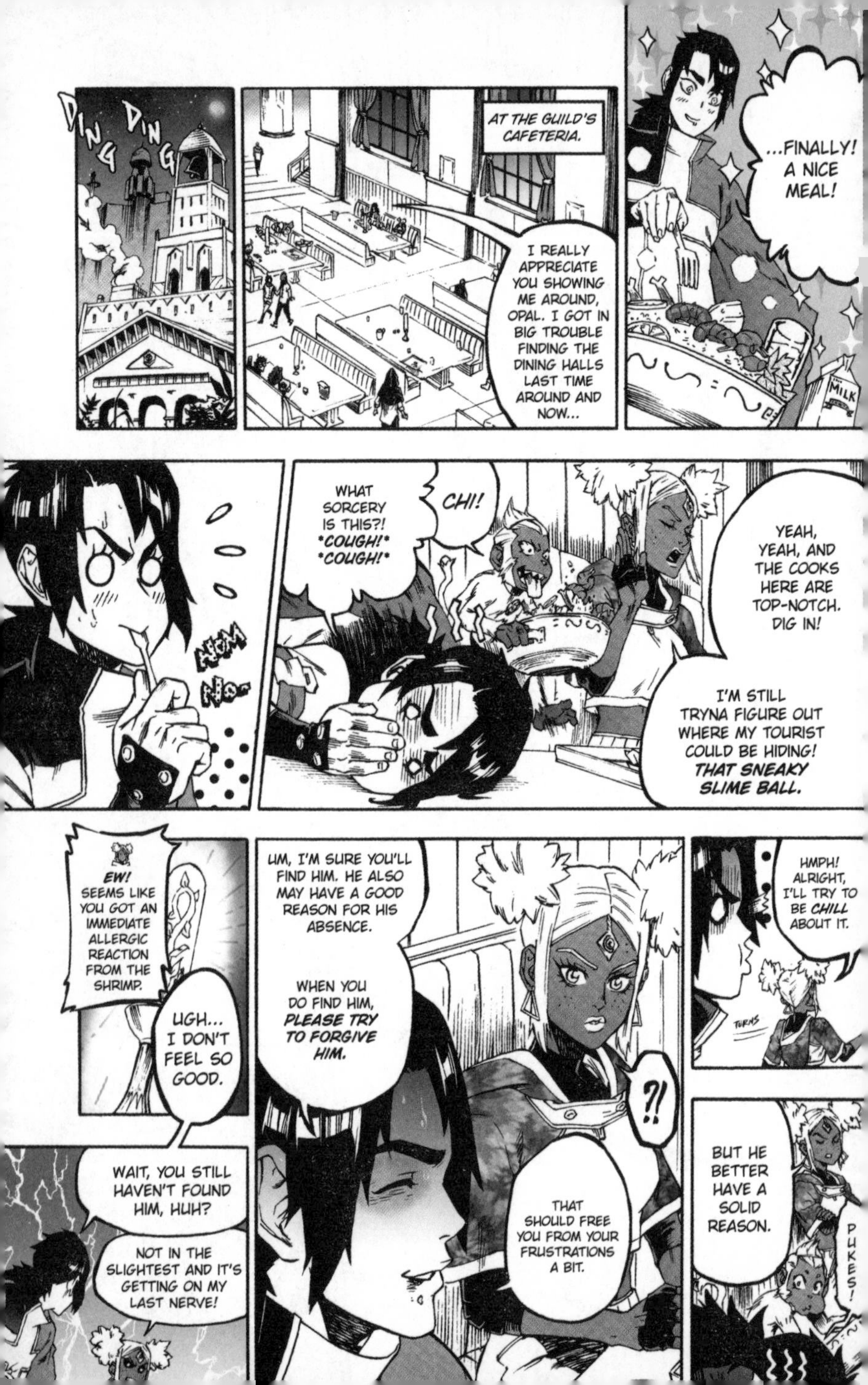
DING DING
AT THE GUILD'S CAFETERIA.
I REALLY APPRECIATE YOU SHOWING ME AROUND, OPAL. I GOT IN BIG TROUBLE FINDING THE DINING HALLS LAST TIME AROUND AND NOW...
...FINALLY! A NICE MEAL!
MILK
NOM NO-
WHAT SORCERY IS THIS?! *COUGH!* *COUGH!*
CHI!
YEAH, YEAH, AND THE COOKS HERE ARE TOP-NOTCH. DIG IN!
I'M STILL TRYNA FIGURE OUT WHERE MY TOURIST COULD BE HIDING! **THAT SNEAKY SLIME BALL.**
**EW!** SEEMS LIKE YOU GOT AN IMMEDIATE ALLERGIC REACTION FROM THE SHRIMP.
UGH... I DON'T FEEL SO GOOD.
WAIT, YOU STILL HAVEN'T FOUND HIM, HUH?
NOT IN THE SLIGHTEST AND IT'S GETTING ON MY LAST NERVE!
UM, I'M SURE YOU'LL FIND HIM. HE ALSO MAY HAVE A GOOD REASON FOR HIS ABSENCE.
WHEN YOU DO FIND HIM, **PLEASE TRY TO FORGIVE HIM.**
?!
THAT SHOULD FREE YOU FROM YOUR FRUSTRATIONS A BIT.
HMPH! ALRIGHT, I'LL TRY TO BE **CHILL** ABOUT IT.
TURNS
BUT HE BETTER HAVE A SOLID REASON.
PUKES!

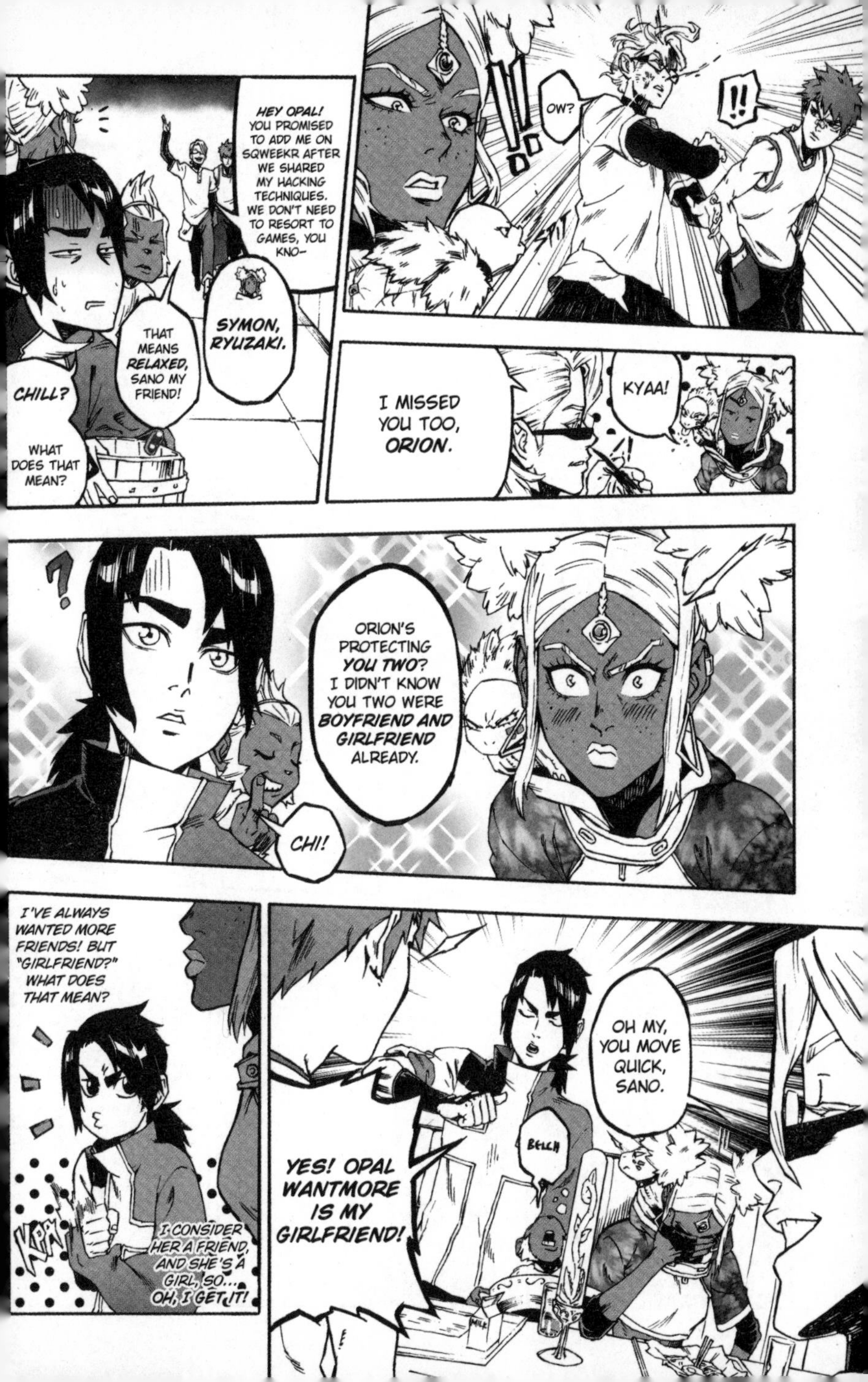
HEY OPAL! YOU PROMISED TO ADD ME ON SQWEEKR AFTER WE SHARED MY HACKING TECHNIQUES. WE DON'T NEED TO RESORT TO GAMES, YOU KNO–
SYMON, RYUZAKI.
THAT MEANS RELAXED, SANO MY FRIEND!
CHILL?
WHAT DOES THAT MEAN?
OW?
!!
I MISSED YOU TOO, ORION.
KYAA!
?
ORION'S PROTECTING YOU TWO? I DIDN'T KNOW YOU TWO WERE BOYFRIEND AND GIRLFRIEND ALREADY.
CHI!
I'VE ALWAYS WANTED MORE FRIENDS! BUT "GIRLFRIEND?" WHAT DOES THAT MEAN?
I CONSIDER HER A FRIEND, AND SHE'S A GIRL, SO... OH, I GET IT!
OH MY, YOU MOVE QUICK, SANO.
BELCH
YES! OPAL WANTMORE IS MY GIRLFRIEND!
MILK

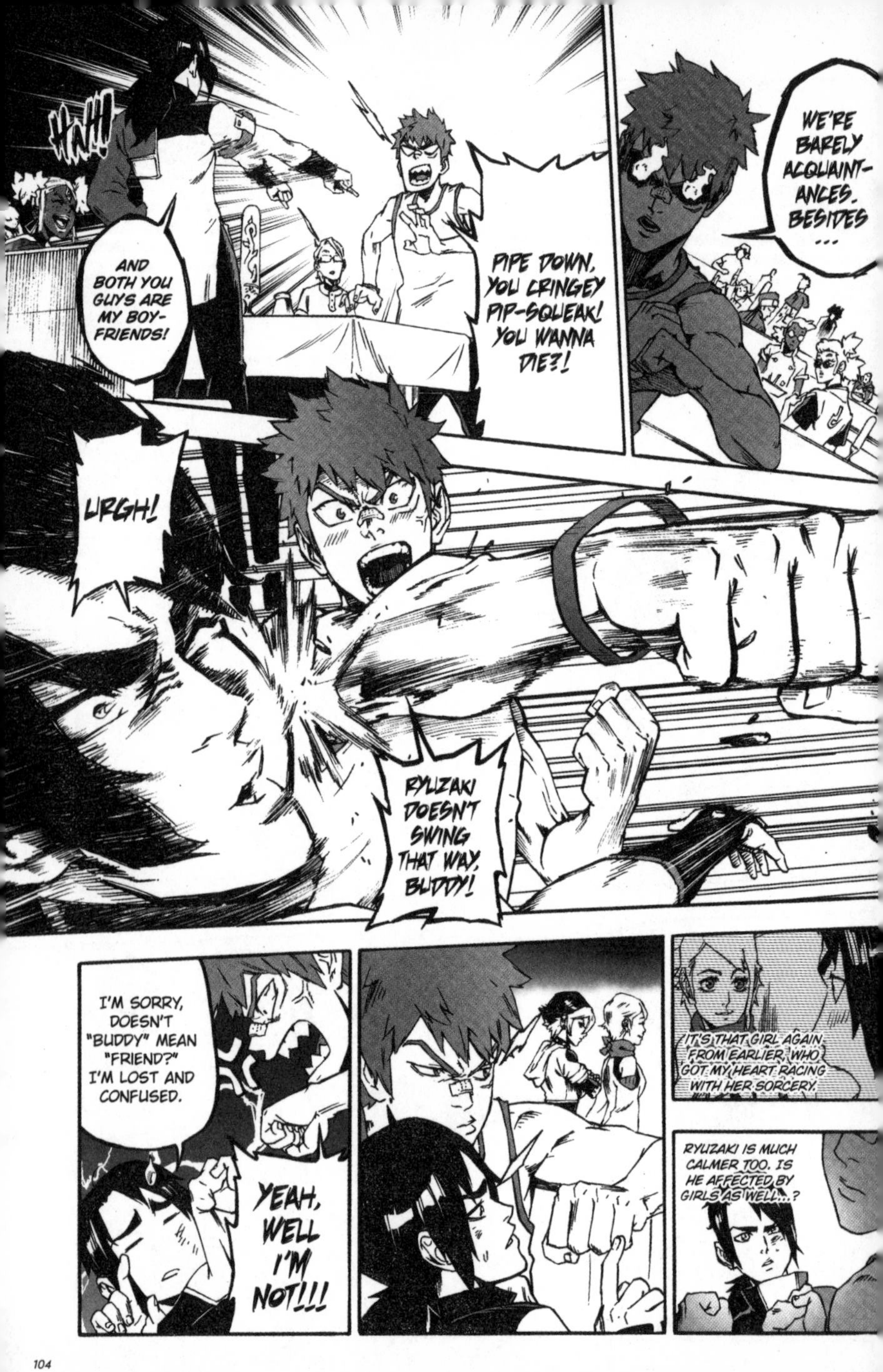
HAH!
AND BOTH YOU GUYS ARE MY BOY-FRIENDS!
PIPE DOWN, YOU CRINGEY PIP-SQUEAK! YOU WANNA DIE?!
WE'RE BARELY ACQUAINT-ANCES. BESIDES...
URGH!
RYUZAKI DOESN'T SWING THAT WAY, BUDDY!
I'M SORRY, DOESN'T "BUDDY" MEAN "FRIEND?" I'M LOST AND CONFUSED.
YEAH, WELL I'M NOT!!!
IT'S THAT GIRL AGAIN FROM EARLIER, WHO GOT MY HEART RACING WITH HER SORCERY.
RYUZAKI IS MUCH CALMER TOO. IS HE AFFECTED BY GIRLS AS WELL...?

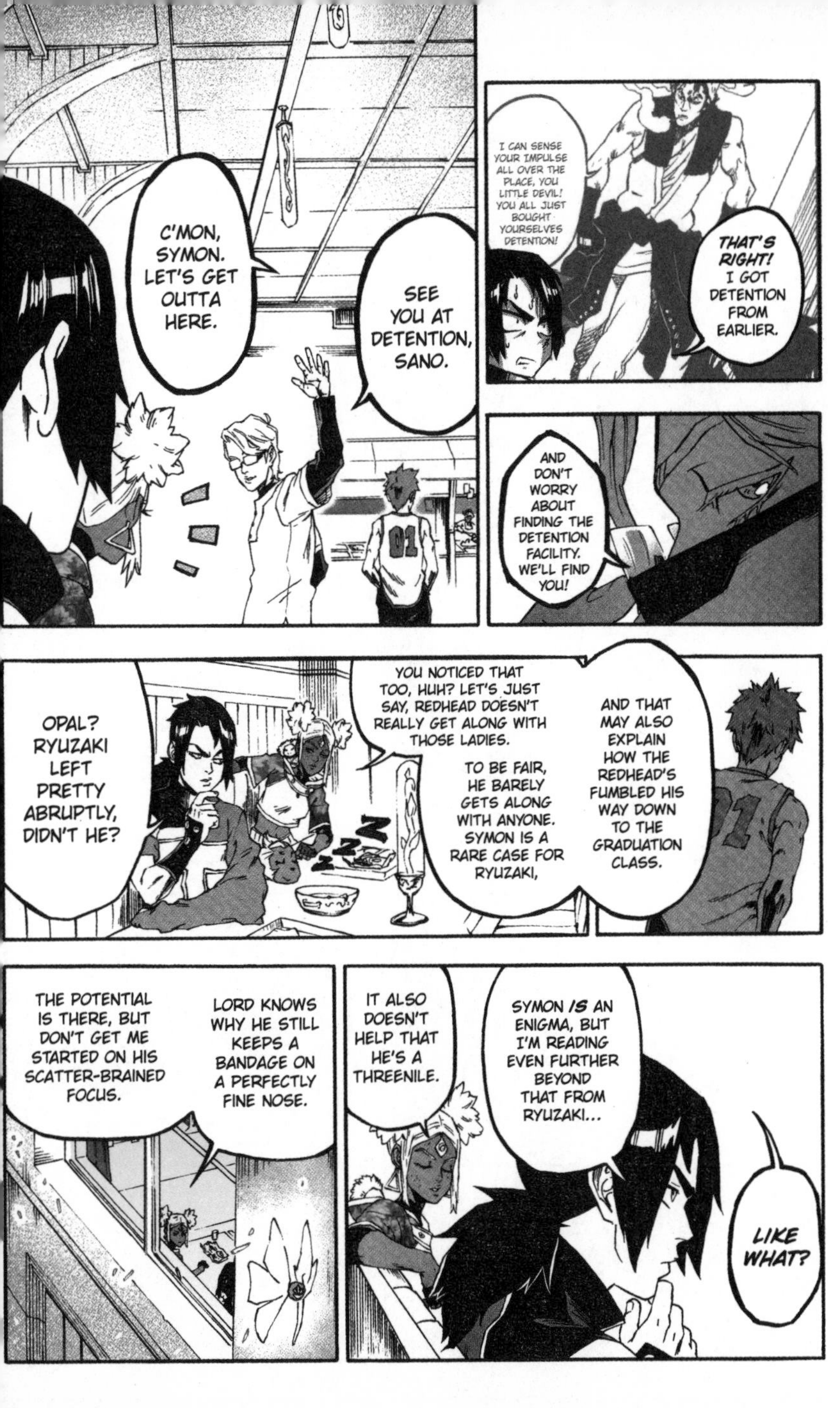
C'MON, SYMON. LET'S GET OUTTA HERE.
SEE YOU AT DETENTION, SANO.
I CAN SENSE YOUR IMPULSE ALL OVER THE PLACE, YOU LITTLE DEVIL! YOU ALL JUST BOUGHT YOURSELVES DETENTION!
THAT'S RIGHT! I GOT DETENTION FROM EARLIER.
AND DON'T WORRY ABOUT FINDING THE DETENTION FACILITY. WE'LL FIND YOU!
OPAL? RYUZAKI LEFT PRETTY ABRUPTLY, DIDN'T HE?
YOU NOTICED THAT TOO, HUH? LET'S JUST SAY, REDHEAD DOESN'T REALLY GET ALONG WITH THOSE LADIES.
TO BE FAIR, HE BARELY GETS ALONG WITH ANYONE. SYMON IS A RARE CASE FOR RYUZAKI,
AND THAT MAY ALSO EXPLAIN HOW THE REDHEAD'S FUMBLED HIS WAY DOWN TO THE GRADUATION CLASS.
THE POTENTIAL IS THERE, BUT DON'T GET ME STARTED ON HIS SCATTER-BRAINED FOCUS.
LORD KNOWS WHY HE STILL KEEPS A BANDAGE ON A PERFECTLY FINE NOSE.
IT ALSO DOESN'T HELP THAT HE'S A THREENILE.
SYMON IS AN ENIGMA, BUT I'M READING EVEN FURTHER BEYOND THAT FROM RYUZAKI...
LIKE WHAT?

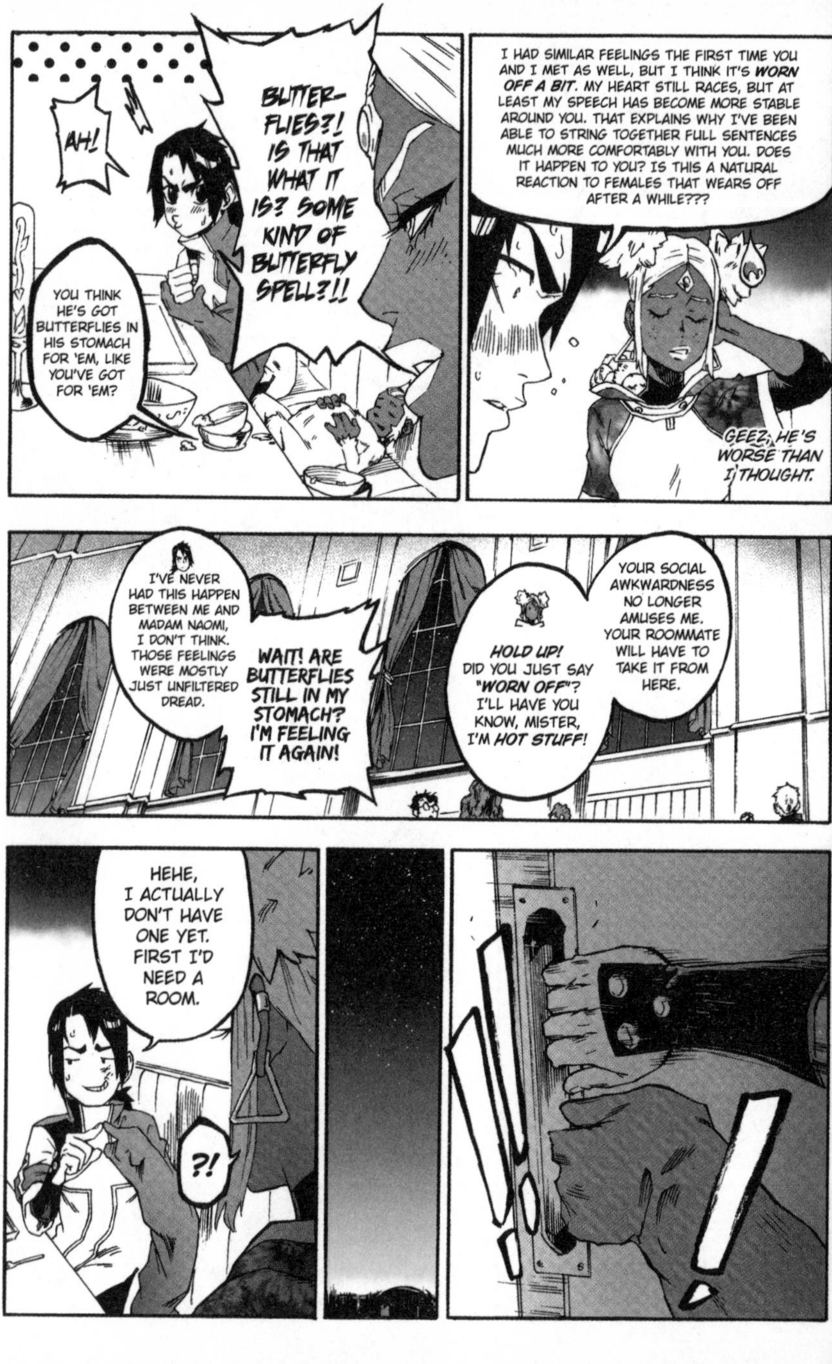
AH!
BUTTER-FLIES?! IS THAT WHAT IT IS? SOME KIND OF BUTTERFLY SPELL?!!
YOU THINK HE'S GOT BUTTERFLIES IN HIS STOMACH FOR 'EM, LIKE YOU'VE GOT FOR 'EM?
I HAD SIMILAR FEELINGS THE FIRST TIME YOU AND I MET AS WELL, BUT I THINK IT'S WORN OFF A BIT. MY HEART STILL RACES, BUT AT LEAST MY SPEECH HAS BECOME MORE STABLE AROUND YOU. THAT EXPLAINS WHY I'VE BEEN ABLE TO STRING TOGETHER FULL SENTENCES MUCH MORE COMFORTABLY WITH YOU. DOES IT HAPPEN TO YOU? IS THIS A NATURAL REACTION TO FEMALES THAT WEARS OFF AFTER A WHILE???
GEEZ, HE'S WORSE THAN I THOUGHT.
YOUR SOCIAL AWKWARDNESS NO LONGER AMUSES ME. YOUR ROOMMATE WILL HAVE TO TAKE IT FROM HERE.
HOLD UP! DID YOU JUST SAY "WORN OFF"? I'LL HAVE YOU KNOW, MISTER, I'M HOT STUFF!
I'VE NEVER HAD THIS HAPPEN BETWEEN ME AND MADAM NAOMI, I DON'T THINK. THOSE FEELINGS WERE MOSTLY JUST UNFILTERED DREAD.
WAIT! ARE BUTTERFLIES STILL IN MY STOMACH? I'M FEELING IT AGAIN!
HEHE, I ACTUALLY DON'T HAVE ONE YET. FIRST I'D NEED A ROOM.
?!

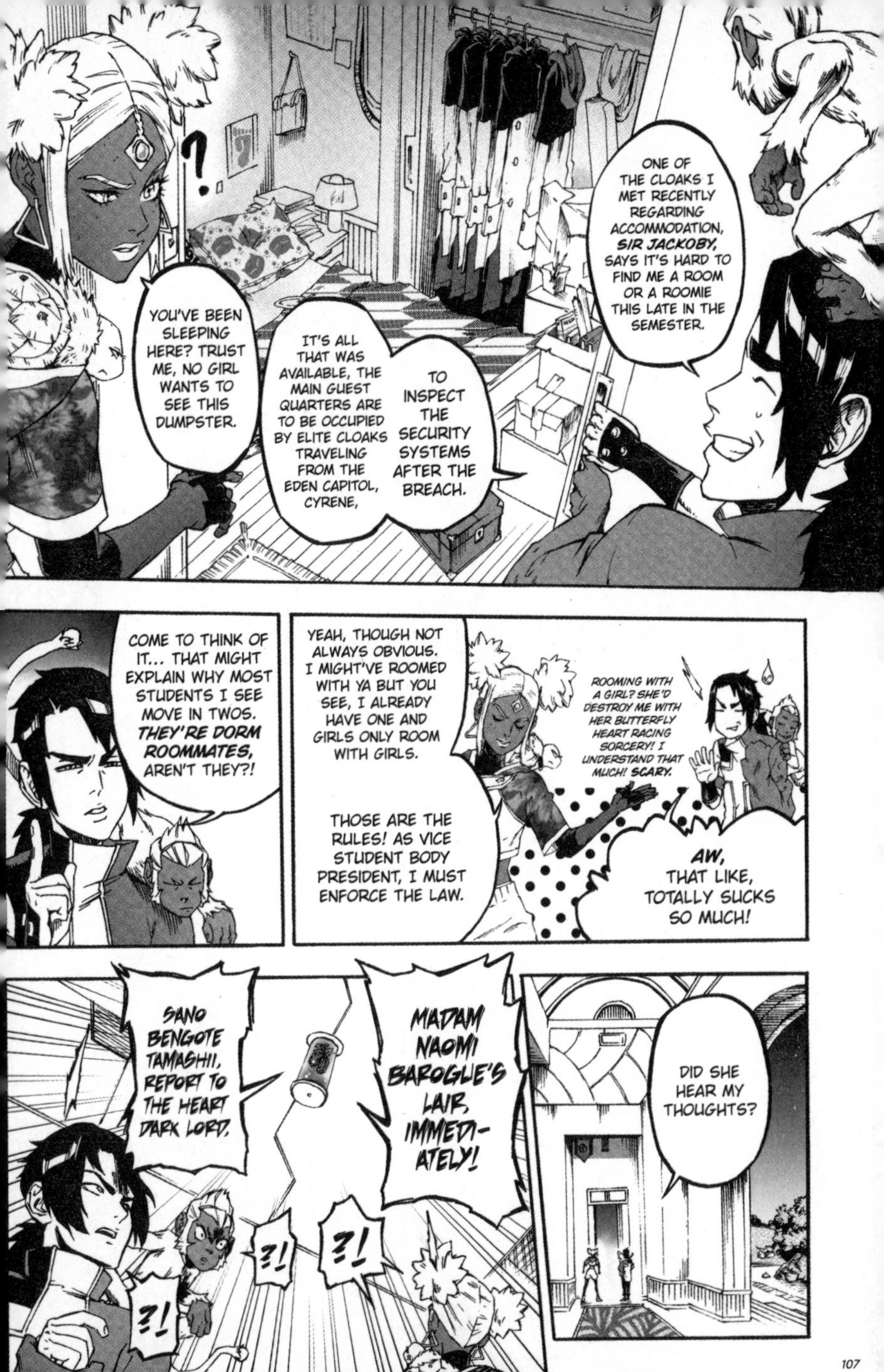
?
YOU'VE BEEN SLEEPING HERE? TRUST ME, NO GIRL WANTS TO SEE THIS DUMPSTER.
IT'S ALL THAT WAS AVAILABLE, THE MAIN GUEST QUARTERS ARE TO BE OCCUPIED BY ELITE CLOAKS TRAVELING FROM THE EDEN CAPITOL, CYRENE,
TO INSPECT THE SECURITY SYSTEMS AFTER THE BREACH.
ONE OF THE CLOAKS I MET RECENTLY REGARDING ACCOMMODATION, **SIR JACKOBY,** SAYS IT'S HARD TO FIND ME A ROOM OR A ROOMIE THIS LATE IN THE SEMESTER.
COME TO THINK OF IT... THAT MIGHT EXPLAIN WHY MOST STUDENTS I SEE MOVE IN TWOS. ***THEY'RE DORM ROOMMATES,*** AREN'T THEY?!
YEAH, THOUGH NOT ALWAYS OBVIOUS. I MIGHT'VE ROOMED WITH YA BUT YOU SEE, I ALREADY HAVE ONE AND GIRLS ONLY ROOM WITH GIRLS.
THOSE ARE THE RULES! AS VICE STUDENT BODY PRESIDENT, I MUST ENFORCE THE LAW.
*ROOMING WITH A GIRL? SHE'D DESTROY ME WITH HER BUTTERFLY HEART RACING SORCERY! I UNDERSTAND THAT MUCH! **SCARY.***
**AW,** THAT LIKE, TOTALLY SUCKS SO MUCH!
SANO BENGOTE TAMASHII, REPORT TO THE HEART DARK LORD.
MADAM NAOMI BAROGUE'S LAIR, IMMEDI-ATELY!
?!
?!
?!
DID SHE HEAR MY THOUGHTS?

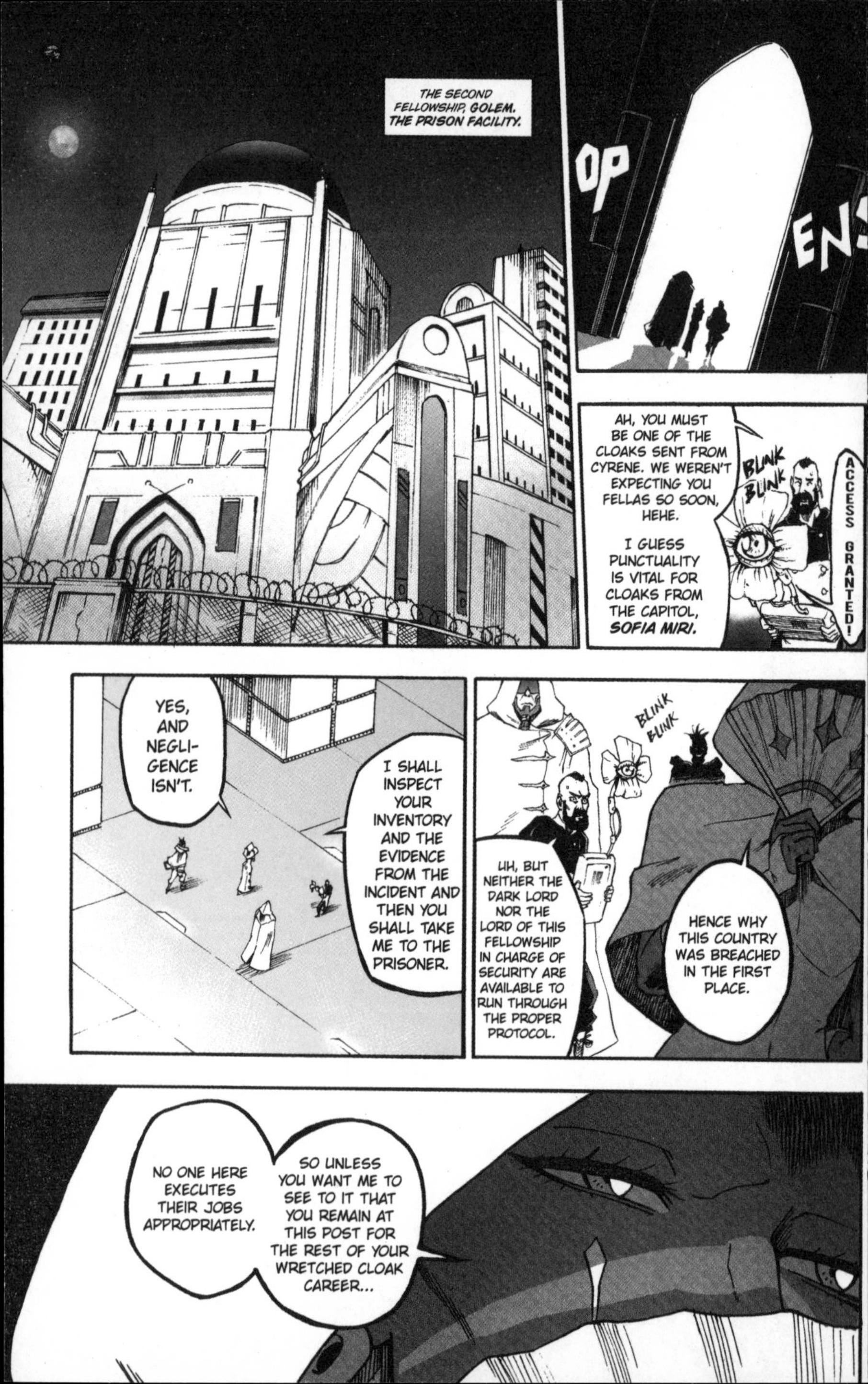
THE SECOND FELLOWSHIP, GOLEM. THE PRISON FACILITY.
OP
ENS
AH, YOU MUST BE ONE OF THE CLOAKS SENT FROM CYRENE. WE WEREN'T EXPECTING YOU FELLAS SO SOON, HEHE.
I GUESS PUNCTUALITY IS VITAL FOR CLOAKS FROM THE CAPITOL, SOFIA MIRI.
BLINK BLINK
ACCESS GRANTED!
YES, AND NEGLI-GENCE ISN'T.
I SHALL INSPECT YOUR INVENTORY AND THE EVIDENCE FROM THE INCIDENT AND THEN YOU SHALL TAKE ME TO THE PRISONER.
BLINK BLINK
UH, BUT NEITHER THE DARK LORD NOR THE LORD OF THIS FELLOWSHIP IN CHARGE OF SECURITY ARE AVAILABLE TO RUN THROUGH THE PROPER PROTOCOL.
HENCE WHY THIS COUNTRY WAS BREACHED IN THE FIRST PLACE.
NO ONE HERE EXECUTES THEIR JOBS APPROPRIATELY.
SO UNLESS YOU WANT ME TO SEE TO IT THAT YOU REMAIN AT THIS POST FOR THE REST OF YOUR WRETCHED CLOAK CAREER...

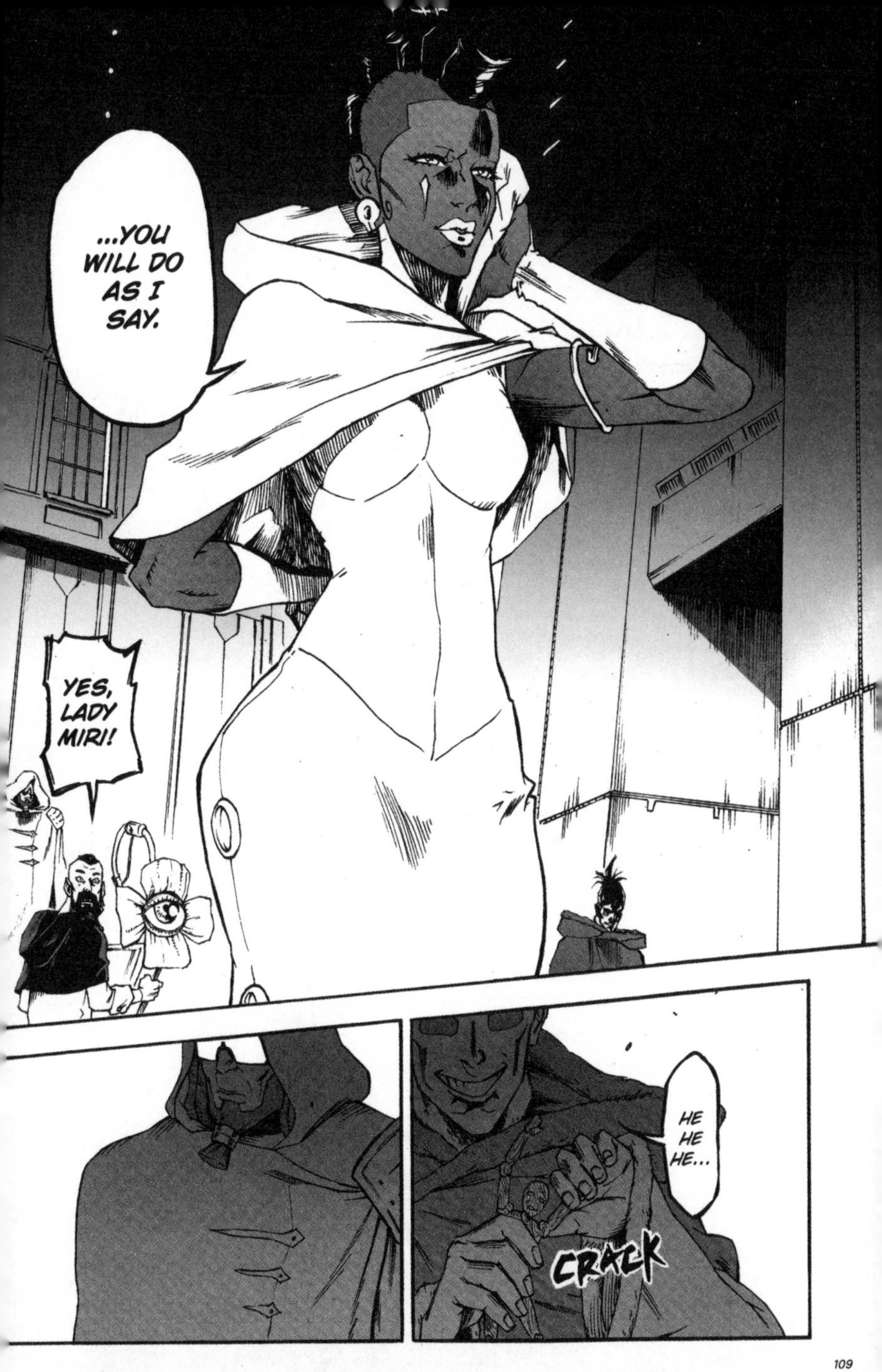
...YOU WILL DO AS I SAY.
YES, LADY MIRI!
HE HE HE...
CRACK

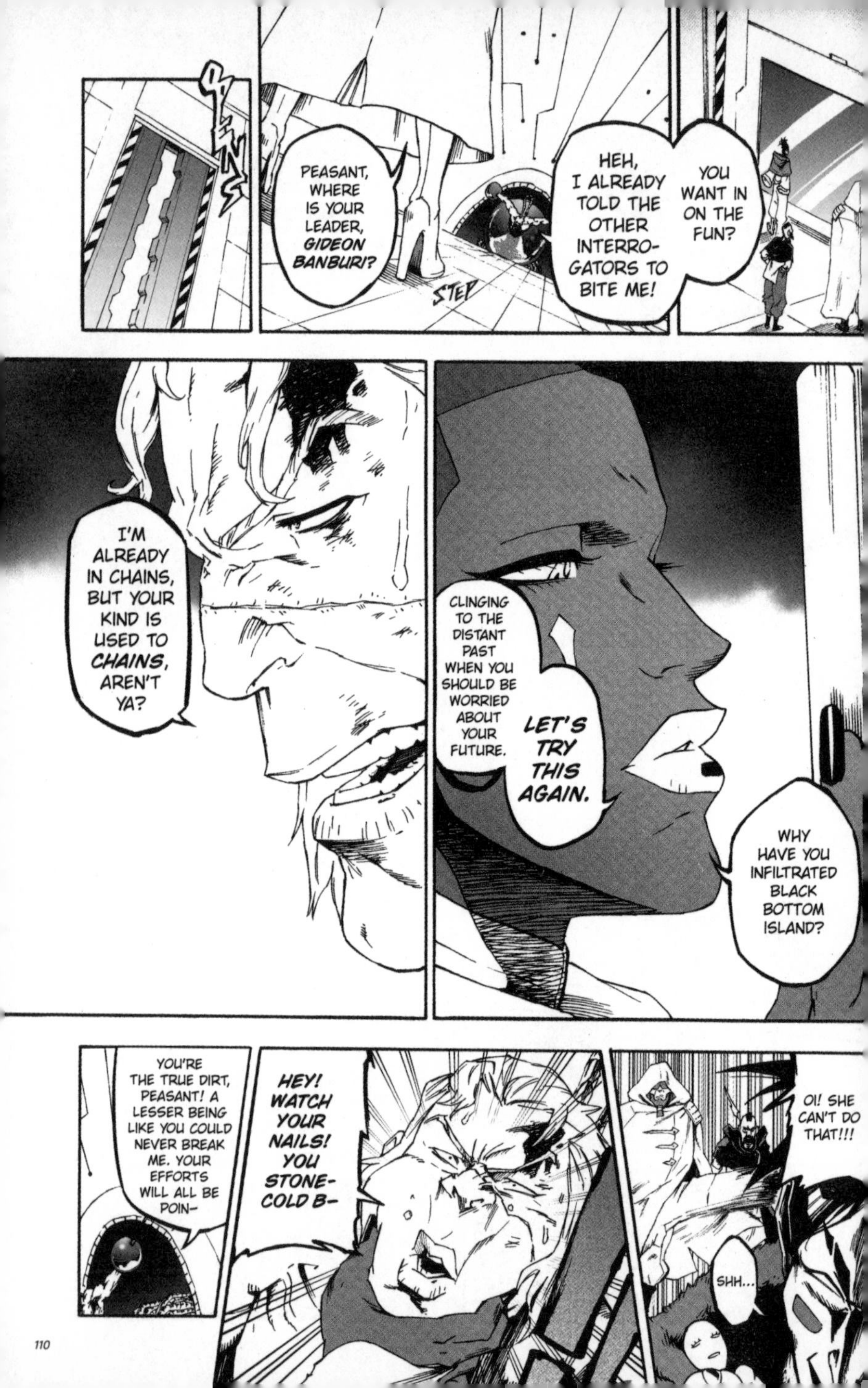
PEASANT, WHERE IS YOUR LEADER, GIDEON BANBURI?
STEP
HEH, I ALREADY TOLD THE OTHER INTERROGATORS TO BITE ME!
YOU WANT IN ON THE FUN?
I'M ALREADY IN CHAINS, BUT YOUR KIND IS USED TO CHAINS, AREN'T YA?
CLINGING TO THE DISTANT PAST WHEN YOU SHOULD BE WORRIED ABOUT YOUR FUTURE.
LET'S TRY THIS AGAIN.
WHY HAVE YOU INFILTRATED BLACK BOTTOM ISLAND?
YOU'RE THE TRUE DIRT, PEASANT! A LESSER BEING LIKE YOU COULD NEVER BREAK ME. YOUR EFFORTS WILL ALL BE POIN-
HEY! WATCH YOUR NAILS! YOU STONE-COLD B-
OI! SHE CAN'T DO THAT!!!
SHH...

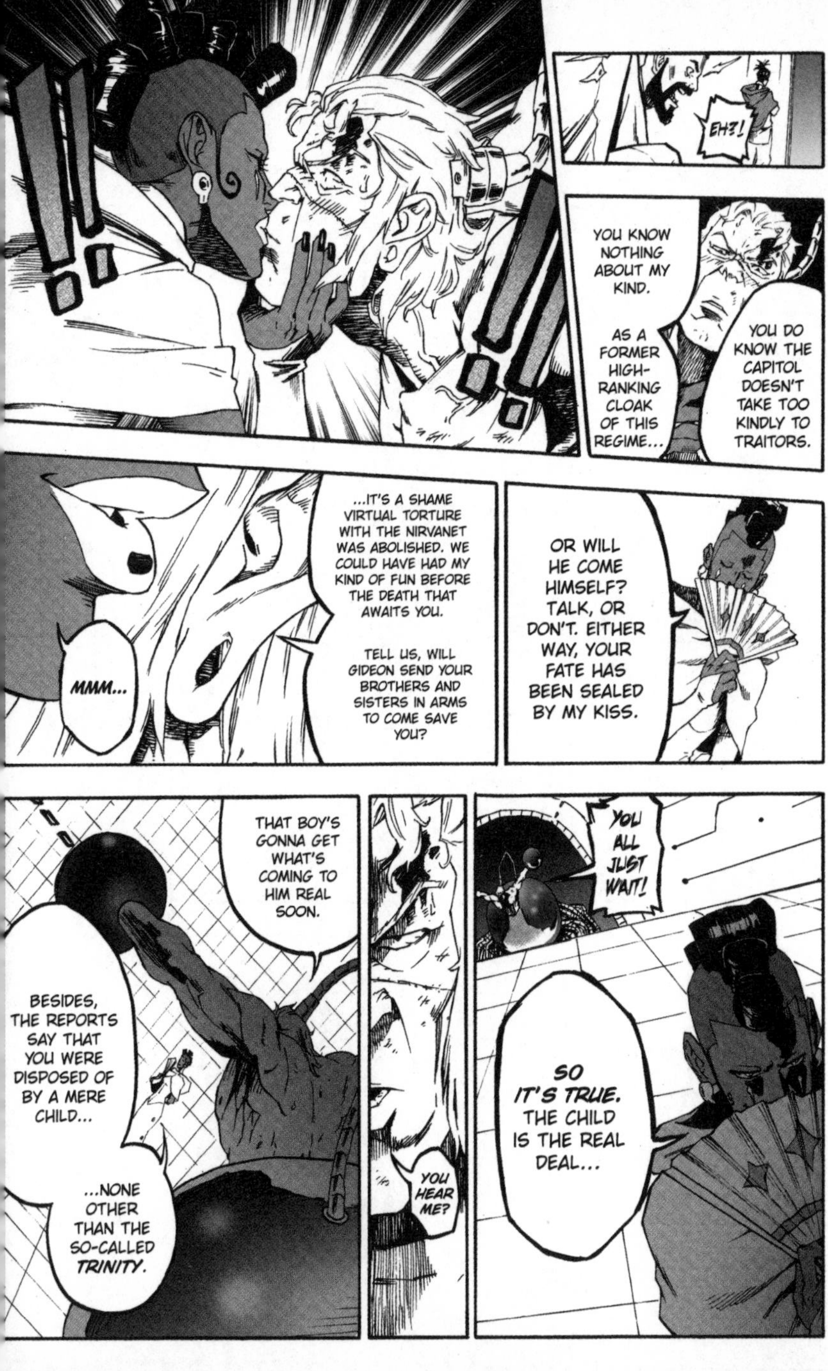
EH?!
YOU KNOW NOTHING ABOUT MY KIND.
AS A FORMER HIGH-RANKING CLOAK OF THIS REGIME...
YOU DO KNOW THE CAPITOL DOESN'T TAKE TOO KINDLY TO TRAITORS.
MMM...
...IT'S A SHAME VIRTUAL TORTURE WITH THE NIRVANET WAS ABOLISHED. WE COULD HAVE HAD MY KIND OF FUN BEFORE THE DEATH THAT AWAITS YOU.
TELL US, WILL GIDEON SEND YOUR BROTHERS AND SISTERS IN ARMS TO COME SAVE YOU?
OR WILL HE COME HIMSELF? TALK, OR DON'T. EITHER WAY, YOUR FATE HAS BEEN SEALED BY MY KISS.
BESIDES, THE REPORTS SAY THAT YOU WERE DISPOSED OF BY A MERE CHILD...
...NONE OTHER THAN THE SO-CALLED TRINITY.
THAT BOY'S GONNA GET WHAT'S COMING TO HIM REAL SOON.
YOU HEAR ME?
YOU ALL JUST WAIT!
SO IT'S TRUE. THE CHILD IS THE REAL DEAL...

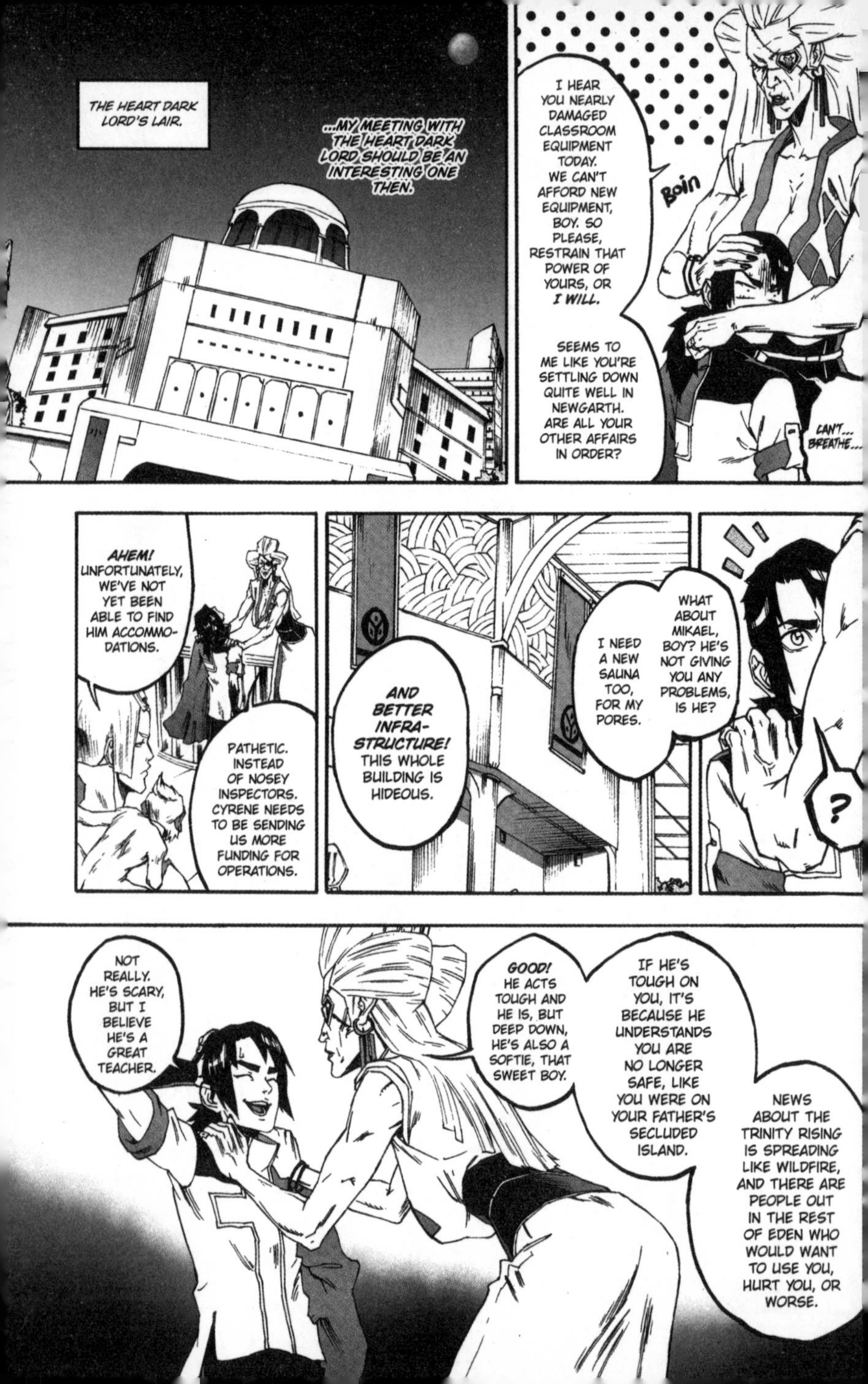
THE HEART DARK LORD'S LAIR.
...MY MEETING WITH THE HEART DARK LORD SHOULD BE AN INTERESTING ONE THEN.
I HEAR YOU NEARLY DAMAGED CLASSROOM EQUIPMENT TODAY. WE CAN'T AFFORD NEW EQUIPMENT, BOY. SO PLEASE, RESTRAIN THAT POWER OF YOURS, OR I WILL.
Boin
SEEMS TO ME LIKE YOU'RE SETTLING DOWN QUITE WELL IN NEWGARTH. ARE ALL YOUR OTHER AFFAIRS IN ORDER?
CAN'T... BREATHE...
AHEM! UNFORTUNATELY, WE'VE NOT YET BEEN ABLE TO FIND HIM ACCOMMODATIONS.
PATHETIC. INSTEAD OF NOSEY INSPECTORS. CYRENE NEEDS TO BE SENDING US MORE FUNDING FOR OPERATIONS.
AND BETTER INFRASTRUCTURE! THIS WHOLE BUILDING IS HIDEOUS.
I NEED A NEW SAUNA TOO, FOR MY PORES.
WHAT ABOUT MIKAEL, BOY? HE'S NOT GIVING YOU ANY PROBLEMS, IS HE?
?
NOT REALLY. HE'S SCARY, BUT I BELIEVE HE'S A GREAT TEACHER.
GOOD! HE ACTS TOUGH AND HE IS, BUT DEEP DOWN, HE'S ALSO A SOFTIE, THAT SWEET BOY.
IF HE'S TOUGH ON YOU, IT'S BECAUSE HE UNDERSTANDS YOU ARE NO LONGER SAFE, LIKE YOU WERE ON YOUR FATHER'S SECLUDED ISLAND.
NEWS ABOUT THE TRINITY RISING IS SPREADING LIKE WILDFIRE, AND THERE ARE PEOPLE OUT IN THE REST OF EDEN WHO WOULD WANT TO USE YOU, HURT YOU, OR WORSE.

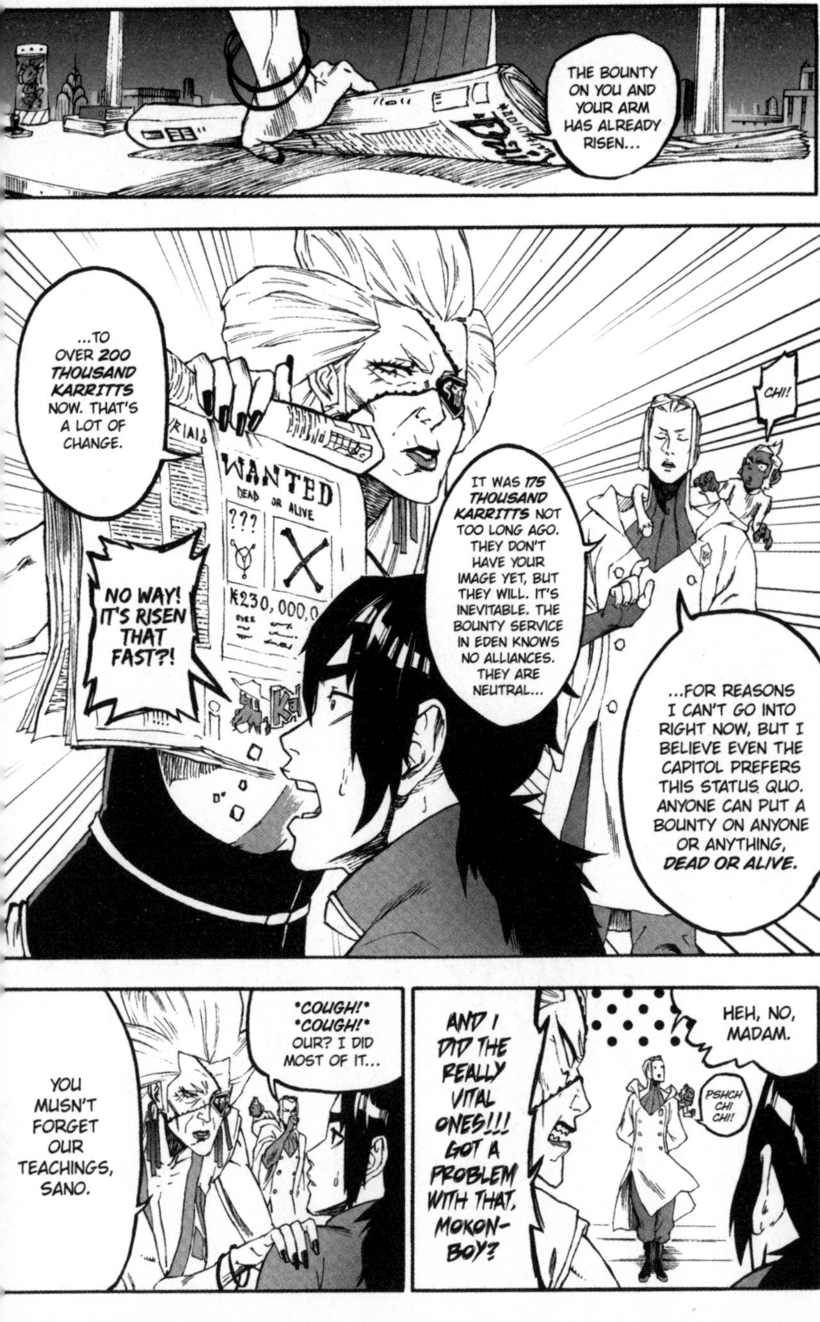
THE BOUNTY ON YOU AND YOUR ARM HAS ALREADY RISEN...
...TO OVER 200 THOUSAND KARRITTS NOW. THAT'S A LOT OF CHANGE.
WANTED
DEAD OR ALIVE
???
₭230,000.0
CHI!
NO WAY! IT'S RISEN THAT FAST?!
IT WAS 175 THOUSAND KARRITTS NOT TOO LONG AGO. THEY DON'T HAVE YOUR IMAGE YET, BUT THEY WILL. IT'S INEVITABLE. THE BOUNTY SERVICE IN EDEN KNOWS NO ALLIANCES. THEY ARE NEUTRAL...
...FOR REASONS I CAN'T GO INTO RIGHT NOW, BUT I BELIEVE EVEN THE CAPITOL PREFERS THIS STATUS QUO. ANYONE CAN PUT A BOUNTY ON ANYONE OR ANYTHING, DEAD OR ALIVE.
YOU MUSN'T FORGET OUR TEACHINGS, SANO.
*COUGH!* *COUGH!* OUR? I DID MOST OF IT...
AND I DID THE REALLY VITAL ONES!!! GOT A PROBLEM WITH THAT, MOKON-BOY?
HEH, NO, MADAM.
PSHCH CHI CHI!

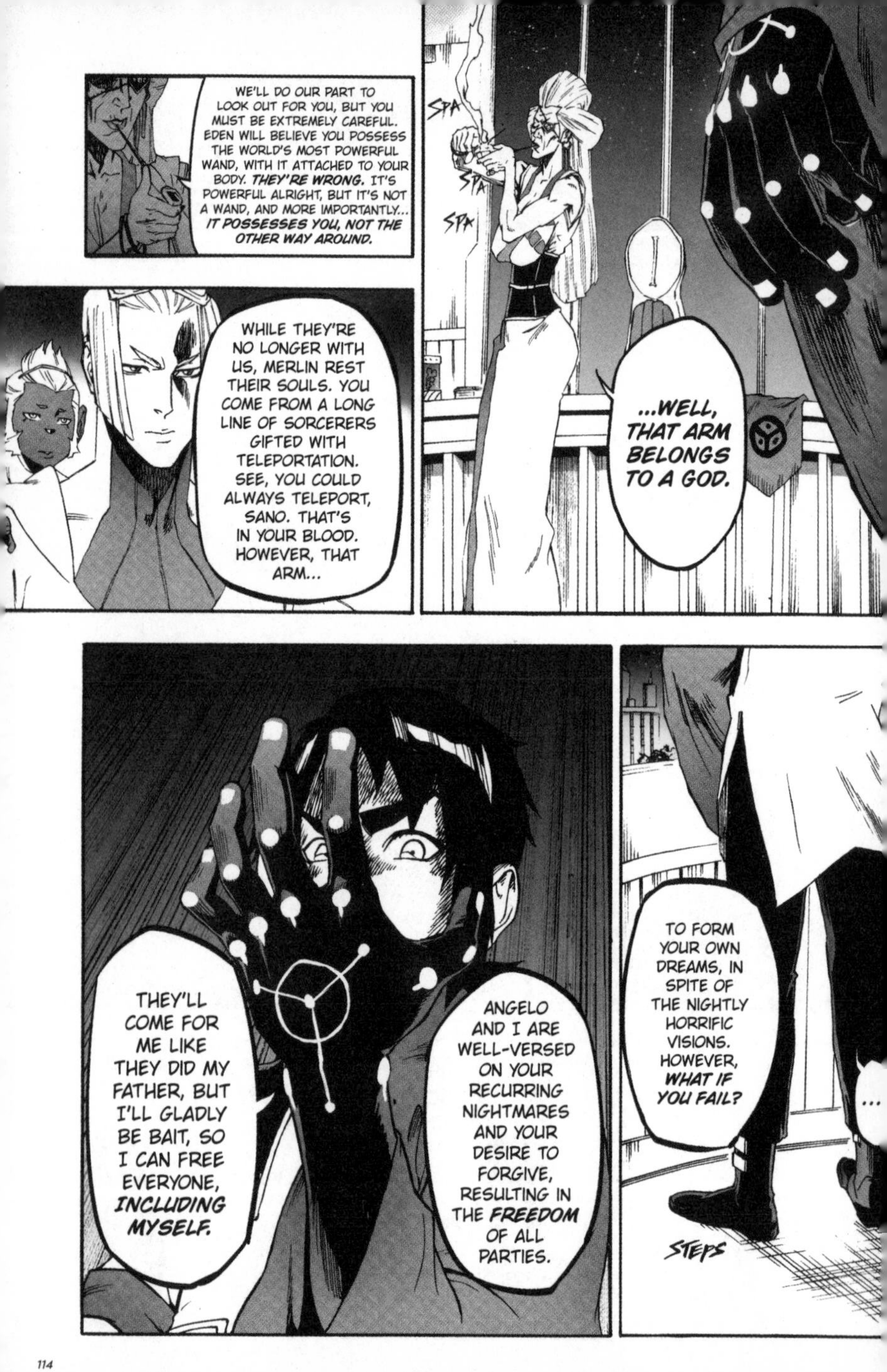
WE'LL DO OUR PART TO LOOK OUT FOR YOU, BUT YOU MUST BE EXTREMELY CAREFUL. EDEN WILL BELIEVE YOU POSSESS THE WORLD'S MOST POWERFUL WAND, WITH IT ATTACHED TO YOUR BODY. THEY'RE WRONG. IT'S POWERFUL ALRIGHT, BUT IT'S NOT A WAND, AND MORE IMPORTANTLY... IT POSSESSES YOU, NOT THE OTHER WAY AROUND.
WHILE THEY'RE NO LONGER WITH US, MERLIN REST THEIR SOULS. YOU COME FROM A LONG LINE OF SORCERERS GIFTED WITH TELEPORTATION. SEE, YOU COULD ALWAYS TELEPORT, SANO. THAT'S IN YOUR BLOOD. HOWEVER, THAT ARM...
SPA
SPA
SPA
...WELL, THAT ARM BELONGS TO A GOD.
THEY'LL COME FOR ME LIKE THEY DID MY FATHER, BUT I'LL GLADLY BE BAIT, SO I CAN FREE EVERYONE, INCLUDING MYSELF.
ANGELO AND I ARE WELL-VERSED ON YOUR RECURRING NIGHTMARES AND YOUR DESIRE TO FORGIVE, RESULTING IN THE FREEDOM OF ALL PARTIES.
TO FORM YOUR OWN DREAMS, IN SPITE OF THE NIGHTLY HORRIFIC VISIONS. HOWEVER, WHAT IF YOU FAIL?
...
STEPS

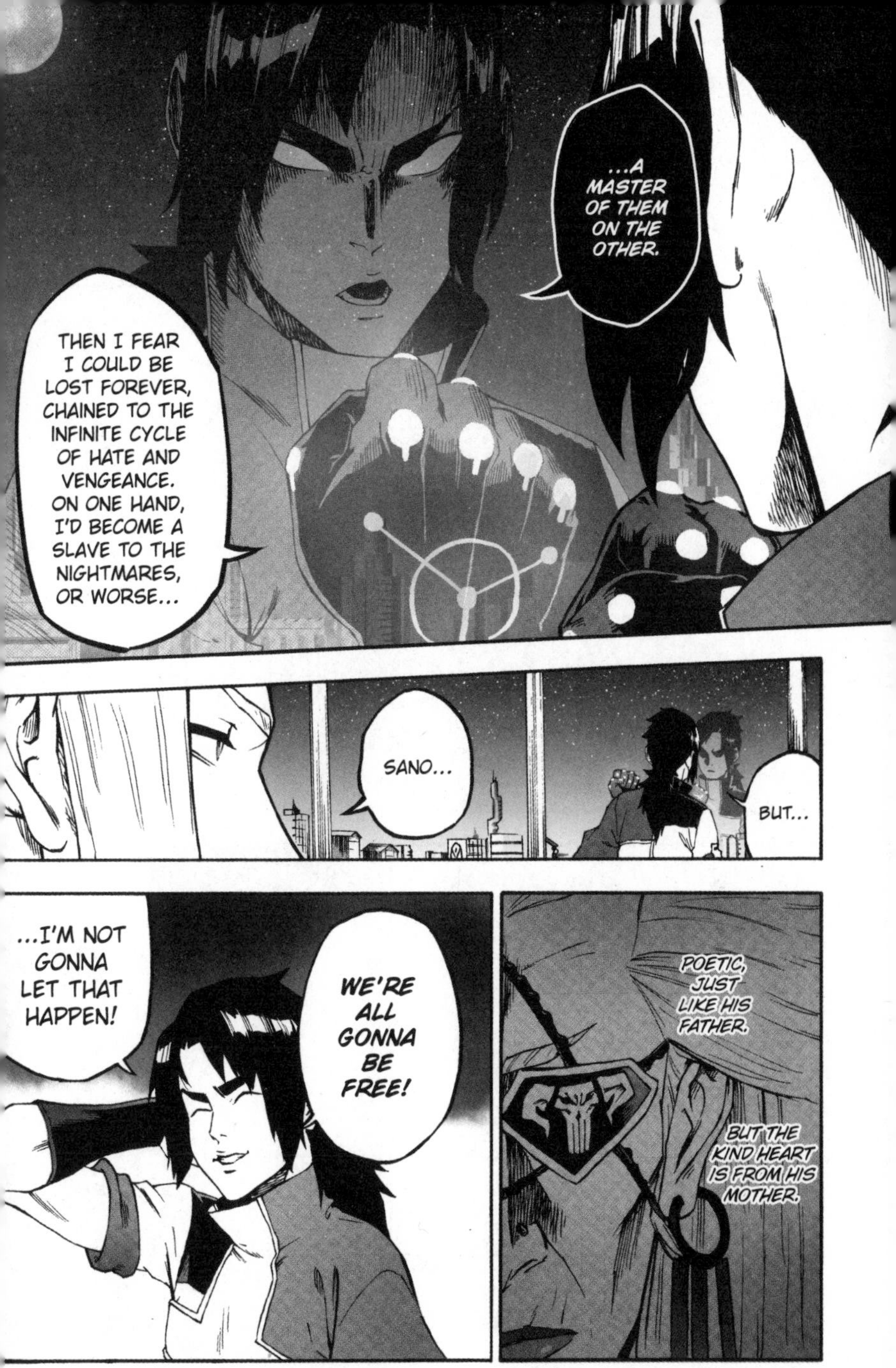
THEN I FEAR I COULD BE LOST FOREVER, CHAINED TO THE INFINITE CYCLE OF HATE AND VENGEANCE. ON ONE HAND, I'D BECOME A SLAVE TO THE NIGHTMARES, OR WORSE...
...A MASTER OF THEM ON THE OTHER.
SANO...
BUT...
...I'M NOT GONNA LET THAT HAPPEN!
WE'RE ALL GONNA BE FREE!
POETIC, JUST LIKE HIS FATHER.
BUT THE KIND HEART IS FROM HIS MOTHER.

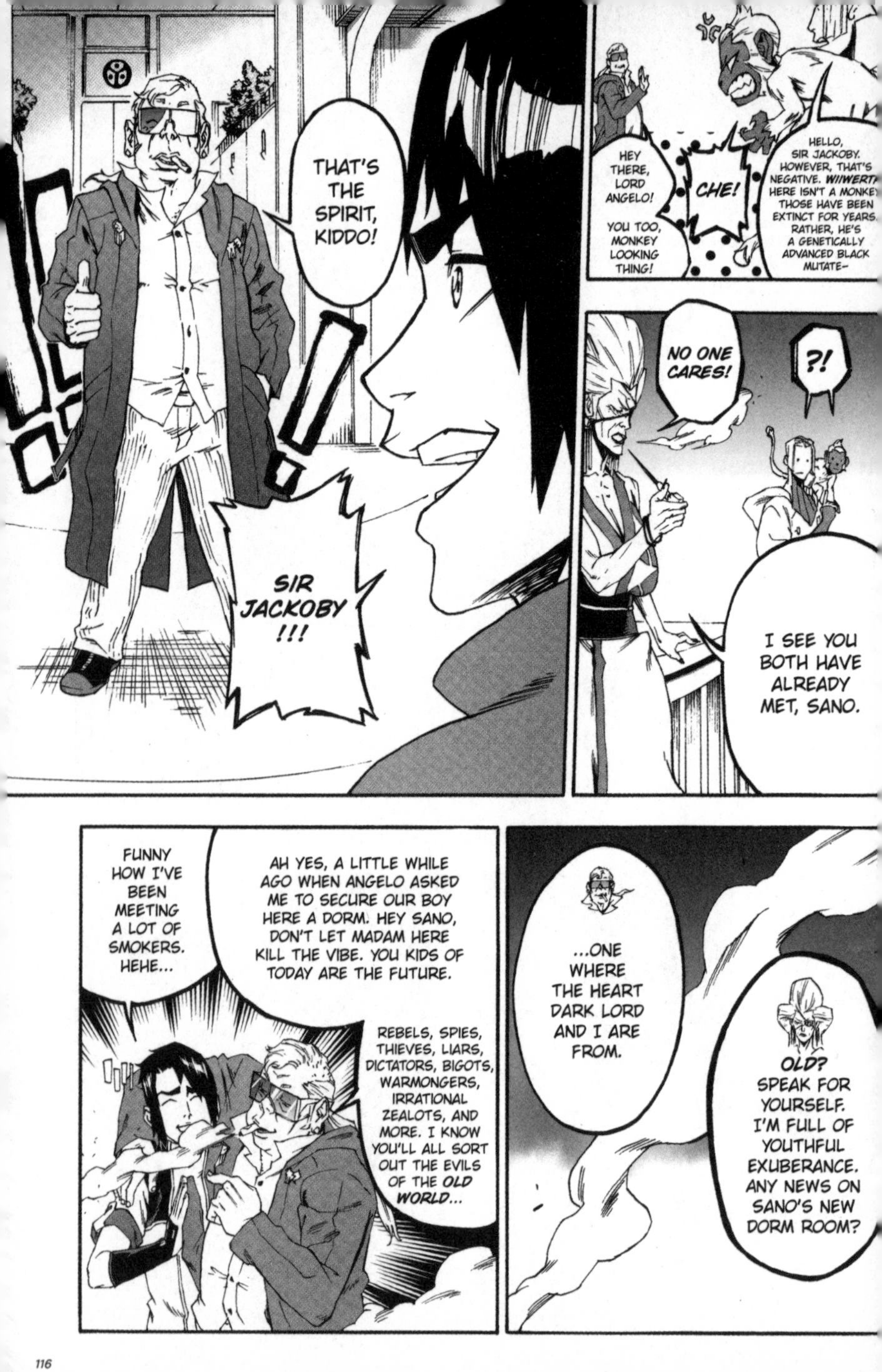

THAT'S THE SPIRIT, KIDDO!
SIR JACKOBY!!!
HEY THERE, LORD ANGELO!
YOU TOO, MONKEY LOOKING THING!
CHE!
HELLO, SIR JACKOBY. HOWEVER, THAT'S NEGATIVE. WIIWERT HERE ISN'T A MONKEY THOSE HAVE BEEN EXTINCT FOR YEARS. RATHER, HE'S A GENETICALLY ADVANCED BLACK MUTATE–
NO ONE CARES!
?!
I SEE YOU BOTH HAVE ALREADY MET, SANO.
FUNNY HOW I'VE BEEN MEETING A LOT OF SMOKERS. HEHE...
AH YES, A LITTLE WHILE AGO WHEN ANGELO ASKED ME TO SECURE OUR BOY HERE A DORM. HEY SANO, DON'T LET MADAM HERE KILL THE VIBE. YOU KIDS OF TODAY ARE THE FUTURE.
REBELS, SPIES, THIEVES, LIARS, DICTATORS, BIGOTS, WARMONGERS, IRRATIONAL ZEALOTS, AND MORE. I KNOW YOU'LL ALL SORT OUT THE EVILS OF THE OLD WORLD...
...ONE WHERE THE HEART DARK LORD AND I ARE FROM.
OLD? SPEAK FOR YOURSELF. I'M FULL OF YOUTHFUL EXUBERANCE. ANY NEWS ON SANO'S NEW DORM ROOM?

WELL, YES. IN FACT, WE HAVE.

YEAH, FINALLY !!!

AND I GET A NEW ROOMMATE, RIGHT?

REALLY? THAT'S GOOD NEWS.

CHIH !!!

WELL, IT'S ABOUT TIME! THAT TOOK TOO LONG, I'M TELLING YOU...

...CYRENE NEEDS TO COUGH UP MORE FUNDING FOR OUR INFRASTRUC-TURE.

HAHA!

YOU JUST WANT ANOTHER SPA.

HEHE, YEAH... WE TRIED TO FIND ALTERNATIVES BUT NOTHING ELSE MADE SENSE.

KEEP IN MIND, THERE ARE A COUPLE PROS AND CONS TO THIS, SO...

HERE'S WHAT I FOUND!

SHINNN

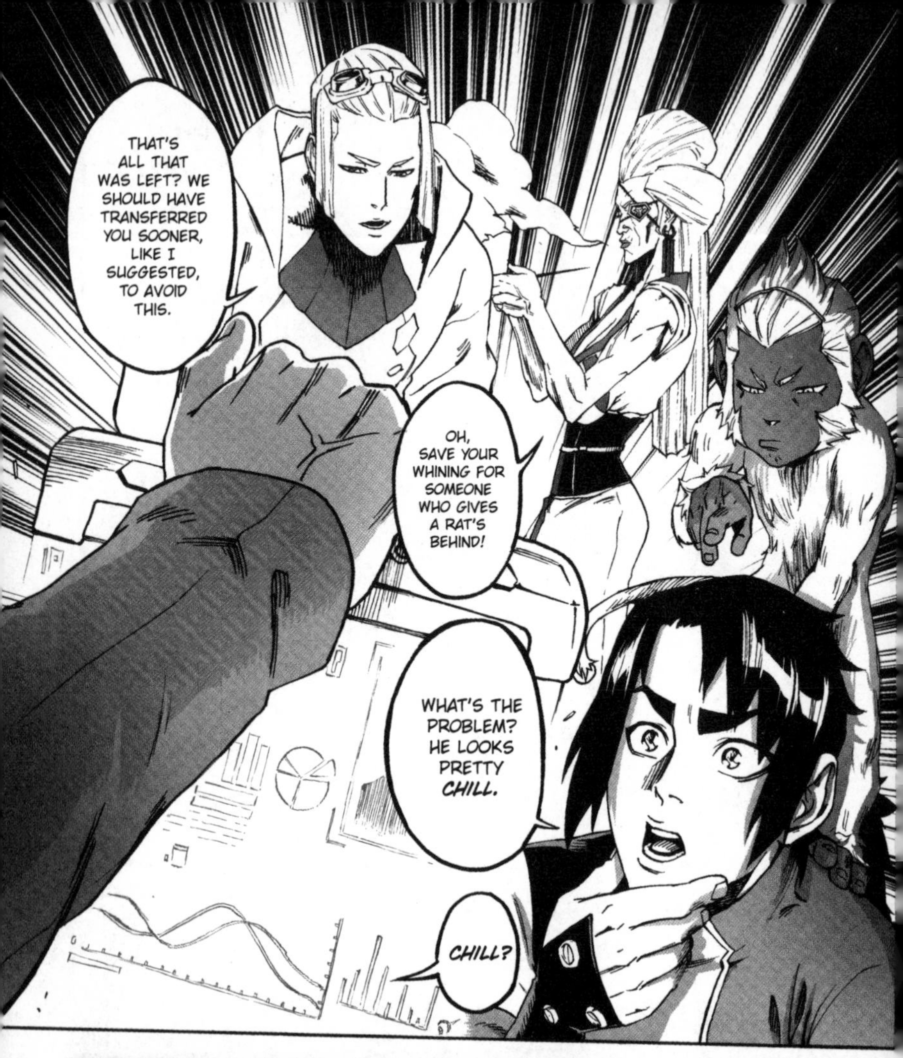
THAT'S ALL THAT WAS LEFT? WE SHOULD HAVE TRANSFERRED YOU SOONER, LIKE I SUGGESTED, TO AVOID THIS.
OH, SAVE YOUR WHINING FOR SOMEONE WHO GIVES A RAT'S BEHIND!
WHAT'S THE PROBLEM? HE LOOKS PRETTY CHILL.
CHILL?
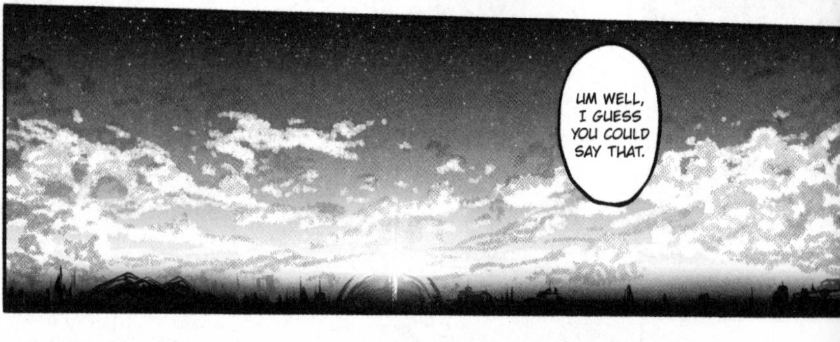
UM WELL, I GUESS YOU COULD SAY THAT.

# APPLE BLACK

**CHAPTER 4** | *HARBINGER*

APPLE BLACK

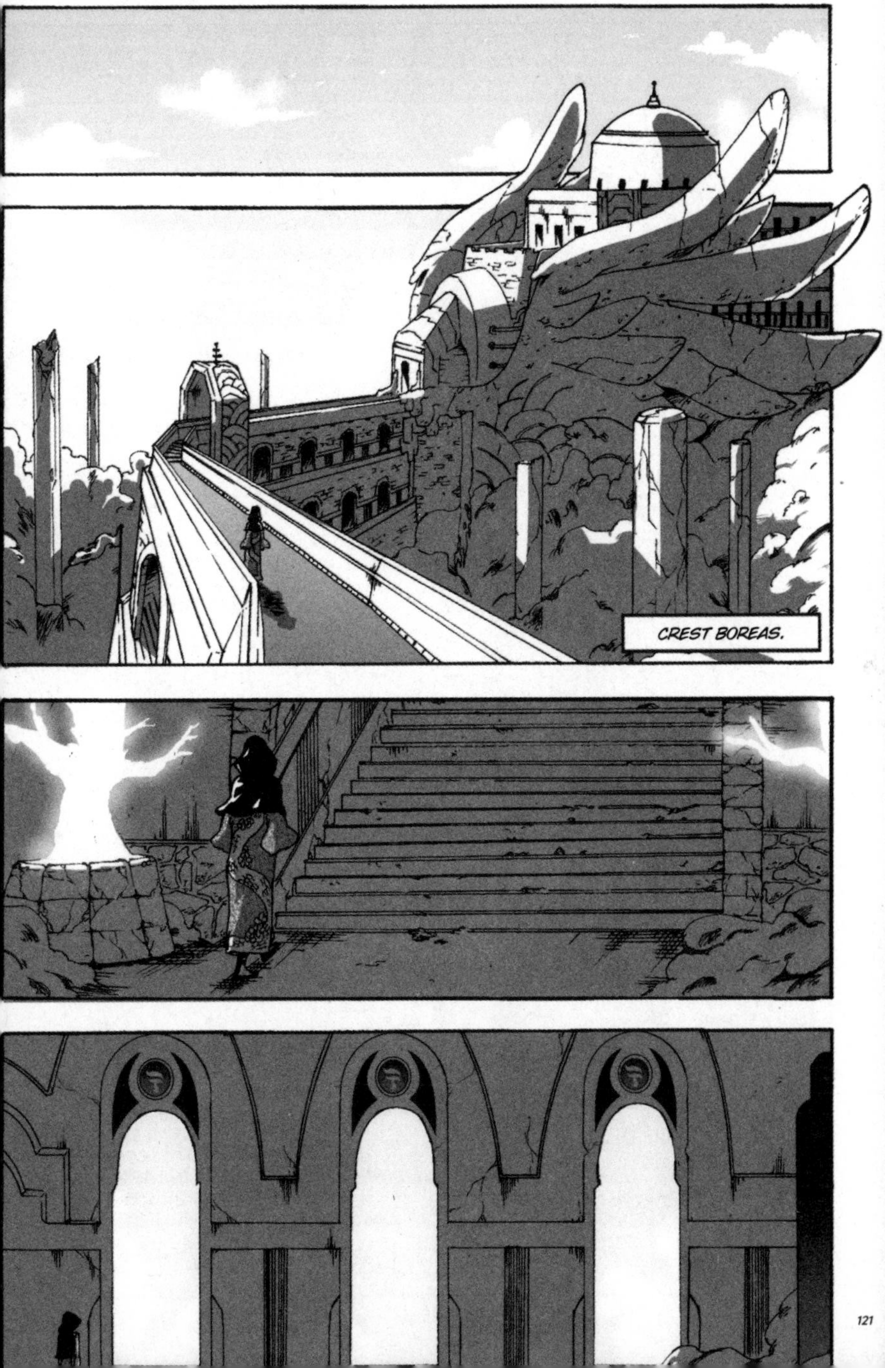
CREST BOREAS.

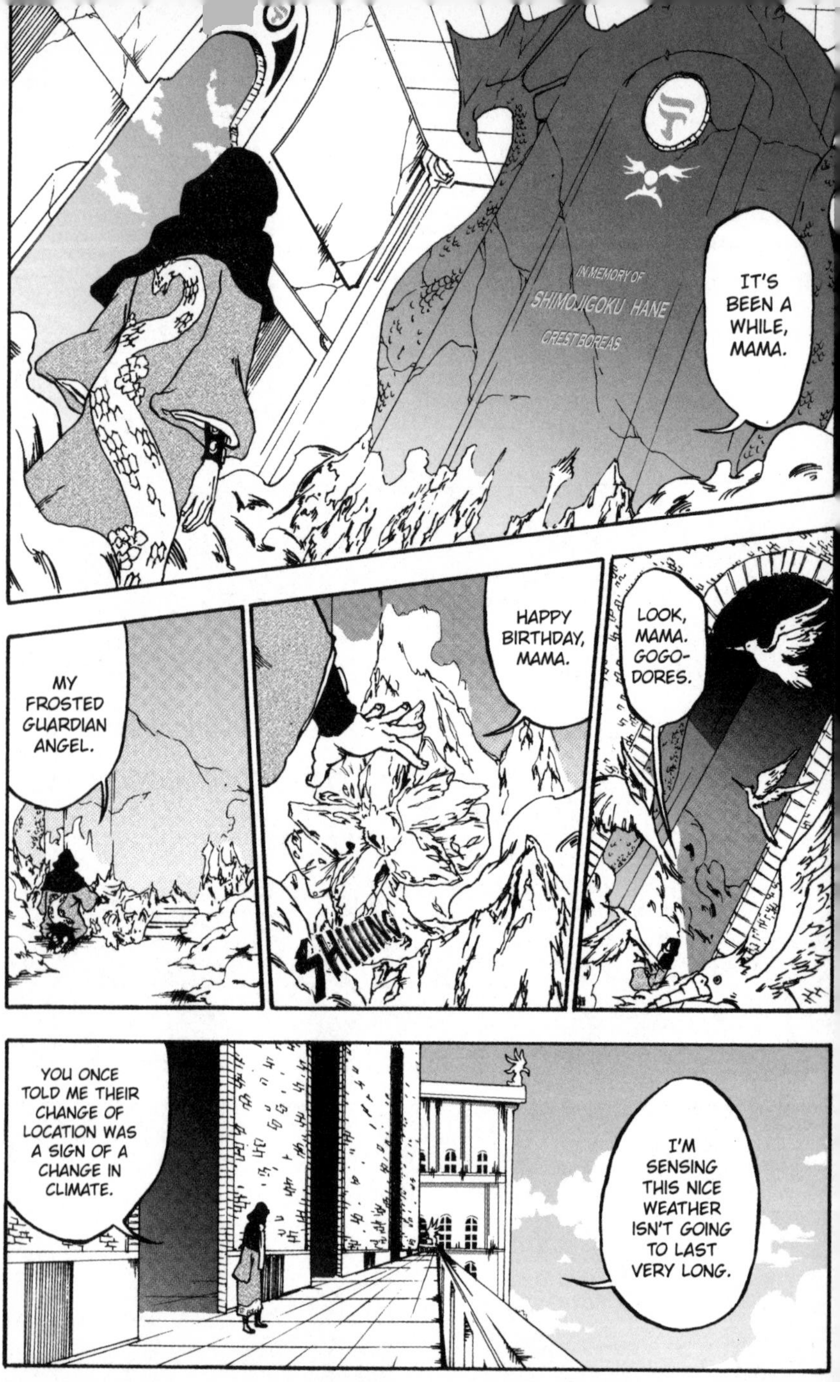
IN MEMORY OF
SHIMOJIGOKU HANE
CREST BOREAS
IT'S BEEN A WHILE, MAMA.
MY FROSTED GUARDIAN ANGEL.
HAPPY BIRTHDAY, MAMA.
SHIIING
LOOK, MAMA. GOGO-DORES.
YOU ONCE TOLD ME THEIR CHANGE OF LOCATION WAS A SIGN OF A CHANGE IN CLIMATE.
I'M SENSING THIS NICE WEATHER ISN'T GOING TO LAST VERY LONG.

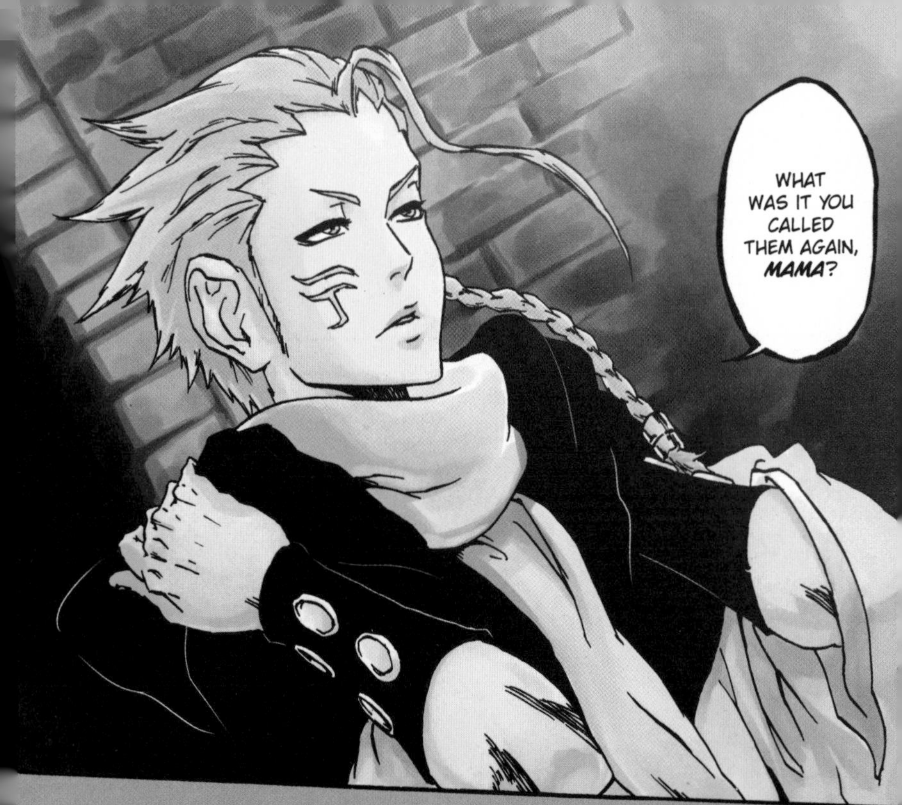
WHAT WAS IT YOU CALLED THEM AGAIN, ***MAMA***?
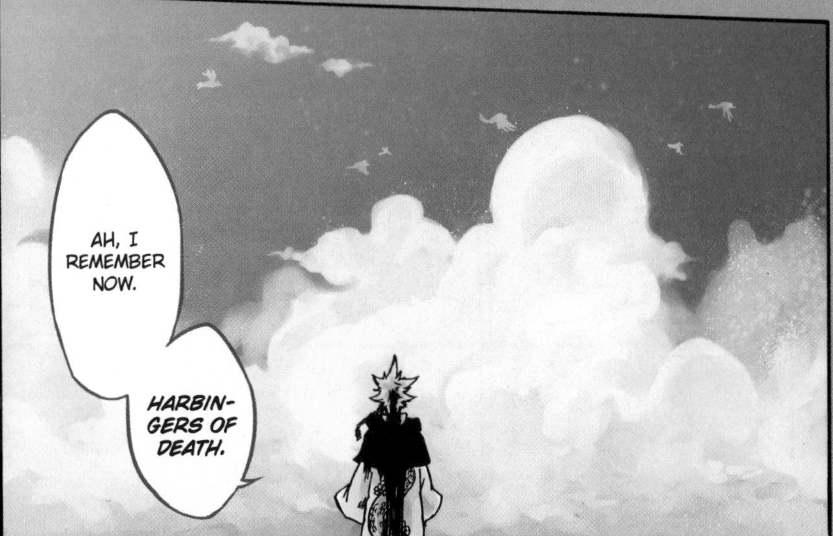
AH, I REMEMBER NOW.
***HARBIN-GERS OF DEATH.***

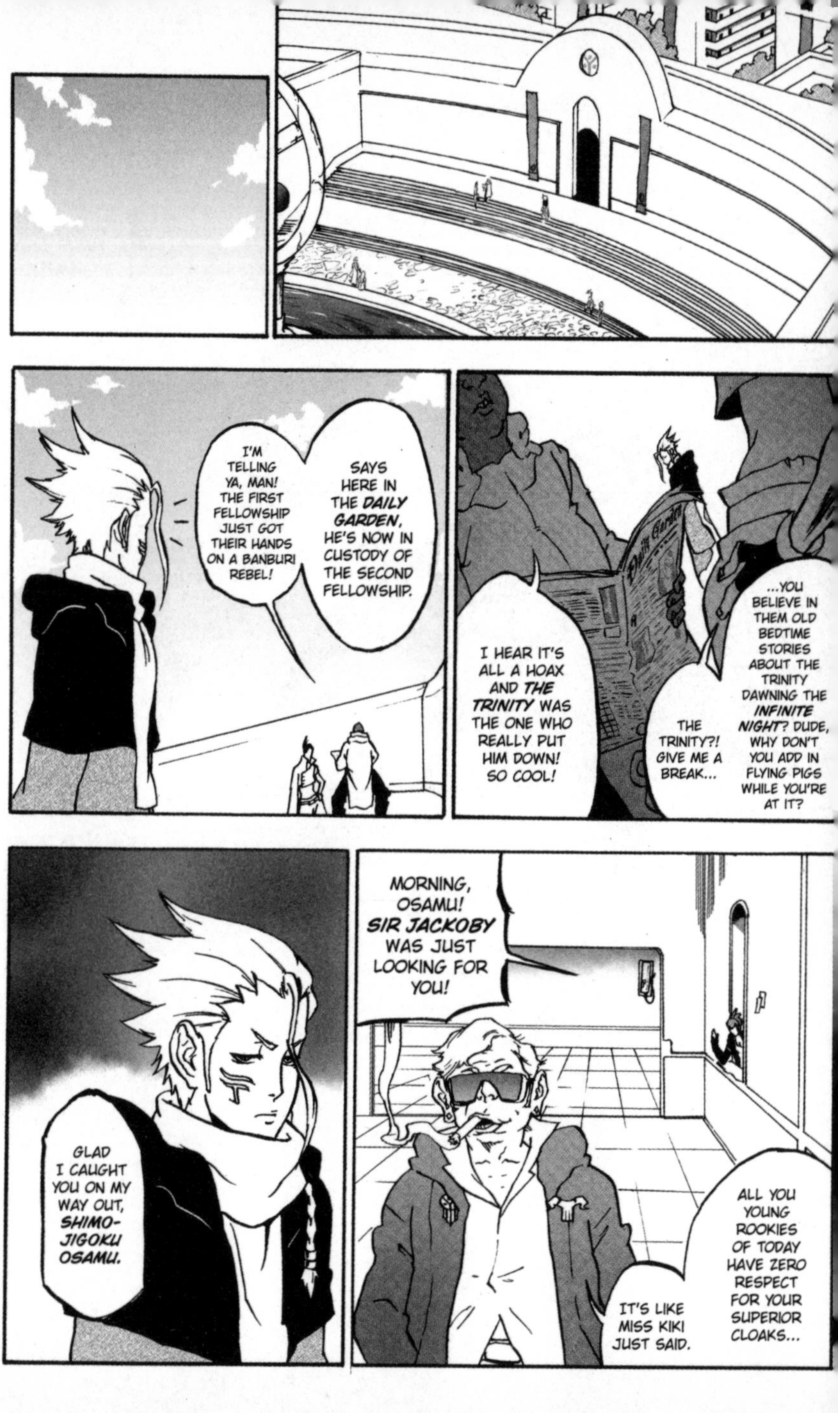

I'M TELLING YA, MAN! THE FIRST FELLOWSHIP JUST GOT THEIR HANDS ON A BANBURI REBEL!
SAYS HERE IN THE ***DAILY GARDEN***, HE'S NOW IN CUSTODY OF THE SECOND FELLOWSHIP.
Daily Garden
I HEAR IT'S ALL A HOAX AND ***THE TRINITY*** WAS THE ONE WHO REALLY PUT HIM DOWN! SO COOL!
THE TRINITY?! GIVE ME A BREAK...
...YOU BELIEVE IN THEM OLD BEDTIME STORIES ABOUT THE TRINITY DAWNING THE ***INFINITE NIGHT***? DUDE, WHY DON'T YOU ADD IN FLYING PIGS WHILE YOU'RE AT IT?
GLAD I CAUGHT YOU ON MY WAY OUT, ***SHIMO-JIGOKU OSAMU.***
MORNING, OSAMU! ***SIR JACKOBY*** WAS JUST LOOKING FOR YOU!
IT'S LIKE MISS KIKI JUST SAID.
ALL YOU YOUNG ROOKIES OF TODAY HAVE ZERO RESPECT FOR YOUR SUPERIOR CLOAKS...

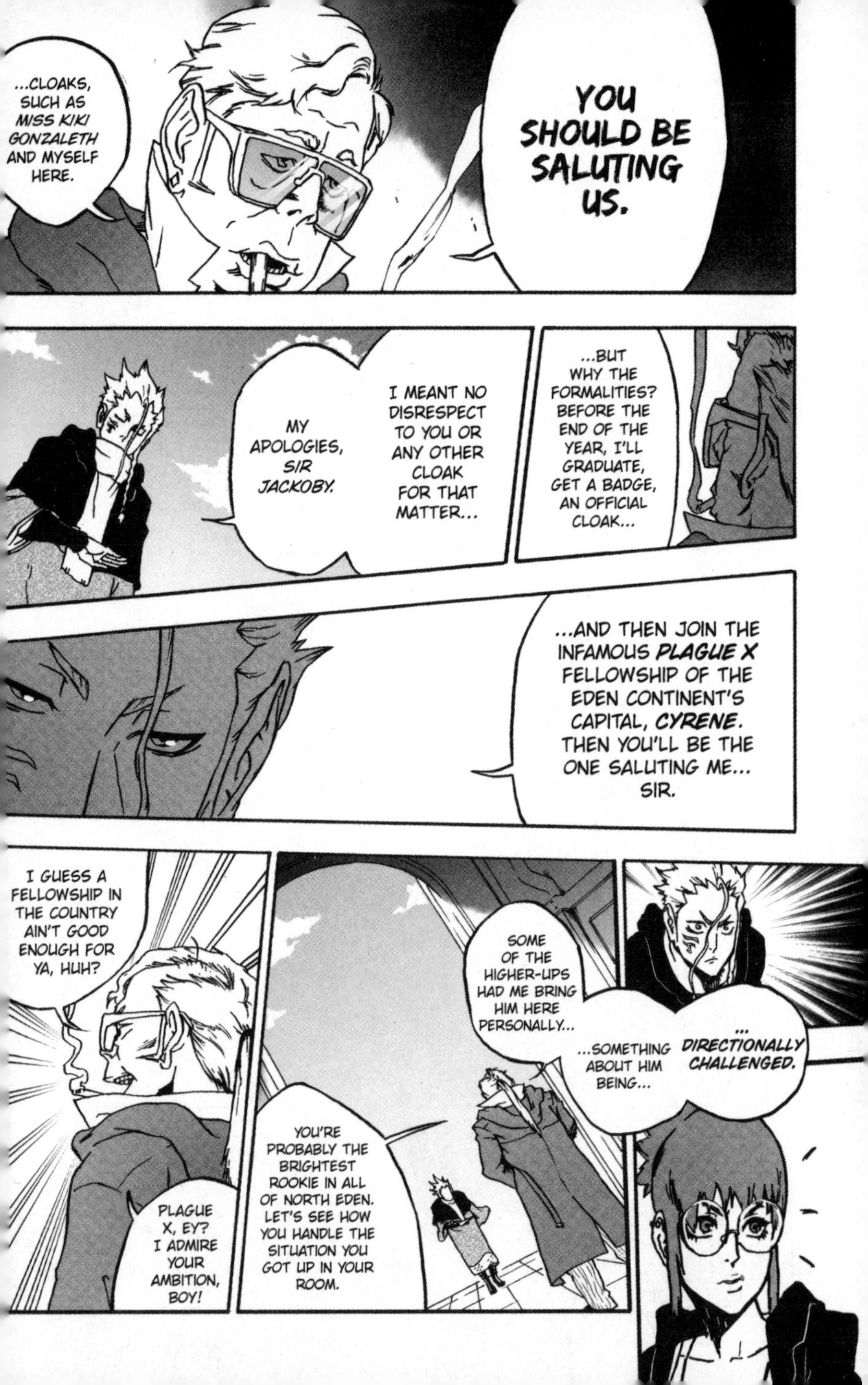
...CLOAKS, SUCH AS MISS KIKI GONZALETH AND MYSELF HERE.
YOU SHOULD BE SALUTING US.
MY APOLOGIES, SIR JACKOBY.
I MEANT NO DISRESPECT TO YOU OR ANY OTHER CLOAK FOR THAT MATTER...
...BUT WHY THE FORMALITIES? BEFORE THE END OF THE YEAR, I'LL GRADUATE, GET A BADGE, AN OFFICIAL CLOAK...
...AND THEN JOIN THE INFAMOUS PLAGUE X FELLOWSHIP OF THE EDEN CONTINENT'S CAPITAL, CYRENE. THEN YOU'LL BE THE ONE SALUTING ME... SIR.
I GUESS A FELLOWSHIP IN THE COUNTRY AIN'T GOOD ENOUGH FOR YA, HUH?
PLAGUE X, EY? I ADMIRE YOUR AMBITION, BOY!
YOU'RE PROBABLY THE BRIGHTEST ROOKIE IN ALL OF NORTH EDEN. LET'S SEE HOW YOU HANDLE THE SITUATION YOU GOT UP IN YOUR ROOM.
SOME OF THE HIGHER-UPS HAD ME BRING HIM HERE PERSONALLY...
...SOMETHING ABOUT HIM BEING...
... DIRECTIONALLY CHALLENGED.

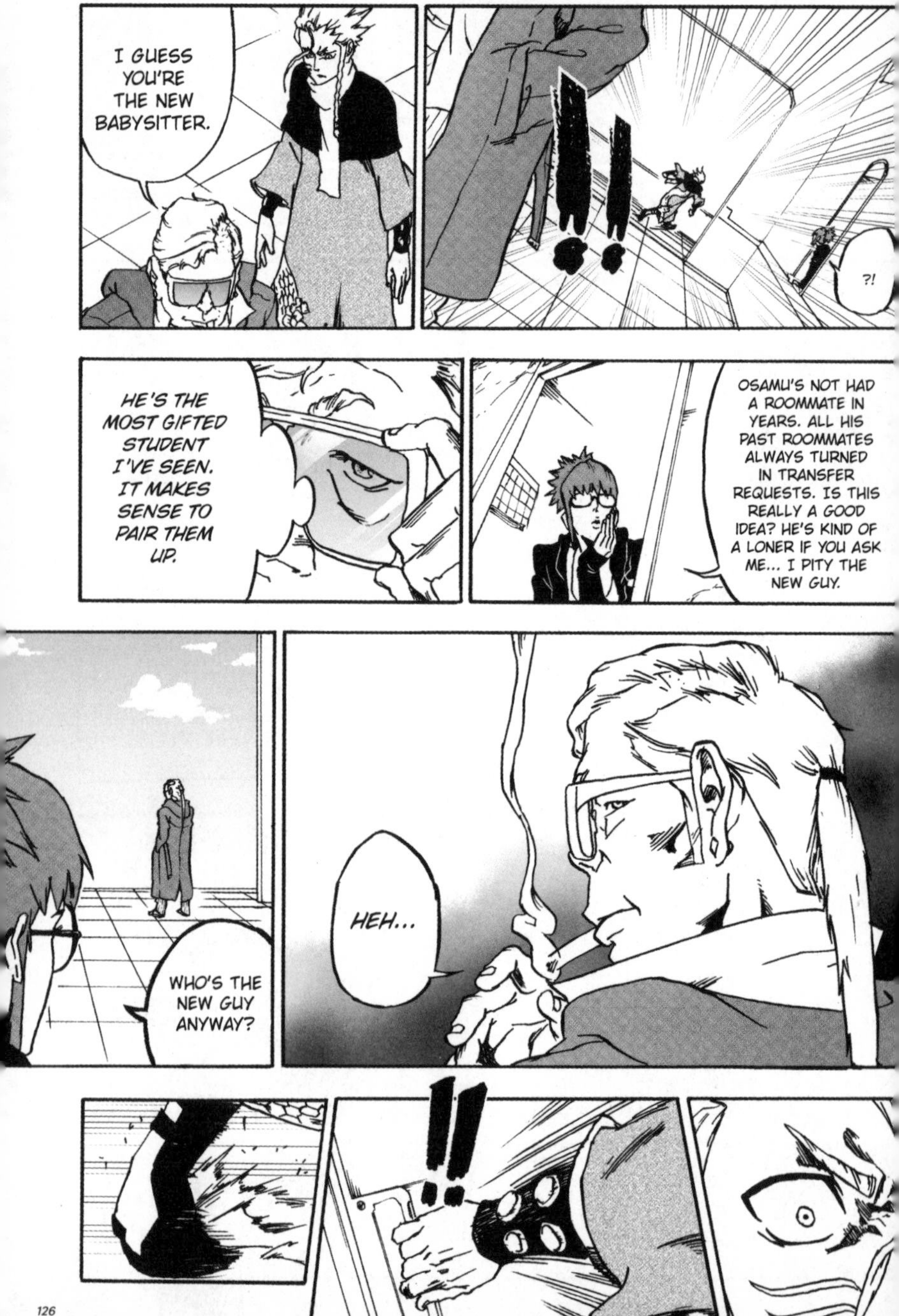
I GUESS YOU'RE THE NEW BABYSITTER.
?!
HE'S THE MOST GIFTED STUDENT I'VE SEEN. IT MAKES SENSE TO PAIR THEM UP.
OSAMU'S NOT HAD A ROOMMATE IN YEARS. ALL HIS PAST ROOMMATES ALWAYS TURNED IN TRANSFER REQUESTS. IS THIS REALLY A GOOD IDEA? HE'S KIND OF A LONER IF YOU ASK ME... I PITY THE NEW GUY.
WHO'S THE NEW GUY ANYWAY?
HEH...

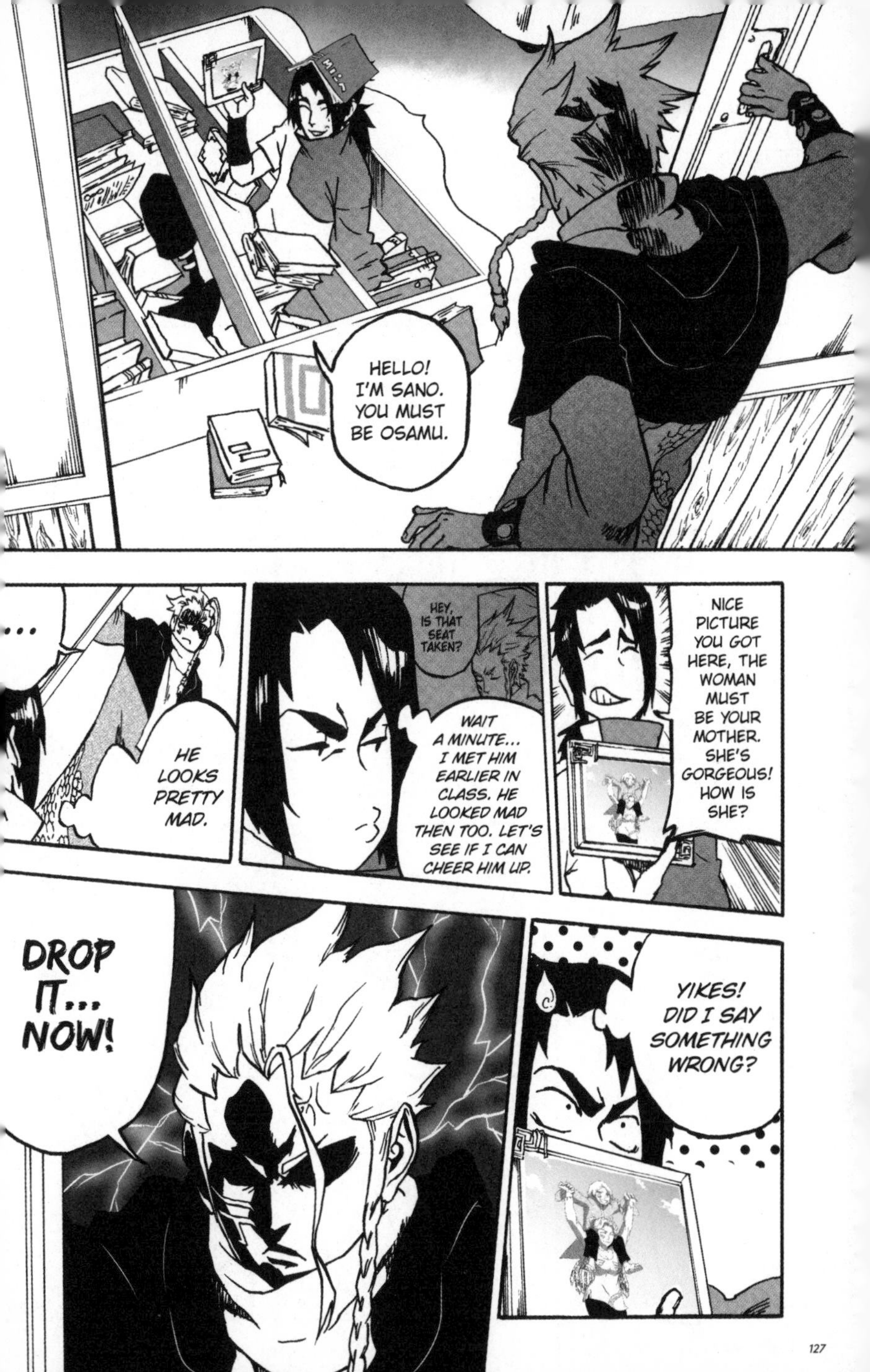
HELLO! I'M SANO. YOU MUST BE OSAMU.
...
HE LOOKS PRETTY MAD.
HEY, IS THAT SEAT TAKEN?
WAIT A MINUTE... I MET HIM EARLIER IN CLASS. HE LOOKED MAD THEN TOO. LET'S SEE IF I CAN CHEER HIM UP.
NICE PICTURE YOU GOT HERE, THE WOMAN MUST BE YOUR MOTHER. SHE'S GORGEOUS! HOW IS SHE?
DROP IT... NOW!
YIKES! DID I SAY SOMETHING WRONG?

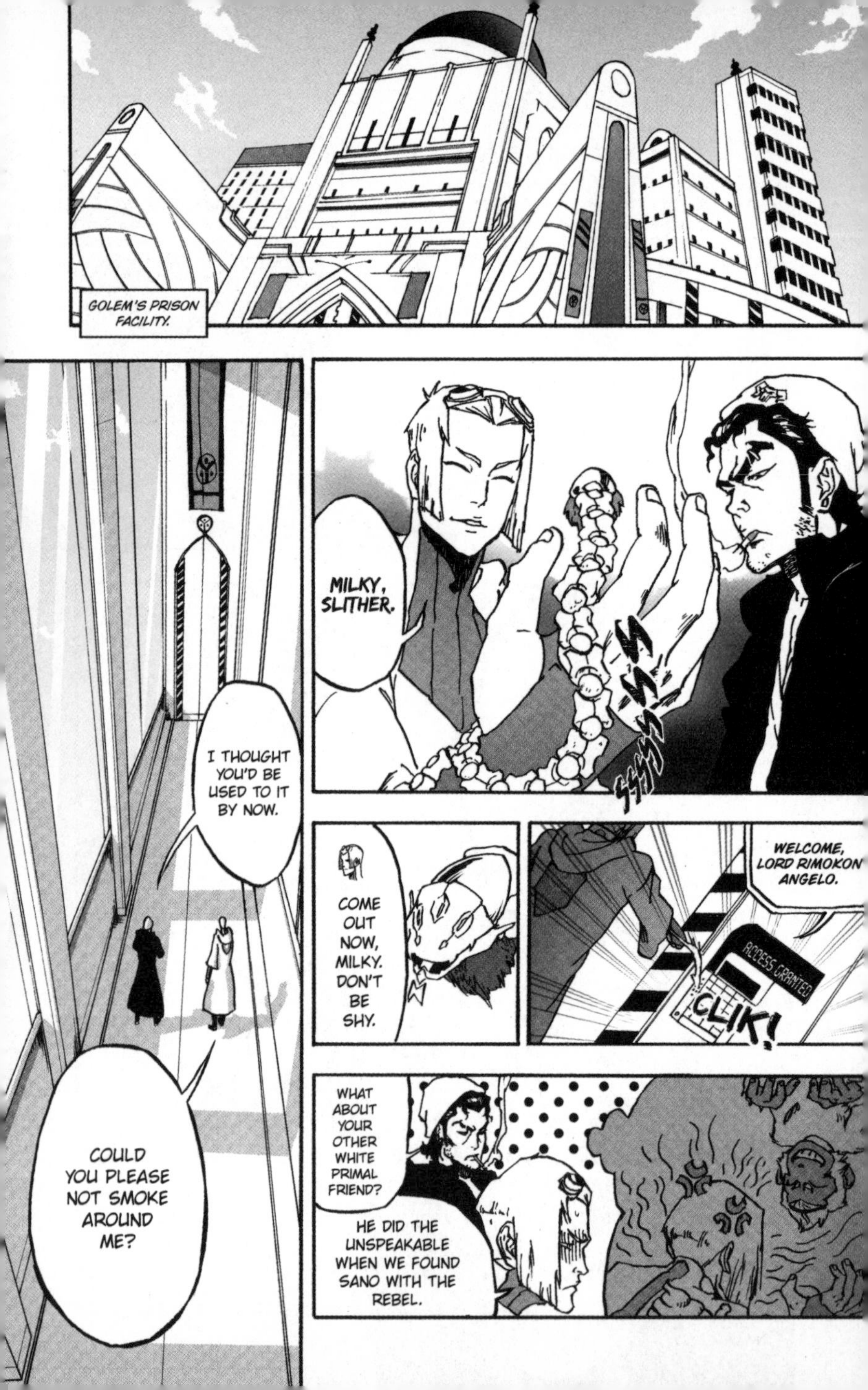
GOLEM'S PRISON FACILITY.
I THOUGHT YOU'D BE USED TO IT BY NOW.
COULD YOU PLEASE NOT SMOKE AROUND ME?
MILKY, SLITHER.
COME OUT NOW, MILKY. DON'T BE SHY.
WELCOME, LORD RIMOKON ANGELO.
ACCESS GRANTED
CLIK!
WHAT ABOUT YOUR OTHER WHITE PRIMAL FRIEND?
HE DID THE UNSPEAKABLE WHEN WE FOUND SANO WITH THE REBEL.

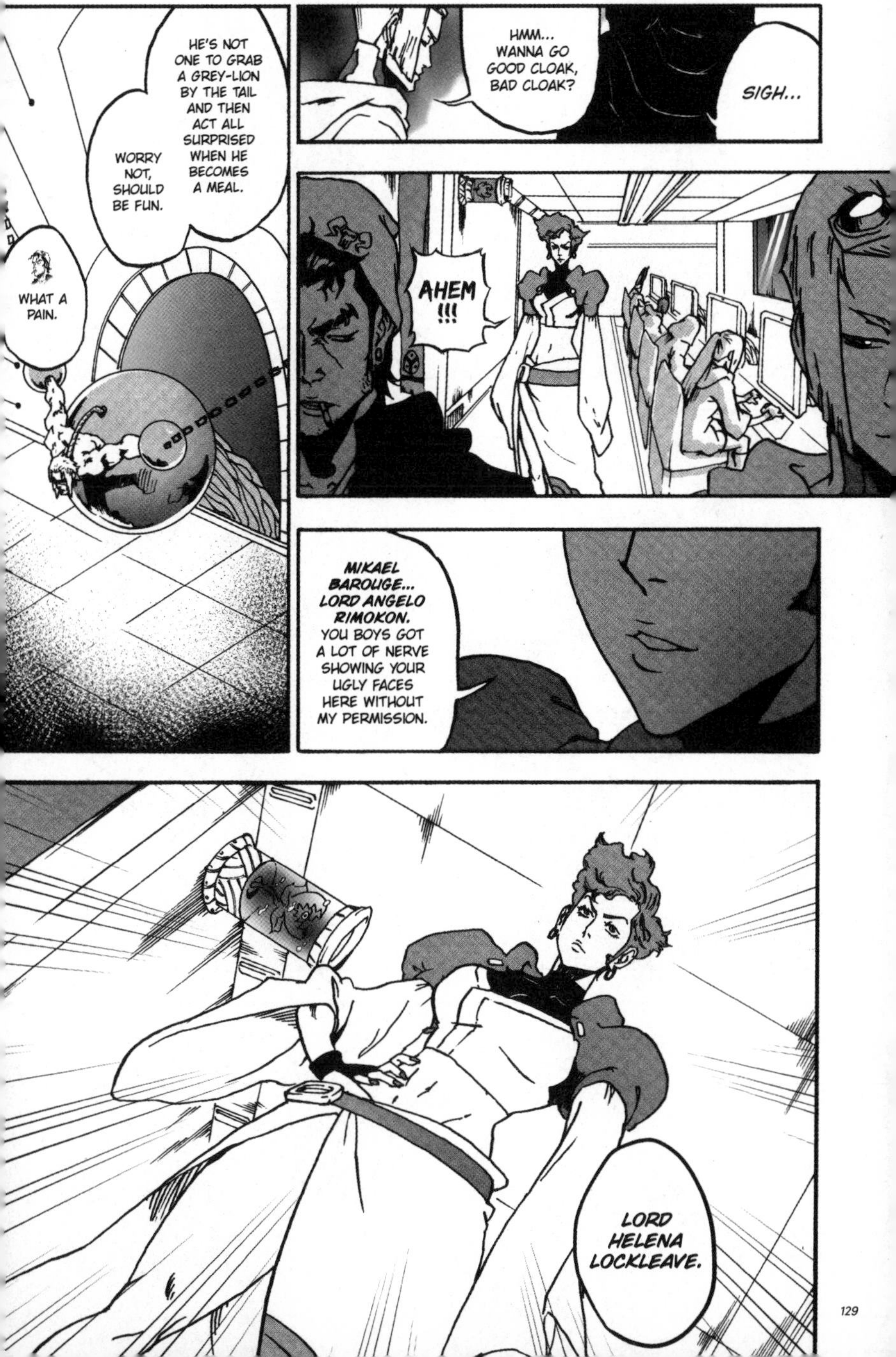
HE'S NOT ONE TO GRAB A GREY-LION BY THE TAIL AND THEN ACT ALL SURPRISED WHEN HE BECOMES A MEAL.
WORRY NOT, SHOULD BE FUN.
WHAT A PAIN.
HMM... WANNA GO GOOD CLOAK, BAD CLOAK?
SIGH...
AHEM !!!
MIKAEL BAROUGE... LORD ANGELO RIMOKON. YOU BOYS GOT A LOT OF NERVE SHOWING YOUR UGLY FACES HERE WITHOUT MY PERMISSION.
LORD HELENA LOCKLEAVE.

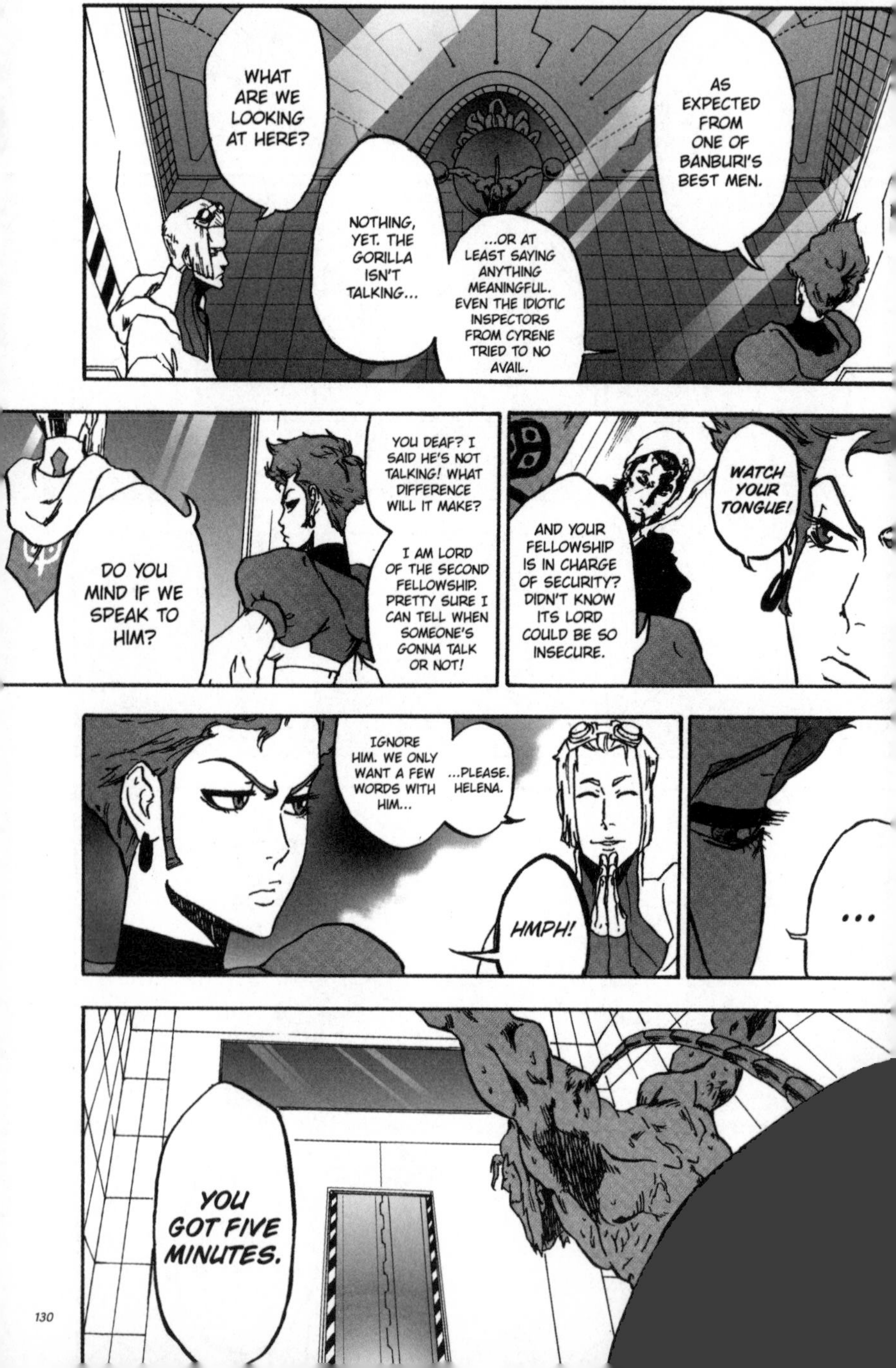
WHAT ARE WE LOOKING AT HERE?
NOTHING, YET. THE GORILLA ISN'T TALKING...
...OR AT LEAST SAYING ANYTHING MEANINGFUL. EVEN THE IDIOTIC INSPECTORS FROM CYRENE TRIED TO NO AVAIL.
AS EXPECTED FROM ONE OF BANBURI'S BEST MEN.
DO YOU MIND IF WE SPEAK TO HIM?
YOU DEAF? I SAID HE'S NOT TALKING! WHAT DIFFERENCE WILL IT MAKE?
I AM LORD OF THE SECOND FELLOWSHIP. PRETTY SURE I CAN TELL WHEN SOMEONE'S GONNA TALK OR NOT!
AND YOUR FELLOWSHIP IS IN CHARGE OF SECURITY? DIDN'T KNOW ITS LORD COULD BE SO INSECURE.
WATCH YOUR TONGUE!
IGNORE HIM. WE ONLY WANT A FEW WORDS WITH HIM...
...PLEASE. HELENA.
HMPH!
...
YOU GOT FIVE MINUTES.

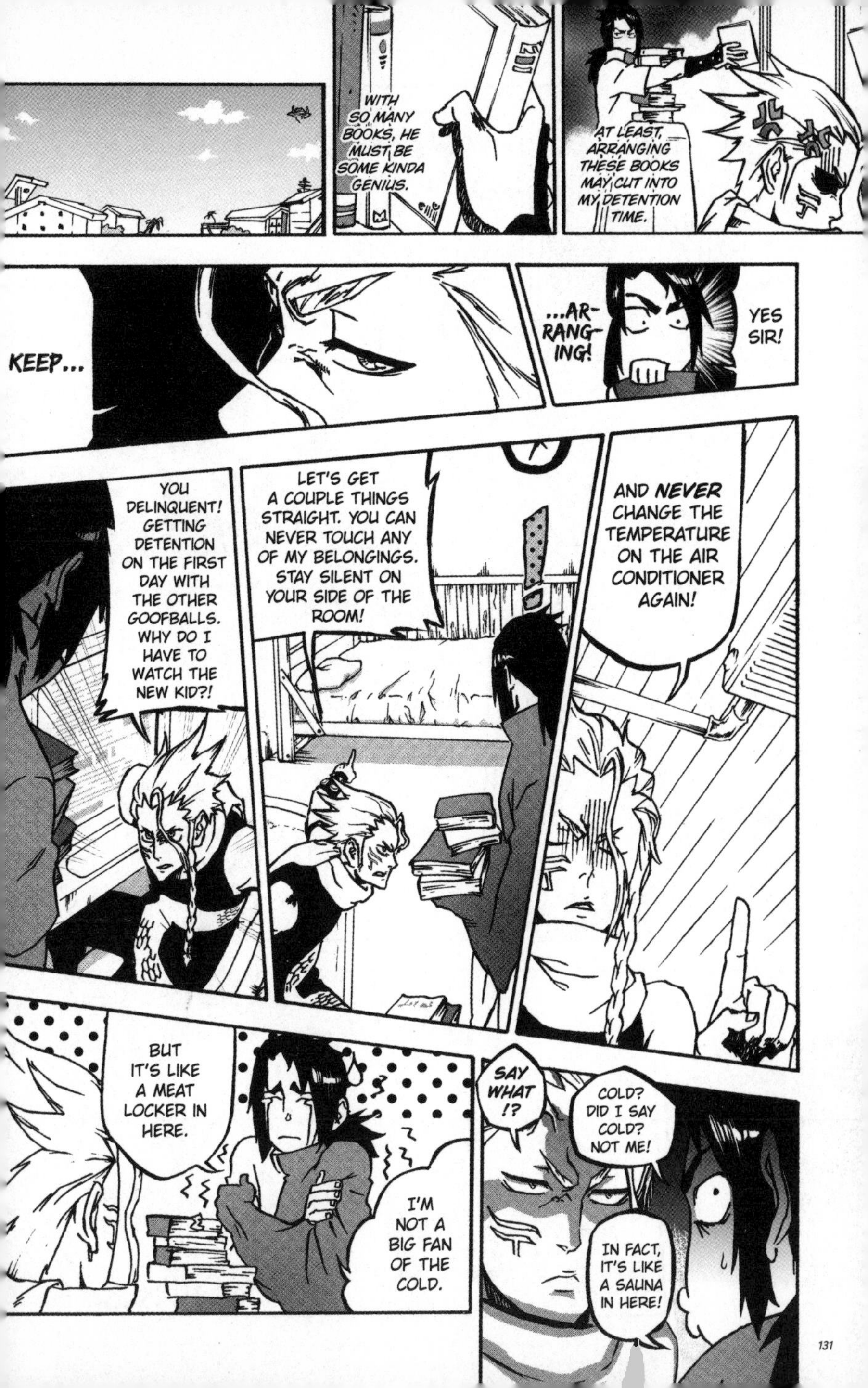
WITH SO MANY BOOKS, HE MUST BE SOME KINDA GENIUS.
AT LEAST, ARRANGING THESE BOOKS MAY CUT INTO MY DETENTION TIME.
KEEP...
...AR-RANG-ING!
YES SIR!
YOU DELINQUENT! GETTING DETENTION ON THE FIRST DAY WITH THE OTHER GOOFBALLS. WHY DO I HAVE TO WATCH THE NEW KID?!
LET'S GET A COUPLE THINGS STRAIGHT. YOU CAN NEVER TOUCH ANY OF MY BELONGINGS. STAY SILENT ON YOUR SIDE OF THE ROOM!
AND NEVER CHANGE THE TEMPERATURE ON THE AIR CONDITIONER AGAIN!
BUT IT'S LIKE A MEAT LOCKER IN HERE.
I'M NOT A BIG FAN OF THE COLD.
SAY WHAT!?
COLD? DID I SAY COLD? NOT ME!
IN FACT, IT'S LIKE A SAUNA IN HERE!

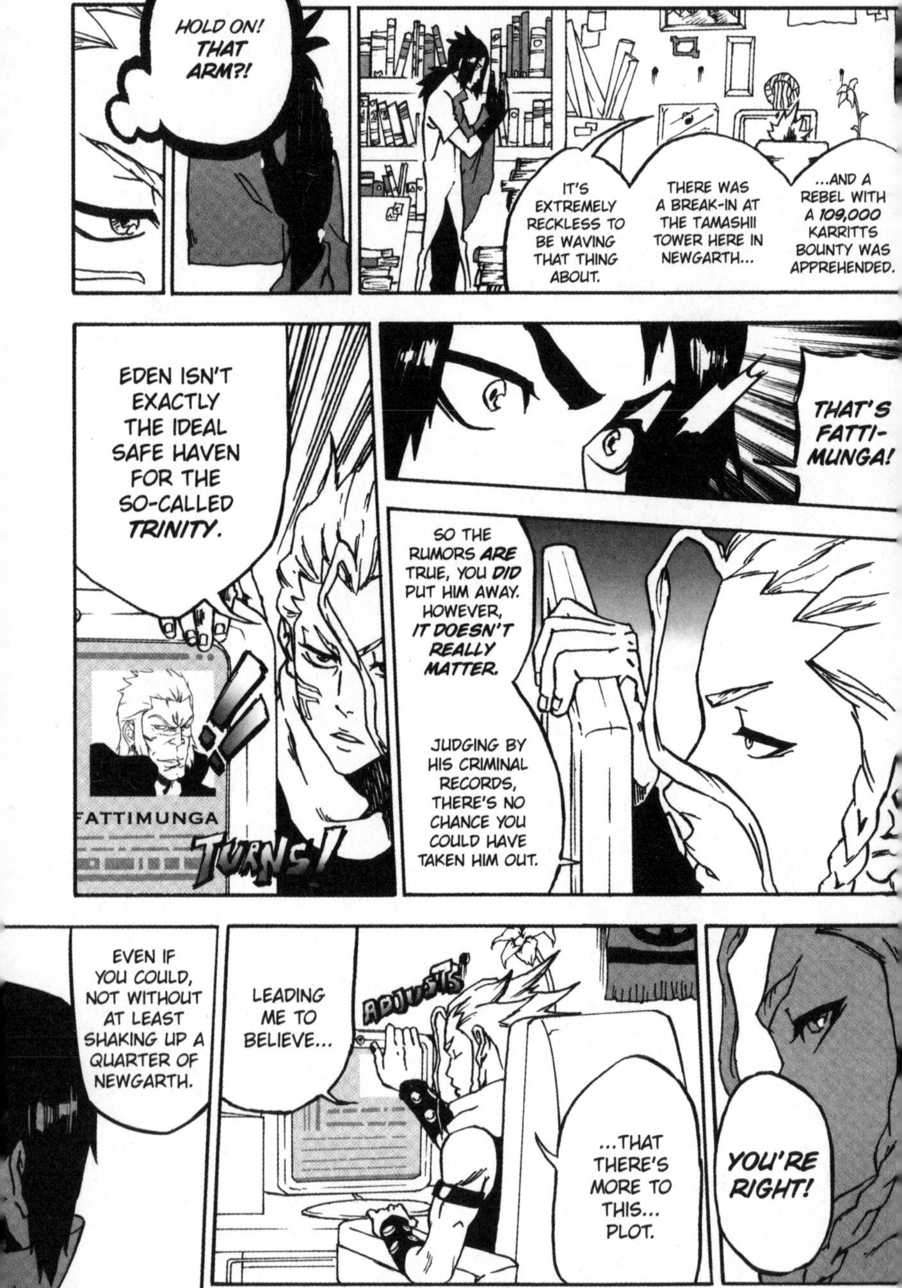
HOLD ON! THAT ARM?!
IT'S EXTREMELY RECKLESS TO BE WAVING THAT THING ABOUT.
THERE WAS A BREAK-IN AT THE TAMASHII TOWER HERE IN NEWGARTH...
...AND A REBEL WITH A 109,000 KARRITTS BOUNTY WAS APPREHENDED.
EDEN ISN'T EXACTLY THE IDEAL SAFE HAVEN FOR THE SO-CALLED TRINITY.
FATTIMUNGA
TURNS!
THAT'S FATTI-MUNGA!
SO THE RUMORS ARE TRUE, YOU DID PUT HIM AWAY. HOWEVER, IT DOESN'T REALLY MATTER.
JUDGING BY HIS CRIMINAL RECORDS, THERE'S NO CHANCE YOU COULD HAVE TAKEN HIM OUT.
EVEN IF YOU COULD, NOT WITHOUT AT LEAST SHAKING UP A QUARTER OF NEWGARTH.
LEADING ME TO BELIEVE...
ADJUSTS
...THAT THERE'S MORE TO THIS... PLOT.
YOU'RE RIGHT!

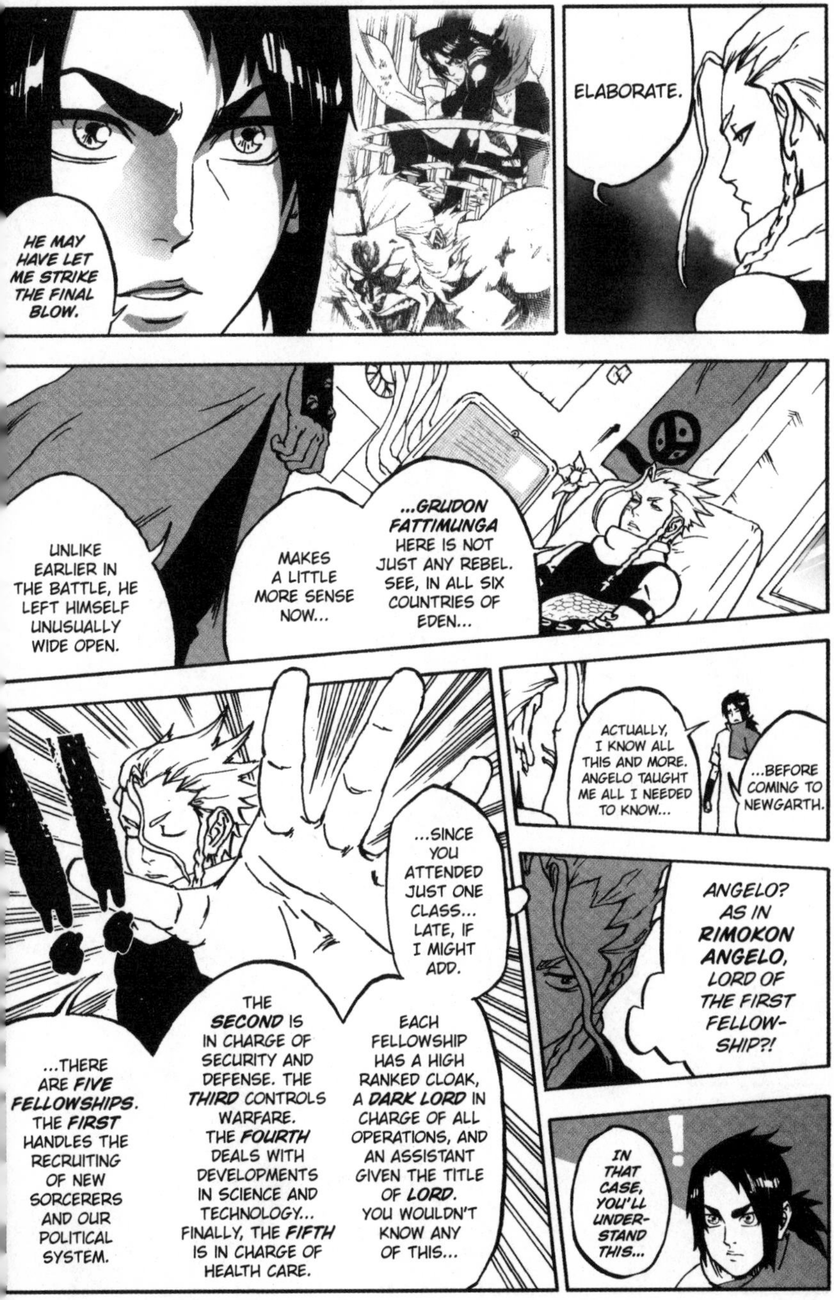
HE MAY HAVE LET ME STRIKE THE FINAL BLOW.
ELABORATE.
UNLIKE EARLIER IN THE BATTLE, HE LEFT HIMSELF UNUSUALLY WIDE OPEN.
MAKES A LITTLE MORE SENSE NOW...
...GRUDON FATTIMUNGA HERE IS NOT JUST ANY REBEL. SEE, IN ALL SIX COUNTRIES OF EDEN...
...SINCE YOU ATTENDED JUST ONE CLASS... LATE, IF I MIGHT ADD.
...THERE ARE FIVE FELLOWSHIPS. THE FIRST HANDLES THE RECRUITING OF NEW SORCERERS AND OUR POLITICAL SYSTEM.
THE SECOND IS IN CHARGE OF SECURITY AND DEFENSE. THE THIRD CONTROLS WARFARE. THE FOURTH DEALS WITH DEVELOPMENTS IN SCIENCE AND TECHNOLOGY... FINALLY, THE FIFTH IS IN CHARGE OF HEALTH CARE.
EACH FELLOWSHIP HAS A HIGH RANKED CLOAK, A DARK LORD IN CHARGE OF ALL OPERATIONS, AND AN ASSISTANT GIVEN THE TITLE OF LORD. YOU WOULDN'T KNOW ANY OF THIS...
ACTUALLY, I KNOW ALL THIS AND MORE. ANGELO TAUGHT ME ALL I NEEDED TO KNOW...
...BEFORE COMING TO NEWGARTH.
ANGELO? AS IN RIMOKON ANGELO, LORD OF THE FIRST FELLOWSHIP?!
!
IN THAT CASE, YOU'LL UNDERSTAND THIS...

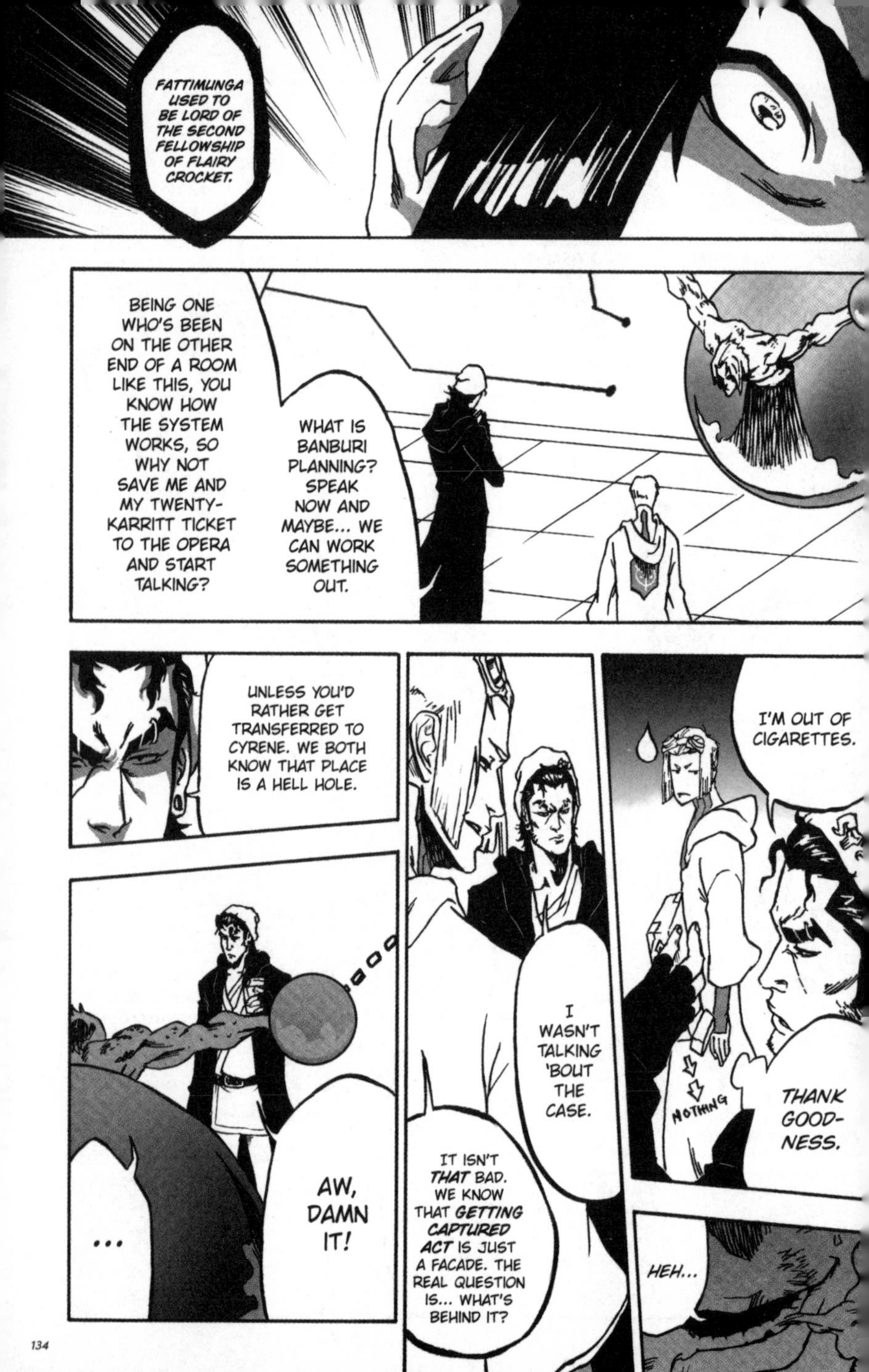
FATTIMUNGA USED TO BE LORD OF THE SECOND FELLOWSHIP OF FLAIRY CROCKET.
BEING ONE WHO'S BEEN ON THE OTHER END OF A ROOM LIKE THIS, YOU KNOW HOW THE SYSTEM WORKS, SO WHY NOT SAVE ME AND MY TWENTY-KARRITT TICKET TO THE OPERA AND START TALKING?
WHAT IS BANBURI PLANNING? SPEAK NOW AND MAYBE... WE CAN WORK SOMETHING OUT.
UNLESS YOU'D RATHER GET TRANSFERRED TO CYRENE. WE BOTH KNOW THAT PLACE IS A HELL HOLE.
...
AW, DAMN IT!
IT ISN'T THAT BAD. WE KNOW THAT GETTING CAPTURED ACT IS JUST A FACADE. THE REAL QUESTION IS... WHAT'S BEHIND IT?
I WASN'T TALKING 'BOUT THE CASE.
I'M OUT OF CIGARETTES.
NOTHING
THANK GOODNESS.
HEH...

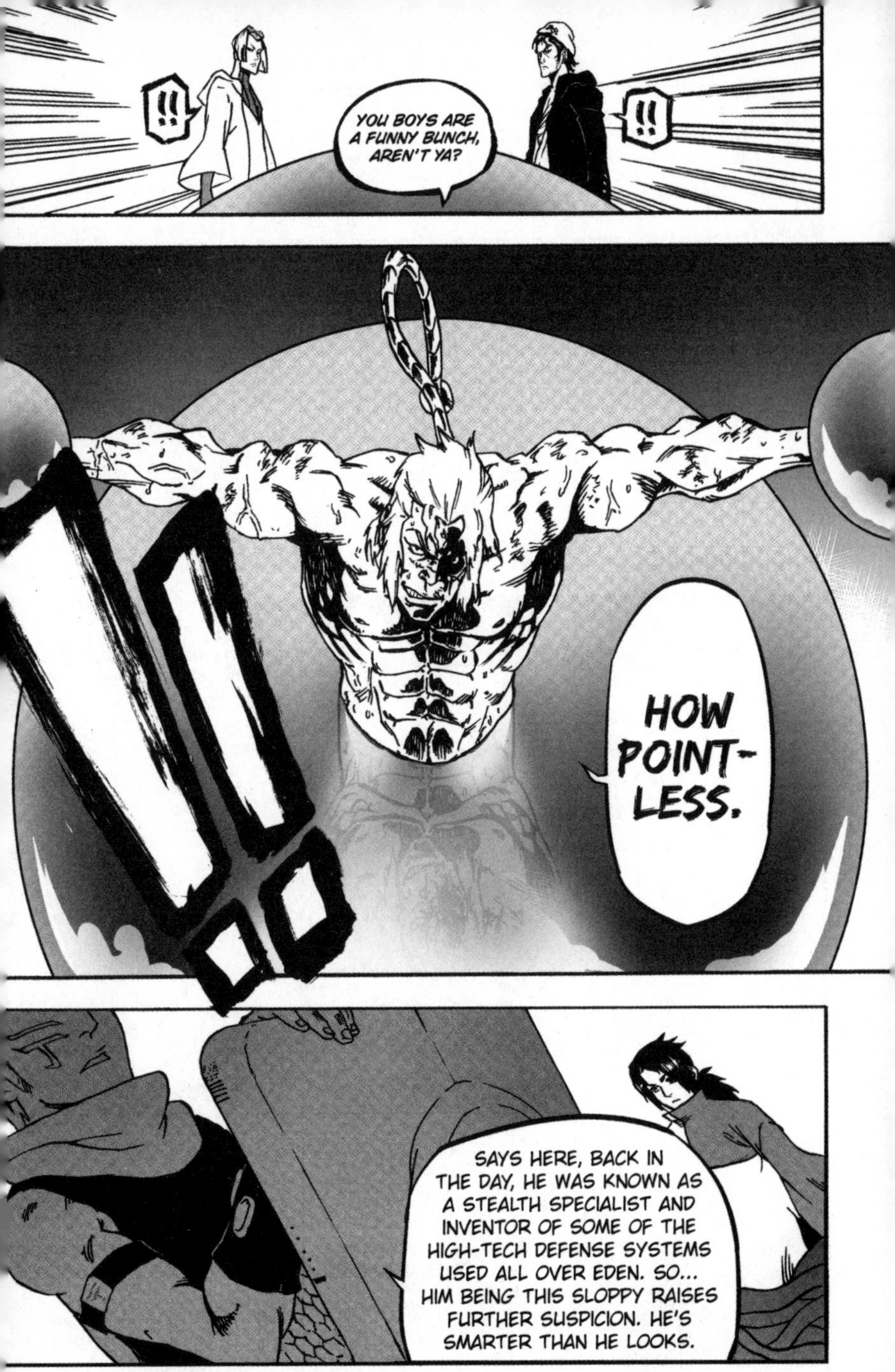
!!
YOU BOYS ARE A FUNNY BUNCH, AREN'T YA?
!!
HOW POINT-LESS.
SAYS HERE, BACK IN THE DAY, HE WAS KNOWN AS A STEALTH SPECIALIST AND INVENTOR OF SOME OF THE HIGH-TECH DEFENSE SYSTEMS USED ALL OVER EDEN. SO... HIM BEING THIS SLOPPY RAISES FURTHER SUSPICION. HE'S SMARTER THAN HE LOOKS.

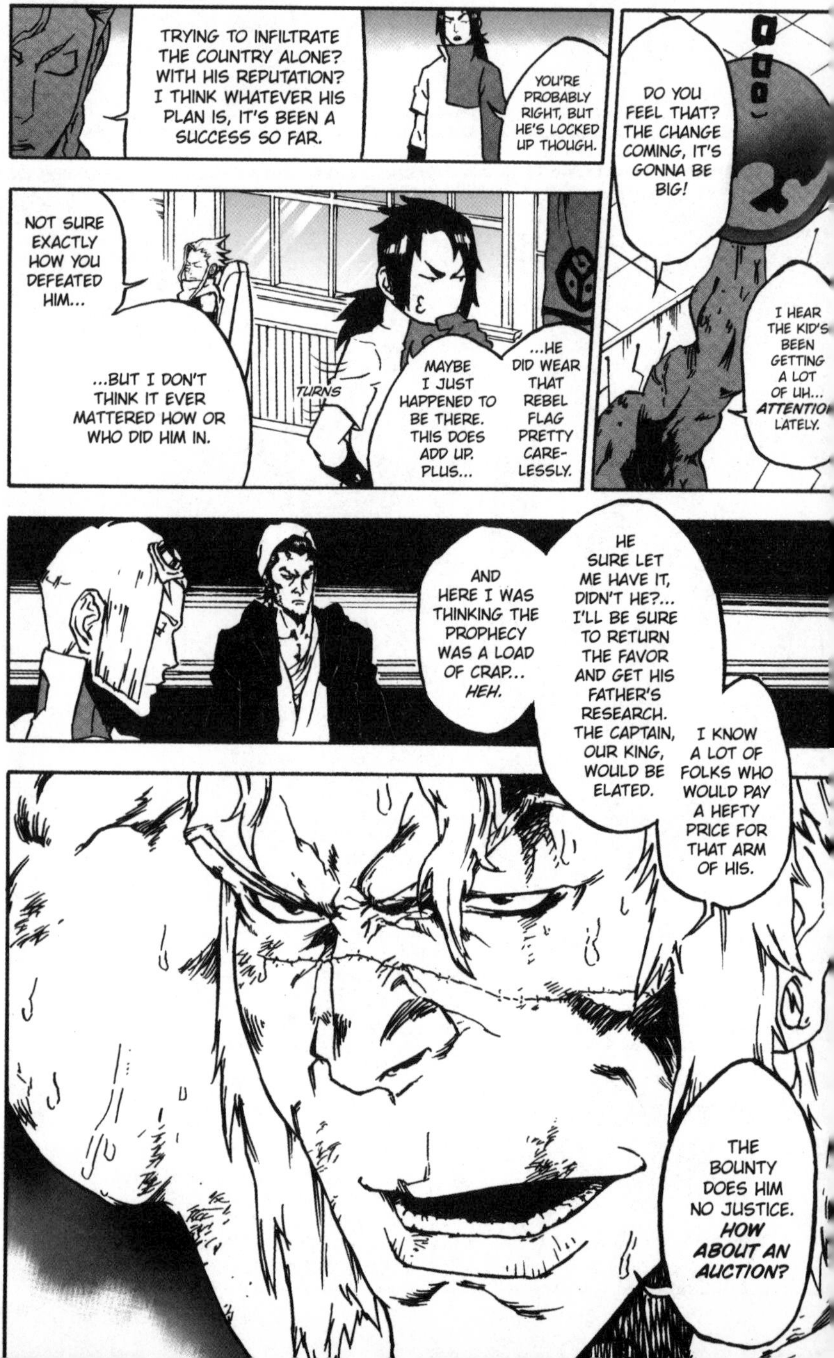

TRYING TO INFILTRATE THE COUNTRY ALONE? WITH HIS REPUTATION? I THINK WHATEVER HIS PLAN IS, IT'S BEEN A SUCCESS SO FAR.
YOU'RE PROBABLY RIGHT, BUT HE'S LOCKED UP THOUGH.
NOT SURE EXACTLY HOW YOU DEFEATED HIM...
...BUT I DON'T THINK IT EVER MATTERED HOW OR WHO DID HIM IN.
TURNS
MAYBE I JUST HAPPENED TO BE THERE. THIS DOES ADD UP. PLUS...
...HE DID WEAR THAT REBEL FLAG PRETTY CARE-LESSLY.
DO YOU FEEL THAT? THE CHANGE COMING, IT'S GONNA BE BIG!
I HEAR THE KID'S BEEN GETTING A LOT OF UH... ATTENTIO LATELY.
AND HERE I WAS THINKING THE PROPHECY WAS A LOAD OF CRAP... HEH.
HE SURE LET ME HAVE IT, DIDN'T HE?... I'LL BE SURE TO RETURN THE FAVOR AND GET HIS FATHER'S RESEARCH. THE CAPTAIN, OUR KING, WOULD BE ELATED.
I KNOW A LOT OF FOLKS WHO WOULD PAY A HEFTY PRICE FOR THAT ARM OF HIS.
THE BOUNTY DOES HIM NO JUSTICE. HOW ABOUT AN AUCTION?

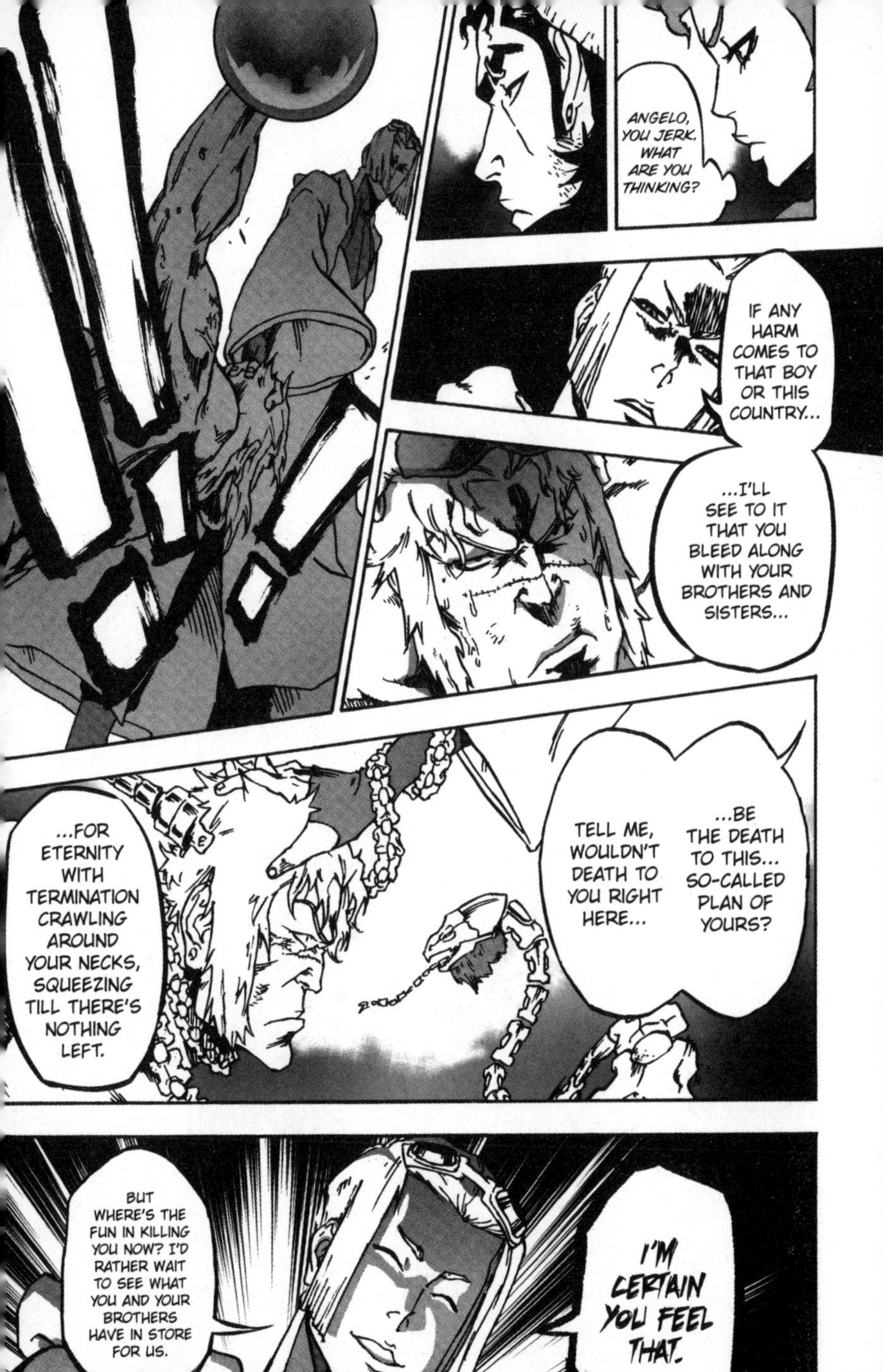

ANGELO, YOU JERK. WHAT ARE YOU THINKING?
IF ANY HARM COMES TO THAT BOY OR THIS COUNTRY...
...I'LL SEE TO IT THAT YOU BLEED ALONG WITH YOUR BROTHERS AND SISTERS...
...FOR ETERNITY WITH TERMINATION CRAWLING AROUND YOUR NECKS, SQUEEZING TILL THERE'S NOTHING LEFT.
TELL ME, WOULDN'T DEATH TO YOU RIGHT HERE...
...BE THE DEATH TO THIS... SO-CALLED PLAN OF YOURS?
BUT WHERE'S THE FUN IN KILLING YOU NOW? I'D RATHER WAIT TO SEE WHAT YOU AND YOUR BROTHERS HAVE IN STORE FOR US.
I'M CERTAIN YOU FEEL THAT.

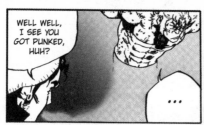

WELL WELL, I SEE YOU GOT PUNKED, HUH?

...

WE'RE DONE HERE.

AND I THOUGHT I'D BE PLAYING BAD CLOAK.

I MUST ADMIT...

...FOR SOMEONE AS WORTHLESS AS YOURSELF...

...YOU'RE NOT TOO STUPID.

THANKS!

YOU'RE NOT AS SCARY AS THE OTHERS. WE'LL GET ALONG JUST FINE!

I'M SORRY ABOUT YOUR MOM. I HAD NO IDEA.

HOW DID YOU-?

TAP! TAP!

NOW, TO TELL ANGELO ALL THIS. HE'S PROBABLY FIGURED THE WHOLE THING OUT.

NOT TO MENTION MIKAEL, NOT AN EASY READ BY ANY MEANS, BUT SEEMS EXTREMELY SMART AS WELL.

SANO... AREN'T YOU FORGETTING SOMETHING?

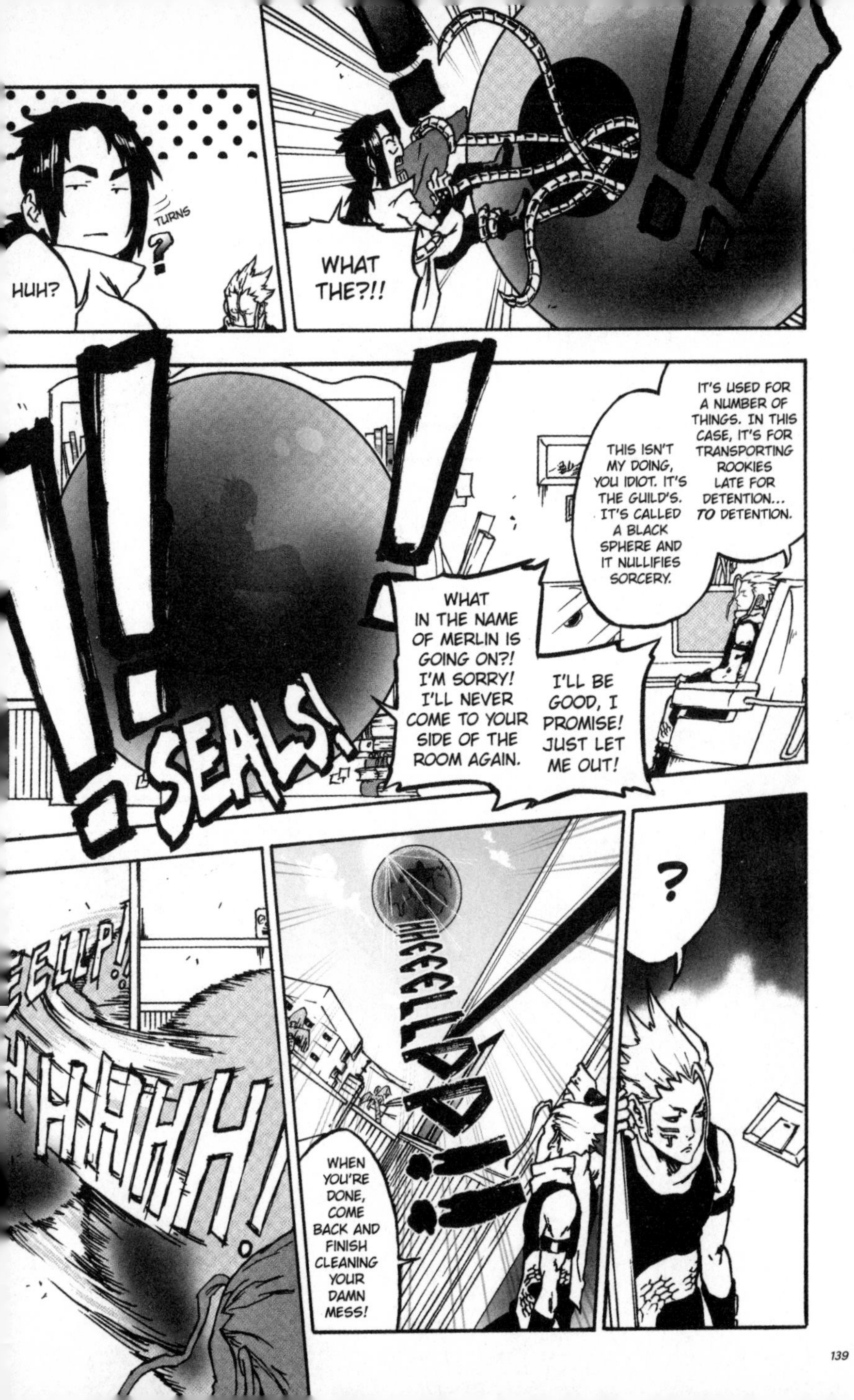
TURNS
?
HUH?
WHAT THE?!!
SEALS!
WHAT IN THE NAME OF MERLIN IS GOING ON?! I'M SORRY! I'LL NEVER COME TO YOUR SIDE OF THE ROOM AGAIN.
I'LL BE GOOD, I PROMISE! JUST LET ME OUT!
THIS ISN'T MY DOING, YOU IDIOT. IT'S THE GUILD'S. IT'S CALLED A BLACK SPHERE AND IT NULLIFIES SORCERY.
IT'S USED FOR A NUMBER OF THINGS. IN THIS CASE, IT'S FOR TRANSPORTING ROOKIES LATE FOR DETENTION... *TO* DETENTION.
HHEEELLLP!!
WHEN YOU'RE DONE, COME BACK AND FINISH CLEANING YOUR DAMN MESS!
?

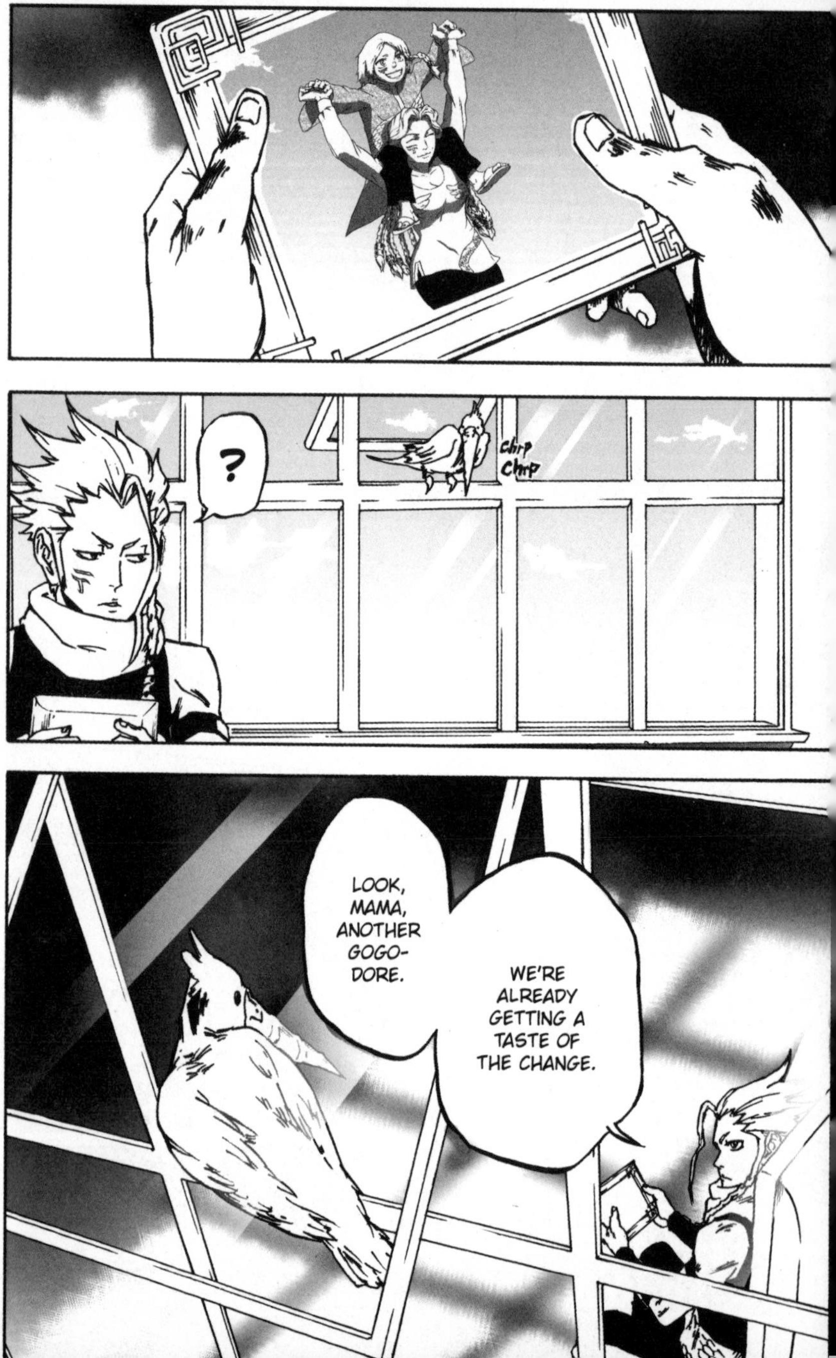
?
Chirp
Chirp
LOOK, MAMA, ANOTHER GOGO-DORE.
WE'RE ALREADY GETTING A TASTE OF THE CHANGE.

# APPLE BLACK

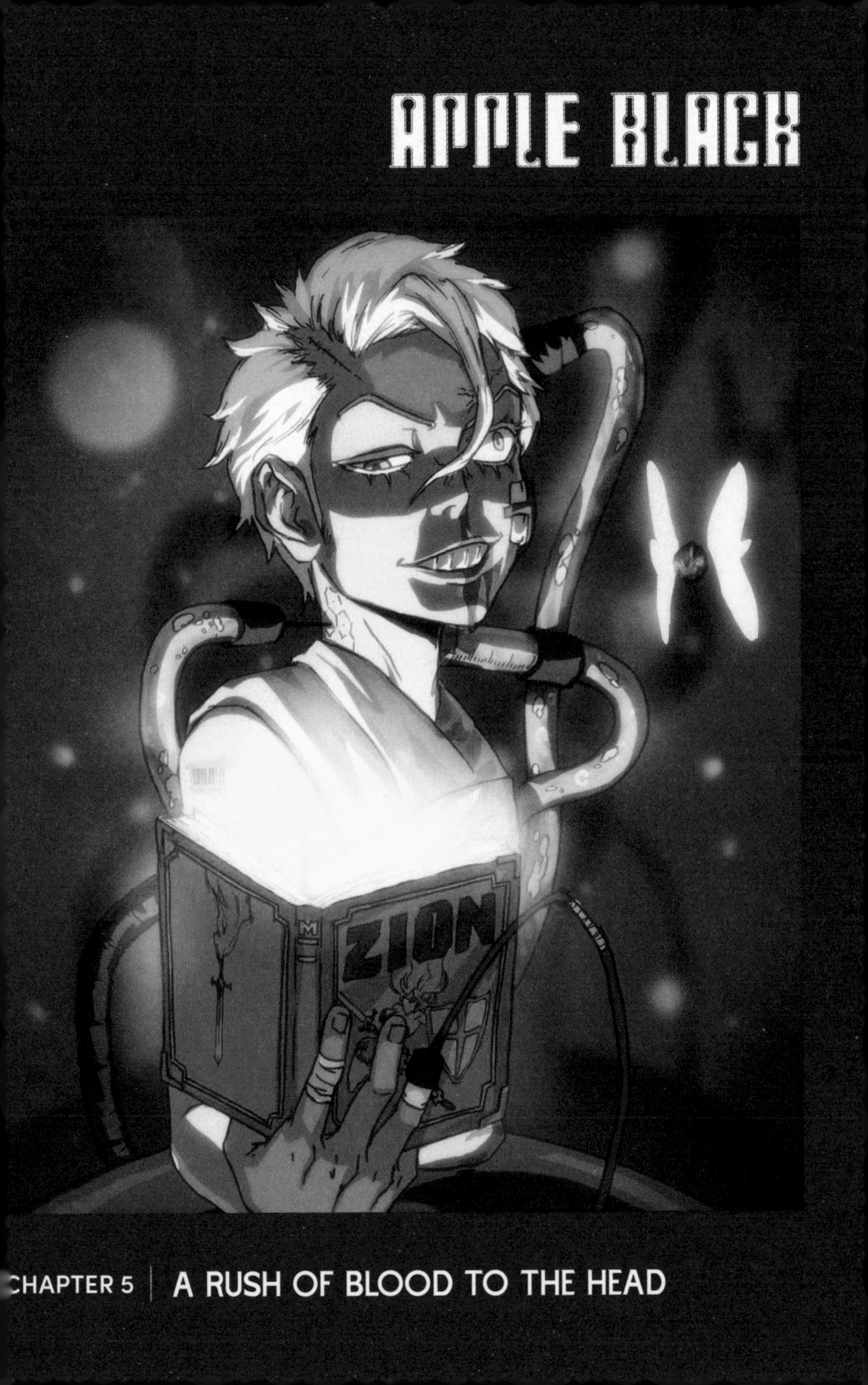

ZION


## CHAPTER 5 | A RUSH OF BLOOD TO THE HEAD

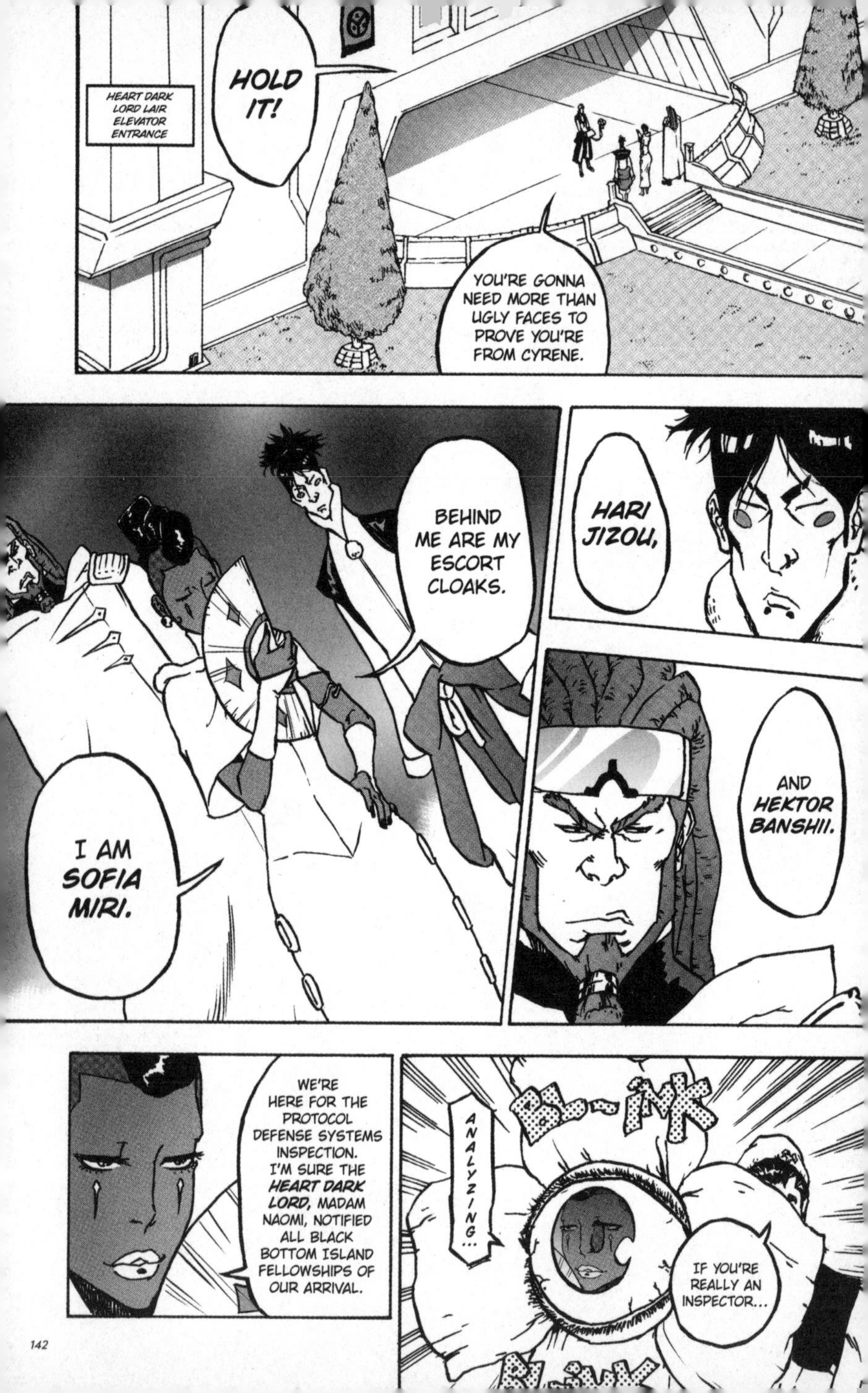

HEART DARK LORD LAIR ELEVATOR ENTRANCE
HOLD IT!
YOU'RE GONNA NEED MORE THAN UGLY FACES TO PROVE YOU'RE FROM CYRENE.
BEHIND ME ARE MY ESCORT CLOAKS.
I AM SOFIA MIRI.
HARI JIZOU,
AND HEKTOR BANSHII.
WE'RE HERE FOR THE PROTOCOL DEFENSE SYSTEMS INSPECTION. I'M SURE THE HEART DARK LORD, MADAM NAOMI, NOTIFIED ALL BLACK BOTTOM ISLAND FELLOWSHIPS OF OUR ARRIVAL.
BL-INK
ANALYZING...
IF YOU'RE REALLY AN INSPECTOR...

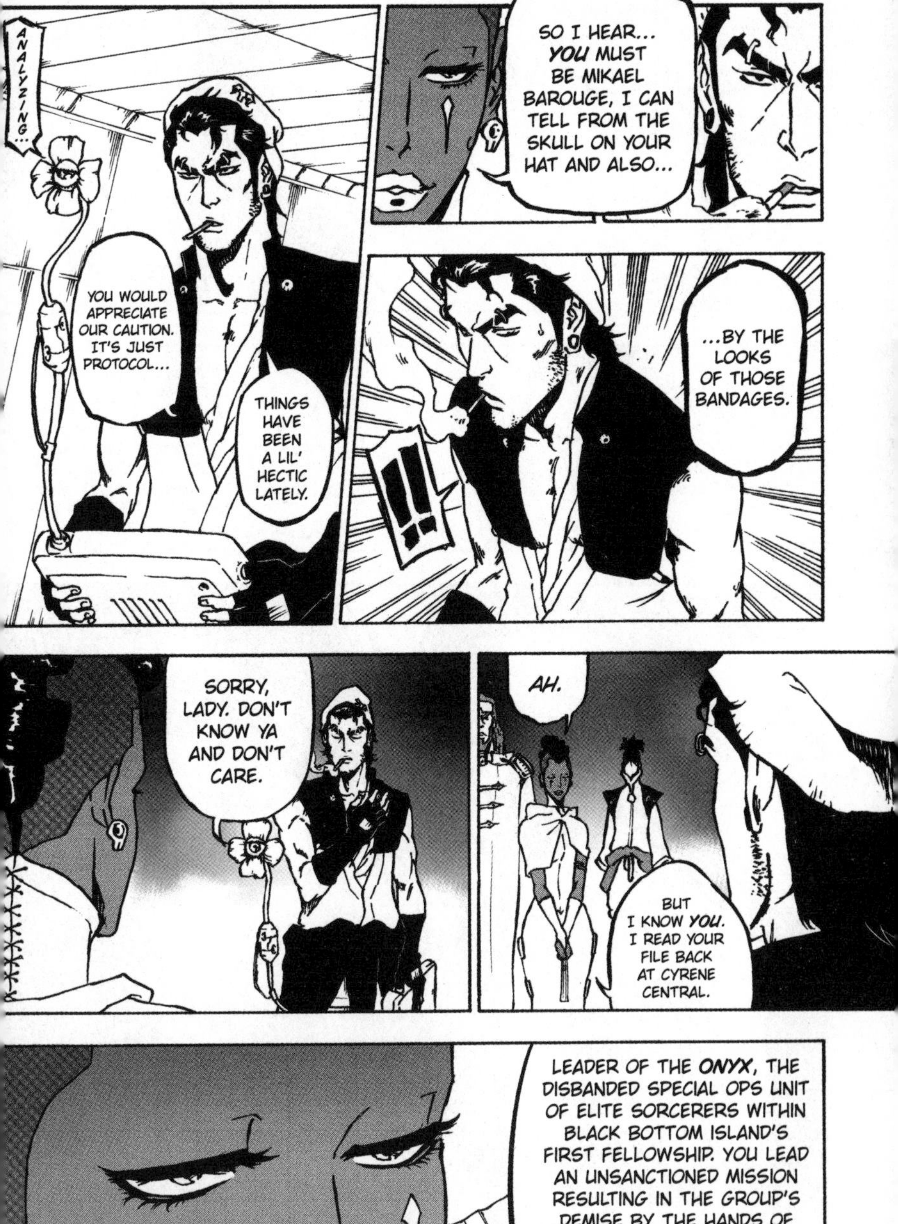
ANALYZING...
YOU WOULD APPRECIATE OUR CAUTION. IT'S JUST PROTOCOL...
THINGS HAVE BEEN A LIL' HECTIC LATELY.
SO I HEAR... *YOU* MUST BE MIKAEL BAROUGE, I CAN TELL FROM THE SKULL ON YOUR HAT AND ALSO...
...BY THE LOOKS OF THOSE BANDAGES.
!!
SORRY, LADY. DON'T KNOW YA AND DON'T CARE.
AH.
BUT I KNOW *YOU*. I READ YOUR FILE BACK AT CYRENE CENTRAL.
LEADER OF THE *ONYX*, THE DISBANDED SPECIAL OPS UNIT OF ELITE SORCERERS WITHIN BLACK BOTTOM ISLAND'S FIRST FELLOWSHIP. YOU LEAD AN UNSANCTIONED MISSION RESULTING IN THE GROUP'S DEMISE BY THE HANDS OF THE SECRET ORGANIZATION AGAINST EDEN... *GHOST.*

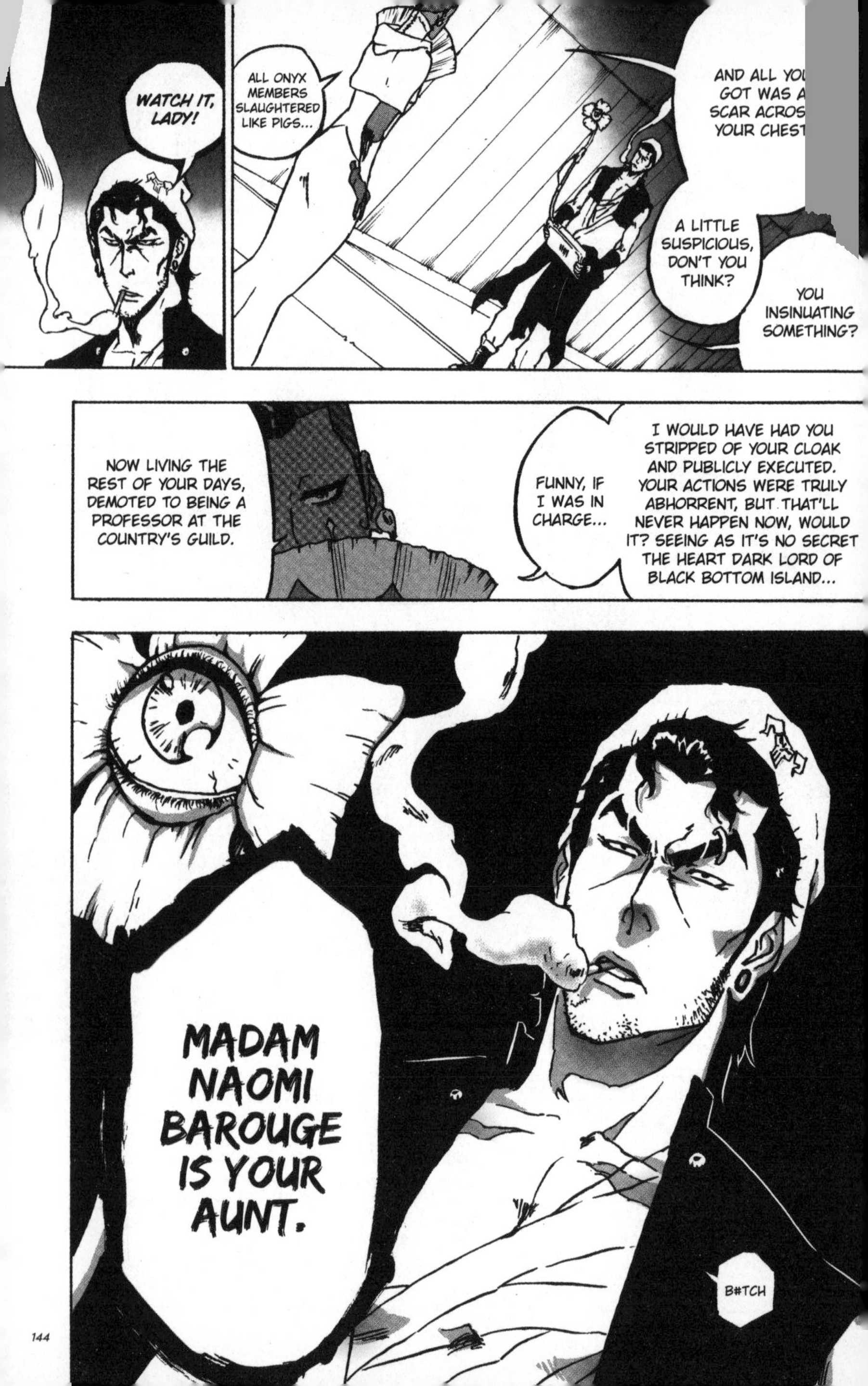
WATCH IT, LADY!
ALL ONYX MEMBERS SLAUGHTERED LIKE PIGS...
AND ALL YOU GOT WAS A SCAR ACROS YOUR CHEST
A LITTLE SUSPICIOUS, DON'T YOU THINK?
YOU INSINUATING SOMETHING?
NOW LIVING THE REST OF YOUR DAYS, DEMOTED TO BEING A PROFESSOR AT THE COUNTRY'S GUILD.
FUNNY, IF I WAS IN CHARGE...
I WOULD HAVE HAD YOU STRIPPED OF YOUR CLOAK AND PUBLICLY EXECUTED. YOUR ACTIONS WERE TRULY ABHORRENT, BUT THAT'LL NEVER HAPPEN NOW, WOULD IT? SEEING AS IT'S NO SECRET THE HEART DARK LORD OF BLACK BOTTOM ISLAND...
MADAM NAOMI BAROUGE IS YOUR AUNT.
B#TCH

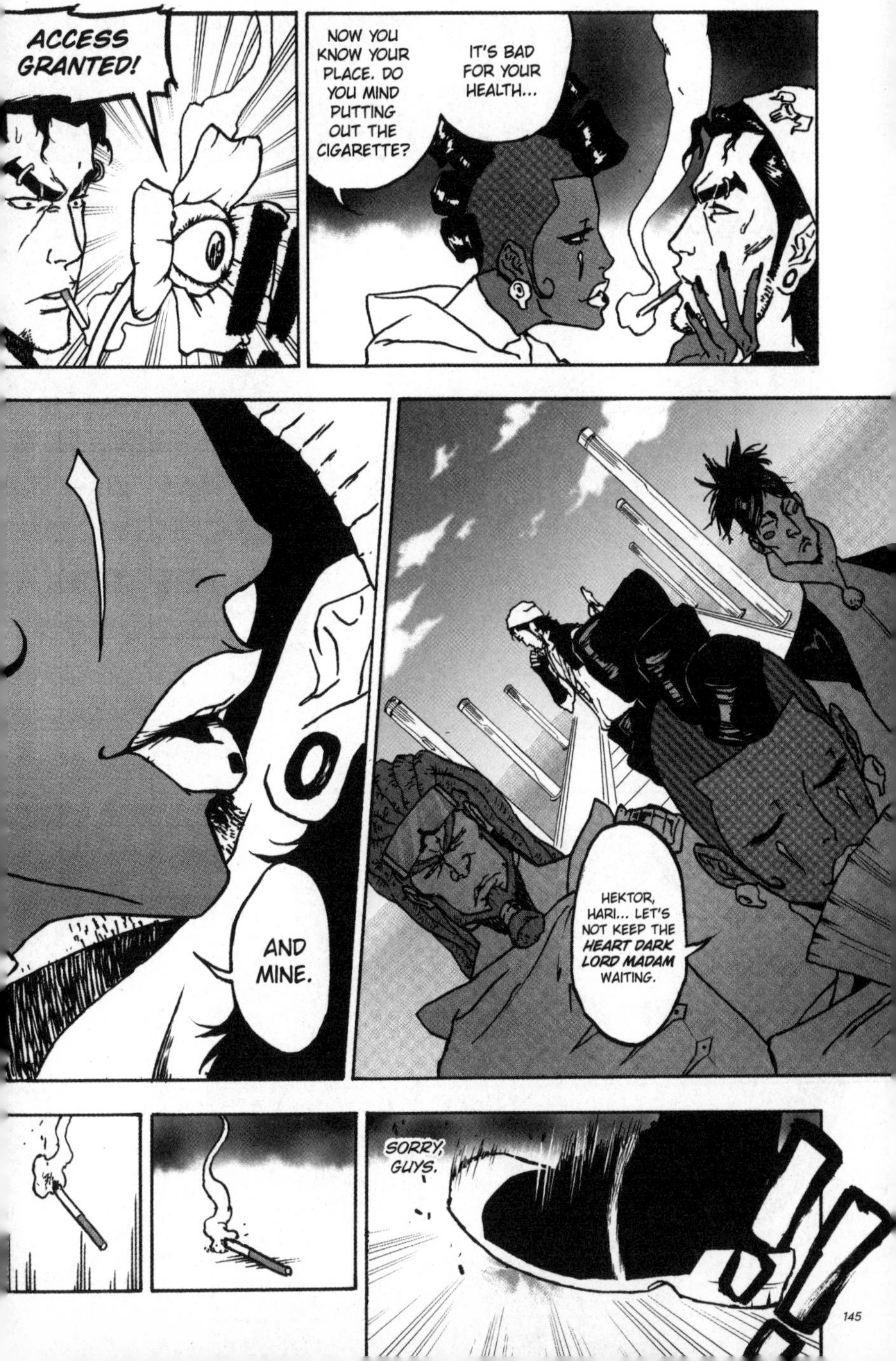
ACCESS GRANTED!
NOW YOU KNOW YOUR PLACE. DO YOU MIND PUTTING OUT THE CIGARETTE?
IT'S BAD FOR YOUR HEALTH...
AND MINE.
HEKTOR, HARI... LET'S NOT KEEP THE HEART DARK LORD MADAM WAITING.
SORRY, GUYS.

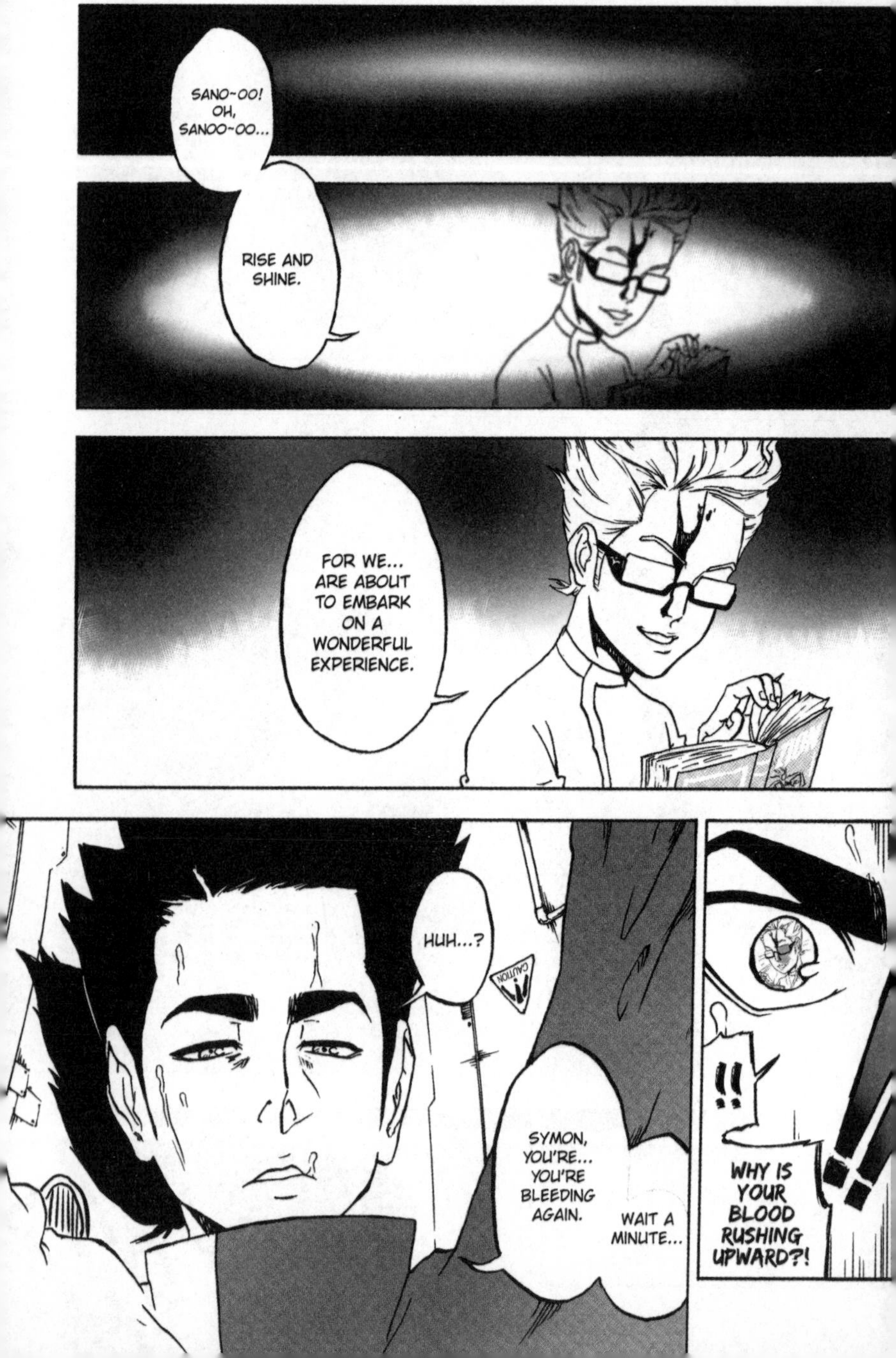
SANO~OO! OH, SANOO~OO...
RISE AND SHINE.
FOR WE... ARE ABOUT TO EMBARK ON A WONDERFUL EXPERIENCE.
HUH...?
CAUTION
SYMON, YOU'RE... YOU'RE BLEEDING AGAIN.
WAIT A MINUTE...
!!
WHY IS YOUR BLOOD RUSHING UPWARD?!

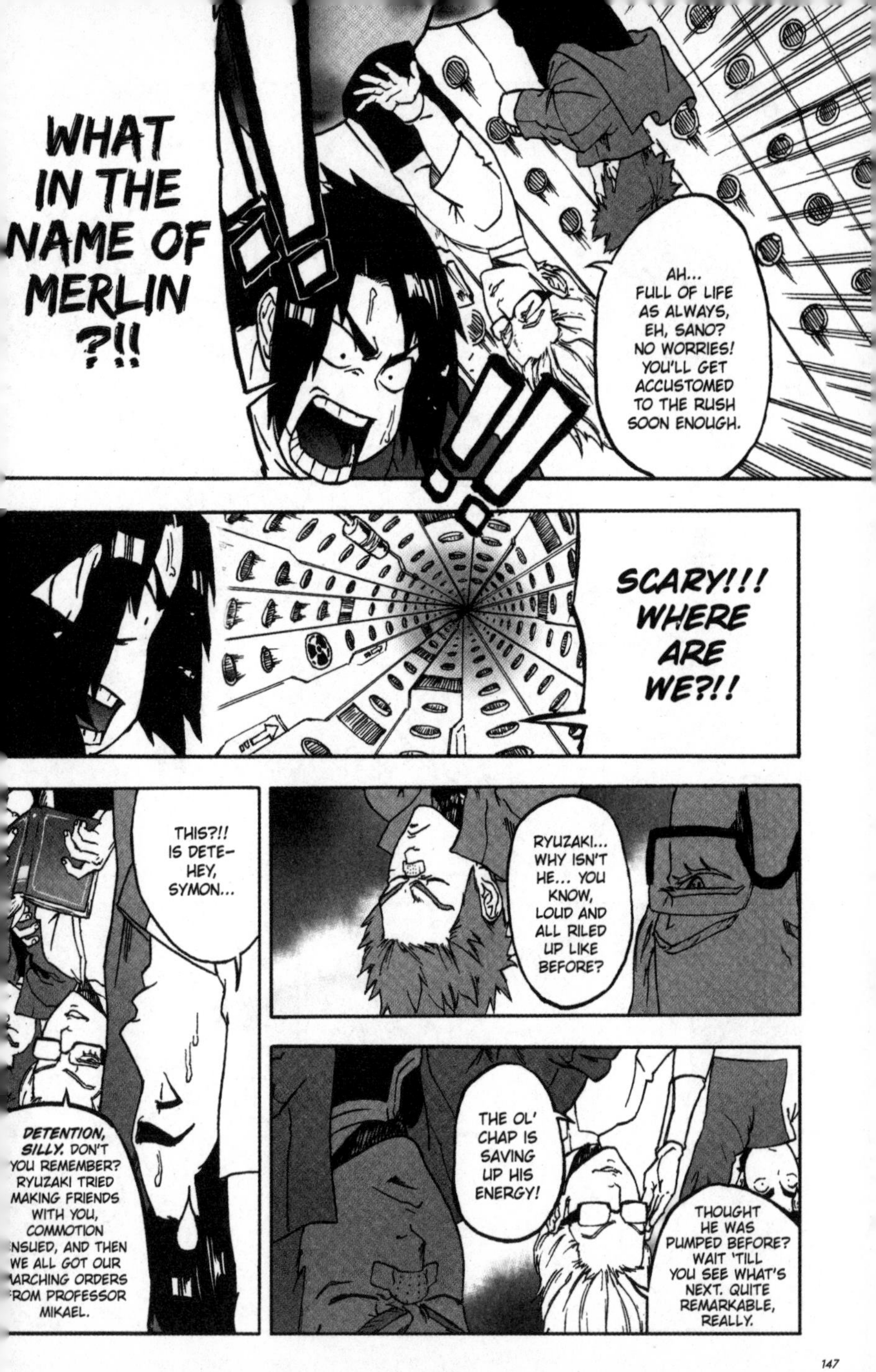
WHAT IN THE NAME OF MERLIN ?!!
AH... FULL OF LIFE AS ALWAYS, EH, SANO? NO WORRIES! YOU'LL GET ACCUSTOMED TO THE RUSH SOON ENOUGH.
SCARY!!! WHERE ARE WE?!!
THIS?!! IS DETE- HEY, SYMON...
***DETENTION, SILLY.*** DON'T YOU REMEMBER? RYUZAKI TRIED MAKING FRIENDS WITH YOU, COMMOTION ENSUED, AND THEN WE ALL GOT OUR MARCHING ORDERS FROM PROFESSOR MIKAEL.
RYUZAKI... WHY ISN'T HE... YOU KNOW, LOUD AND ALL RILED UP LIKE BEFORE?
THE OL' CHAP IS SAVING UP HIS ENERGY!
THOUGHT HE WAS PUMPED BEFORE? WAIT 'TILL YOU SEE WHAT'S NEXT. QUITE REMARKABLE, REALLY.

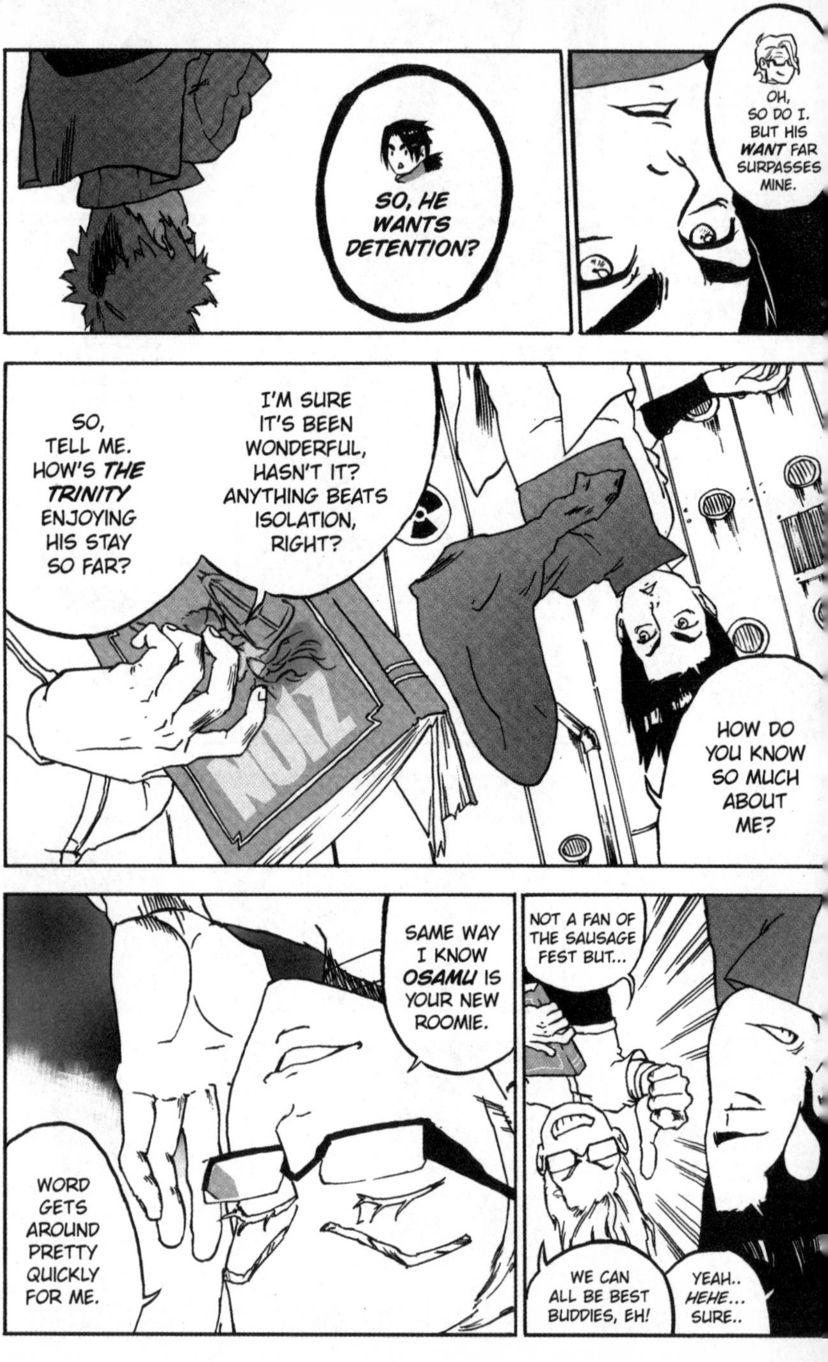
SO, HE WANTS DETENTION?
OH, SO DO I. BUT HIS WANT FAR SURPASSES MINE.
SO, TELL ME. HOW'S THE TRINITY ENJOYING HIS STAY SO FAR?
I'M SURE IT'S BEEN WONDERFUL, HASN'T IT? ANYTHING BEATS ISOLATION, RIGHT?
NOIZ
HOW DO YOU KNOW SO MUCH ABOUT ME?
SAME WAY I KNOW OSAMU IS YOUR NEW ROOMIE.
WORD GETS AROUND PRETTY QUICKLY FOR ME.
NOT A FAN OF THE SAUSAGE FEST BUT...
WE CAN ALL BE BEST BUDDIES, EH!
YEAH.. HEHE... SURE..

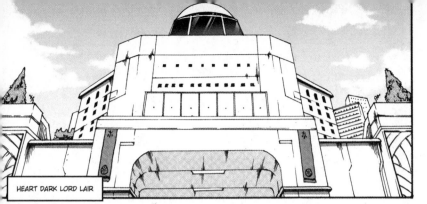

HEART DARK LORD LAIR

FATTIMUNGA'S BREAK-IN IS UNACCEPTABLE. I JUST RECENTLY REVIEWED YOUR COUNTRY'S DEFENSE SYSTEMS AND I MUST SAY...

...THEY'RE AN UTTER EMBARRASS-MENT TO THE CREST OF BLACK BOTTOM ISLAND.

AND YOUR DARK LORD IN CHARGE OF SECURITY IS ABSENT. AVOIDING DUTY IS ALSO...

...UNAC-CEPTABLE!

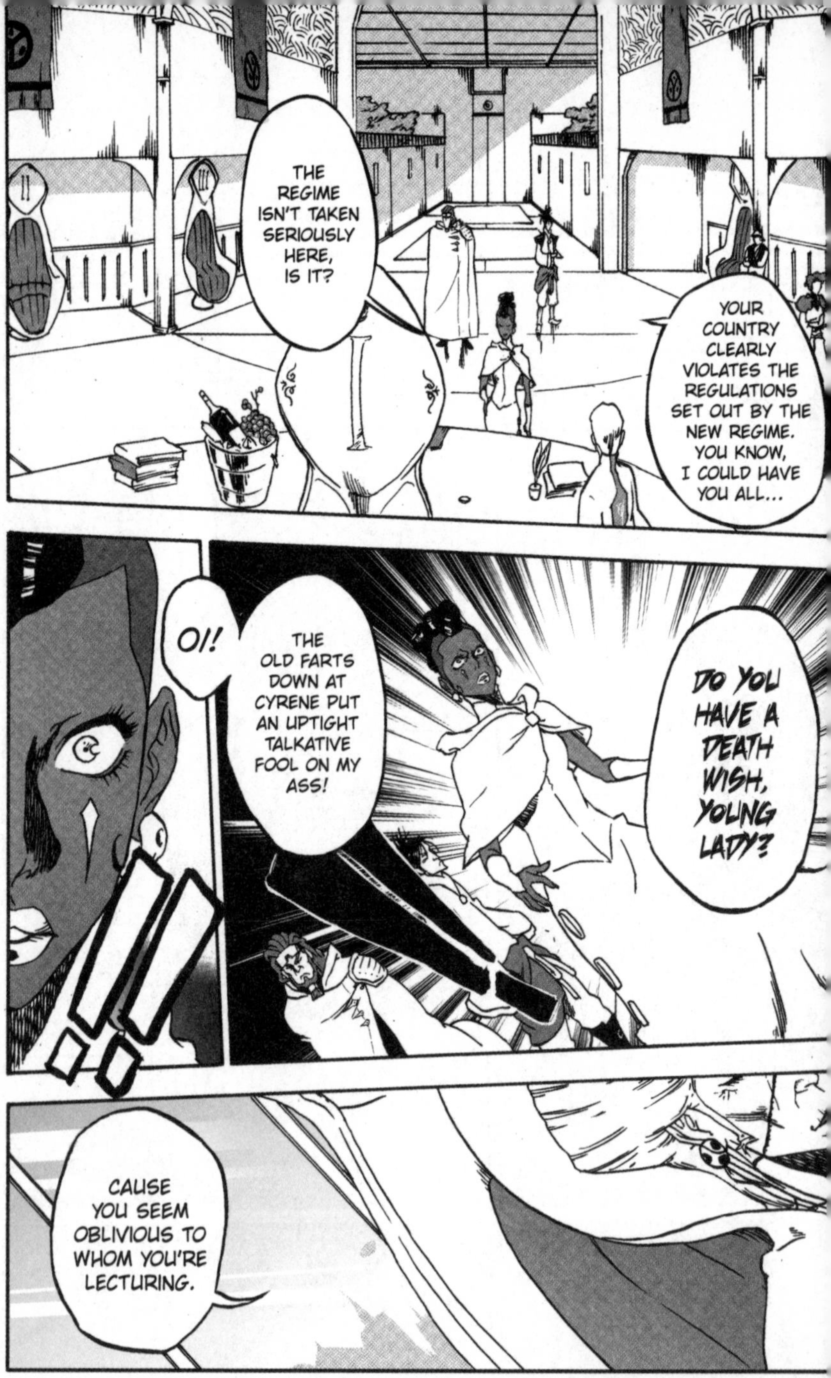
THE REGIME ISN'T TAKEN SERIOUSLY HERE, IS IT?
YOUR COUNTRY CLEARLY VIOLATES THE REGULATIONS SET OUT BY THE NEW REGIME. YOU KNOW, I COULD HAVE YOU ALL...
OI!
THE OLD FARTS DOWN AT CYRENE PUT AN UPTIGHT TALKATIVE FOOL ON MY ASS!
DO YOU HAVE A DEATH WISH, YOUNG LADY?
CAUSE YOU SEEM OBLIVIOUS TO WHOM YOU'RE LECTURING.

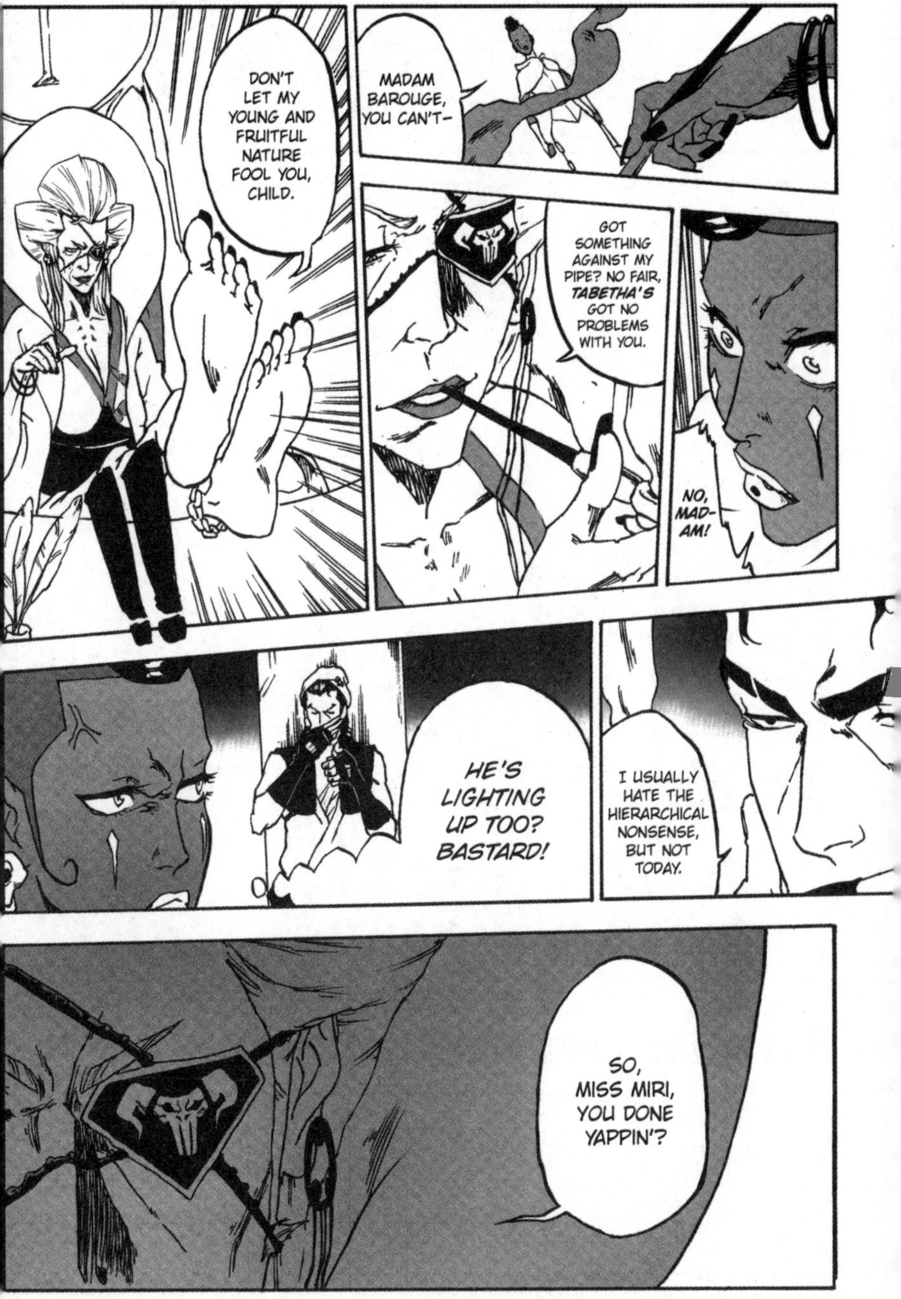
DON'T LET MY YOUNG AND FRUITFUL NATURE FOOL YOU, CHILD.
MADAM BAROUGE, YOU CAN'T–
GOT SOMETHING AGAINST MY PIPE? NO FAIR, TABETHA'S GOT NO PROBLEMS WITH YOU.
NO, MAD-AM!
HE'S LIGHTING UP TOO? BASTARD!
I USUALLY HATE THE HIERARCHICAL NONSENSE, BUT NOT TODAY.
SO, MISS MIRI, YOU DONE YAPPIN'?

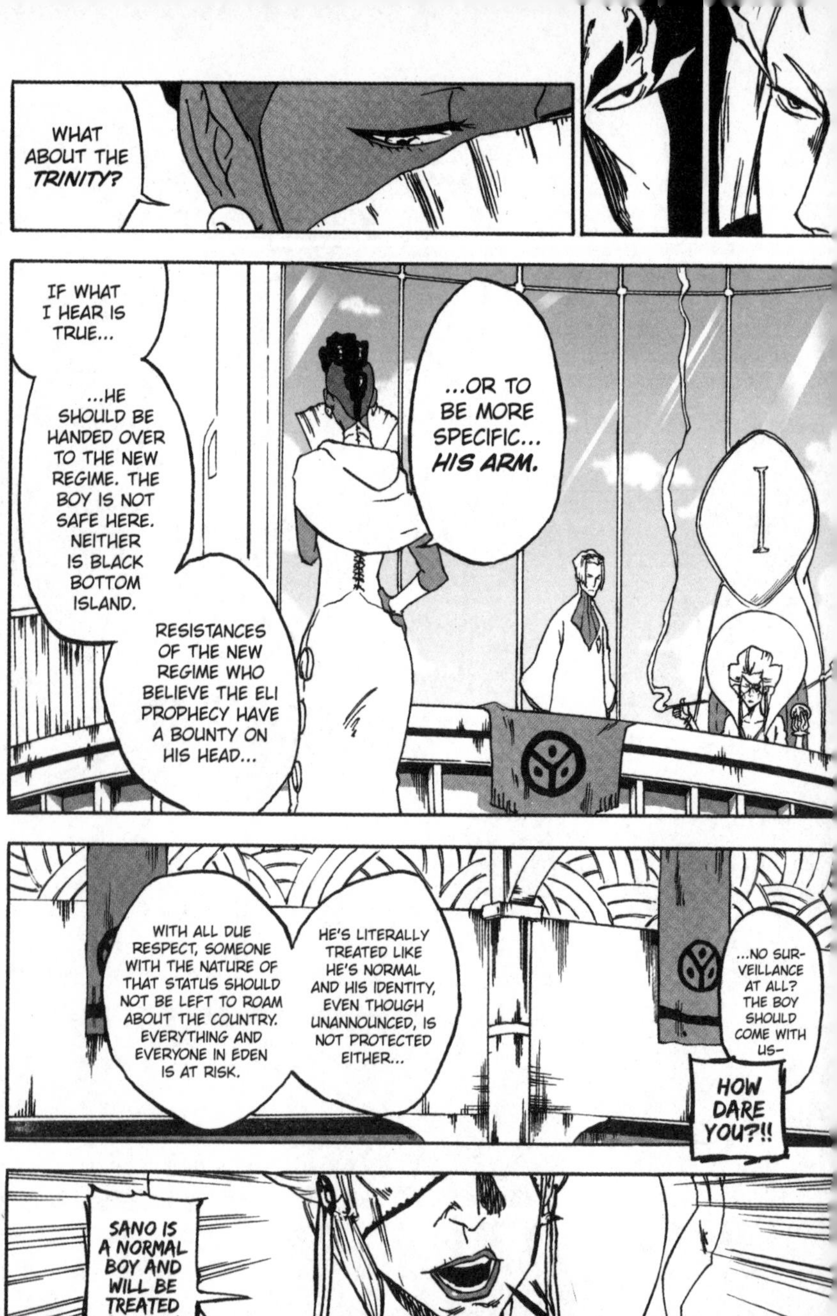

WHAT ABOUT THE *TRINITY?*
IF WHAT I HEAR IS TRUE...
...HE SHOULD BE HANDED OVER TO THE NEW REGIME. THE BOY IS NOT SAFE HERE. NEITHER IS BLACK BOTTOM ISLAND.
RESISTANCES OF THE NEW REGIME WHO BELIEVE THE ELI PROPHECY HAVE A BOUNTY ON HIS HEAD...
...OR TO BE MORE SPECIFIC... ***HIS ARM.***
I
WITH ALL DUE RESPECT, SOMEONE WITH THE NATURE OF THAT STATUS SHOULD NOT BE LEFT TO ROAM ABOUT THE COUNTRY. EVERYTHING AND EVERYONE IN EDEN IS AT RISK.
HE'S LITERALLY TREATED LIKE HE'S NORMAL AND HIS IDENTITY, EVEN THOUGH UNANNOUNCED, IS NOT PROTECTED EITHER...
...NO SURVEILLANCE AT ALL? THE BOY SHOULD COME WITH US—
**HOW DARE YOU?!!**
**SANO IS A NORMAL BOY AND WILL BE TREATED AS SUCH!**

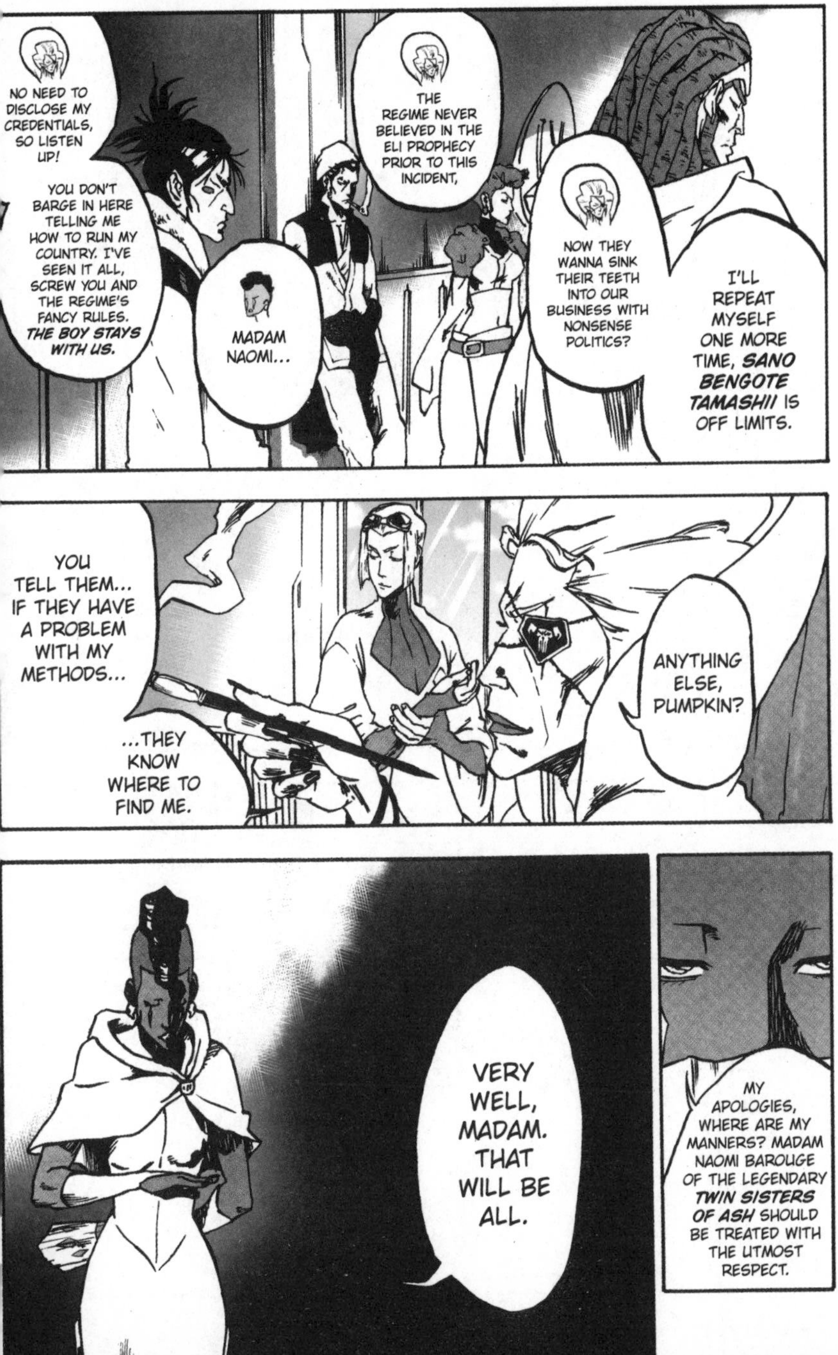
NO NEED TO DISCLOSE MY CREDENTIALS, SO LISTEN UP!
YOU DON'T BARGE IN HERE TELLING ME HOW TO RUN MY COUNTRY. I'VE SEEN IT ALL, SCREW YOU AND THE REGIME'S FANCY RULES. ***THE BOY STAYS WITH US.***
MADAM NAOMI...
THE REGIME NEVER BELIEVED IN THE ELI PROPHECY PRIOR TO THIS INCIDENT,
NOW THEY WANNA SINK THEIR TEETH INTO OUR BUSINESS WITH NONSENSE POLITICS?
I'LL REPEAT MYSELF ONE MORE TIME, ***SANO BENGOTE TAMASHII*** IS OFF LIMITS.
YOU TELL THEM... IF THEY HAVE A PROBLEM WITH MY METHODS...
...THEY KNOW WHERE TO FIND ME.
ANYTHING ELSE, PUMPKIN?
VERY WELL, MADAM. THAT WILL BE ALL.
MY APOLOGIES, WHERE ARE MY MANNERS? MADAM NAOMI BAROUGE OF THE LEGENDARY ***TWIN SISTERS OF ASH*** SHOULD BE TREATED WITH THE UTMOST RESPECT.

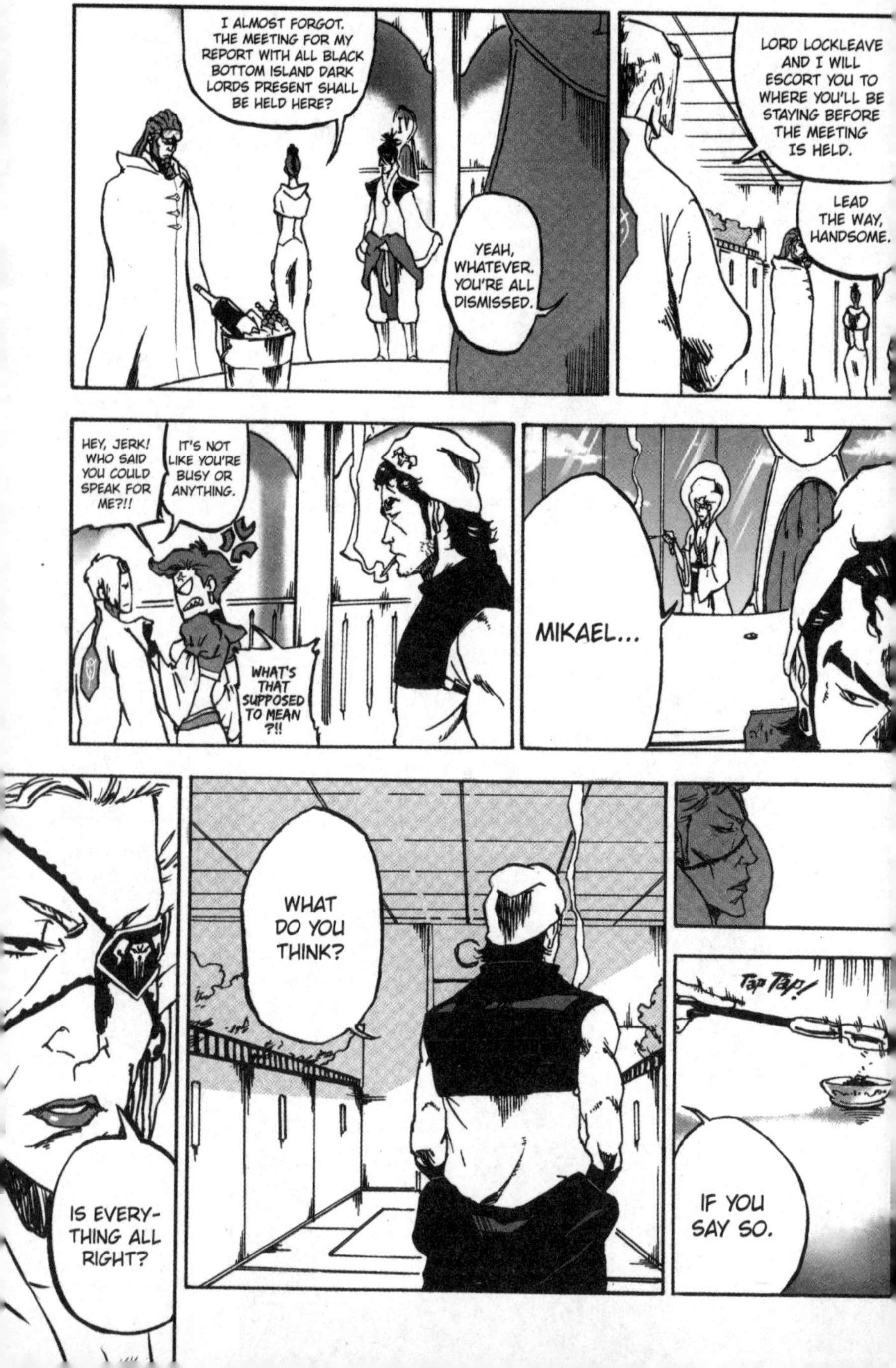
I ALMOST FORGOT. THE MEETING FOR MY REPORT WITH ALL BLACK BOTTOM ISLAND DARK LORDS PRESENT SHALL BE HELD HERE?
YEAH, WHATEVER. YOU'RE ALL DISMISSED.
LORD LOCKLEAVE AND I WILL ESCORT YOU TO WHERE YOU'LL BE STAYING BEFORE THE MEETING IS HELD.
LEAD THE WAY, HANDSOME.
HEY, JERK! WHO SAID YOU COULD SPEAK FOR ME?!!
IT'S NOT LIKE YOU'RE BUSY OR ANYTHING.
WHAT'S THAT SUPPOSED TO MEAN ?!!
MIKAEL...
IS EVERY-THING ALL RIGHT?
WHAT DO YOU THINK?
Tap Tap!
IF YOU SAY SO.

NOOOO!!!! AND JUST WHEN I WAS GETTING ATTACHED TO THE CHARACTER.

UH... I'M A LITTLE FRIGHTENED TO ASK BUT...

WHAT EXACTLY ARE YOU READING?

THOUGHT YOU'D NEVER ASK!

OH MY, HE'S BLEEDING AGAIN.

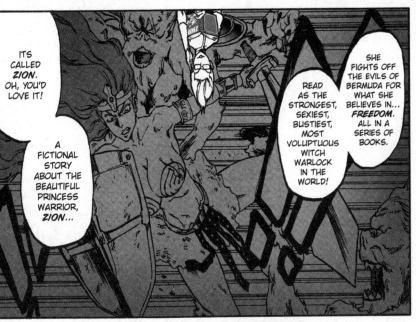

ITS CALLED ZION. OH, YOU'D LOVE IT!

A FICTIONAL STORY ABOUT THE BEAUTIFUL PRINCESS WARRIOR, ZION...

READ AS THE STRONGEST, SEXIEST, BUSTIEST, MOST VOLUPTUOUS WITCH WARLOCK IN THE WORLD!

SHE FIGHTS OFF THE EVILS OF BERMUDA FOR WHAT SHE BELIEVES IN... FREEDOM. ALL IN A SERIES OF BOOKS.

THAT'S THE GIST OF IT, BUT IT'S SO MUCH MORE! YOU SHOULD TRY IT. I GUARANTEE AMAZEMENT!

PROBABLY NOT. I'M MORE INTO BOOKS OF MERLIN. EVER HEARD OF THEM? I HAVE A LOT, USED TO BE MY FATHER'S.

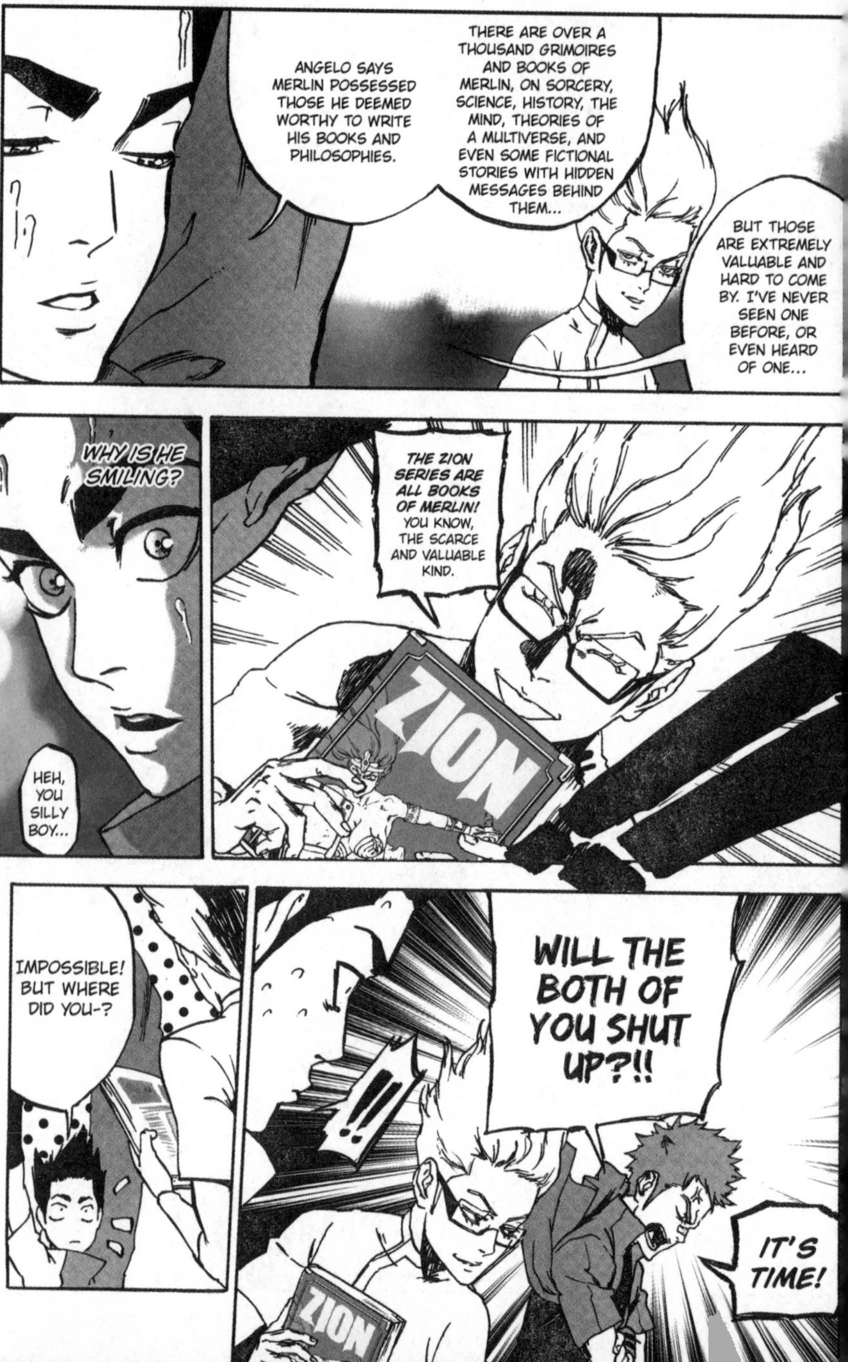

ANGELO SAYS MERLIN POSSESSED THOSE HE DEEMED WORTHY TO WRITE HIS BOOKS AND PHILOSOPHIES.
THERE ARE OVER A THOUSAND GRIMOIRES AND BOOKS OF MERLIN, ON SORCERY, SCIENCE, HISTORY, THE MIND, THEORIES OF A MULTIVERSE, AND EVEN SOME FICTIONAL STORIES WITH HIDDEN MESSAGES BEHIND THEM...
BUT THOSE ARE EXTREMELY VALUABLE AND HARD TO COME BY. I'VE NEVER SEEN ONE BEFORE, OR EVEN HEARD OF ONE...
WHY IS HE SMILING?
HEH, YOU SILLY BOY...
THE ZION SERIES ARE ALL BOOKS OF MERLIN! YOU KNOW, THE SCARCE AND VALUABLE KIND.
ZION
IMPOSSIBLE! BUT WHERE DID YOU-?
!!
WILL THE BOTH OF YOU SHUT UP?!!
IT'S TIME!
ZION

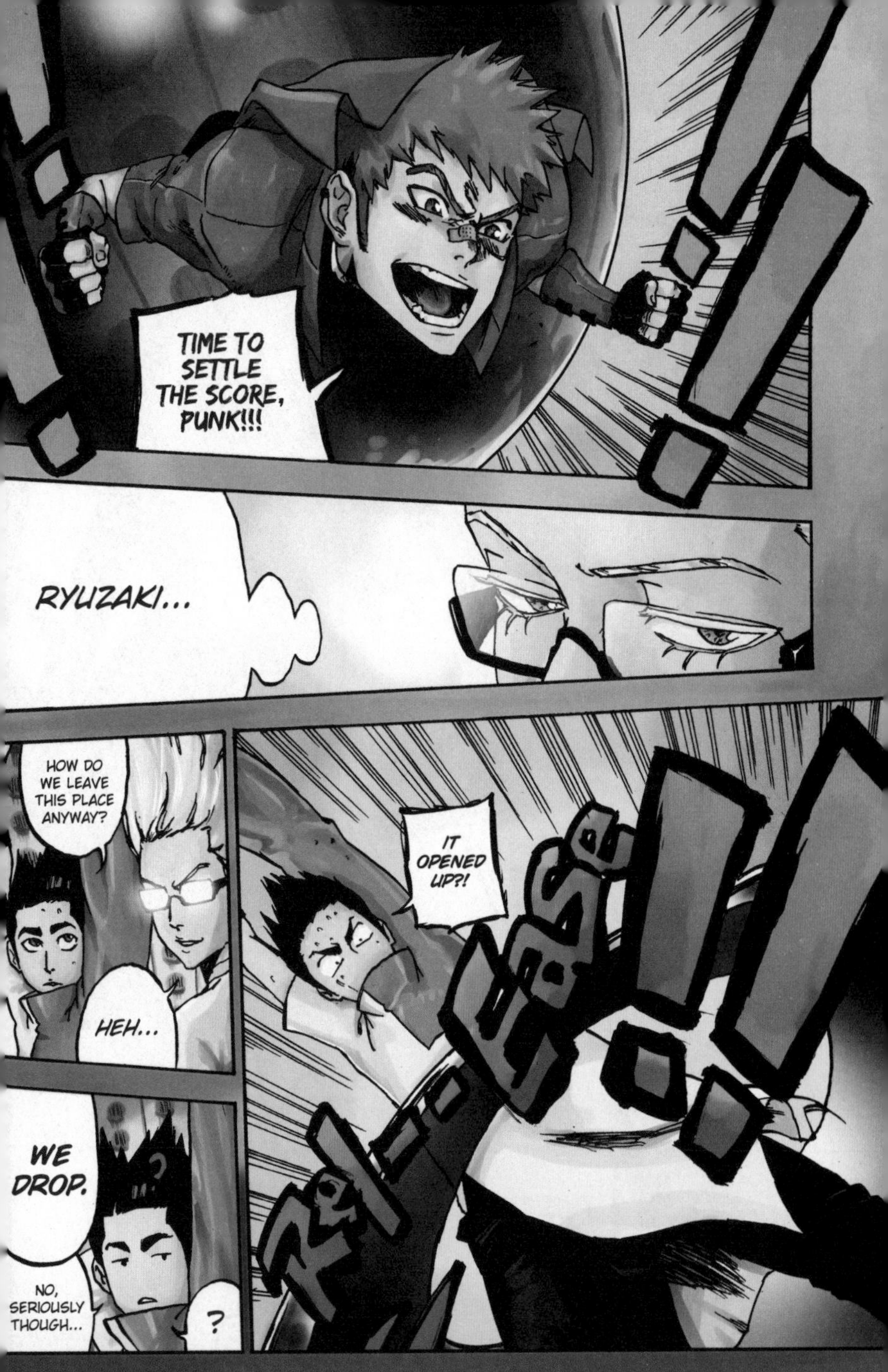
TIME TO SETTLE THE SCORE, PUNK!!!
RYUZAKI...
HOW DO WE LEAVE THIS PLACE ANYWAY?
HEH...
WE DROP.
NO, SERIOUSLY THOUGH...
?
IT OPENED UP?!

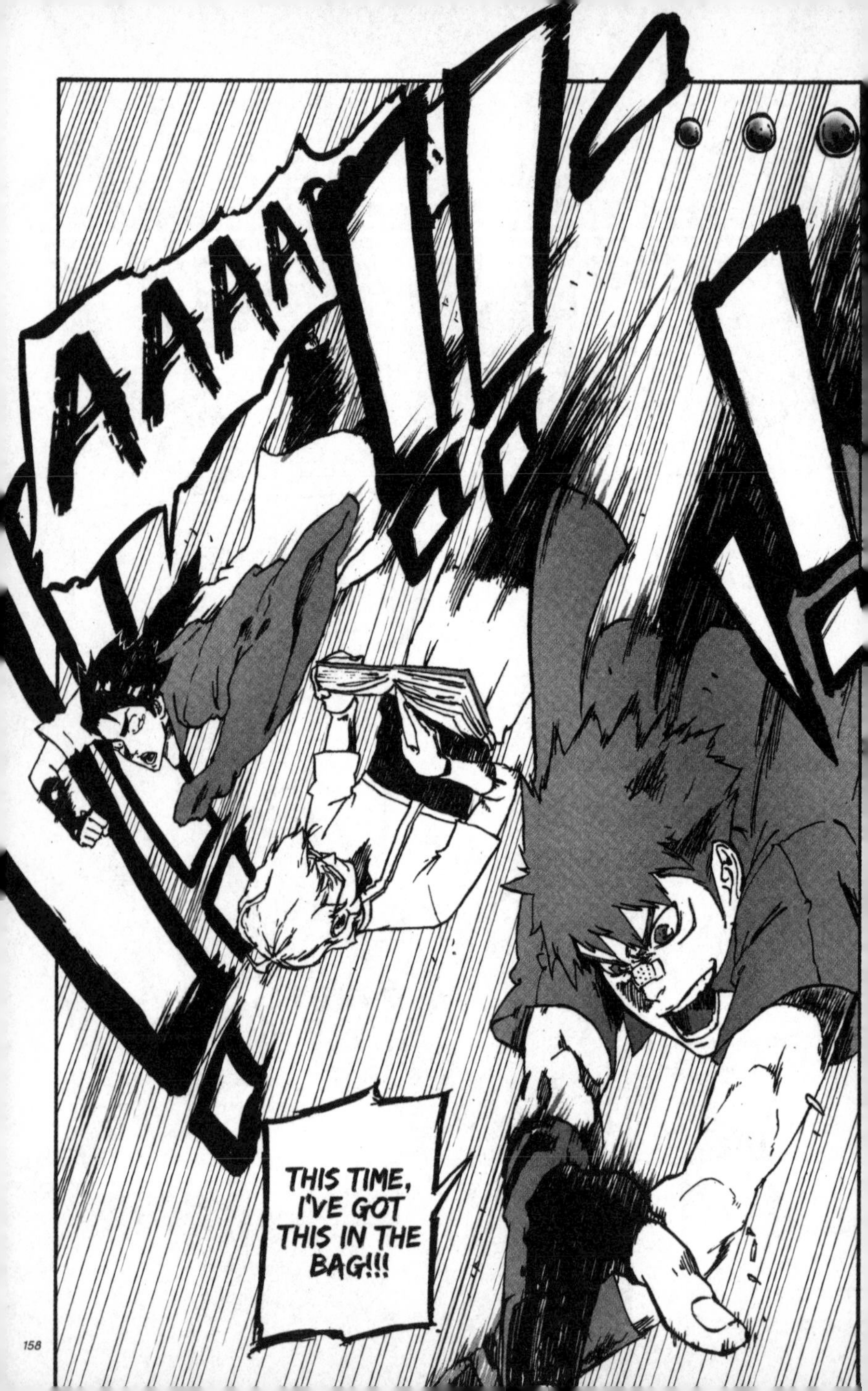
AAAA
THIS TIME, I'VE GOT THIS IN THE BAG!!!

# APPLE BLACK

CHAPTER 6 | NIRVANA RED

APPLE BLACK

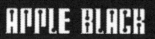

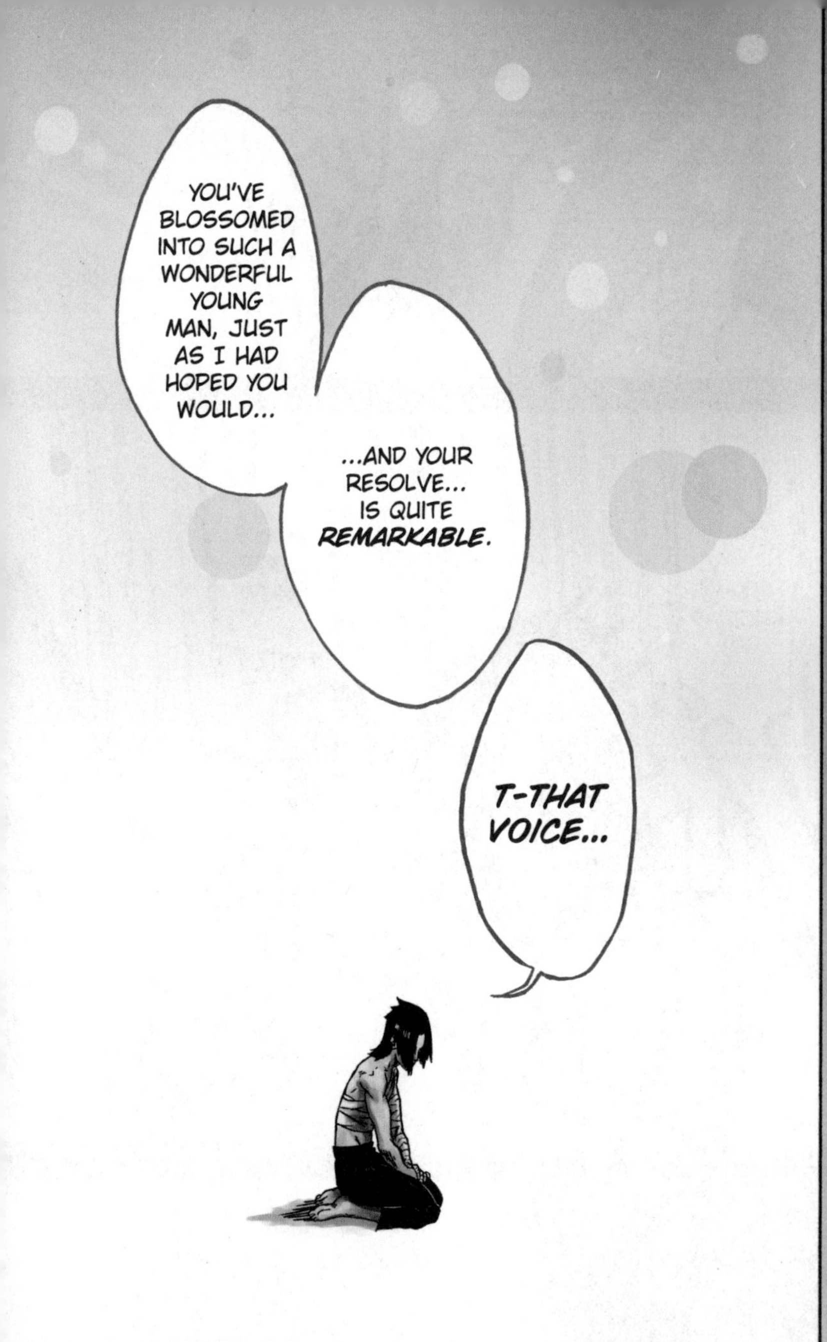
YOU'VE BLOSSOMED INTO SUCH A WONDERFUL YOUNG MAN, JUST AS I HAD HOPED YOU WOULD...
...AND YOUR RESOLVE... IS QUITE REMARKABLE.
T-THAT VOICE...

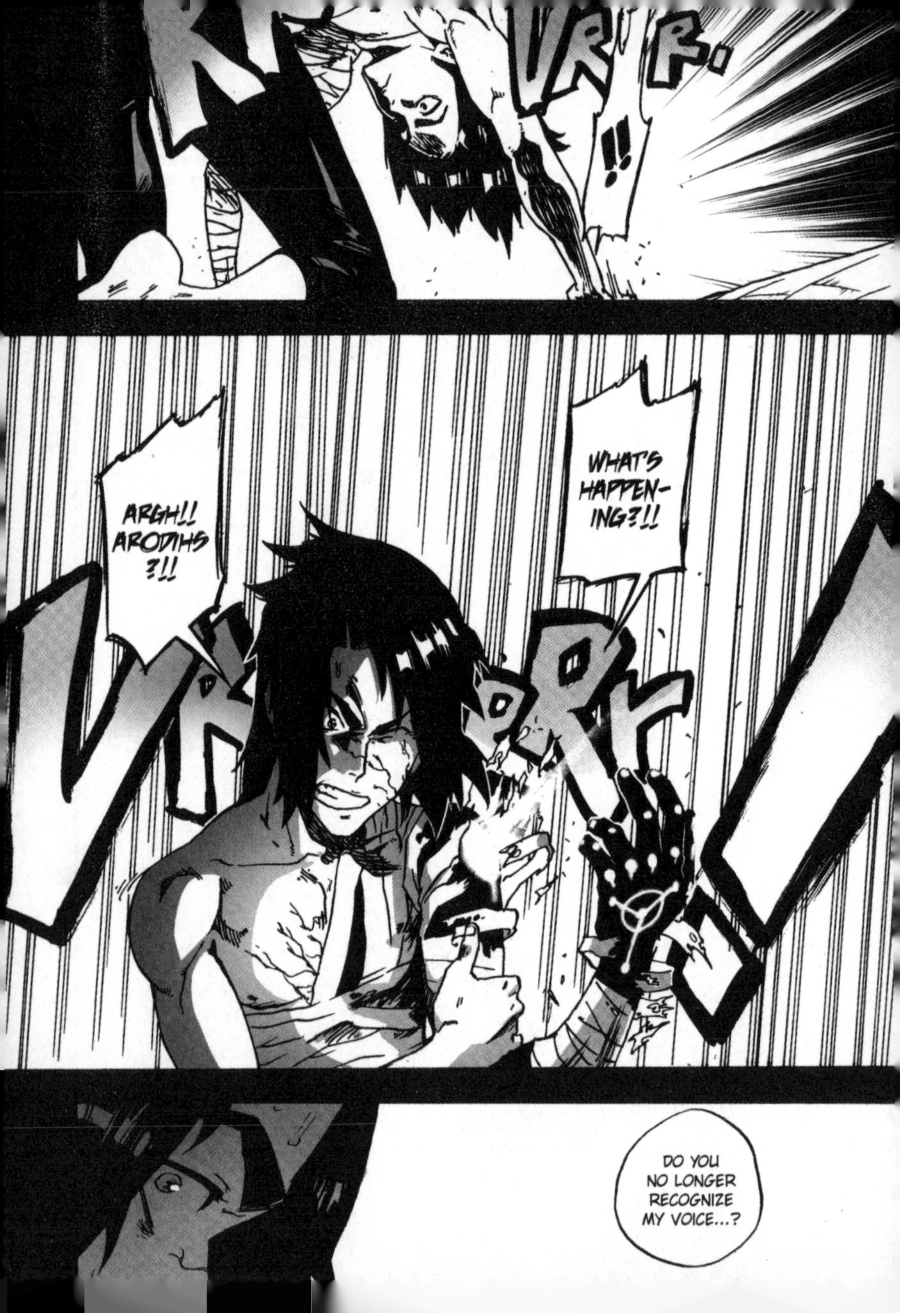
!!
ARGH!! ARODIHS ?!!
WHAT'S HAPPEN-ING?!!
DO YOU NO LONGER RECOGNIZE MY VOICE...?

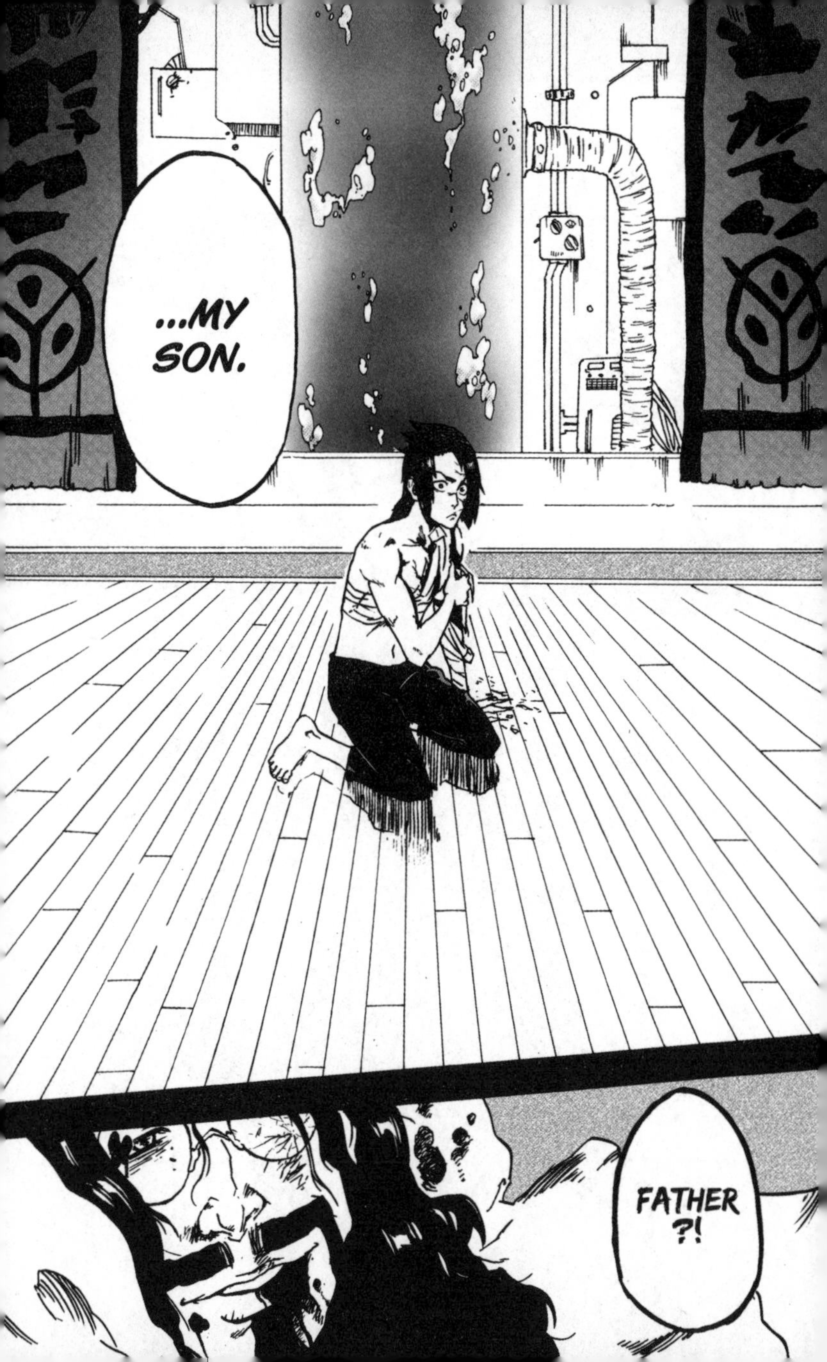
...MY SON.
FATHER ?!

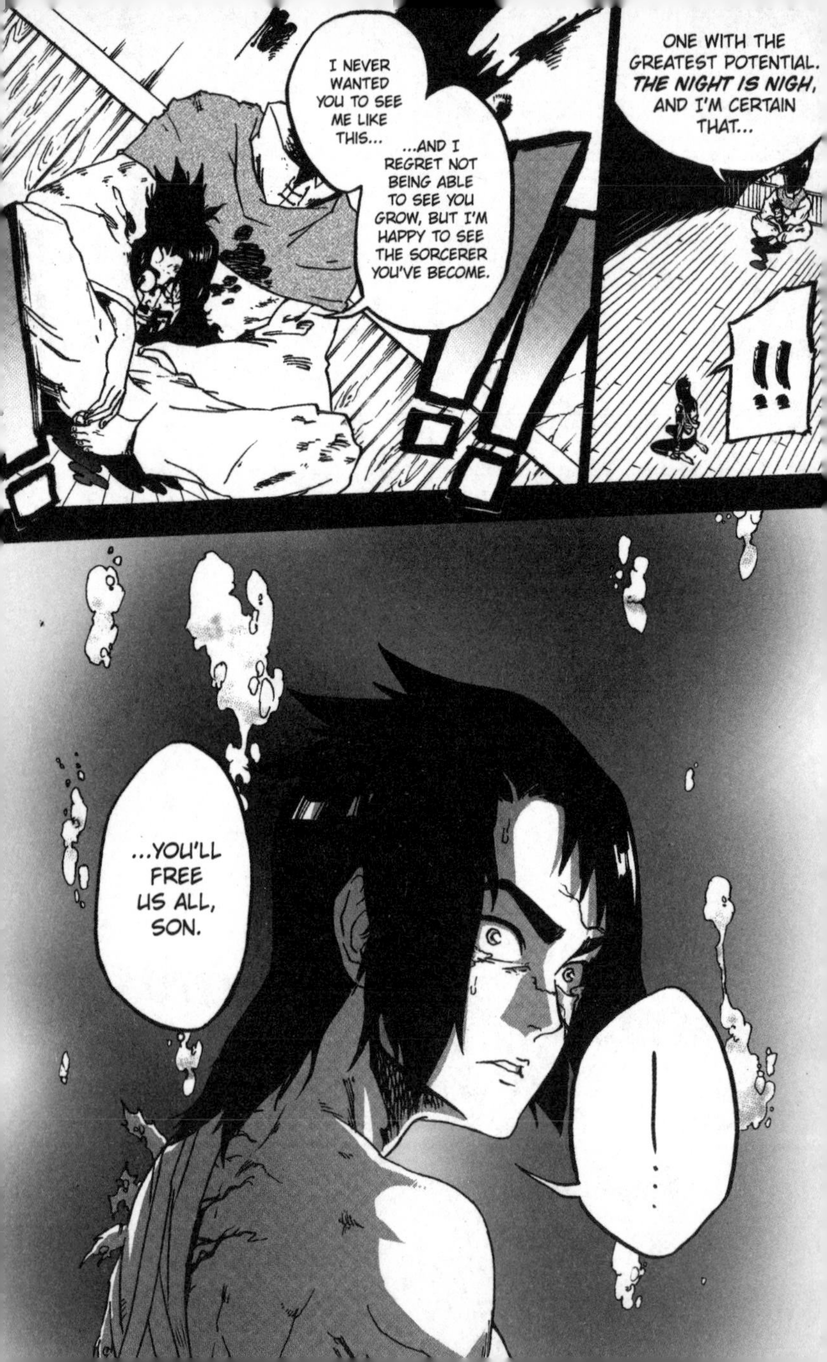
I NEVER WANTED YOU TO SEE ME LIKE THIS...
...AND I REGRET NOT BEING ABLE TO SEE YOU GROW, BUT I'M HAPPY TO SEE THE SORCERER YOU'VE BECOME.
!!
ONE WITH THE GREATEST POTENTIAL. *THE NIGHT IS NIGH*, AND I'M CERTAIN THAT...
!!
...YOU'LL FREE US ALL, SON.
!...

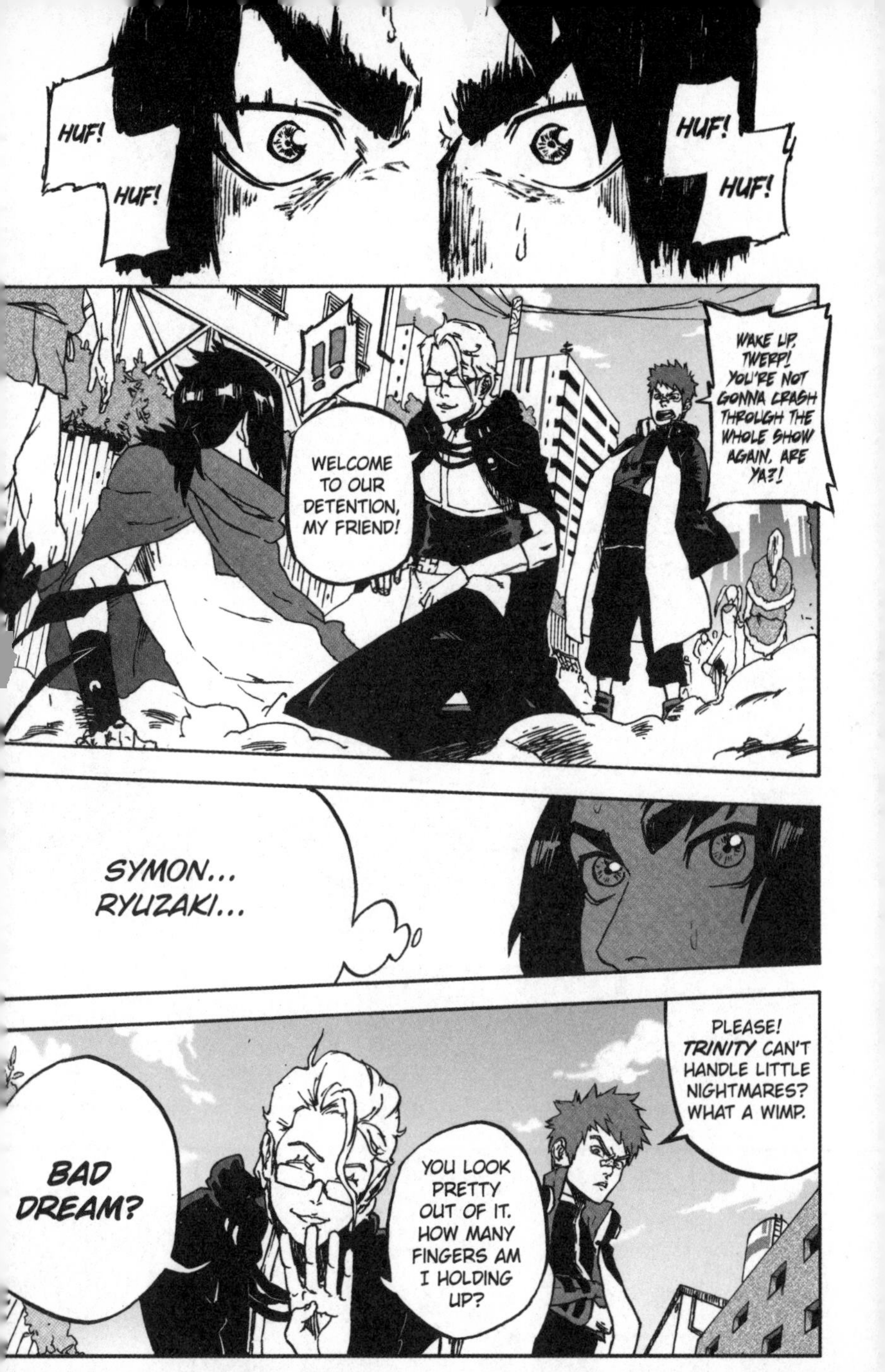
HUF!
HUF!
HUF!
HUF!
!!
WELCOME TO OUR DETENTION, MY FRIEND!
WAKE UP, TWERP! YOU'RE NOT GONNA CRASH THROUGH THE WHOLE SHOW AGAIN, ARE YA?!
SYMON... RYUZAKI...
BAD DREAM?
YOU LOOK PRETTY OUT OF IT. HOW MANY FINGERS AM I HOLDING UP?
PLEASE! *TRINITY* CAN'T HANDLE LITTLE NIGHTMARES? WHAT A WIMP.

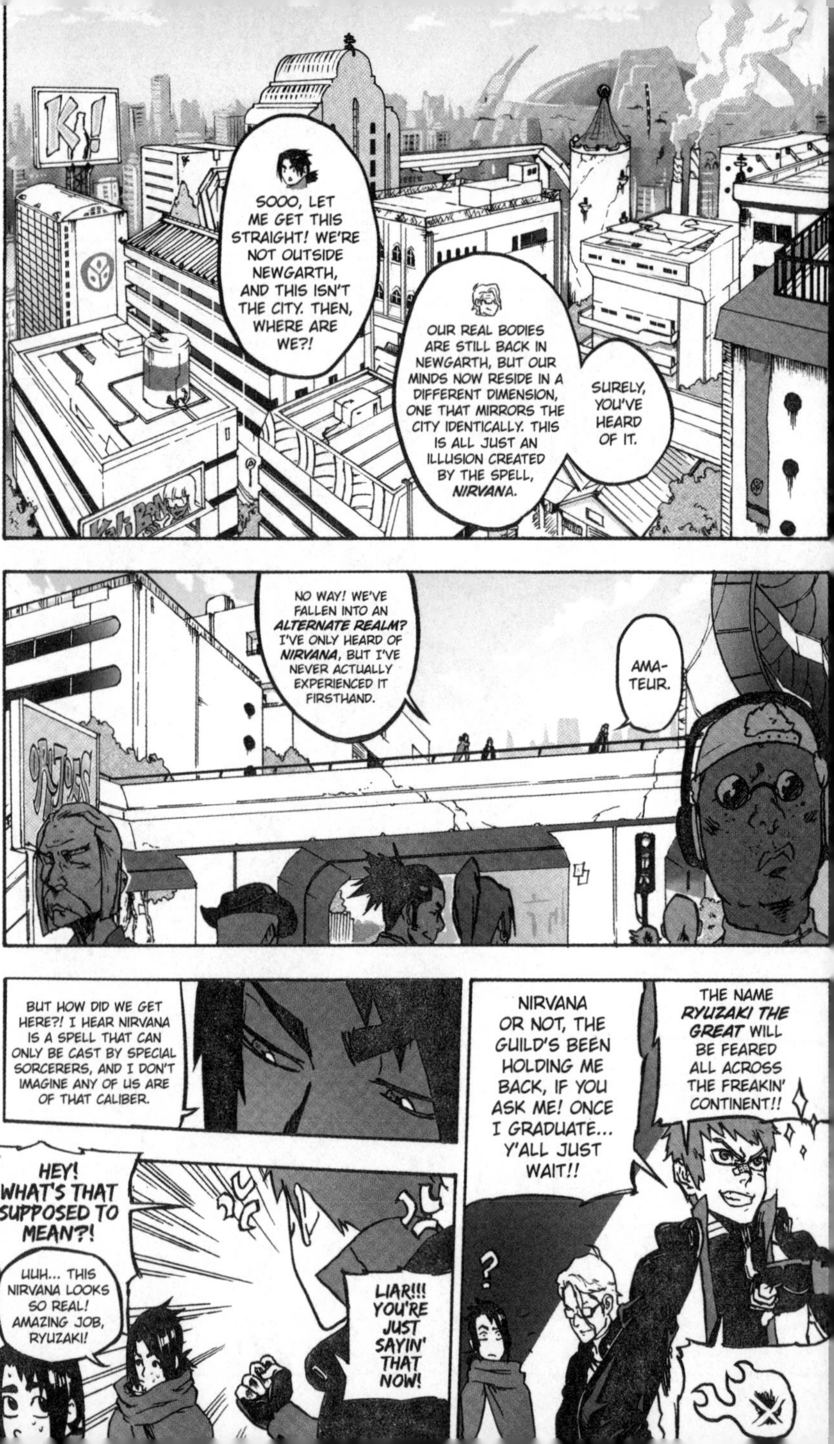
SOOO, LET ME GET THIS STRAIGHT! WE'RE NOT OUTSIDE NEWGARTH, AND THIS ISN'T THE CITY. THEN, WHERE ARE WE?!
OUR REAL BODIES ARE STILL BACK IN NEWGARTH, BUT OUR MINDS NOW RESIDE IN A DIFFERENT DIMENSION, ONE THAT MIRRORS THE CITY IDENTICALLY. THIS IS ALL JUST AN ILLUSION CREATED BY THE SPELL, NIRVANA.
SURELY, YOU'VE HEARD OF IT.
NO WAY! WE'VE FALLEN INTO AN ALTERNATE REALM? I'VE ONLY HEARD OF NIRVANA, BUT I'VE NEVER ACTUALLY EXPERIENCED IT FIRSTHAND.
AMA-TEUR.
BUT HOW DID WE GET HERE?! I HEAR NIRVANA IS A SPELL THAT CAN ONLY BE CAST BY SPECIAL SORCERERS, AND I DON'T IMAGINE ANY OF US ARE OF THAT CALIBER.
HEY! WHAT'S THAT SUPPOSED TO MEAN?!
UUH... THIS NIRVANA LOOKS SO REAL! AMAZING JOB, RYUZAKI!
LIAR!!! YOU'RE JUST SAYIN' THAT NOW!
NIRVANA OR NOT, THE GUILD'S BEEN HOLDING ME BACK, IF YOU ASK ME! ONCE I GRADUATE... Y'ALL JUST WAIT!!
THE NAME RYUZAKI THE GREAT WILL BE FEARED ALL ACROSS THE FREAKIN' CONTINENT!!

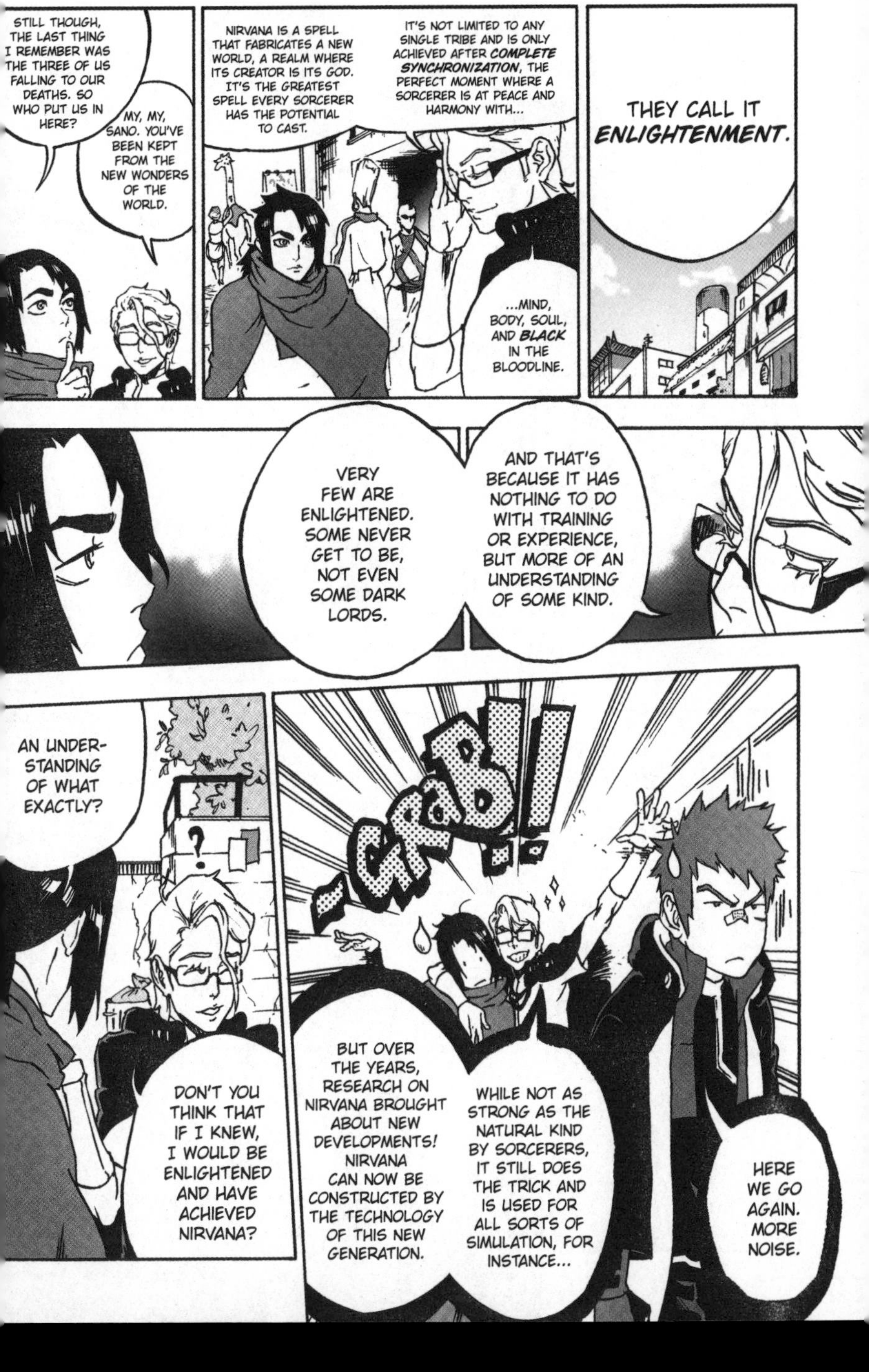
STILL THOUGH, THE LAST THING I REMEMBER WAS THE THREE OF US FALLING TO OUR DEATHS. SO WHO PUT US IN HERE?
MY, MY, SANO. YOU'VE BEEN KEPT FROM THE NEW WONDERS OF THE WORLD.
NIRVANA IS A SPELL THAT FABRICATES A NEW WORLD, A REALM WHERE ITS CREATOR IS ITS GOD. IT'S THE GREATEST SPELL EVERY SORCERER HAS THE POTENTIAL TO CAST.
IT'S NOT LIMITED TO ANY SINGLE TRIBE AND IS ONLY ACHIEVED AFTER ***COMPLETE SYNCHRONIZATION***, THE PERFECT MOMENT WHERE A SORCERER IS AT PEACE AND HARMONY WITH...
...MIND, BODY, SOUL, AND ***BLACK*** IN THE BLOODLINE.
THEY CALL IT ***ENLIGHTENMENT***.
VERY FEW ARE ENLIGHTENED. SOME NEVER GET TO BE, NOT EVEN SOME DARK LORDS.
AND THAT'S BECAUSE IT HAS NOTHING TO DO WITH TRAINING OR EXPERIENCE, BUT MORE OF AN UNDERSTANDING OF SOME KIND.
AN UNDER-STANDING OF WHAT EXACTLY?
DON'T YOU THINK THAT IF I KNEW, I WOULD BE ENLIGHTENED AND HAVE ACHIEVED NIRVANA?
GRAB!!
BUT OVER THE YEARS, RESEARCH ON NIRVANA BROUGHT ABOUT NEW DEVELOPMENTS! NIRVANA CAN NOW BE CONSTRUCTED BY THE TECHNOLOGY OF THIS NEW GENERATION.
WHILE NOT AS STRONG AS THE NATURAL KIND BY SORCERERS, IT STILL DOES THE TRICK AND IS USED FOR ALL SORTS OF SIMULATION, FOR INSTANCE...
HERE WE GO AGAIN. MORE NOISE.

TRAINING SESSIONS, MISSIONS, EVENTS, DETENTION IN OUR CASE! HEH.

EVEN NIRVANA CONNECTED COMPUTER NETWORKS, WE CALL *THE NIRVANET.* ITS ACTUALLY PRETTY AMAZING.

WHICH REMINDS ME...

EH?

...ZAKI-BRO, YOU HAVEN'T FOLLOWED ME BACK ON *SQWEEKR!*

THOSE THINGS ARE FOR PUNKS. YOU KNOW I DON'T HAVE ONE.

OH!

I CREATED AN ACCOUNT FOR HIM AND YOU TOO, SANO. DON'T WORRY, IT'S A SOCIAL THING ON THE NIRVANET. YOU'LL LOVE IT!

**YOU WHAT?!**

YEAH, YOUR USERNAME IS *CRAZYRED-HEAD13*

DELETE IT, YOU TROLL! OR I'LL DELETE YOU!

C'MON, CALM DOWN, RYUZAKI. I THINK THE NAME FITS PERFECTLY!

SYMON...

...IF WE *ARE* IN A *NIRVANA,* THEN WE HAVE EVEN BIGGER ISSUES THAN I THOUGHT.

I REMEMBER ANGELO MENTIONING THAT ANYONE DELETED HERE BECOMES A VEGETABLE IN REALITY.

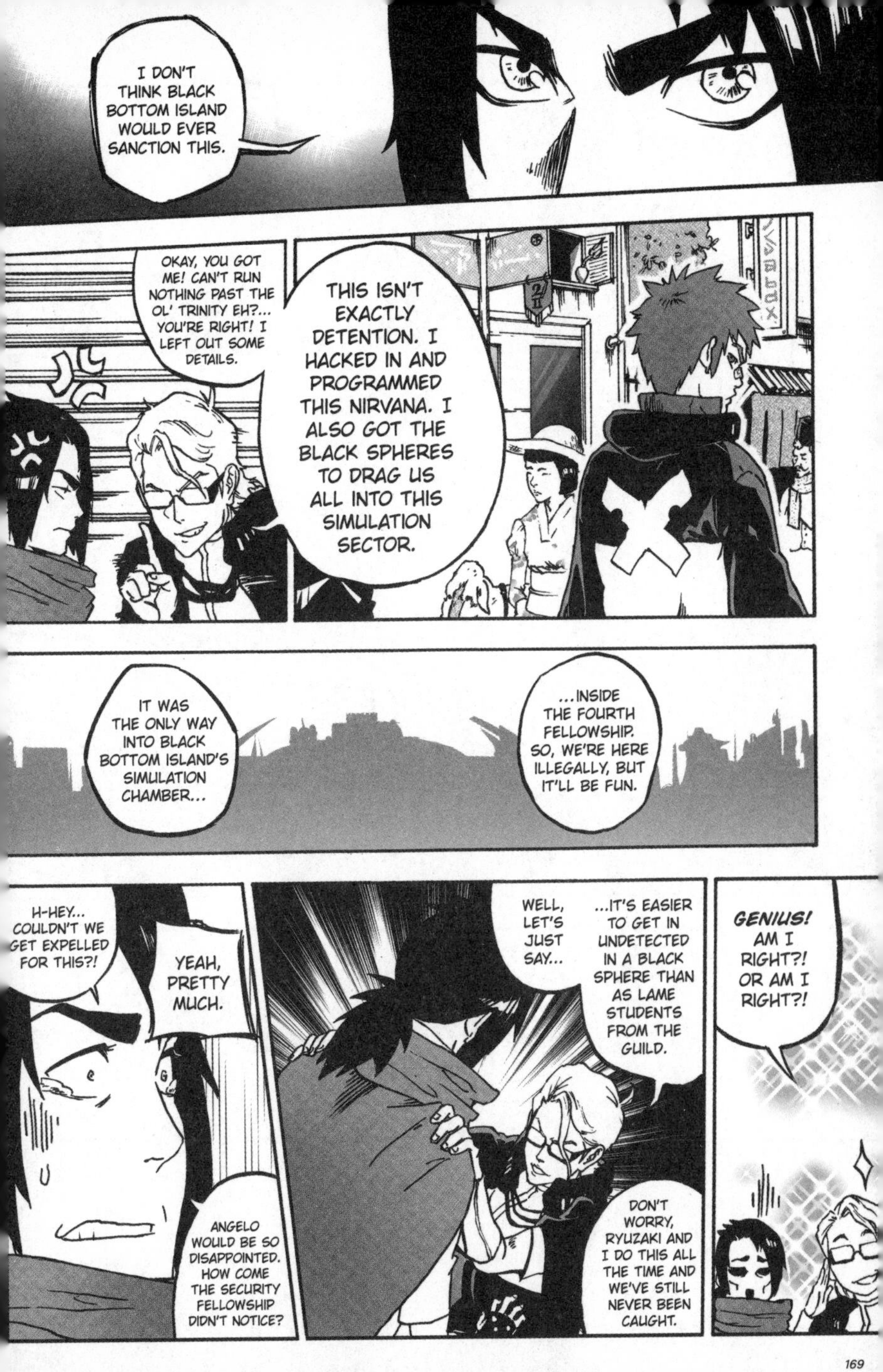
I DON'T THINK BLACK BOTTOM ISLAND WOULD EVER SANCTION THIS.
OKAY, YOU GOT ME! CAN'T RUN NOTHING PAST THE OL' TRINITY EH?... YOU'RE RIGHT! I LEFT OUT SOME DETAILS.
THIS ISN'T EXACTLY DETENTION. I HACKED IN AND PROGRAMMED THIS NIRVANA. I ALSO GOT THE BLACK SPHERES TO DRAG US ALL INTO THIS SIMULATION SECTOR.
IT WAS THE ONLY WAY INTO BLACK BOTTOM ISLAND'S SIMULATION CHAMBER...
...INSIDE THE FOURTH FELLOWSHIP. SO, WE'RE HERE ILLEGALLY, BUT IT'LL BE FUN.
H-HEY... COULDN'T WE GET EXPELLED FOR THIS?!
YEAH, PRETTY MUCH.
ANGELO WOULD BE SO DISAPPOINTED. HOW COME THE SECURITY FELLOWSHIP DIDN'T NOTICE?
WELL, LET'S JUST SAY...
...IT'S EASIER TO GET IN UNDETECTED IN A BLACK SPHERE THAN AS LAME STUDENTS FROM THE GUILD.
DON'T WORRY, RYUZAKI AND I DO THIS ALL THE TIME AND WE'VE STILL NEVER BEEN CAUGHT.
GENIUS! AM I RIGHT?! OR AM I RIGHT?!

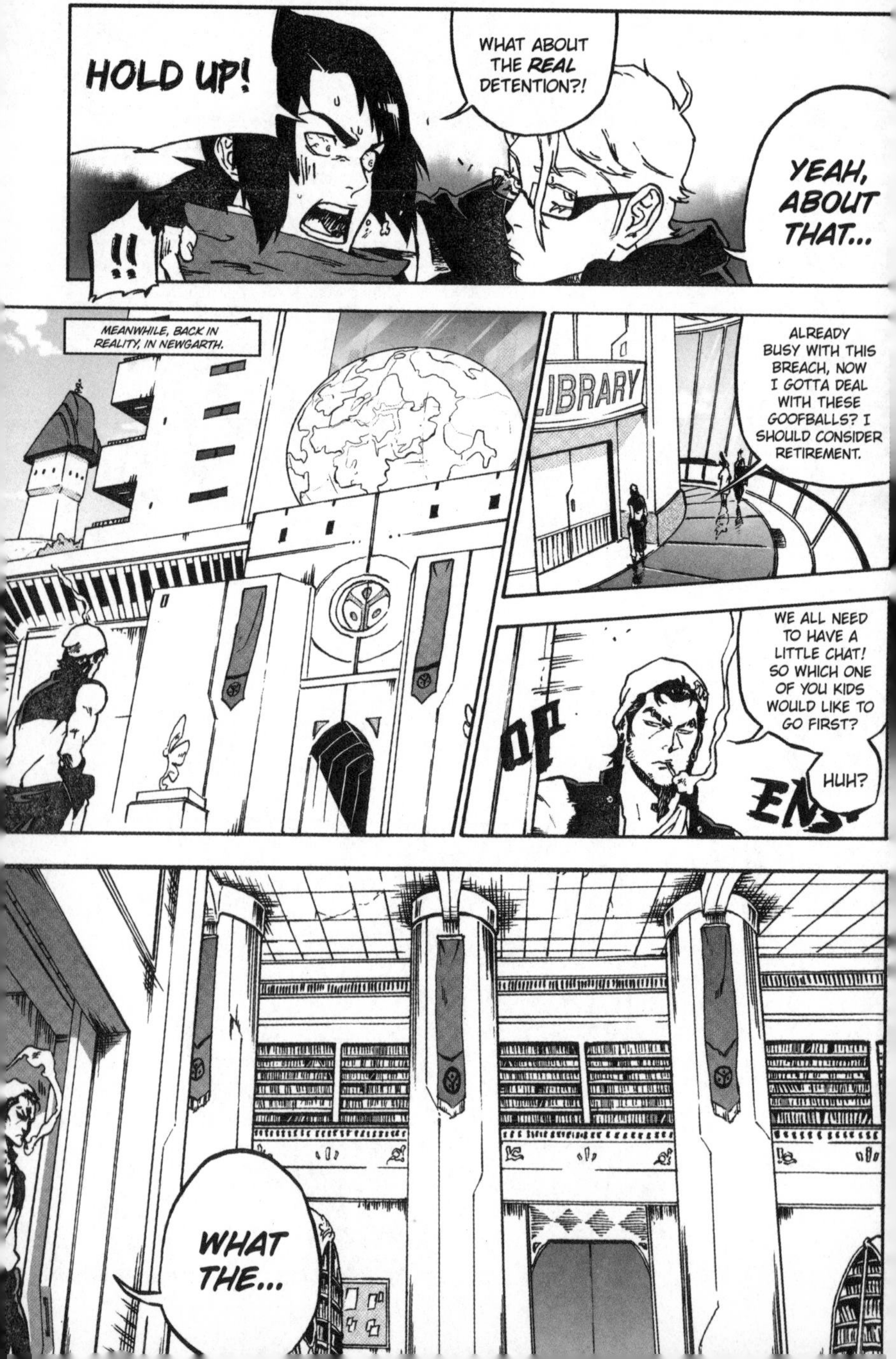
HOLD UP!
!!
WHAT ABOUT THE *REAL* DETENTION?!
YEAH, ABOUT THAT...
MEANWHILE, BACK IN REALITY, IN NEWGARTH.
ALREADY BUSY WITH THIS BREACH, NOW I GOTTA DEAL WITH THESE GOOFBALLS? I SHOULD CONSIDER RETIREMENT.
OP
WE ALL NEED TO HAVE A LITTLE CHAT! SO WHICH ONE OF YOU KIDS WOULD LIKE TO GO FIRST?
HUH?
ENS
WHAT THE...

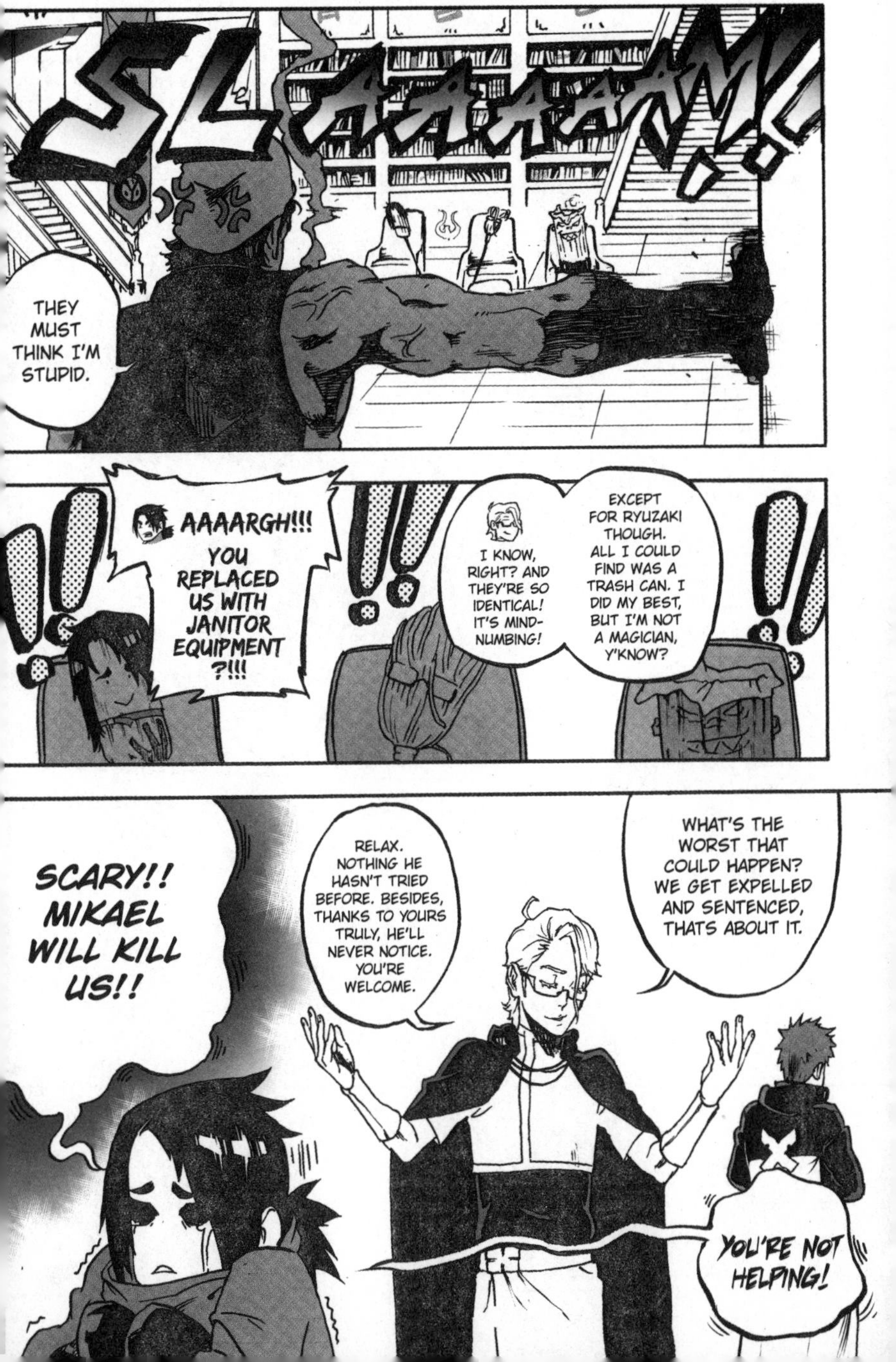
SLAAAAAM!!
THEY MUST THINK I'M STUPID.
AAAARGH!!! YOU REPLACED US WITH JANITOR EQUIPMENT?!!!
I KNOW, RIGHT? AND THEY'RE SO IDENTICAL! IT'S MIND-NUMBING!
EXCEPT FOR RYUZAKI THOUGH. ALL I COULD FIND WAS A TRASH CAN. I DID MY BEST, BUT I'M NOT A MAGICIAN, Y'KNOW?
SCARY!! MIKAEL WILL KILL US!!
RELAX. NOTHING HE HASN'T TRIED BEFORE. BESIDES, THANKS TO YOURS TRULY, HE'LL NEVER NOTICE. YOU'RE WELCOME.
WHAT'S THE WORST THAT COULD HAPPEN? WE GET EXPELLED AND SENTENCED, THATS ABOUT IT.
YOU'RE NOT HELPING!

IT DOESN'T MATTER. WE'RE A UNIT NOW...

...WE HAVE EACH OTHER'S BACKS FROM NOW ON.

ARE THE BOTH OF YOU GONNA KEEP BLABBIN' LIKE LITTLE KIDS THE WHOLE TIME? JEEZ, SHUT UP!

LET'S NOT FORGET WHY WE CAME HERE IN THE FIRST PLACE!

COME TO THINK OF IT, WHY ARE WE HERE—

SKREEEEEEEE—

IS... THAT... RYUZAKI?!

HEH!

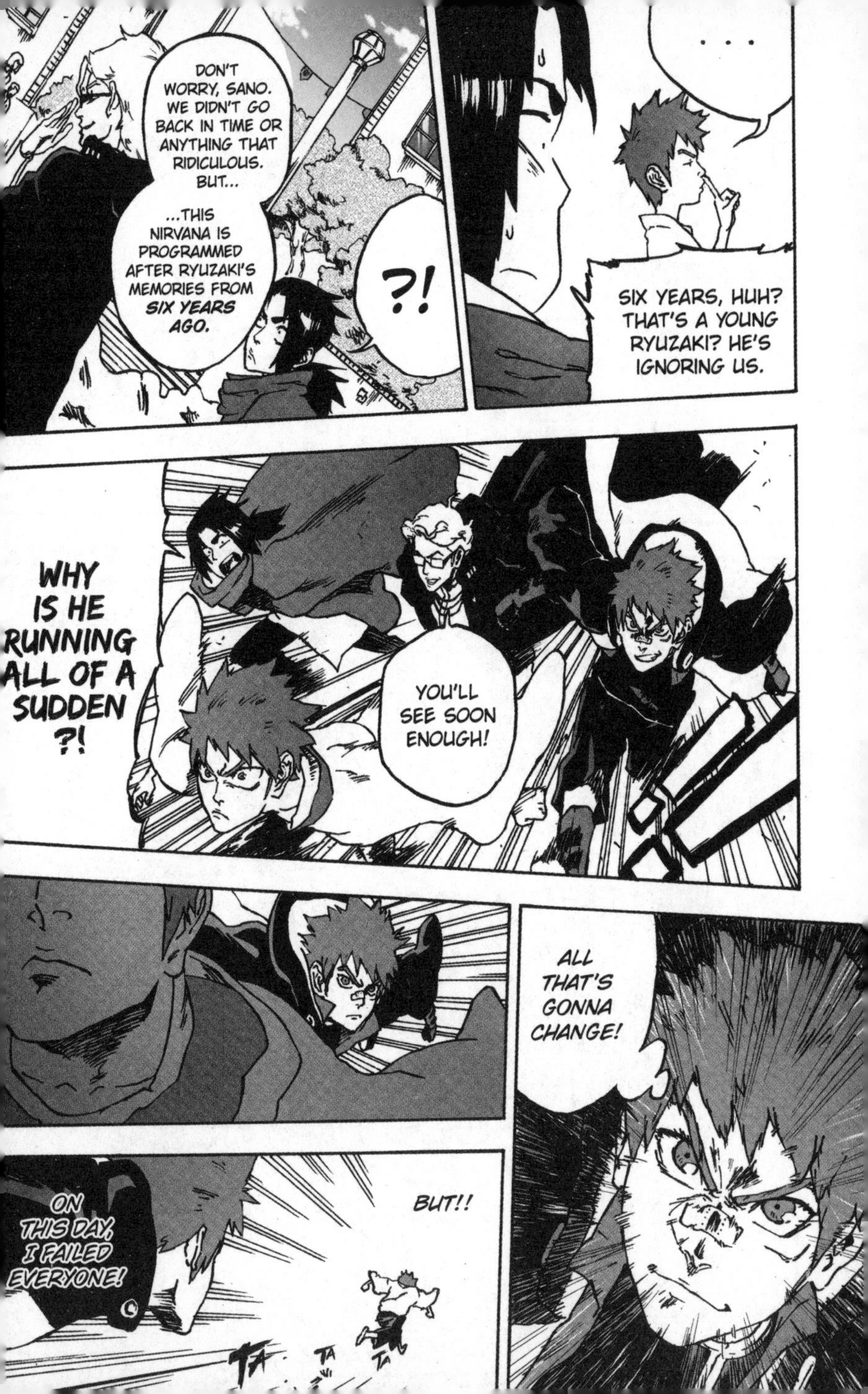
DON'T WORRY, SANO. WE DIDN'T GO BACK IN TIME OR ANYTHING THAT RIDICULOUS. BUT...
...THIS NIRVANA IS PROGRAMMED AFTER RYUZAKI'S MEMORIES FROM SIX YEARS AGO.
?!
...
SIX YEARS, HUH? THAT'S A YOUNG RYUZAKI? HE'S IGNORING US.
WHY IS HE RUNNING ALL OF A SUDDEN ?!
YOU'LL SEE SOON ENOUGH!
ALL THAT'S GONNA CHANGE!
ON THIS DAY, I FAILED EVERYONE!
BUT!!
TA
TA
TA

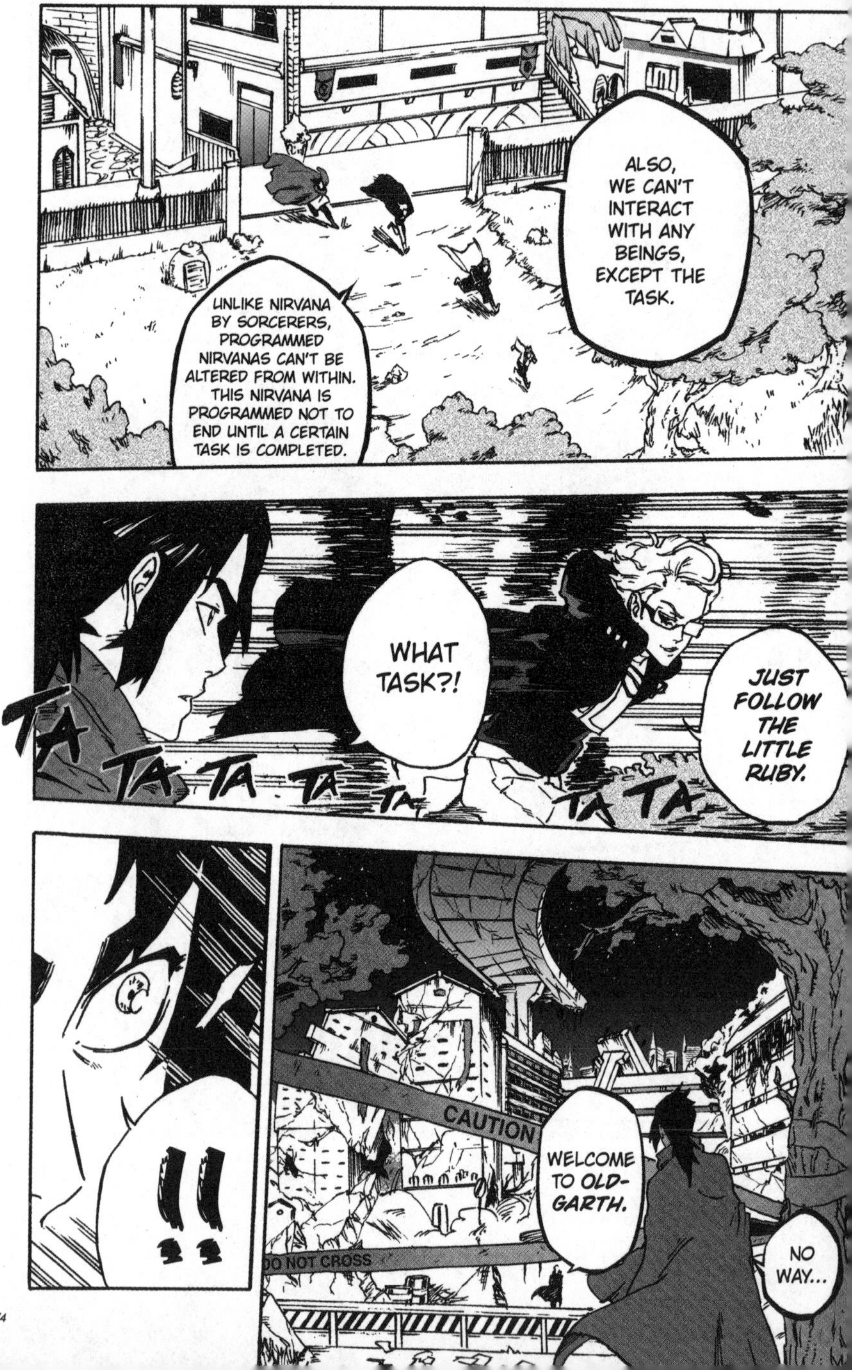
UNLIKE NIRVANA BY SORCERERS, PROGRAMMED NIRVANAS CAN'T BE ALTERED FROM WITHIN. THIS NIRVANA IS PROGRAMMED NOT TO END UNTIL A CERTAIN TASK IS COMPLETED.
ALSO, WE CAN'T INTERACT WITH ANY BEINGS, EXCEPT THE TASK.
TA TA TA TA TA
WHAT TASK?!
TA TA
JUST FOLLOW THE LITTLE RUBY.
CAUTION
WELCOME TO OLD-GARTH.
DO NOT CROSS
NO WAY...

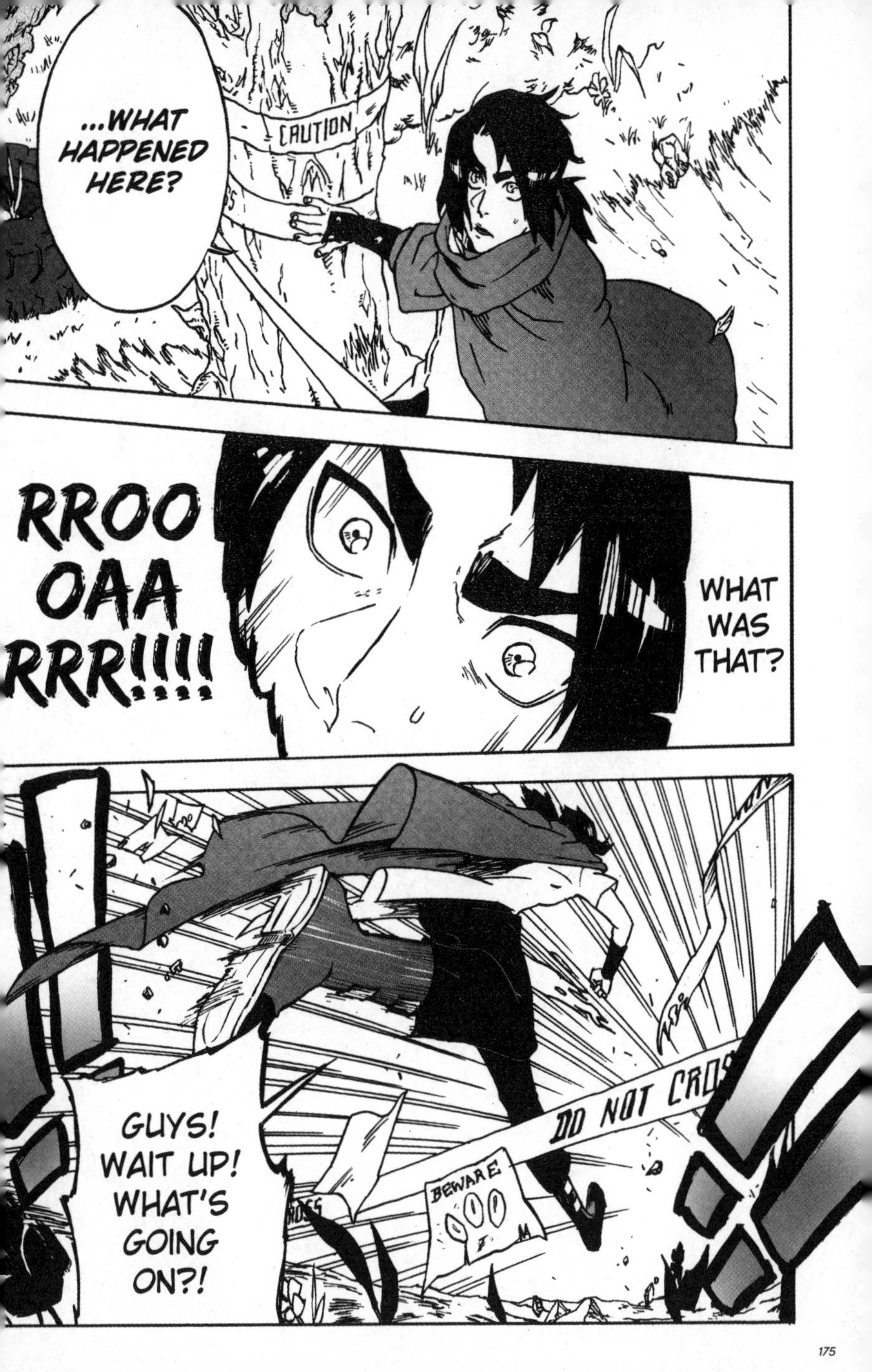

...WHAT HAPPENED HERE?
CAUTION
RROO OAA RRR!!!!
WHAT WAS THAT?
GUYS! WAIT UP! WHAT'S GOING ON?!
DO NOT CROS
BEWARE

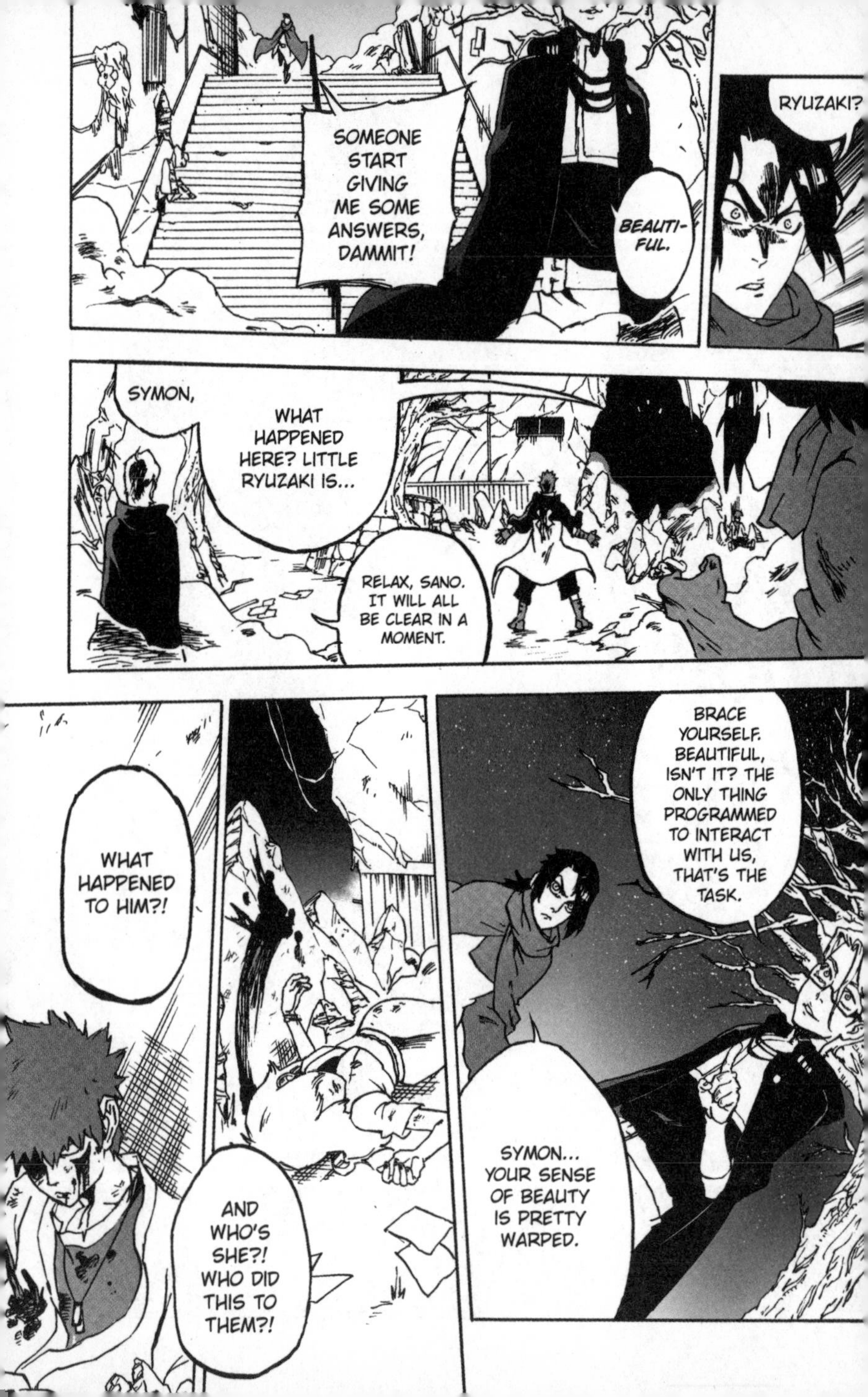
SOMEONE START GIVING ME SOME ANSWERS, DAMMIT!
BEAUTI-FUL.
RYUZAKI?
SYMON,
WHAT HAPPENED HERE? LITTLE RYUZAKI IS...
RELAX, SANO. IT WILL ALL BE CLEAR IN A MOMENT.
WHAT HAPPENED TO HIM?!
AND WHO'S SHE?! WHO DID THIS TO THEM?!
BRACE YOURSELF. BEAUTIFUL, ISN'T IT? THE ONLY THING PROGRAMMED TO INTERACT WITH US, THAT'S THE TASK.
SYMON... YOUR SENSE OF BEAUTY IS PRETTY WARPED.

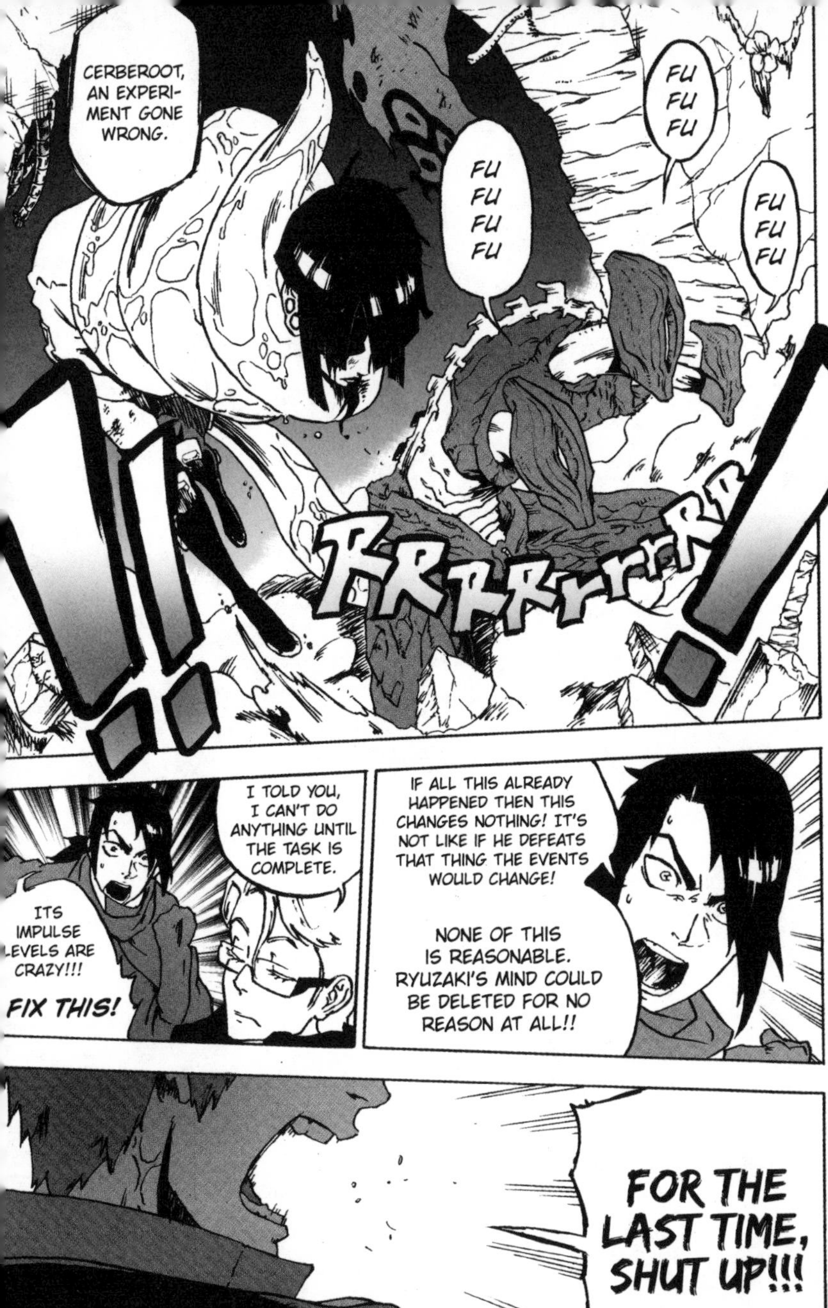
CERBEROOT, AN EXPERIMENT GONE WRONG.
FU FU FU FU
FU FU FU
FU FU FU
BRRRRrrrRR
I TOLD YOU, I CAN'T DO ANYTHING UNTIL THE TASK IS COMPLETE.
ITS IMPULSE LEVELS ARE CRAZY!!!
FIX THIS!
IF ALL THIS ALREADY HAPPENED THEN THIS CHANGES NOTHING! IT'S NOT LIKE IF HE DEFEATS THAT THING THE EVENTS WOULD CHANGE!
NONE OF THIS IS REASONABLE. RYUZAKI'S MIND COULD BE DELETED FOR NO REASON AT ALL!!
FOR THE LAST TIME, SHUT UP!!!

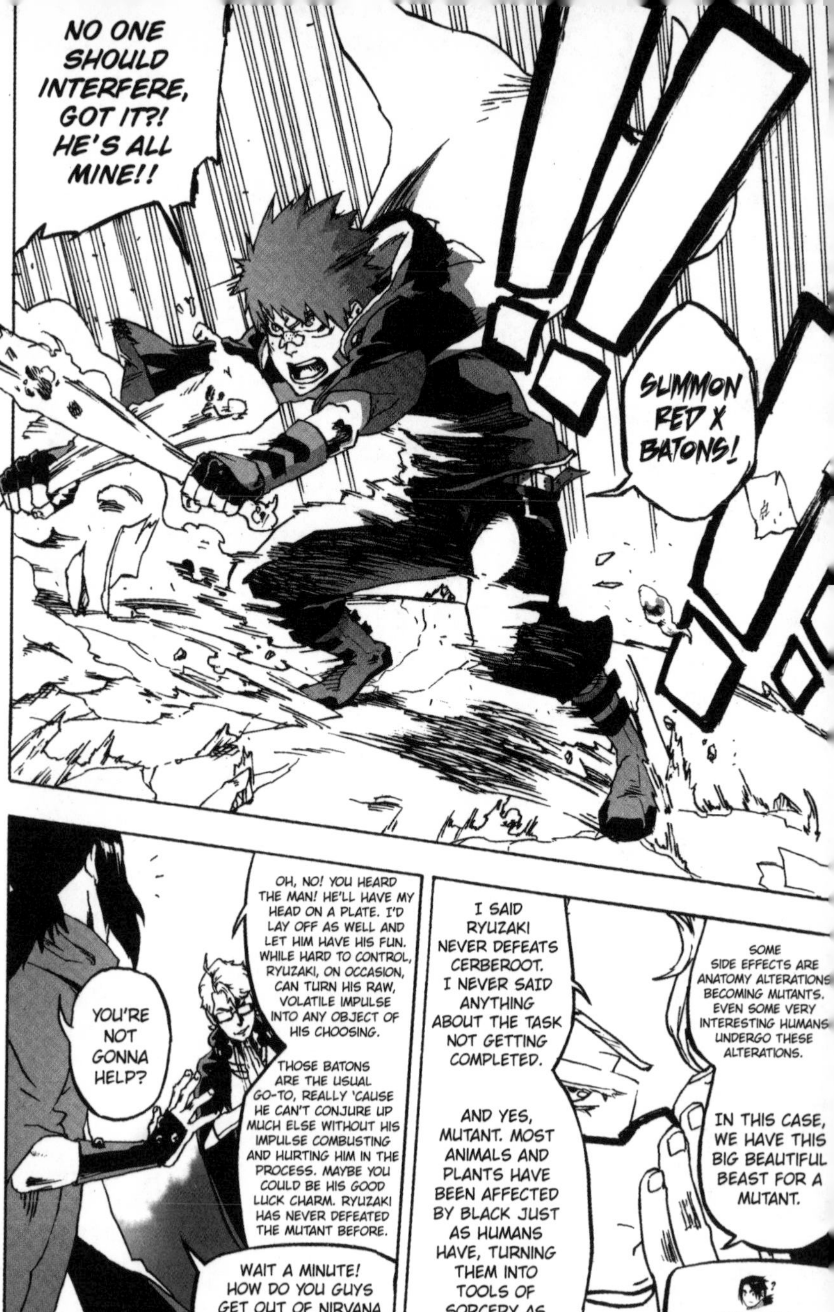

NO ONE SHOULD INTERFERE, GOT IT?! HE'S ALL MINE!!
SUMMON RED X BATONS!
YOU'RE NOT GONNA HELP?
OH, NO! YOU HEARD THE MAN! HE'LL HAVE MY HEAD ON A PLATE. I'D LAY OFF AS WELL AND LET HIM HAVE HIS FUN. WHILE HARD TO CONTROL, RYUZAKI, ON OCCASION, CAN TURN HIS RAW, VOLATILE IMPULSE INTO ANY OBJECT OF HIS CHOOSING.
THOSE BATONS ARE THE USUAL GO-TO, REALLY 'CAUSE HE CAN'T CONJURE UP MUCH ELSE WITHOUT HIS IMPULSE COMBUSTING AND HURTING HIM IN THE PROCESS. MAYBE YOU COULD BE HIS GOOD LUCK CHARM. RYUZAKI HAS NEVER DEFEATED THE MUTANT BEFORE.
WAIT A MINUTE! HOW DO YOU GUYS GET OUT OF NIRVANA IF HE NEVER WINS?! AND A MUTANT?!
I SAID RYUZAKI NEVER DEFEATS CERBEROOT. I NEVER SAID ANYTHING ABOUT THE TASK NOT GETTING COMPLETED.
AND YES, MUTANT. MOST ANIMALS AND PLANTS HAVE BEEN AFFECTED BY BLACK JUST AS HUMANS HAVE, TURNING THEM INTO TOOLS OF SORCERY AS WELL.
SOME SIDE EFFECTS ARE ANATOMY ALTERATIONS BECOMING MUTANTS. EVEN SOME VERY INTERESTING HUMANS UNDERGO THESE ALTERATIONS.
IN THIS CASE, WE HAVE THIS BIG BEAUTIFUL BEAST FOR A MUTANT.
I'M STILL CONFUSED.

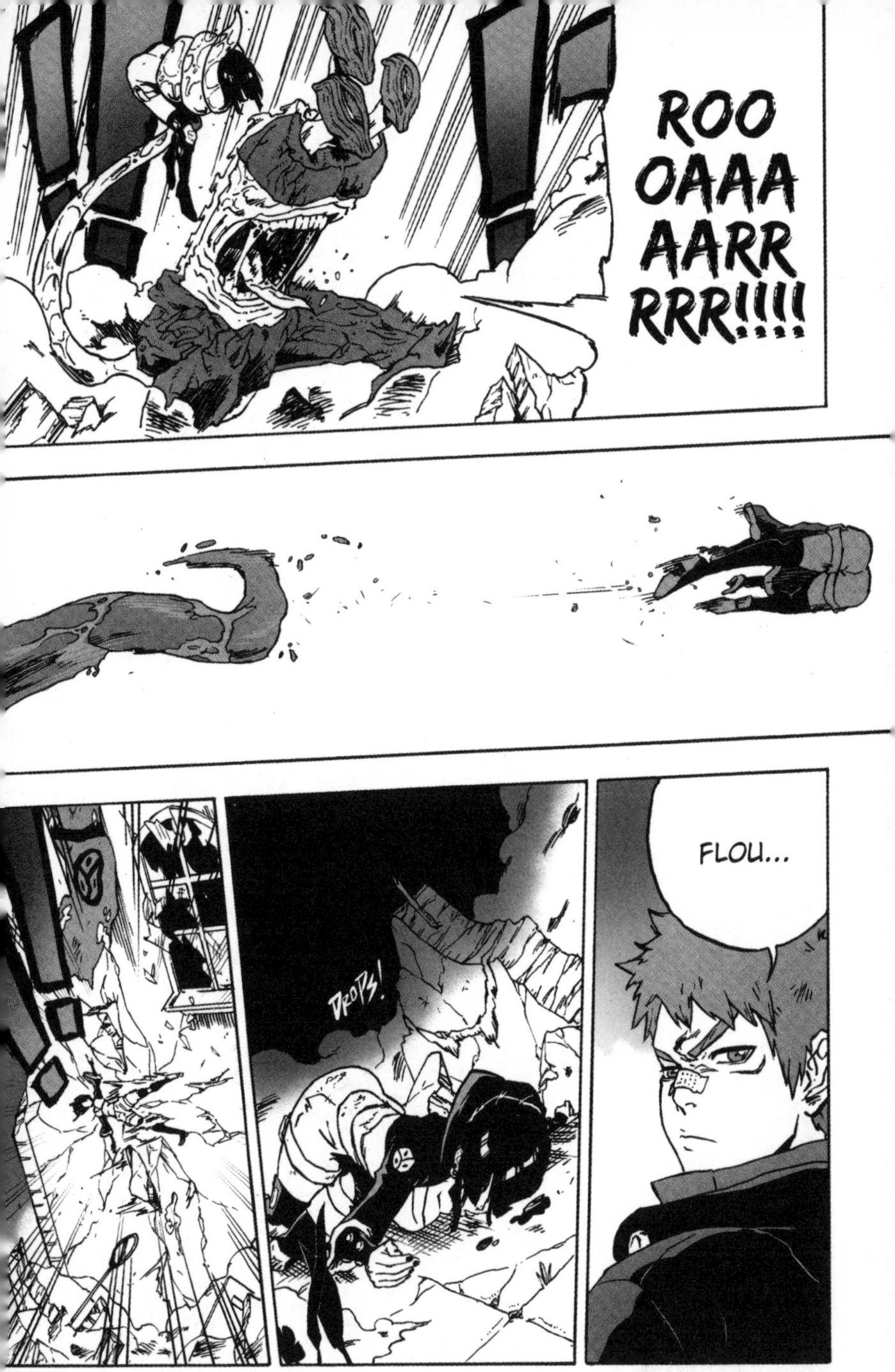
ROO
OAAA
AARR
RRR!!!!
DROPS!
FLOU...

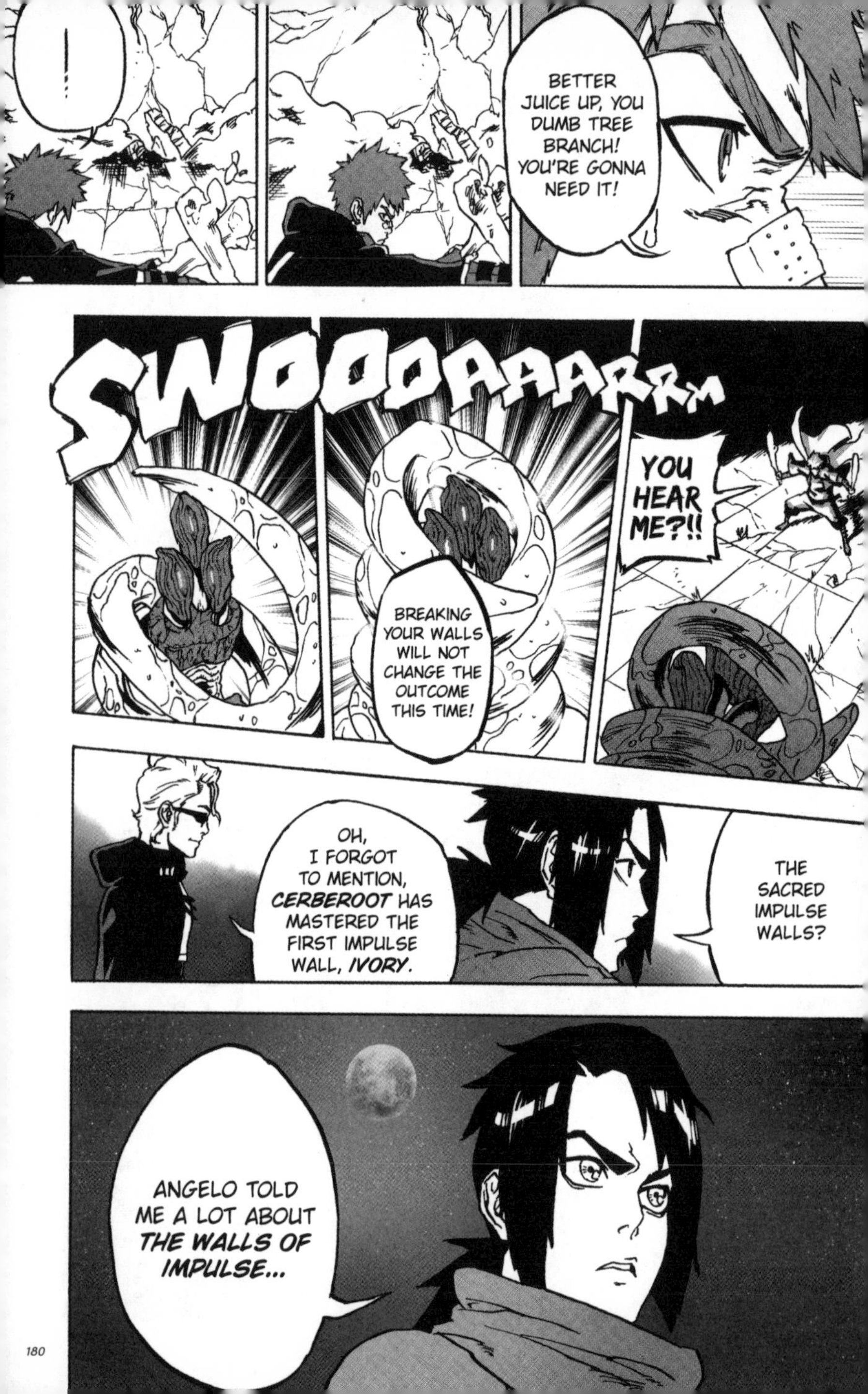
!!
BETTER JUICE UP, YOU DUMB TREE BRANCH! YOU'RE GONNA NEED IT!
SWOOOAAARRM
BREAKING YOUR WALLS WILL NOT CHANGE THE OUTCOME THIS TIME!
YOU HEAR ME?!!
OH, I FORGOT TO MENTION, CERBEROOT HAS MASTERED THE FIRST IMPULSE WALL, IVORY.
THE SACRED IMPULSE WALLS?
ANGELO TOLD ME A LOT ABOUT THE WALLS OF IMPULSE...

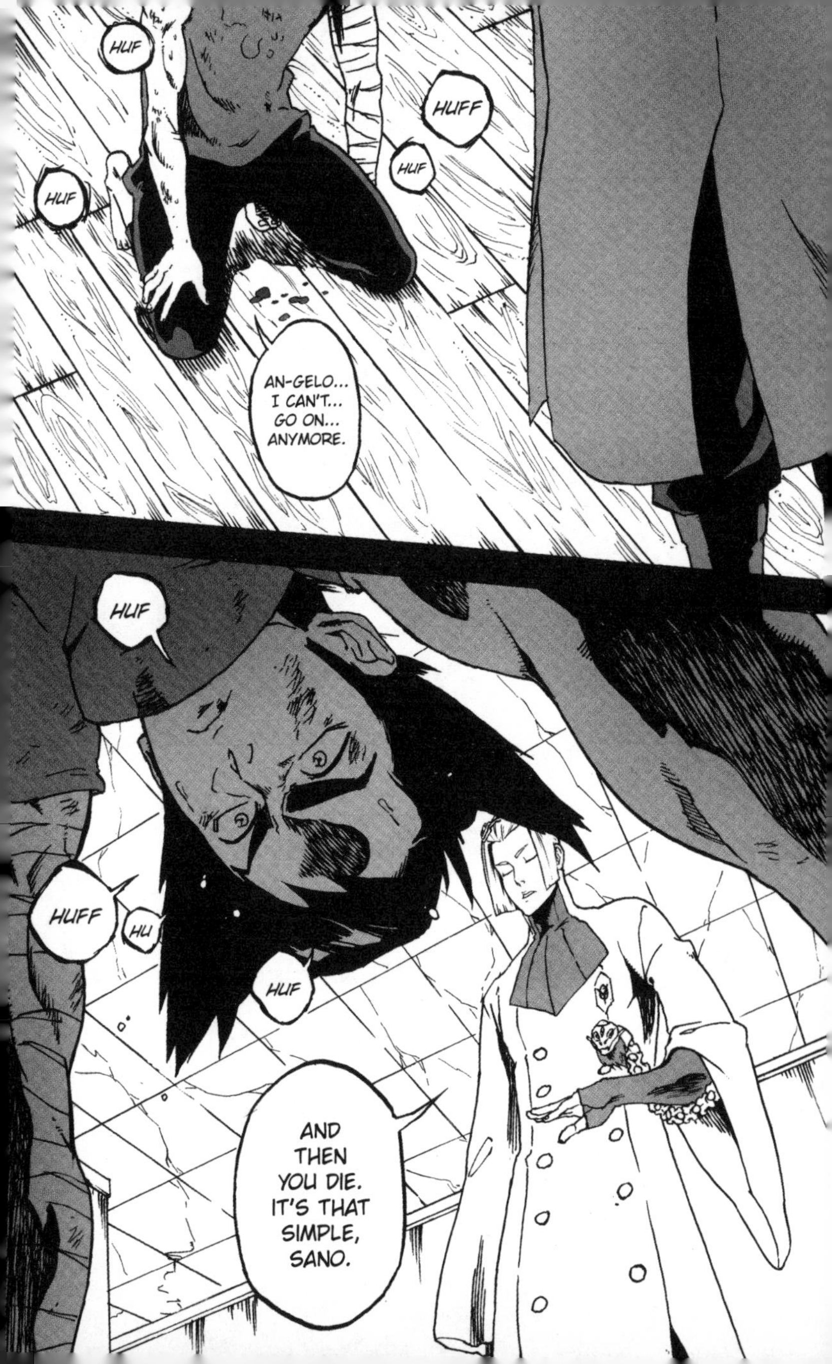
HUF
HUFF
HUF
HUF
AN-GELO... I CAN'T... GO ON... ANYMORE.
HUF
HUFF
HU
HUF
AND THEN YOU DIE. IT'S THAT SIMPLE, SANO.

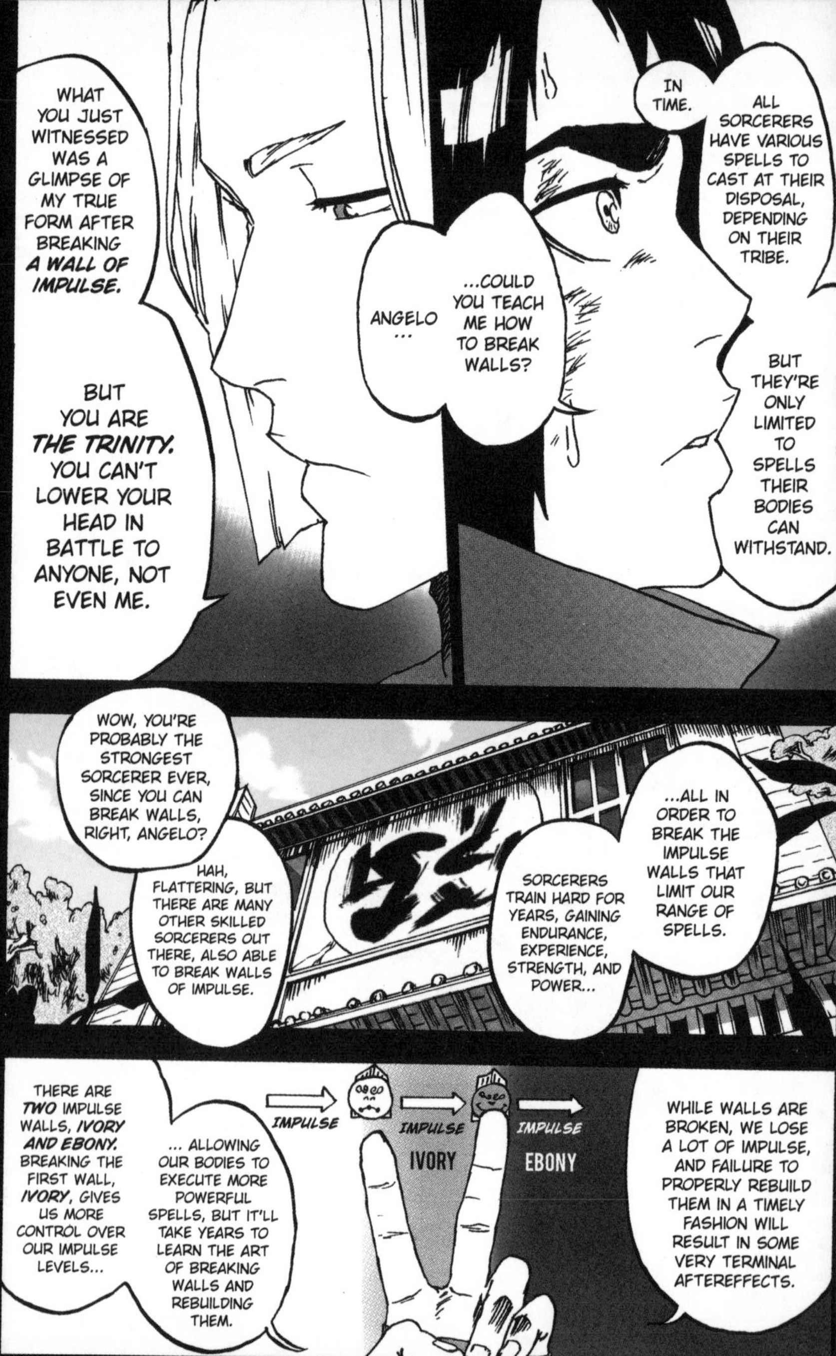

WHAT YOU JUST WITNESSED WAS A GLIMPSE OF MY TRUE FORM AFTER BREAKING ***A WALL OF IMPULSE.***
BUT YOU ARE ***THE TRINITY.*** YOU CAN'T LOWER YOUR HEAD IN BATTLE TO ANYONE, NOT EVEN ME.
ANGELO ...
...COULD YOU TEACH ME HOW TO BREAK WALLS?
IN TIME.
ALL SORCERERS HAVE VARIOUS SPELLS TO CAST AT THEIR DISPOSAL, DEPENDING ON THEIR TRIBE.
BUT THEY'RE ONLY LIMITED TO SPELLS THEIR BODIES CAN WITHSTAND.
WOW, YOU'RE PROBABLY THE STRONGEST SORCERER EVER, SINCE YOU CAN BREAK WALLS, RIGHT, ANGELO?
HAH, FLATTERING, BUT THERE ARE MANY OTHER SKILLED SORCERERS OUT THERE, ALSO ABLE TO BREAK WALLS OF IMPULSE.
SORCERERS TRAIN HARD FOR YEARS, GAINING ENDURANCE, EXPERIENCE, STRENGTH, AND POWER...
...ALL IN ORDER TO BREAK THE IMPULSE WALLS THAT LIMIT OUR RANGE OF SPELLS.
THERE ARE ***TWO*** IMPULSE WALLS, ***IVORY AND EBONY.*** BREAKING THE FIRST WALL, ***IVORY***, GIVES US MORE CONTROL OVER OUR IMPULSE LEVELS...
... ALLOWING OUR BODIES TO EXECUTE MORE POWERFUL SPELLS, BUT IT'LL TAKE YEARS TO LEARN THE ART OF BREAKING WALLS AND REBUILDING THEM.
IMPULSE
IMPULSE
IMPULSE
IVORY
EBONY
WHILE WALLS ARE BROKEN, WE LOSE A LOT OF IMPULSE, AND FAILURE TO PROPERLY REBUILD THEM IN A TIMELY FASHION WILL RESULT IN SOME VERY TERMINAL AFTEREFFECTS.

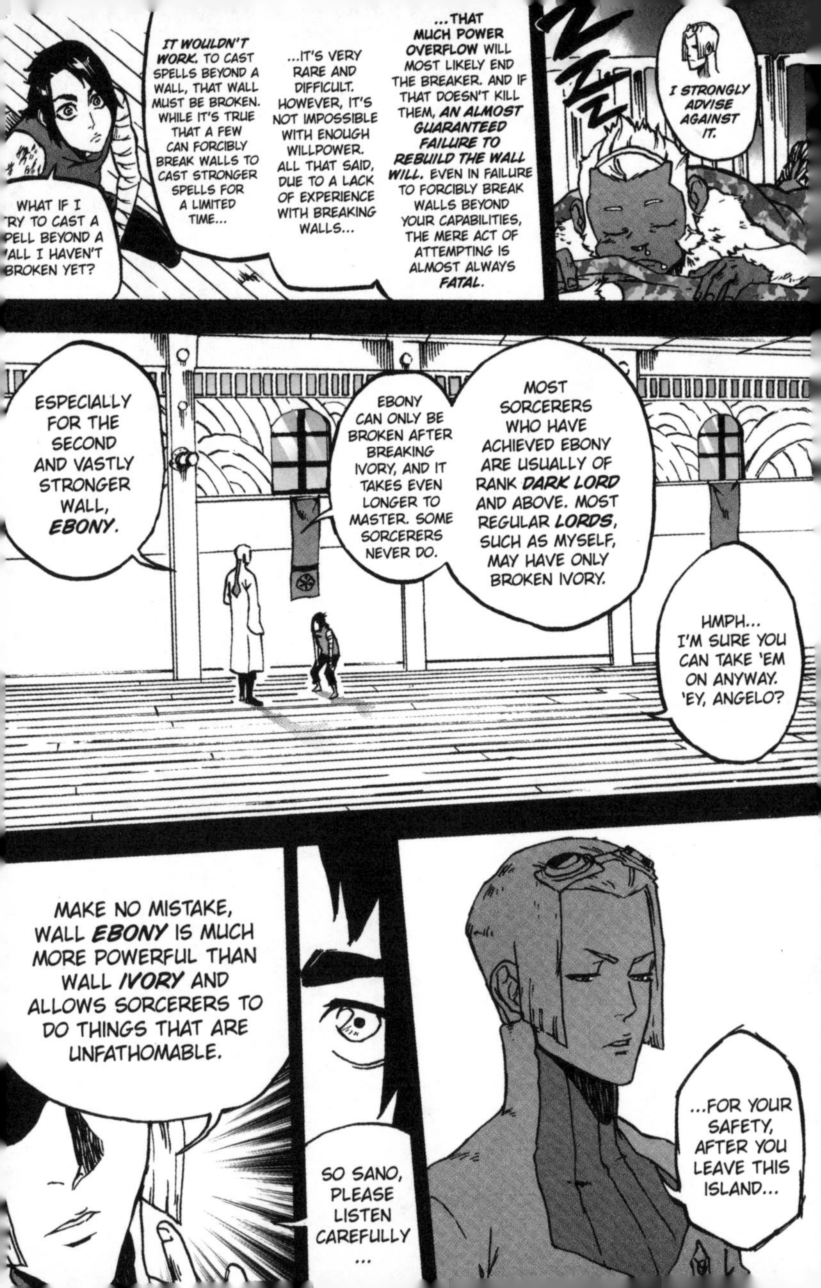
WHAT IF I TRY TO CAST A SPELL BEYOND A WALL I HAVEN'T BROKEN YET?
IT WOULDN'T WORK. TO CAST SPELLS BEYOND A WALL, THAT WALL MUST BE BROKEN. WHILE IT'S TRUE THAT A FEW CAN FORCIBLY BREAK WALLS TO CAST STRONGER SPELLS FOR A LIMITED TIME...
...IT'S VERY RARE AND DIFFICULT. HOWEVER, IT'S NOT IMPOSSIBLE WITH ENOUGH WILLPOWER. ALL THAT SAID, DUE TO A LACK OF EXPERIENCE WITH BREAKING WALLS...
...THAT MUCH POWER OVERFLOW WILL MOST LIKELY END THE BREAKER. AND IF THAT DOESN'T KILL THEM, AN ALMOST GUARANTEED FAILURE TO REBUILD THE WALL WILL. EVEN IN FAILURE TO FORCIBLY BREAK WALLS BEYOND YOUR CAPABILITIES, THE MERE ACT OF ATTEMPTING IS ALMOST ALWAYS FATAL.
ZZZ
I STRONGLY ADVISE AGAINST IT.
ESPECIALLY FOR THE SECOND AND VASTLY STRONGER WALL, EBONY.
EBONY CAN ONLY BE BROKEN AFTER BREAKING IVORY, AND IT TAKES EVEN LONGER TO MASTER. SOME SORCERERS NEVER DO.
MOST SORCERERS WHO HAVE ACHIEVED EBONY ARE USUALLY OF RANK DARK LORD AND ABOVE. MOST REGULAR LORDS, SUCH AS MYSELF, MAY HAVE ONLY BROKEN IVORY.
HMPH... I'M SURE YOU CAN TAKE 'EM ON ANYWAY. 'EY, ANGELO?
MAKE NO MISTAKE, WALL EBONY IS MUCH MORE POWERFUL THAN WALL IVORY AND ALLOWS SORCERERS TO DO THINGS THAT ARE UNFATHOMABLE.
SO SANO, PLEASE LISTEN CAREFULLY...
...FOR YOUR SAFETY, AFTER YOU LEAVE THIS ISLAND...

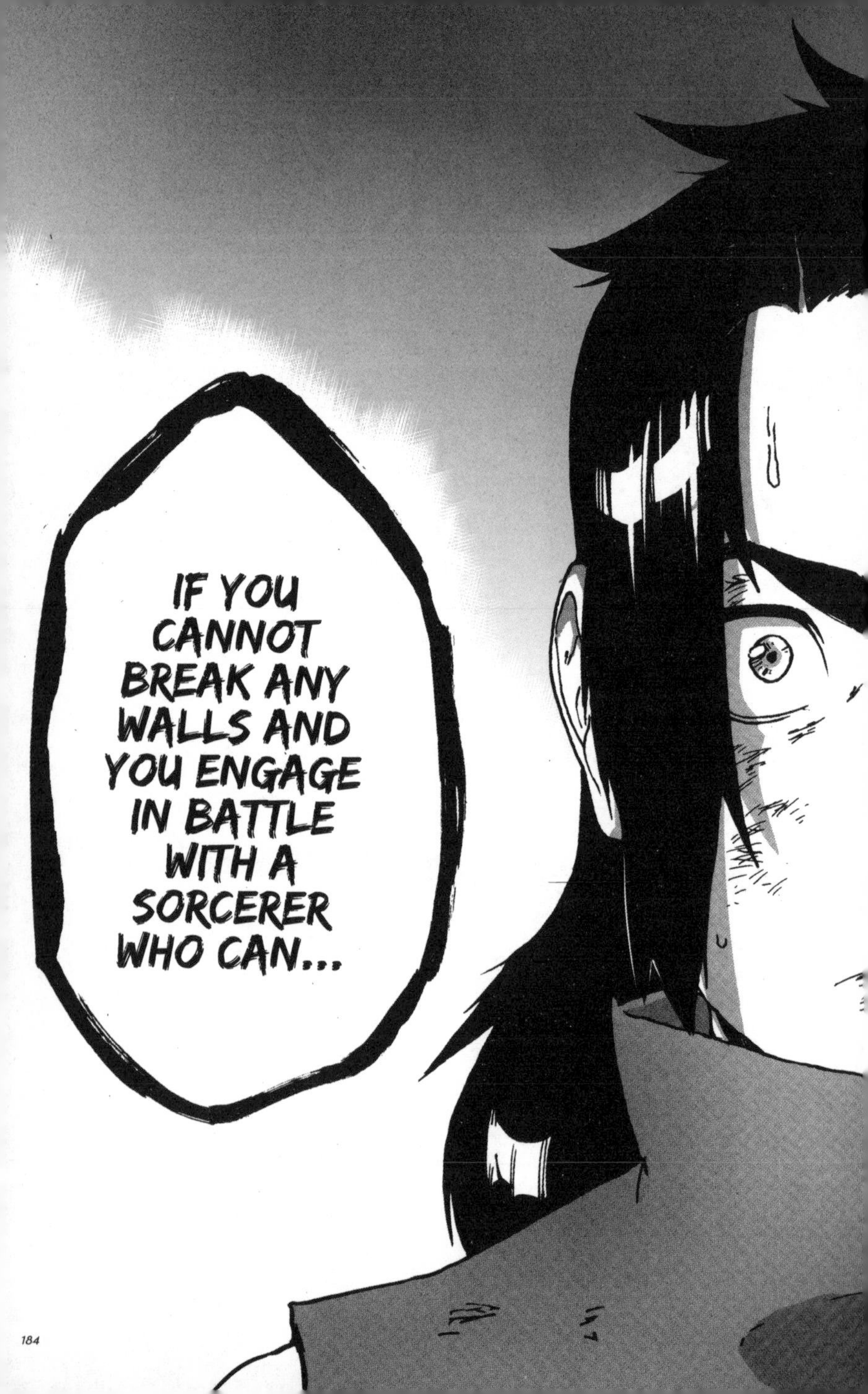
IF YOU CANNOT BREAK ANY WALLS AND YOU ENGAGE IN BATTLE WITH A SORCERER WHO CAN...

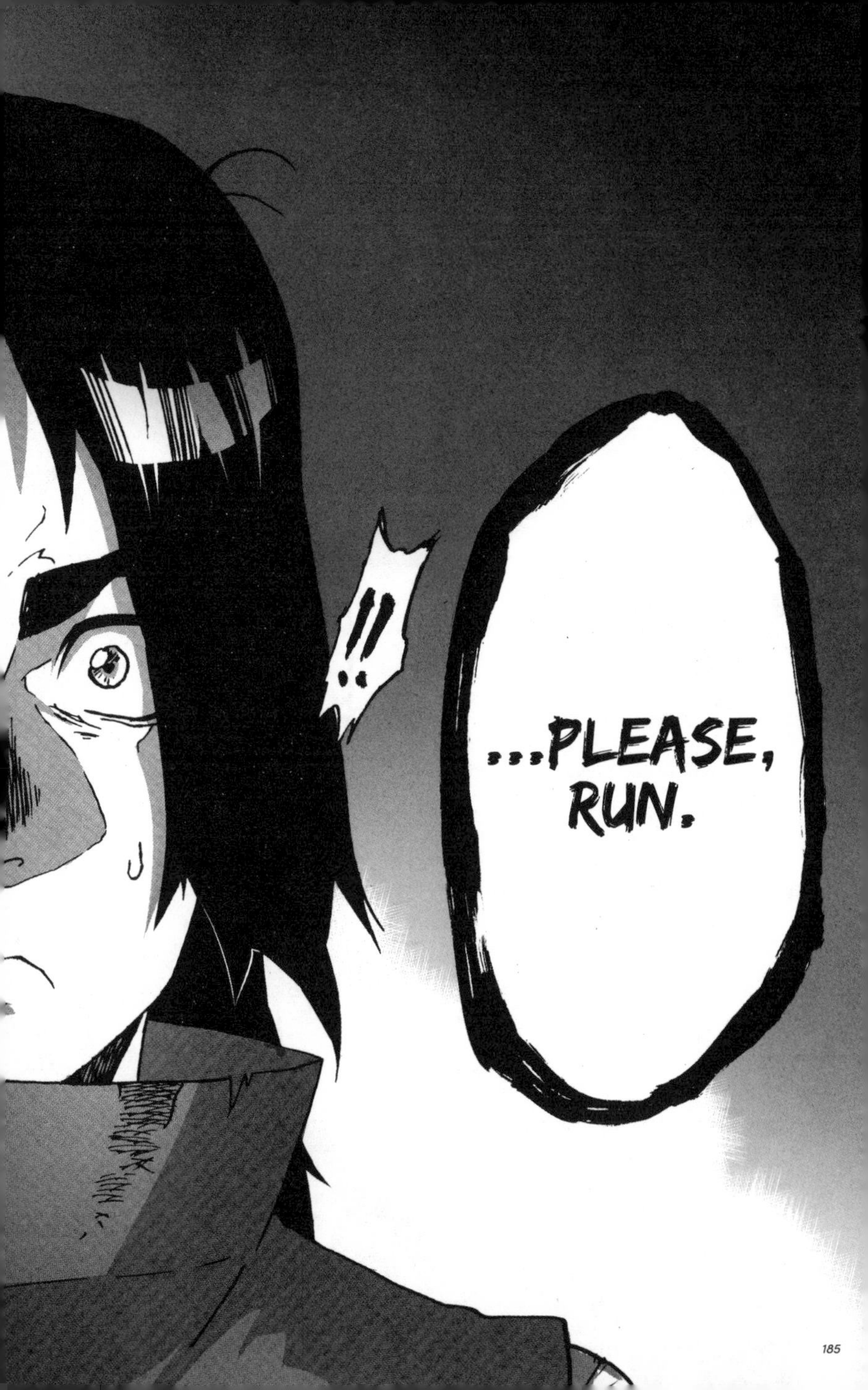
!!
...PLEASE,
RUN.

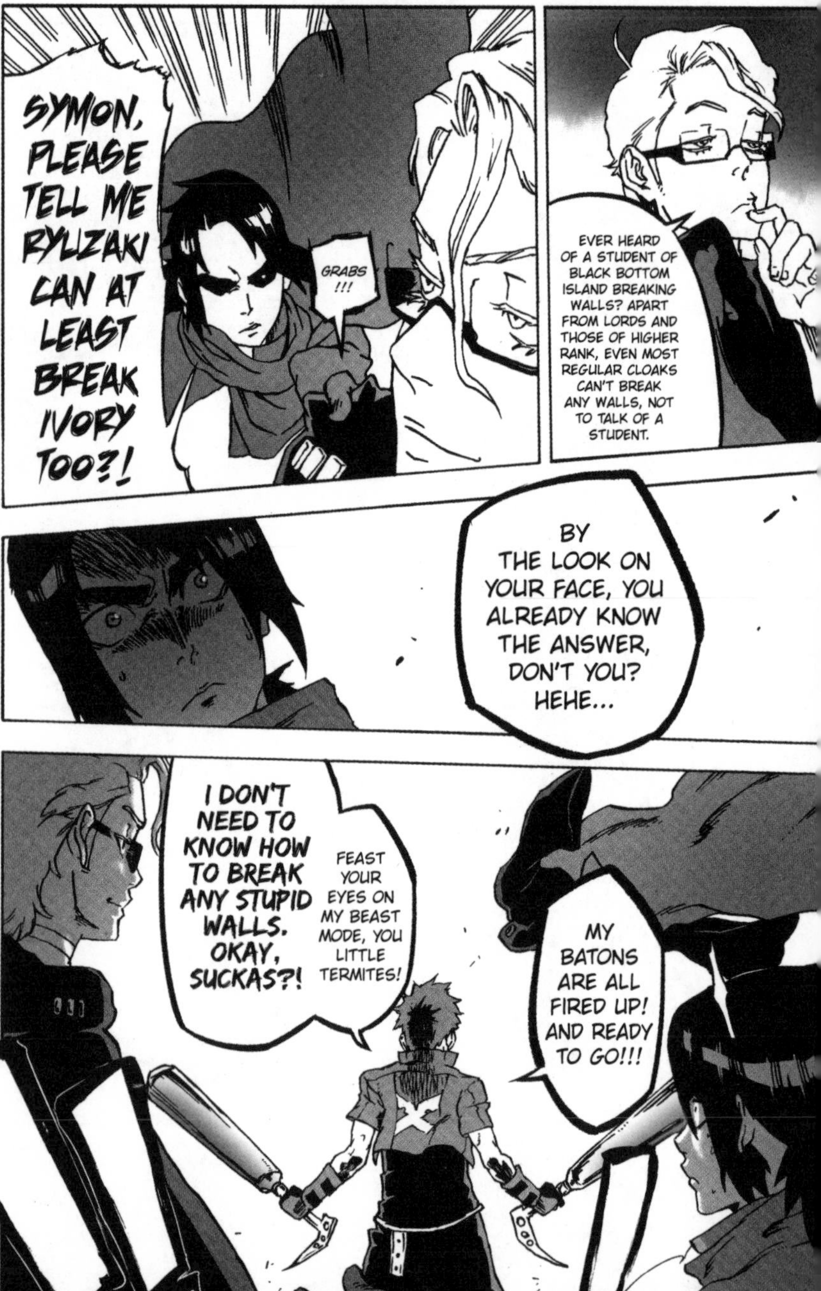
SYMON, PLEASE TELL ME RYUZAKI CAN AT LEAST BREAK IVORY TOO?!
GRABS !!!
EVER HEARD OF A STUDENT OF BLACK BOTTOM ISLAND BREAKING WALLS? APART FROM LORDS AND THOSE OF HIGHER RANK, EVEN MOST REGULAR CLOAKS CAN'T BREAK ANY WALLS, NOT TO TALK OF A STUDENT.
BY THE LOOK ON YOUR FACE, YOU ALREADY KNOW THE ANSWER, DON'T YOU? HEHE...
I DON'T NEED TO KNOW HOW TO BREAK ANY STUPID WALLS. OKAY, SUCKAS?!
FEAST YOUR EYES ON MY BEAST MODE, YOU LITTLE TERMITES!
MY BATONS ARE ALL FIRED UP! AND READY TO GO!!!

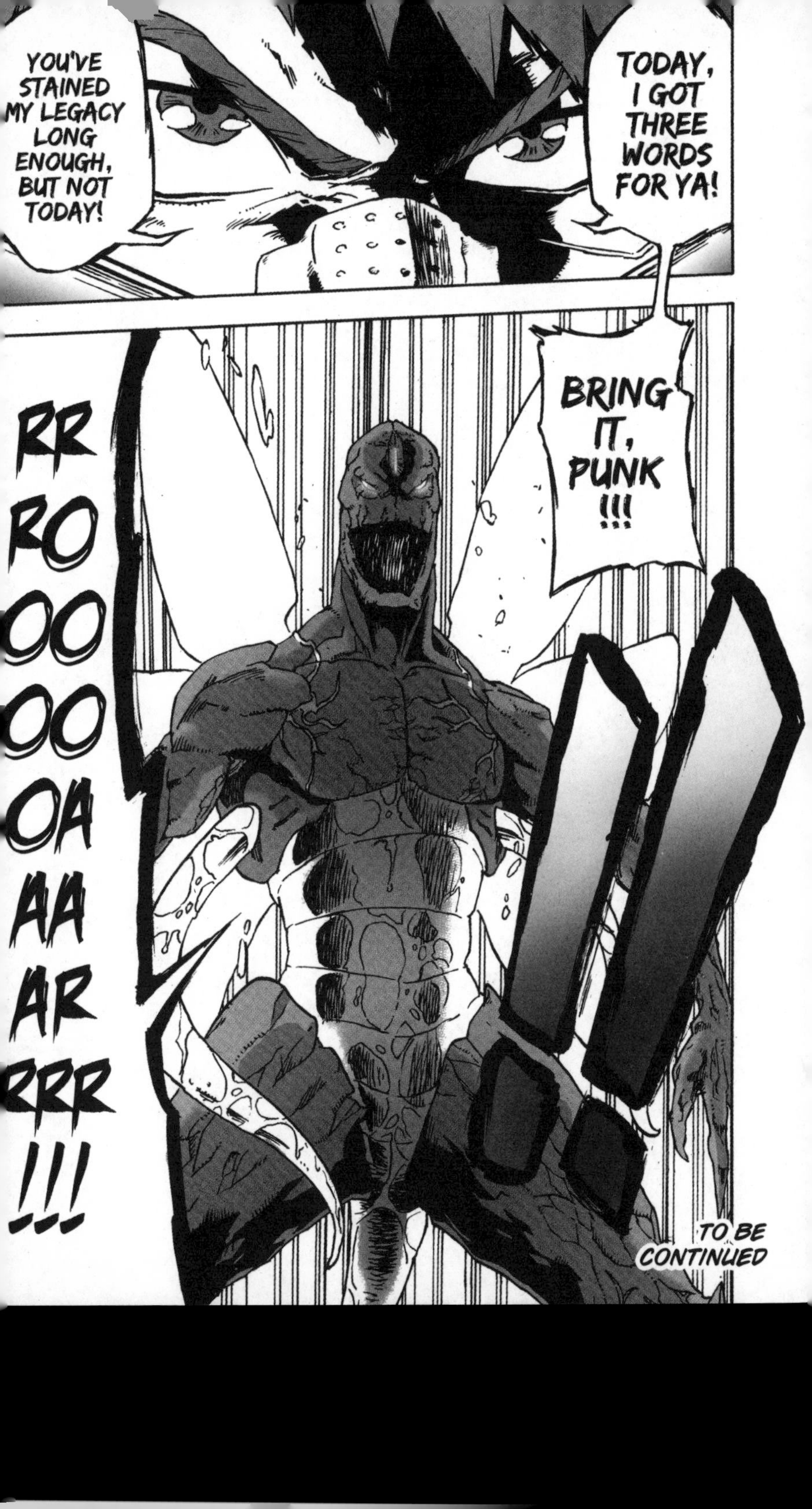
YOU'VE STAINED MY LEGACY LONG ENOUGH, BUT NOT TODAY!
TODAY, I GOT THREE WORDS FOR YA!
RRROOOOOOOAAAARRRR!!!
BRING IT, PUNK!!!
TO BE CONTINUED

# APPLE BLACK

## END OF VOLUME 1

ABOUT THE AUTHOR

# ODUNZE OGUGUO

Nigerian artist **Odunze Oguguo** (aka Whyt Manga)
is the creator of hit manga series *Apple Black*
and *Bacassi*. Odunze is one of the co-founders of
MyFutprint Entertainment, LLC, and a central figure
in developing its brands, including Saturday AM.
He holds both bachelor's and master's degrees
from the University of Texas at Arlington.

## ACKNOWLEDGMENTS

THE FIRST-EVER APPLE BLACK PAGE WAS DRAWN IN 2012. A FEW YEARS, IMPROVEMENTS, AND EDITS LATER, HERE WE ARE! WE'VE WORKED SO HARD TO BRING YOU THESE BOOKS, AND WE'RE PROUD OF ALL WE'VE DONE AND ACCOMPLISHED. BIG THANKS TO OUR SUPPORTERS WHO'VE STOOD BY THIS SERIES OVER THE YEARS

I HOPE YOU GUYS ENJOY IT!

-Odunze Oguguo (Whyt Manga)

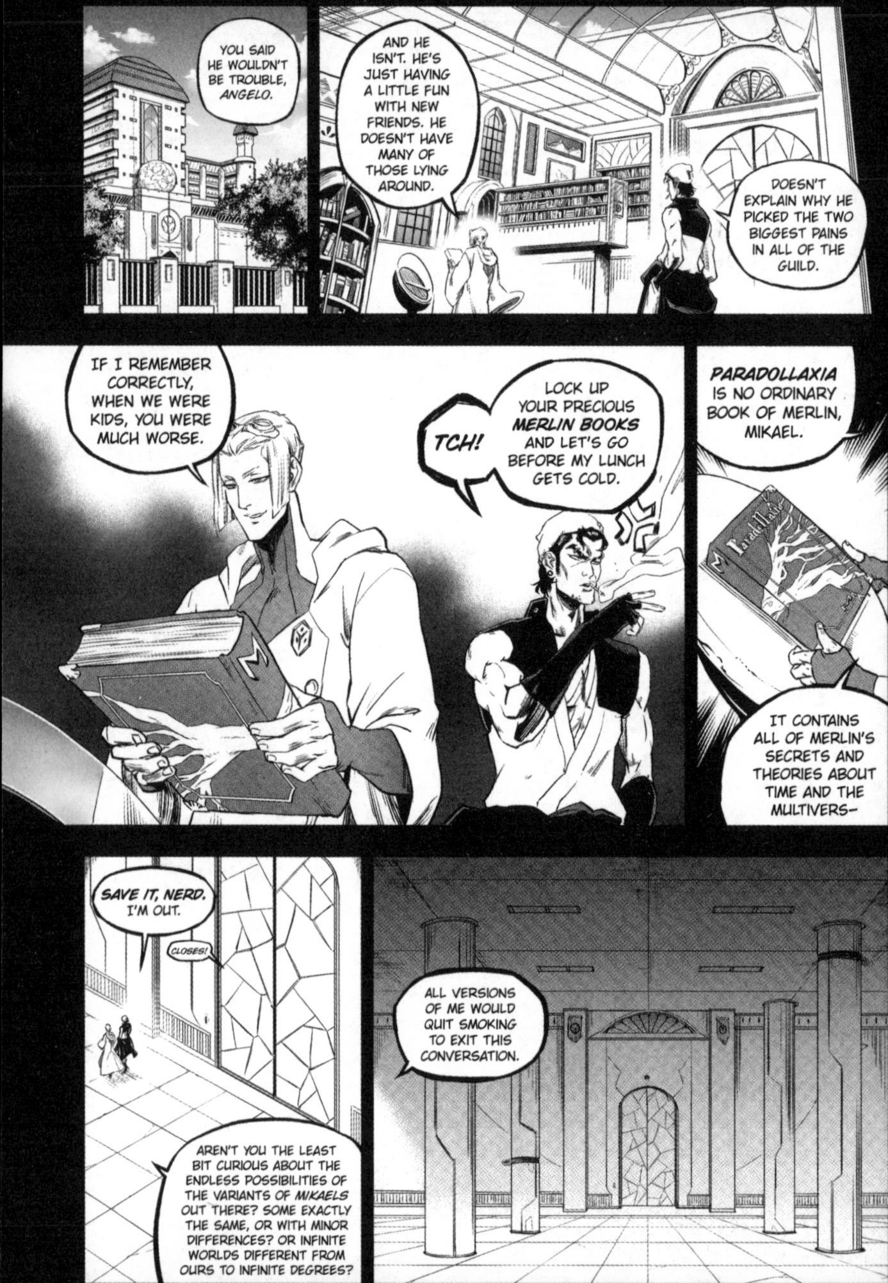
YOU SAID HE WOULDN'T BE TROUBLE, *ANGELO.*
AND HE ISN'T. HE'S JUST HAVING A LITTLE FUN WITH NEW FRIENDS. HE DOESN'T HAVE MANY OF THOSE LYING AROUND.
DOESN'T EXPLAIN WHY HE PICKED THE TWO BIGGEST PAINS IN ALL OF THE GUILD.
IF I REMEMBER CORRECTLY, WHEN WE WERE KIDS, YOU WERE MUCH WORSE.
TCH!
LOCK UP YOUR PRECIOUS *MERLIN BOOKS* AND LET'S GO BEFORE MY LUNCH GETS COLD.
*PARADOLLAXIA* IS NO ORDINARY BOOK OF MERLIN, MIKAEL.
IT CONTAINS ALL OF MERLIN'S SECRETS AND THEORIES ABOUT TIME AND THE MULTIVERS–
*SAVE IT, NERD.* I'M OUT.
CLOSES!
ALL VERSIONS OF ME WOULD QUIT SMOKING TO EXIT THIS CONVERSATION.
AREN'T YOU THE LEAST BIT CURIOUS ABOUT THE ENDLESS POSSIBILITIES OF THE VARIANTS OF *MIKAELS* OUT THERE? SOME EXACTLY THE SAME, OR WITH MINOR DIFFERENCES? OR INFINITE WORLDS DIFFERENT FROM OURS TO INFINITE DEGREES?

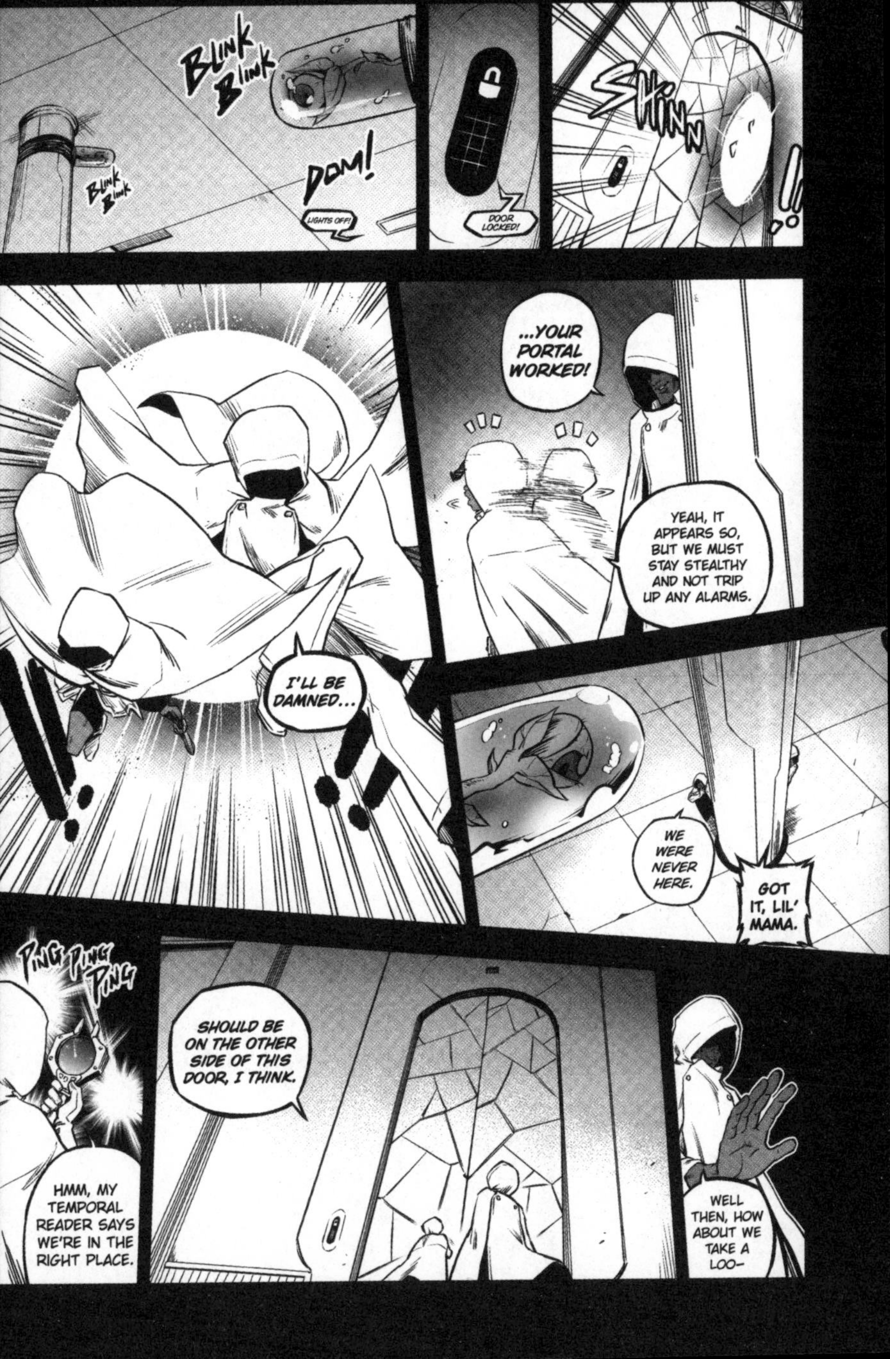
BLINK BLINK
BLINK BLINK
DOM!
LIGHTS OFF!
DOOR LOCKED!
SHINN
!!
...YOUR PORTAL WORKED!
YEAH, IT APPEARS SO, BUT WE MUST STAY STEALTHY AND NOT TRIP UP ANY ALARMS.
I'LL BE DAMNED...
WE WERE NEVER HERE.
GOT IT, LIL' MAMA.
PING PING PING
HMM, MY TEMPORAL READER SAYS WE'RE IN THE RIGHT PLACE.
SHOULD BE ON THE OTHER SIDE OF THIS DOOR, I THINK.
WELL THEN, HOW ABOUT WE TAKE A LOO–

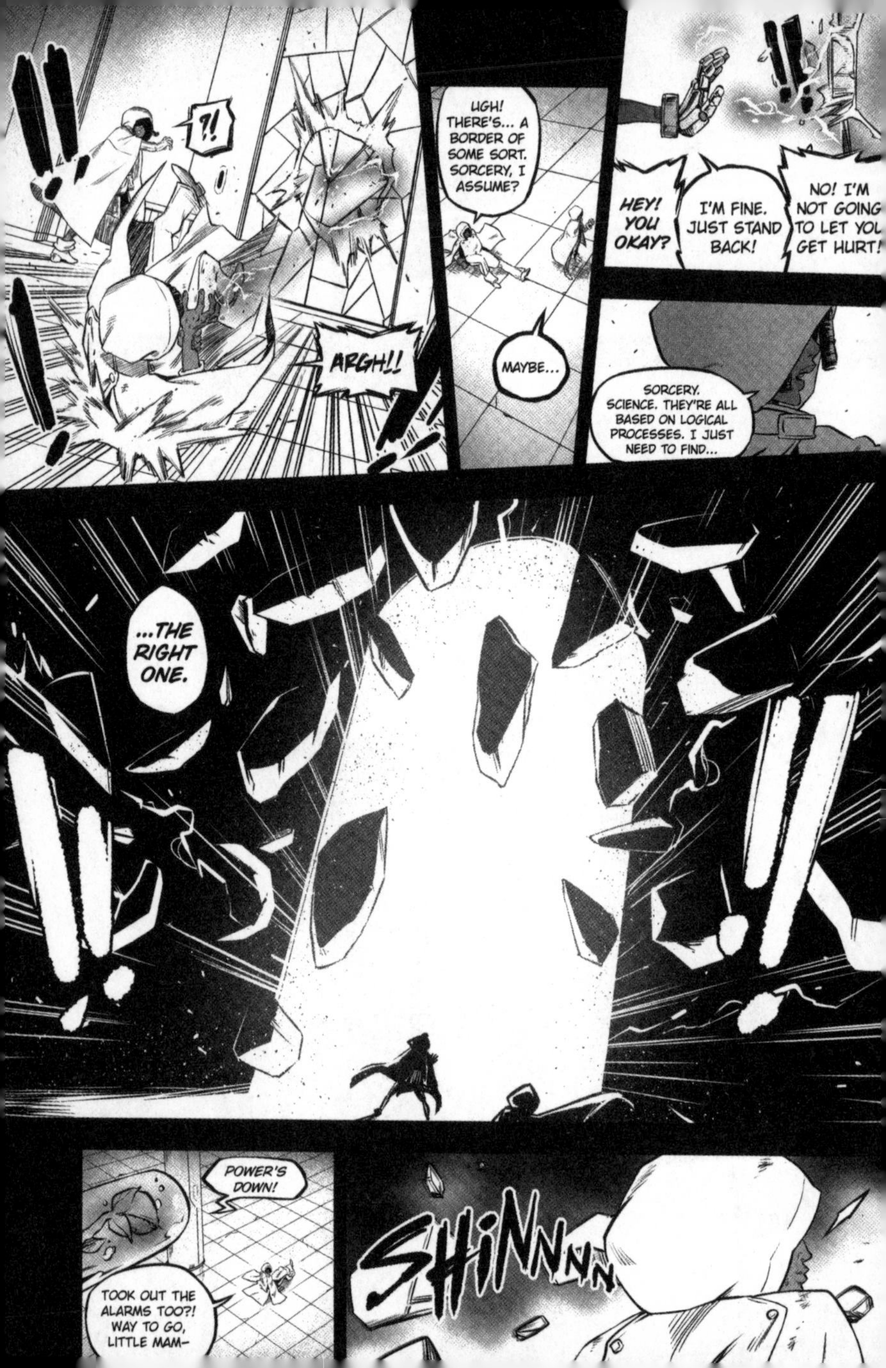
?!
ARGH!!
UGH! THERE'S... A BORDER OF SOME SORT. SORCERY, I ASSUME?
MAYBE...
HEY! YOU OKAY?
I'M FINE. JUST STAND BACK!
NO! I'M NOT GOING TO LET YOU GET HURT!
SORCERY. SCIENCE. THEY'RE ALL BASED ON LOGICAL PROCESSES. I JUST NEED TO FIND...
...THE RIGHT ONE.
POWER'S DOWN!
TOOK OUT THE ALARMS TOO?! WAY TO GO, LITTLE MAM—
SHINNNNN

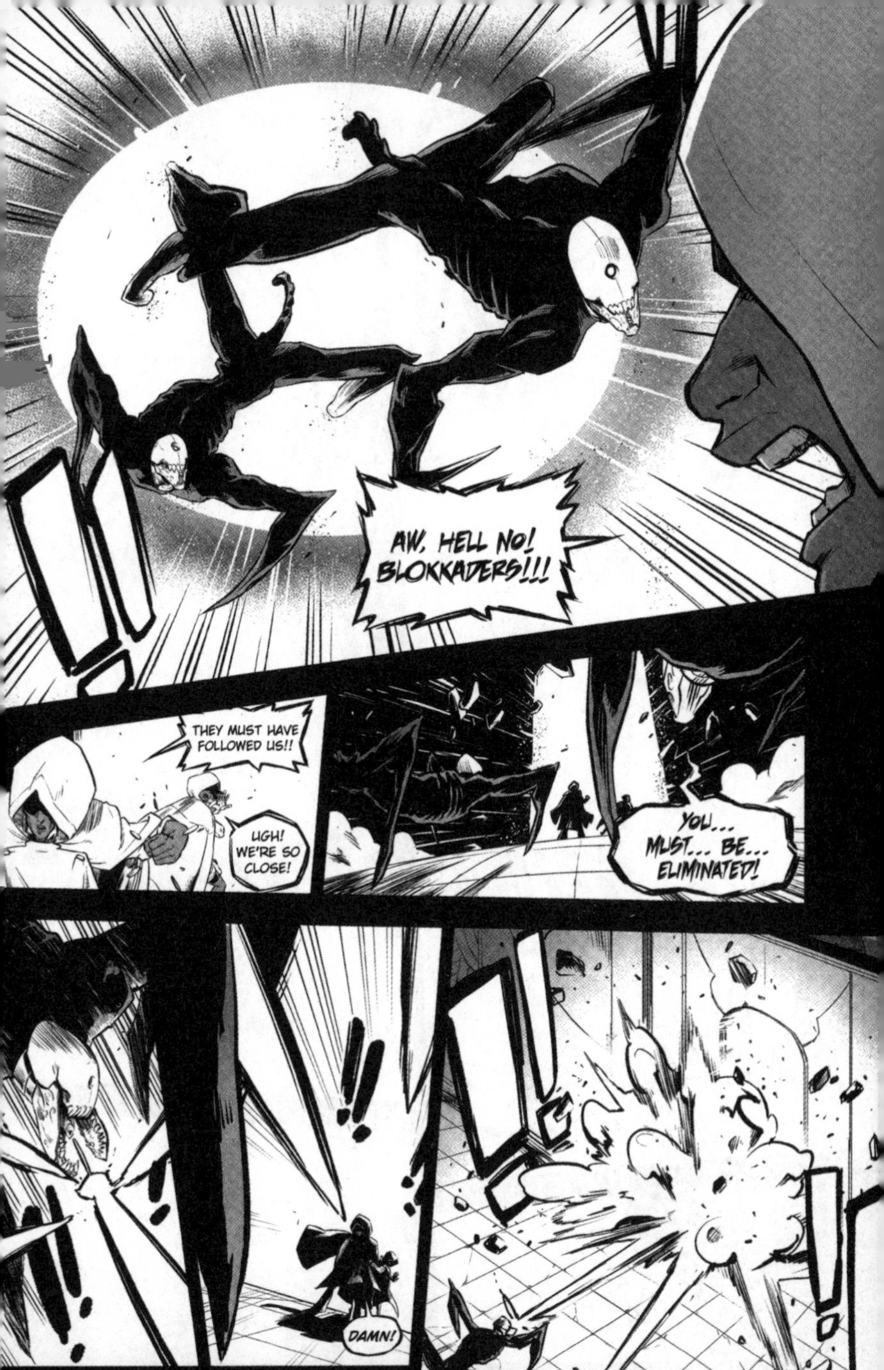
AW, HELL NO! BLOKKADERS!!!
THEY MUST HAVE FOLLOWED US!!
UGH! WE'RE SO CLOSE!
YOU... MUST... BE... ELIMINATED!
DAMN!

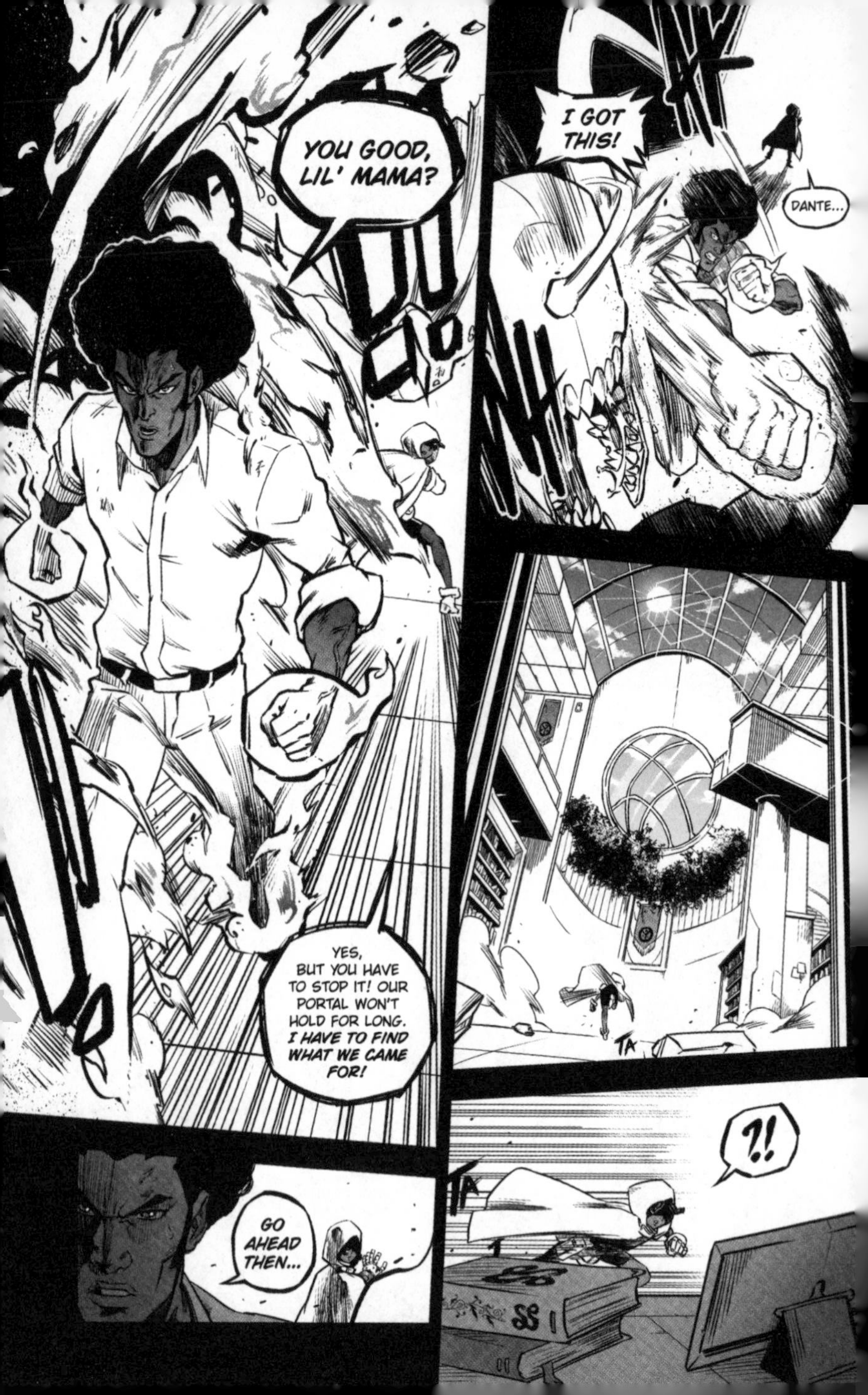
YOU GOOD, LIL' MAMA?
YES, BUT YOU HAVE TO STOP IT! OUR PORTAL WON'T HOLD FOR LONG. I HAVE TO FIND WHAT WE CAME FOR!
I GOT THIS!
DANTE...
TA
GO AHEAD THEN...
TA
?!

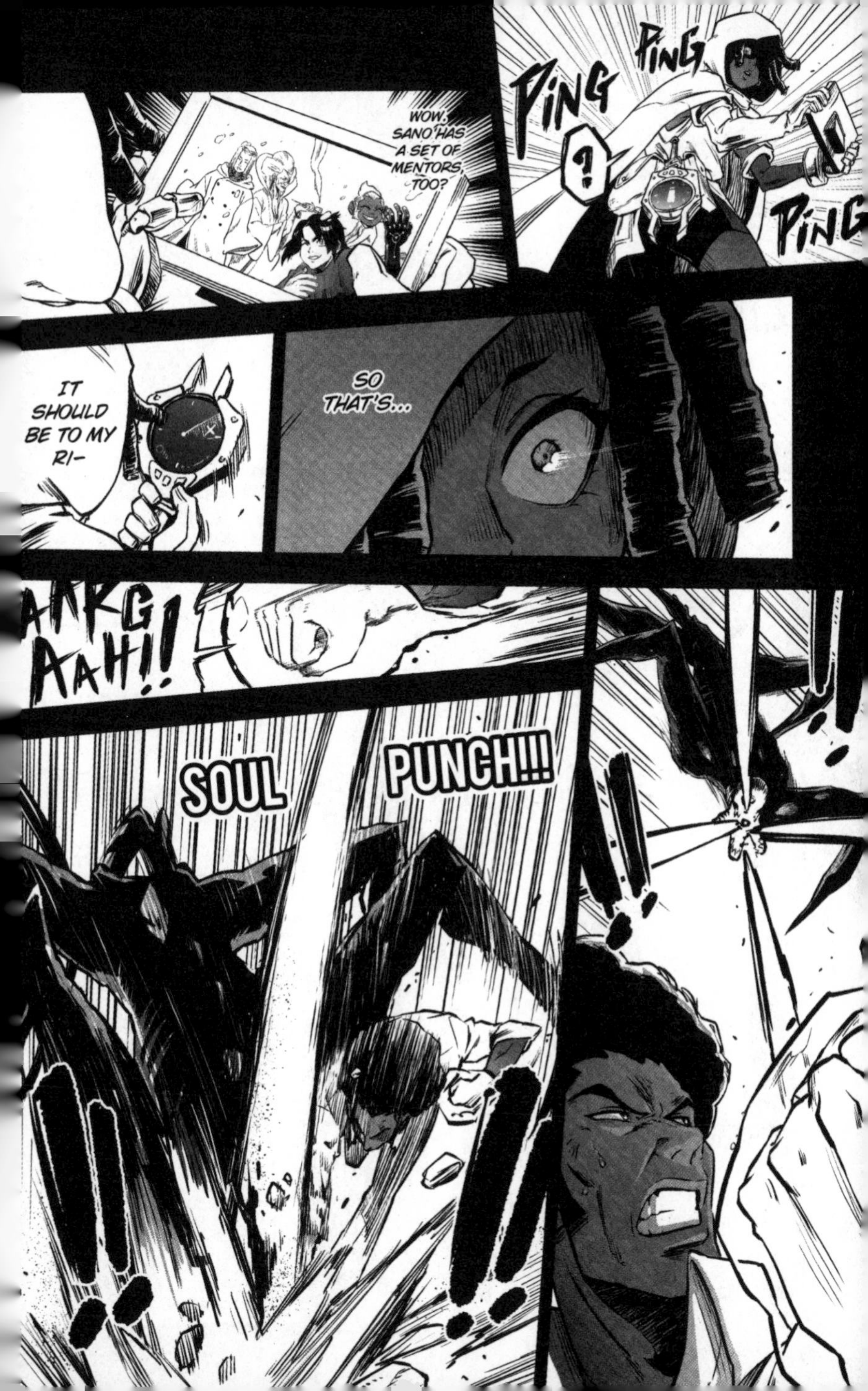
WOW. SANO HAS A SET OF MENTORS, TOO?
PING PING
?
PING
IT SHOULD BE TO MY RI-
SO THAT'S...
AHRG AAH!!
SOUL
PUNCH!!!

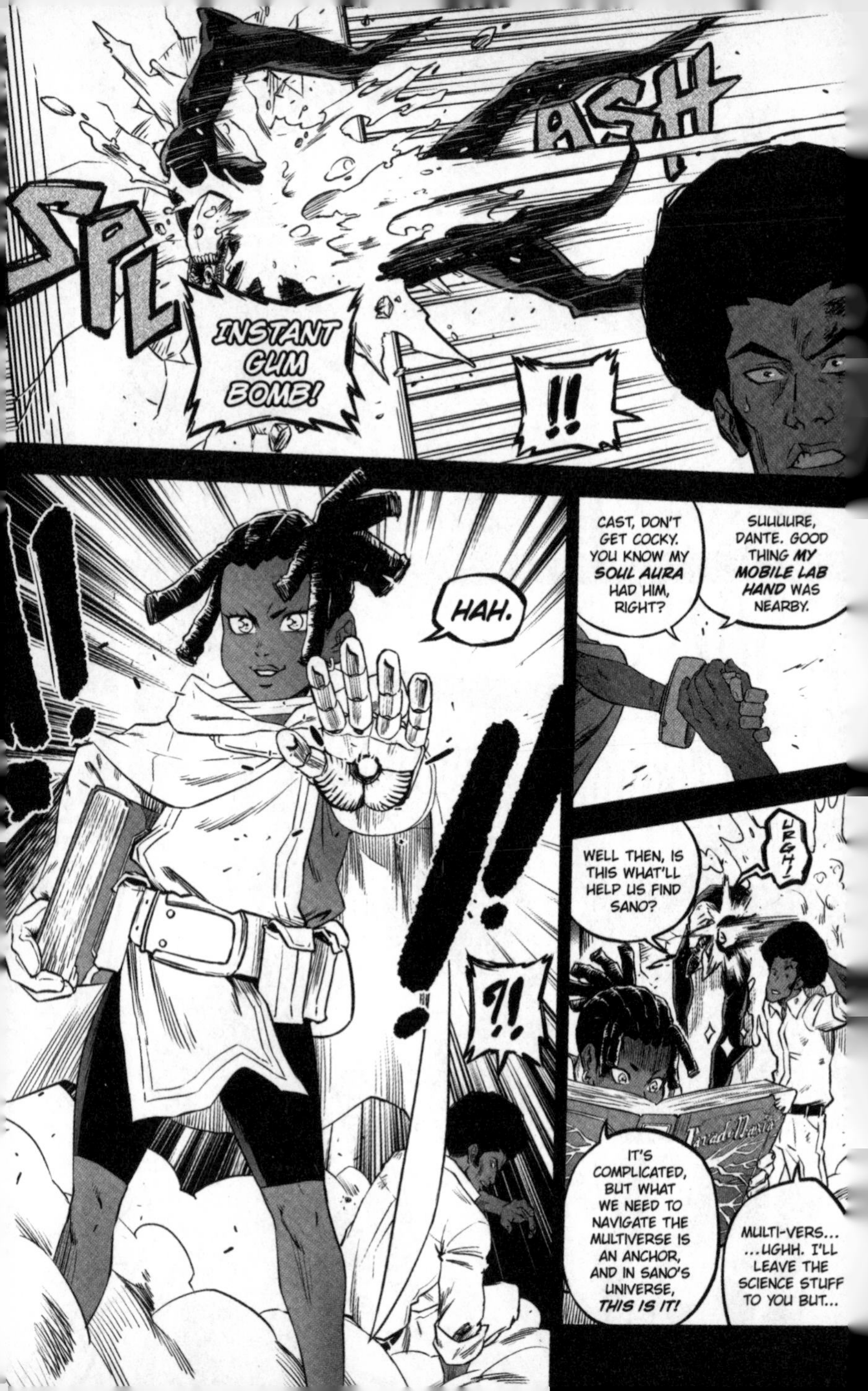
SPL
ASH
INSTANT GUM BOMB!
!!
!!
HAH.
!!
?!
CAST, DON'T GET COCKY. YOU KNOW MY SOUL AURA HAD HIM, RIGHT?
SUUUURE, DANTE. GOOD THING MY MOBILE LAB HAND WAS NEARBY.
URGH!
WELL THEN, IS THIS WHAT'LL HELP US FIND SANO?
IT'S COMPLICATED, BUT WHAT WE NEED TO NAVIGATE THE MULTIVERSE IS AN ANCHOR, AND IN SANO'S UNIVERSE, THIS IS IT!
MULTI-VERS... ...UGHH. I'LL LEAVE THE SCIENCE STUFF TO YOU BUT...

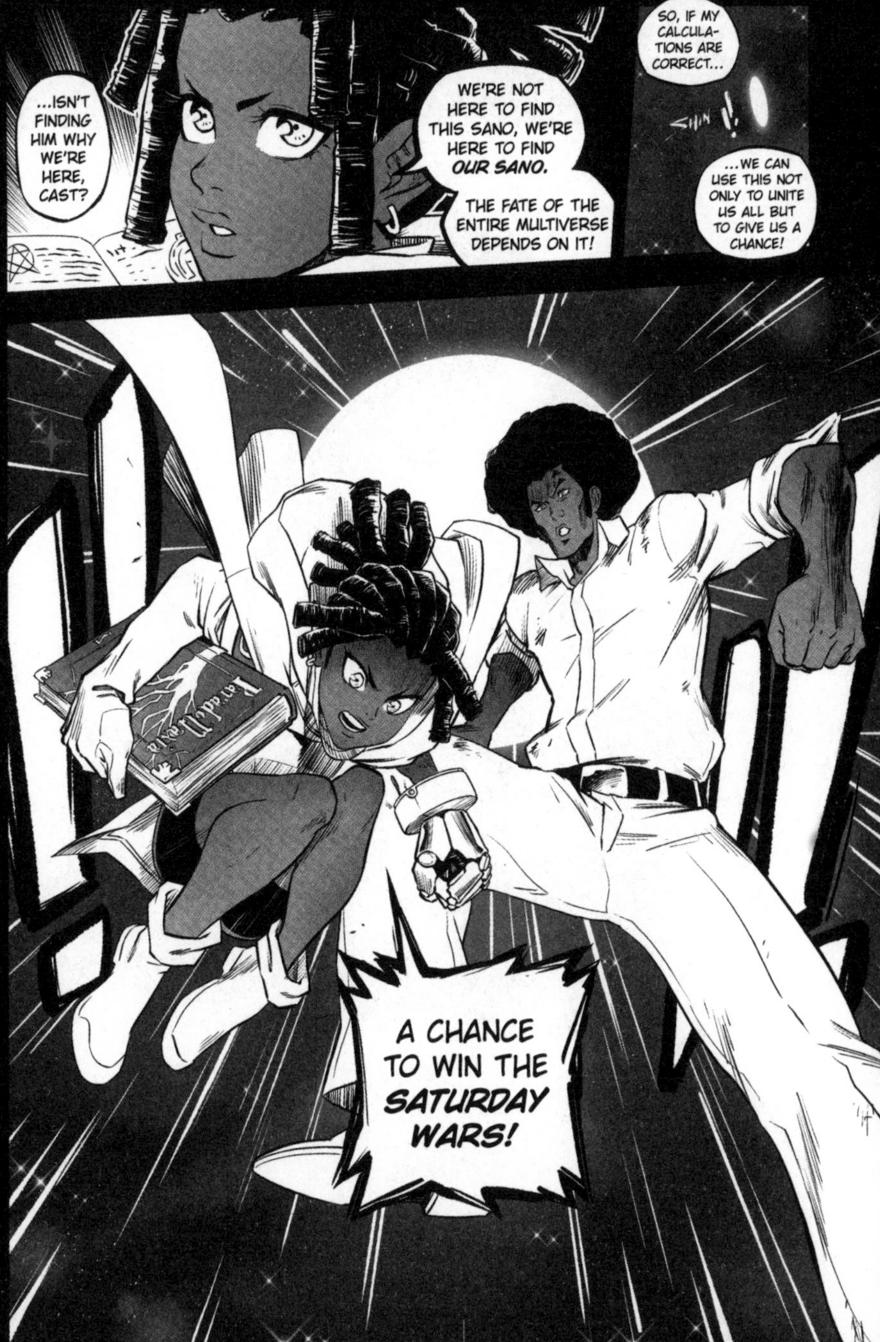
...ISN'T FINDING HIM WHY WE'RE HERE, CAST?
WE'RE NOT HERE TO FIND THIS SANO, WE'RE HERE TO FIND **OUR SANO.**
THE FATE OF THE ENTIRE MULTIVERSE DEPENDS ON IT!
SO, IF MY CALCULATIONS ARE CORRECT...
SHIN
...WE CAN USE THIS NOT ONLY TO UNITE US ALL BUT TO GIVE US A CHANCE!
A CHANCE TO WIN THE **SATURDAY WARS!**

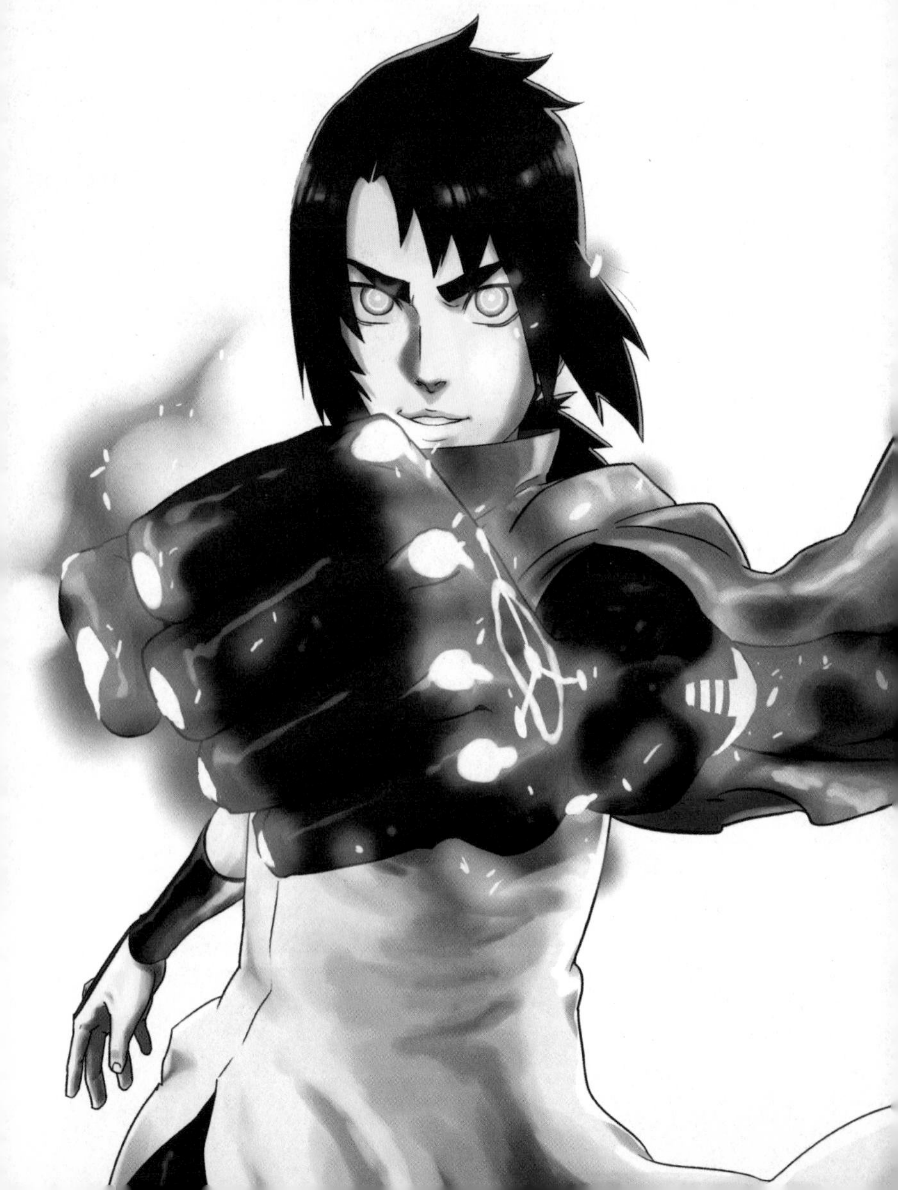

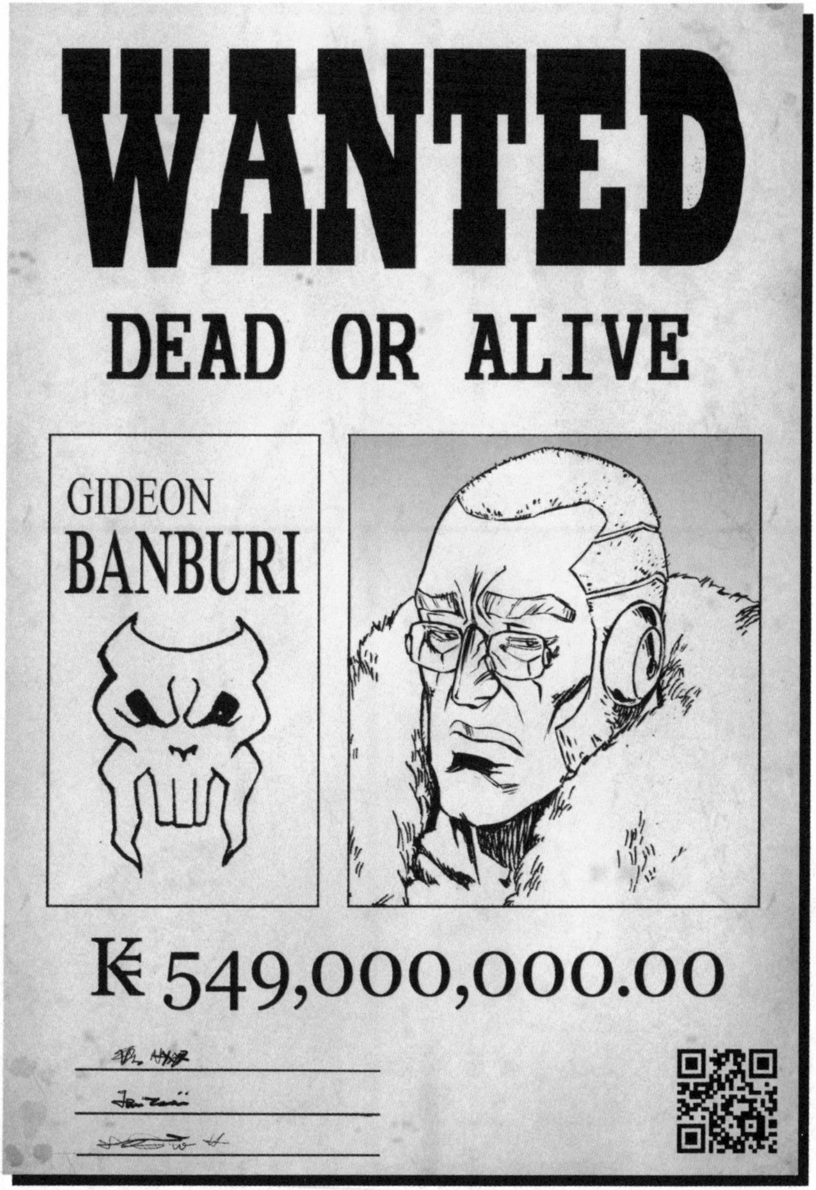

# WANTED

## DEAD OR ALIVE

GIDEON
**BANBURI**

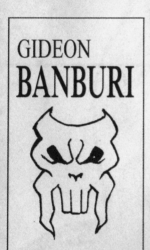

₭ 549,000,000.00

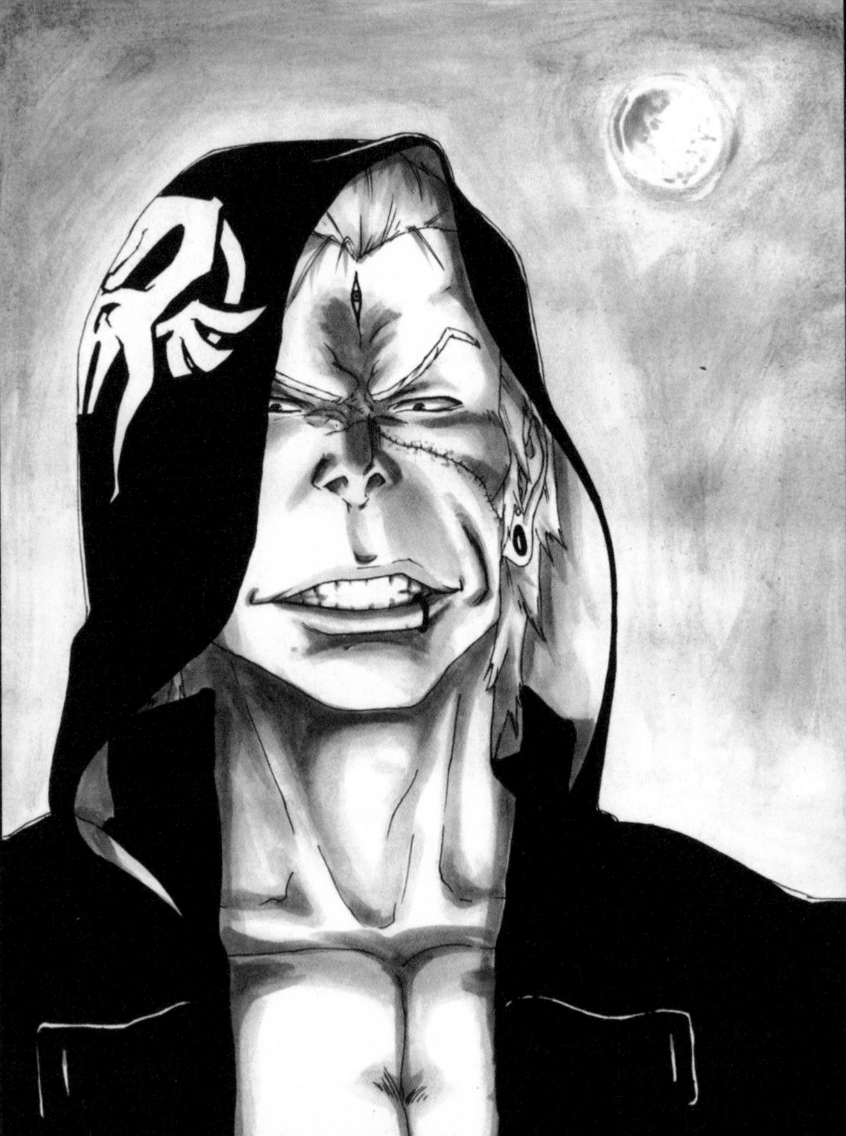

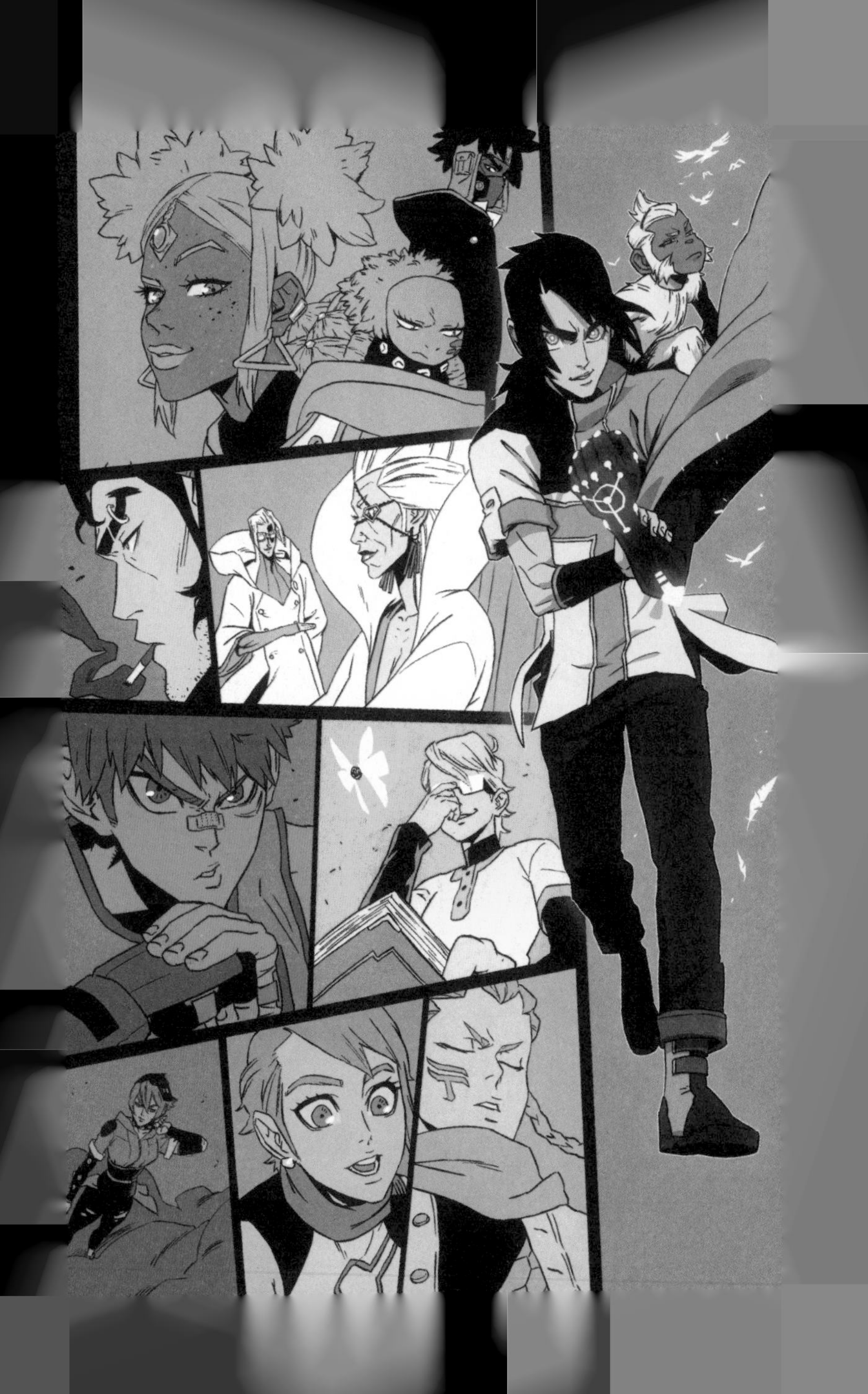

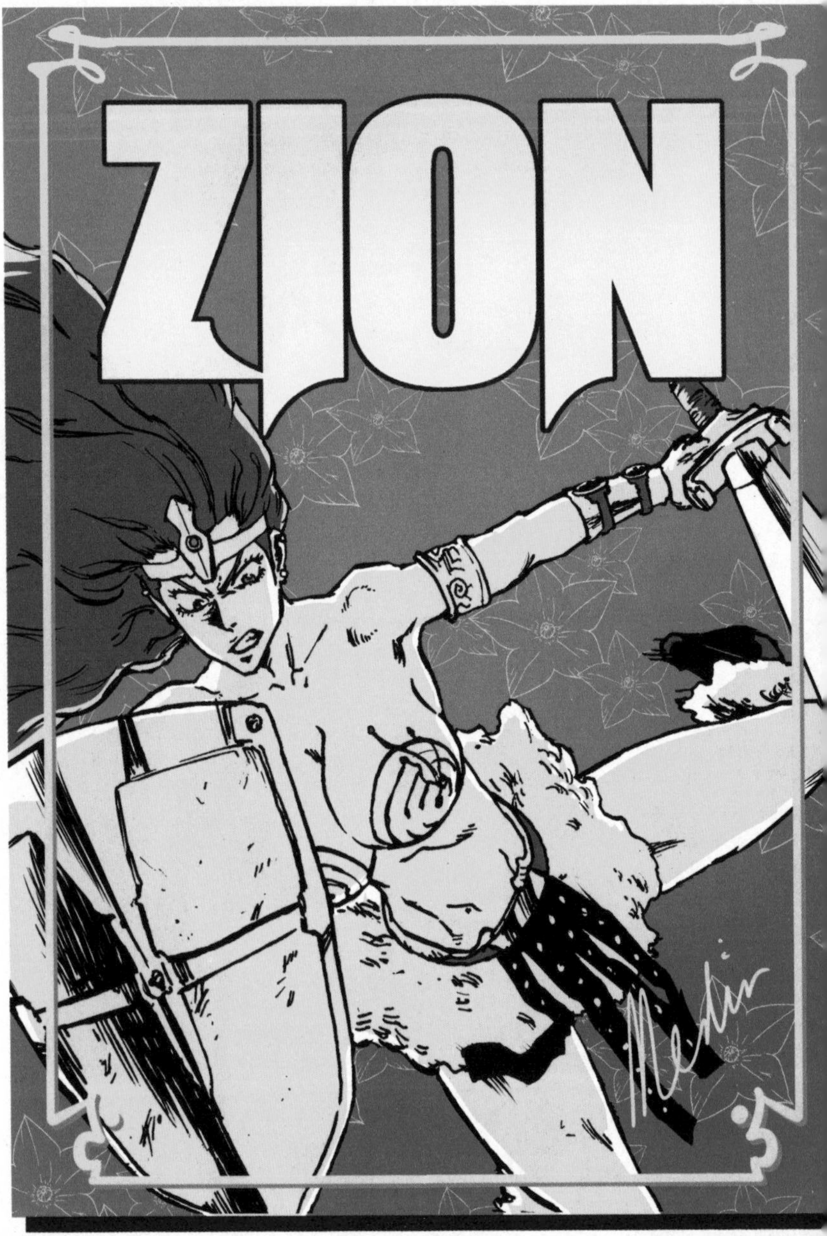
ZION

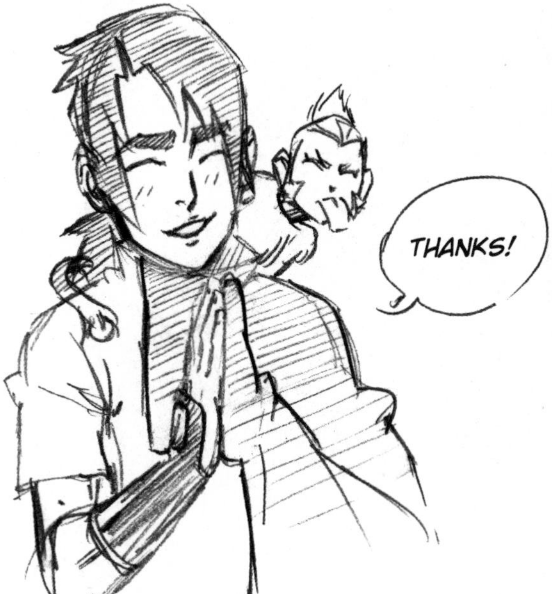
THANKS!

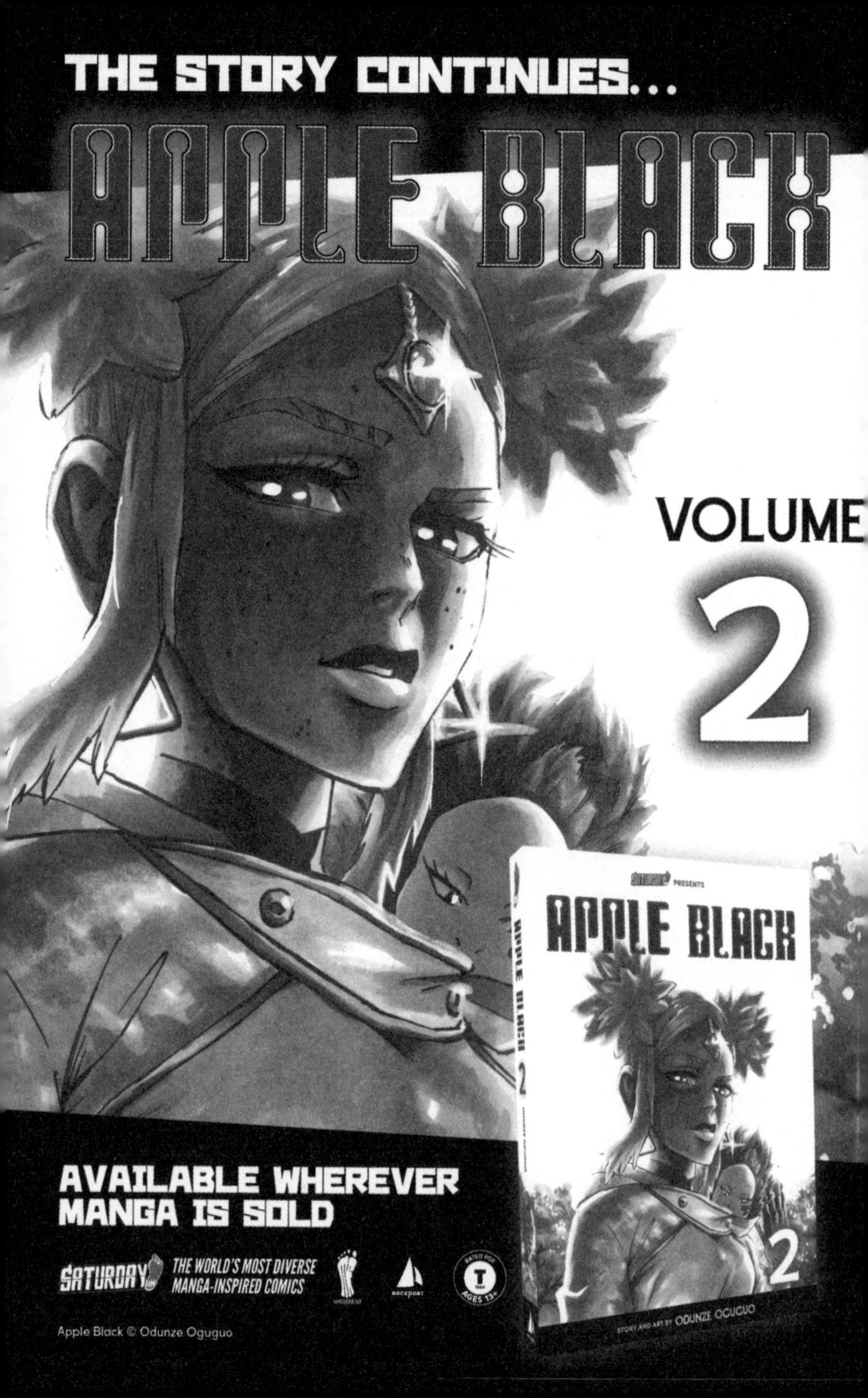

THE STORY CONTINUES...
APPLE BLACK
VOLUME
2
AVAILABLE WHEREVER MANGA IS SOLD
SATURDAY
THE WORLD'S MOST DIVERSE MANGA-INSPIRED COMICS
RATED FOR
T
AGES 13+
PRESENTS
APPLE BLACK
2
STORY AND ART BY ODUNZE OGUGUO
Apple Black © Odunze Oguguo

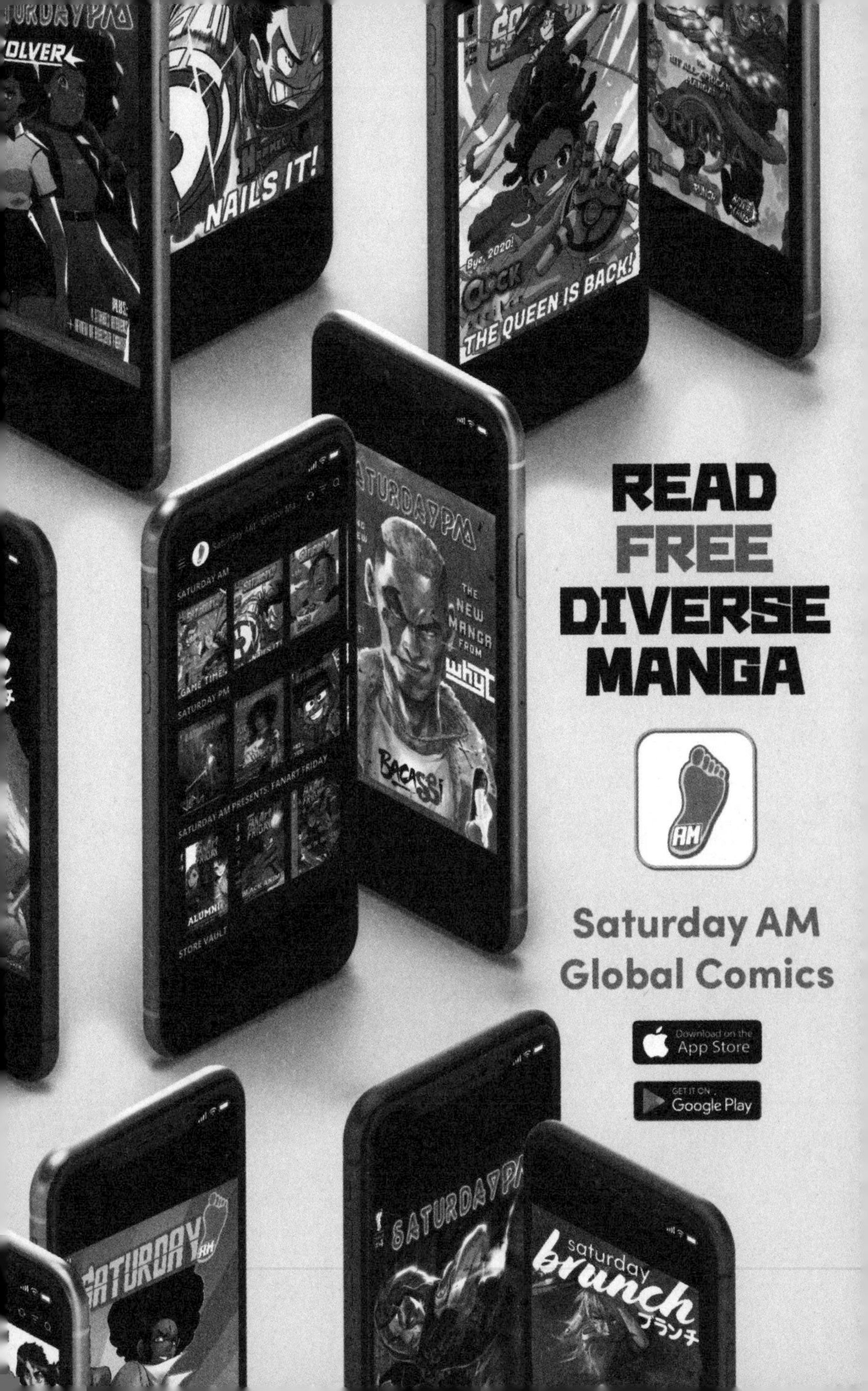
READ
FREE
DIVERSE
MANGA
Saturday AM
Global Comics
Download on the App Store
GET IT ON Google Play

© 2022 Odunze Oguguo

First published in 2022 by Rockport Publishers,
an imprint of The Quarto Group,
100 Cummings Center, Suite 265-D, Beverly, MA 01915, USA.
T (978) 282-9590 F (978) 283-2742 Quarto.com

Rockport Publishers titles are also available at discount for retail, wholesale, promotional, and bulk purchase. For details, contact the Special Sales Manager by email at specialsales@quarto.com or by mail at The Quarto Group, Attn: Special Sales Manager, 100 Cummings Center, Suite 265-D, Beverly, MA 01915, USA.

10 9 8 7 6 5 4 3 2 1

ISBN: 978-0-7603-7684-3

Library of Congress Cataloging-in-Publication Data is available.

Story and Art: Odunze Oguguo (Whyt Manga)
Lettering: Sara Linsley
Design and Additional Lettering: Mitch Proctor
Editors: Frederick L. Jones, Peter Doney, and Austin Harvey

Printed in China

*Apple Black, Volume 1* is rated T for Teen and is recommended for ages 13 and up. It contains mild violence and some mature language.